THE POCKET
B OK OF STONES

ALSO BY ROBERT SIMMONS:

Stones of the New Consciousness: Healing Awakening and Co-creating with Crystals, Minerals and Gems

The Book of Stones: Who They Are & What They Teach (with Naisha Ahsian)

Moldavite: Starborn Stone of Transformation (with Kathy Warner)

Earthfire

THE POCKET
BOOK OF STONES

WHO THEY ARE & WHAT THEY TEACH

A Sacred Planet Book

ROBERT SIMMONS

Destiny Books
Rochester, Vermont

Destiny Books
One Park Street
Rochester, Vermont 05767
www.DestinyBooks.com

Destiny Books is a division of Inner Traditions International

Sacred Planet Books are curated by Richard Grossinger, Inner Traditions editorial board member and cofounder and former publisher of North Atlantic Books. The Sacred Planet collection, published under the umbrella of the Inner Traditions family of imprints, publishes on the themes of consciousness, cosmology, alternative medicine, dreams, climate, permaculture, alchemy, shamanic studies, oracles, astrology, crystals, hyperobjects, locutions, and subtle bodies.

This edition published by Destiny Books by arrangement with Heaven and Earth Publishing, East Montpelier, Vermont

Cataloging-in-Publication Data for this title is available from the Library of Congress

ISBN 978-1-64411-383-7 (print)
ISBN 978-1-64411-386-8 (ebook)

Cover photos by John Goodman, Rob Lavinsky, and Jeff Scovil
Cover and book design by Margery Cantor and Patrick Gaudreault

Printed and bound in Canada by Transcontinental Printing

To send correspondence to the author of this book, mail a first-class letter to the author c/o Inner Traditions • Bear & Company, One Park Street, Rochester, VT 05767, and we will forward the communication, or contact the author directly at **http://heavenandearthjewelry.com**.

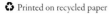 Printed on recycled paper

CONTENTS

SPECIAL ACKNOWLEDGMENT

I wish to thank my friend and sister Naisha Ahsian for her decades of work with crystals, both mineral and human. Your humor, intelligence and spiritual gifts have allowed you to be one of the luminaries of the crystal community. But it was your heart and your will that did the work.

INTRODUCTION

People love stones, and—if the meditative encounters I and thousands of others have experienced mean what they appear to mean—the feeling is mutual.

The lore of the spiritual qualities of crystals, gems and minerals goes back far beyond our written history. Moldavite amulets were discovered in the 25,000-year-old archeological dig that uncovered the Venus of Willendorf, the oldest Goddess statue. Fifteen centuries ago, Hindus believed that diamonds provided their owners with protection from evil spirits, fire, poison, snakes and illness. In ancient Rome, Emerald was viewed as a symbol of fertility and was associated with the goddess Venus. Christian legends speak of Emerald as the stone of resurrection. Ancient legend in Burma held that inserting a Ruby into one's flesh would make one invulnerable. The Christian Mystic Hildegard of Bingen wrote an entire volume on gemstone cures for all sorts of illnesses. Several years after *The Book of Stones* was published, I discovered it was predated by a similar book with the same title, written by the Arabian alchemist Abu Musa Jābir ibn Hayyān, over 1,000 years ago!

My own books are nourished by the roots of these ancient traditions, and are addressed to the large community of spiritually-oriented stone lovers that sprouted in the early 1980s and has grown exponentially since then. Like the alchemists, we look beyond the outer appearances of crystals and minerals to link with their quintessential energies, and to open ourselves to their influence. The hope and intention we carry is for transformation to occur. The sorts of changes we seek run the gamut from self-healing to spiritual awakening, from grounding to ascension. In the process of this inner work, we tend to find more than we seek. We discover new capacities and deeper sensitivities. We experience visions. We begin to feel the awakening of heart awareness and body consciousness. We sense the dawning realization that stones are more than useful objects—there is Someone there, a helping spirit that has its own nature and is ready to join us in cocreation.

After several decades in its initial stages, I feel our current work with stones is ready to be taken to a new level. Now we are prepared to meet the Stones Beings, and to work with them in partnership for the good of the world. We are called in this time to enter, with the help of the stones, into a New Consciousness, a new way of being for which we have been preparing for a very long time. Within this, we will find new modes of healing, new ways of sensing, new insights into our purpose and new ways to participate in bringing forth an awakened Earth.

In light of such a grand vision, what is the purpose of something like *The Pocket Book of Stones?* I see it as a Who's Who or Facebook for the beings of the mineral realm. Each entry provides a kind of character sketch, complete with picture, intended to introduce you to the stone, offering a summary of its qualities and the ways you might be likely to experience it when you meet it. It can help you decide what stones you might want to work with at a particular time, or it may help you understand the crystals and minerals that already grace your surroundings. It can orient you to better translate the inner experiences you undergo when meditating with a stone, and it can help you consider which stones to combine for enhancing their benefits. Finally, it is small enough to take with you on a backpacking trip to the rocky realm of the great outdoors, or a more genteel excursion into a crystal shop.

For me, the Mother of all the Stone Beings, and of all the human beings, is Sophia, ancient Goddess of Wisdom, the Soul of the World. The greatest blessing of my work with stones has been their aid in guiding me to an inner meeting with Her. From that meeting, it became clear to me that each kind of stone has its own archetypal character, a stone soul that knows and loves Sophia and is ready to work and play with Her in cocreative communion. To meet Sophia is to experience joy, and it is also to be welcomed into that same collaboration. As She is the Goddess of the Earth, the stones are her angels, and we can join in partnership with them all. To do so is transformative, awe-inspiring and fun. I recommend it highly.

Think of this book as your engraved invitation. The party has been going on for millennia . . . and it is just getting started.

Robert Simmons

June 24, 2011

Author's Note on Crystal Healing:
There are many references in this book to crystal healing and physical corre-spondences of stones with bodily organs and systems. I want to be sure that readers understand my perspective on this. I work with the stones intuitively, and I listen to their "voices" inwardly. What I write about healing properties is what I hear inwardly while meditating with the stones. None of these intu-itions have been scientifically tested, and when I test them on myself, it is as an adjunct to good medical care, not as a substitute for it. Using crystals is, in my view, not like taking pills. I think that any effects they may have for healing are spiritual, like the effects of prayer. People who want to try out these intu-itions, like myself, are free to do so. But please do not look at the writings in this book as prescriptions, or as any sort of promise that a stone will cure anything. At best, we don't know that yet. I advise anyone in need of medical or psychological care to do what I do and get the best professional help you can. If you want to add stones, or prayer, or both, why not? And to those who practice stone layouts or crystal healing, I strongly suggest that your clients be similarly advised.

DISCLAIMER: This book is not a substitute for professional medical or psychological advice and care. The author of this book does not dispense medical advice or prescribe the use of stones as a form of treatment for medical or psychological conditions. Readers should regularly consult a physician and seek professional medical advice about any physical, medical, psychological, or emotional matters that may require diagnosis or medical attention. The statements in this book have not been evaluated by the Food and Drug Administration. This book is not intended to be used to diagnose, treat, cure or prevent disease.

The information discussed in this book regarding the metaphysical properties of stones is intuitively derived and has not been scientifically evaluated. Readers are advised to view this information as speculative in nature, and to evaluate it in light of their own experiences. The author's intent is only to offer information of a general nature to help readers in their spiritual quest for higher consciousness and well-being. In the event that you use any of this information in this book for yourself, the author and publishers assume no responsibility for your actions.

THE STONES

ADAMITE

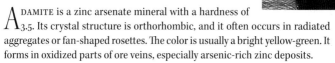

KEY WORDS Joy, love, creativity, enthusiasm, perseverance
CHAKRAS Solar Plexus (3rd) and Heart (4th)
ELEMENT Fire, Wind **PHYSICAL** Supports heart, stomach, small intestine **EMOTIONAL** Facilitates lifting one's mood, strengthening the will **SPIRITUAL** Aids conscious connection with spirit guides and angels, facilitating one's capacity to evolve through inner communion with them

A DAMITE is a zinc arsenate mineral with a hardness of 3.5. Its crystal structure is orthorhombic, and it often occurs in radiated aggregates or fan-shaped rosettes. The color is usually a bright yellow-green. It forms in oxidized parts of ore veins, especially arsenic-rich zinc deposits.

Adamite can enhance the alignment of the heart and solar plexus chakras, allowing one to synergize one's will with one's feelings. Such an alignment is particularly helpful for achieving one's "heart's desires"—the aspects of life one longs for but which may seem impossible to realize. Adamite kindles the fires of optimism and determination, assisting one in taking on whatever challenges must be faced, making the necessary leaps of insight and persevering through difficulties.

Adamite facilitates contact with spirits, angels, guides and the souls of those who have passed on. Clairvoyants, readers, psychic healers and shamanic practitioners will find that Adamite increases their sensitivity, enhancing the clarity of the messages one sends to and receives from entities in the higher vibrational realms.

Adamite harmonizes with Moldavite, Rose Quartz, Rhodochrosite, Morganite Emerald, Heliodor, Golden Labradorite, Sulfur and Citrine, Phenacite and Tsavorite Garnet.

AEGIRINE

KEY WORDS Clearing, protection, energy, confidence
CHAKRAS All **ELEMENT** Earth, Fire **PHYSICAL** Supports liver, spleen, gallbladder, recovery from exposure to toxic substances or energies, supports stamina and recovery from addiction **EMOTIONAL** Aids with lifting depression, clearing guilt and shame, building confidence **SPIRITUAL** Assists removal of negative energies and entities

AEGIRINE (also known as Acmite) is a sodium iron silicate mineral with a hardness of 6. Its crystal system is monoclinic and it forms in columnar, prismatic crystals, sometimes striated with pointed terminations. Its color is black, greenish black or brownish black.

Aegirine crystals are wonderful tools for removing negative or stuck energies from all levels of the subtle bodies. They are stones of confidence and strength, allowing one to shine one's Light even in the darkest places—in the inner or outer world. There are few stones as effective as Aegirine for breaking the attachment of negative entities or patterns to one's etheric body. Such attachments are not normal for energetically healthy and balanced individuals, but anyone can become vulnerable in moments of strong fear or anger, or through abuse of alcohol, tobacco or drugs.

Carrying or wearing Aegirine can be an effective stop-gap measure for forcing the release of these vampiric energies, and working with Aegirine in body layouts or in conjunction with other subtle energy healing modalities can, in time, regenerate the damaged protective auric shield.

AGATE, BLUE LACE

KEY WORDS Communication, clarity, confidence
CHAKRAS Throat (5th)   **ELEMENT** Water
PHYSICAL Supports healing of sore throat,
laryngitis, thyroid problems, speech impediments
EMOTIONAL Calms the emotional body, aids
confidence in communication, helpful for
releasing negative habits of interaction and speech
SPIRITUAL Helps one communicate one's deepest truth, enhances communication
with inner guides and connection with one's inner wisdom

Blue lace agate is a member of the Quartz family with a hardness of 7. It is banded in intricate patterns of light blue and white. Most of the best material comes from South Africa.

Blue Lace Agate is beneficial for those who have difficulty making themselves heard by others, or who wish to become more articulate in their speech. It helps one "find the words" to share one's highest truth and it assists one in building the confidence necessary to stand up and speak it in all situations. It helps instill clarity of thought and unwavering intent in regard to the ideals and goals that matter most. It is stone for the enhancement of loyalty and trustworthiness.

For those working with affirmations, Blue Lace Agate can be an excellent tool, because it strengthens the throat chakra and amplifies the power of what comes through it. Like other Agates, Blue Lace works in a slow, steady manner. It may not make one's dreams come true overnight, but it helps one stick with it while the transformation is in progress, and it magnifies the effects of our efforts.

Blue Lace Agate harmonizes with Malachite, Blue Chalcedony, Anandalite, Guardianite, Moldavite and Blue Kyanite.

3

AGATE, DENDRITIC

KEY WORDS Growth and wisdom through inner work **CHAKRAS** All **ELEMENT** Earth **PHYSICAL** Supports healing of back pain, neck problems, low blood count, health issues related to stress, addictive behavior, low self-esteem **EMOTIONAL** Assists with clearing and releasing self-negating and destructive patterns, enhancing self-esteem, building a stronger ego **SPIRITUAL** Aids in seeing oneself with honesty and clarity, encourages development of one's true self and embodiment of one's highest potential

Dendritic agate is a Quartz with a hexagonal crystal system and a hardness of 7. It has branching inclusions of iron or manganese.

Dendritic Agates are ideal tools for strengthening the fiber of the self through inner work. Those involved in therapy, meditation practice, rebirthing, a twelve-step program or any other path of serious inner work will find Dendritic Agate to be a helpful talisman. It can assist one in taking the day-by-day steps necessary to achieve the desired insights and behavior changes. Dendritic Agate helps one to keep a positive, though not unrealistic, attitude while going through needed transformations. It assists in keeping one in touch with the physical world, so one does not live merely in one's thoughts and mental processes. These stones can help reduce stress in difficult times, promoting a good-natured acceptance of one's circumstances, as well as offering long-term help in improving them. The purple varieties of Dendritic Agate are particularly well suited to purification of the body and energy field, and to working toward spiritual transformation.

Dendritic Agate harmonizes with Ellensburg Blue Agate, Satyaloka Azeztulite, Anandalite, Tibetan Tektite and Rosophia. Guardianite can assist with psychic protection, grounding and healing.

AGATE,
ELLENSBURG BLUE

KEY WORDS Eloquent communication of
the heart's truth, soothing the throat chakra,
calming the mind, opening psychic vision
CHAKRAS Throat (5th), Heart (4th), Third
Eye (6th), Crown (7th)   **ELEMENTS** Earth,
Water   **PHYSICAL** Supports healing of skin and throat problems, clearing
pathological neural patterns   **EMOTIONAL** Assists with releasing negative
judgments, fears, anger and encouraging compassion and loving kindness
SPIRITUAL Finding inner truth, courage and freedom

ELLENSBURG BLUE AGATE is a rare amygdaloidal nodule Agate found in Kittitas County near Ellensburg, Washington. It is a silicon dioxide with a
hardness of 7. Its color ranges from light to cornflower blue.

Ellensburg Blue Agate is beneficial for the throat chakra, conveying an
enhanced ability to see and speak the truth without concern for the consequences. It links the throat with the heart, allowing one to communicate
what the heart knows. This stone can also aid artists, poets and musicians to
eloquently express the treasures of their souls and the messages that come
through them from the Soul of the World.

Ellensburg Blue Agate emanates the vibration of peace, soothing the emotional body and releasing stress from the psyche. It can be used to heal burns,
lower fevers and cool hot tempers. It is an excellent antidote for destructive
excesses of passion which are the result of negative judgments. They help one
to see the deeper truth of the suffering of others in a way that leads inevitably
to compassion. The deeper shades of Ellensburg Blue can also stimulate the
third eye, activating psychic abilities and inner visions, as well as the crown
chakra, for spiritual purification and linkage with the Soul body.

5

AGATE, FIRE

KEY WORDS Vitality, sexuality, creativity, will
CHAKRAS Root (1st), Sexual/Creative (2nd),
Solar Plexus (3rd)　**ELEMENT** Fire
PHYSICAL Stimulates youthful energy,
sexual organs, digestion, bowels
EMOTIONAL Intensifies emotions, increases passion, enhances sexual attraction
SPIRITUAL Revitalizes spiritual and physical energies, inspires creativity

Fire AGATE is a silicon dioxide with a hexagonal crystal system and a hardness of 7. It combines a deep brown base hue with flashes of orange, red, green and gold that look like tongues of living flame. The best stones come from Mexico.

Fire Agates vibrate with the vitality of the physical world and are ideal tools for those who need to have an "in-the-body experience." Among the spiritually inclined segment of the population, there are many who attempt or wish to avoid the messy and painful difficulties of life by escaping into the upper realms. Unfortunately, the price one pays is often high, and one can become a spacey, low-energy person who glows with spiritual light but does not generate enough heat to get anything done. For those of us who lament that they don't much like the Earth and they want to go home, Fire Agate is an ideal remedy. Fire Agate awakens the lower chakras and fills one with the zest for living. It lights one's inner fires of life force, creativity, sexuality and will. It activates the senses and increases the pleasure one takes in everyday life. In helping one come fully into the body, Fire Agate assists one in making real the divine blueprint of one's life purpose.

Fire Agate harmonizes with Diamond, Chrysocolla, Anandalite, Crimson Cuprite, Mystic Merlinite, Agnitite and Agni Gold Danburite.

6

AGATE, HOLLY BLUE

KEY WORDS Bringing Spirit into matter, stimulating psychic abilities, exploring the "vertical dimension" **CHAKRAS** Crown (7th), Third Eye (6th), Heart (4th) **ELEMENT** Wind **PHYSICAL** Aids in head and brain problems; may aid in clearing headaches, stress and nervousness; facilitates spiritual help with dementia and psychosis **EMOTIONAL** Encourages calm, inner clarity, compassion, stability; freedom from anxiety, worry, jealousy and fearfulness **SPIRITUAL** Enhancing inner vision, clairvoyance, clairaudience, prophetic vision

Holly blue agate is a blue-violet stone found near Holly, Oregon. It is a Quartz with a hardness of 7. It is one of the rarer varieties of Agate and is highly prized for its rich color. It is a popular jewelry stone.

Holly Blue Agate carries the highest vibration of all the Agates. It is a stone for grounding spiritual energies in the physical world and can be used to link the higher spiritual "bodies" to the physical self, so one can experience multi-level awareness. Holly Blue Agate resonates with the "vertical dimension" and allows one to move up and down the scale, seeing the perfection of the simultaneous operation of the many levels of consciousness which it is possible for one to perceive. It activates the psychic centers in the brain, enhancing ESP, lucid dreaming, mediumship and other paranormal abilities. It also helps one to "hear" the prompting of one's spirit guides.

Holly Blue Agate is a stone of awakening to one's capacity to become a "Divine Human Being," a living incarnation of the partnership between the spiritual and earthly realms.

AGATE, MOSS

KEY WORDS Stability, persistence, grounding   **CHAKRAS** Root (1st), Heart (4th)
ELEMENT Earth   **PHYSICAL** Aids stabilizing of all body systems; enhancement of sensing capacities; aiding circulation, digestion, enuronal activity   **EMOTIONAL** Encourages peaceful temperament, lessens mood swings, helps develop stronger will forces   **SPIRITUAL** Opens inner doors to communion with Nature spirits, helps one find and adhere to one's higher purpose, releases negative karma

Moss AGATE is not technically a true Agate, because it is not banded. It is a chalcedony with dendritic inclusions of moss-colored green minerals. Spots of red also occur in some specimens. It is a Quartz with a hardness of 7. Many of the best Moss Agates come from India.

Moss Agate is one of those stones that would be beneficial to almost everyone. Its energies are modest but wholesome. It emanates the vibrations of balance and stability in the physical domain. It is an excellent stone for individuals convalescing after an illness, or for those in recovery from addictions. Like the tortoise in the old fable, the motto of Moss Agate is "Slow and steady wins the race." Moss Agate can assist those who feel ungrounded or unstable. It enhances mental concentration, persistence, endurance and bringing one's goals to completion. It can be used as a talisman for increasing the effectiveness of physical workouts and even bodybuilding. Meditating with Moss Agate, one can project the image of a completed project or goal into the stone, and the stone will magnify the energy of one's intention, thus assisting in the achievement of the goal.

Moss Agate harmonizes with Moldavite and all other Agates.

AGNITITE

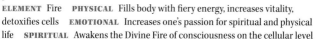

KEY WORDS Infusion of Divine Fire, life force,
purification, transformation **CHAKRAS** All
ELEMENT Fire **PHYSICAL** Fills body with fiery energy, increases vitality,
detoxifies cells **EMOTIONAL** Increases one's passion for spiritual and physical
life **SPIRITUAL** Awakens the Divine Fire of consciousness on the cellular level

AGNITITE is a silicon dioxide with a hexagonal crystal system and a hardness of 7. It is colorless or whitish with streaks of reddish Hematite. It is found in Madagascar.

Agnitite was named for Agni, the Vedic deity of fire. Agni was considered the supreme source of spiritual Light, life force and even immortality. Agni was fervently invited to enter the bodies of the ancient chanters, to illumine their hearts, tissues and consciousness with the sacred fire carrying the Divine nectar. Agnitite carries this Holy Fire.

Agnitite stimulates the entire Liquid Crystal Body Matrix, infusing it with the Divine fire of *prana*. It enhances intuition, healing, strength of will and the awareness of one's shared consciousness with that of the world. Individuals who wish to help in the formation of the Planetary Crystal Grid of Light are urged to work with Agnitite, because of its capacity to awaken the higher vibrational potential of the body. In healing, Agnitite can spiritually purify the blood and cellular tissues. It aids in detoxifying and energizing all of one's systems.

For opening the spinal channel, one can combine Agnitite with Tibetan Tektite. For developing the spiritual capacities of the new human species, Agnitite combines well with Nirvana Quartz, Circle Stones, Cryolite and Herderite. For the additional step of awakening the Light Body, all forms of Azeztulite can be very helpful. For increasing the down flow of the Supramental Force, Spanish Aragonite is also suggested.

AJOITE

KEY WORDS Love, healing, emotional support, goddess and angelic connections **ELEMENT** Storm **CHAKRAS** Heart (4th), Throat (5th), Third Eye (6th), Crown (7th), Etheric (8th–14th) **PHYSICAL** Aids in alleviation of physical symptoms of stress or depression **EMOTIONAL** Supports healing, calming and balancing the emotional body **SPIRITUAL** Links one's awareness with Divine guidance, facilitates empathic connection with the Soul of the World

Ajoite is a blue or blue-green copper silicate mineral named after Ajo, Arizona, where it was first identified. It is a rare mineral, most frequently seen as an inclusion in Quartz. The most beautiful and plentiful Ajoite specimens in Quartz crystal points came from the Messina Copper Mine in South Africa.

Ajoite in Quartz emanates one of the sweetest, most nurturing and loving energies of any stone in the mineral kingdom. It is a pure bearer of the vibrations of the Earth Mother or Soul of the World. Ajoite can cleanse the heart of sorrow, wash negativity out of one's thoughts and open the floodgates for the ocean of love to lift one to the higher planes. It clears and activates the throat chakra, assisting one in communicating one's deepest inner truth.

Ajoite can clear the auric field and align the Light Body with the physical. It can harmonize the energies of any chakra, disperse contracted thought forms that are creating pain, dispel any amount of negativity, and call forth the truth from oneself and others. All of Ajoite's work is accomplished in the most soft and loving manner. It can harmonize the emotional body, drawing out the poisons of one's sorrows, fears, rage and old wounds, replacing them with love and forgiveness.

ALEXANDRITE

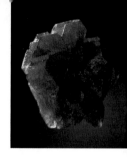

KEY WORDS Joy and wisdom, release of sorrow
CHAKRAS Heart (4th), Third Eye (6th), Crown (7th)
ELEMENT Wind, Water **PHYSICAL** Stimulates pineal
and pituitary glands, helps balance brain functions
EMOTIONAL Aids with relieving stress, encouraging trust,
awakening joy **SPIRITUAL** Enhancing awareness of Divine
Love, recalling past lives, accessing Akashic records

ALEXANDRITE is a variety of Chrysoberyl, a beryllium aluminum oxide with a hardness of 8.5. Its crystal pattern is orthorhombic, and it sometimes forms in hexagonal-looking twinned crystals. It was named after the Russian Czar Alexander II. The magic of gem-quality Alexandrite is in its property of color change—it is light red or red-purple in incandescent artificial light and green or blue-green in daylight.

It is true that Alexandrites are stones of joy, and for that reason they ought to be taken seriously. These stones have a connection to Source energies of the higher dimensions, where the atmosphere is most rapturous. However, one must be careful to do more than just enjoy the happy feelings. Alexandrite's window to the ecstasies of the higher realms can and should be the springboard to inner exploration. Alexandrite invites one on a quest into the Self. It can help one realize that the joy of the celestial realms is also simultaneously here at every moment, and one's reality depends greatly upon the levels at which one chooses to receive. Alexandrite teaches us to take in all energies that come to us, to transmute them into such harmony and beauty as is possible, and to do this with the inner resilience of a commitment to joy. This commitment, with the assistance of Alexandrite's link to the higher realms, makes us into sources, rather than mere receivers, of joy.

AMAZONITE

KEY WORDS Truth, communication, harmony
CHAKRAS Heart (4th), Throat (5th)   **ELEMENT** Water
PHYSICAL Aids cellular regeneration, healing from trauma, gout, arthritis   **EMOTIONAL** Facilitates releasing fear of judgment or conflict, finding inner freedom   **SPIRITUAL** Receiving and communicating higher knowledge, speaking truth

AMAZONITE is an alkali feldspar mineral, a potassium aluminum silicate with a hardness of 6 to 6.5. Its crystal system is triclinic and prismatic. Its color is green or blue-green. Its name derives from the Amazon River in Brazil, where there are important Amazonite deposits.

Amazonite is a stone of harmony, both within the self and among people. It is a truth-teller and a peacemaker, assisting one in communicating one's true thoughts and feelings without overemotionalism. Amazonite awakens compassion through stimulation of the heart chakra. Sleeping with Amazonite can bring one's competing unconscious tendencies into focus through the symbolism of dreams. Meditation with Amazonite makes everything more conscious, so one can listen to and integrate all aspects of the self. Because it is a stone of truth, one can trust the visions, dreams and intuitions that surface while working with it.

Amazonite can also empower us in manifesting our dreams and desires. It is a magnifier of our intentions, and because it works through the throat chakra, these intentions must be spoken aloud. Holding an Amazonite while affirming aloud what one wishes to create can powerfully enhance one's ability to bring it into being. The power of the spoken word is a great and mystical thing—remember that Genesis affirms that the Universe was brought into being by the word of God. Amazonite teaches us to speak the truth and to make what we speak come true.

AMBER

KEY WORDS Light, warmth, solar energies, clarification, healing **CHAKRAS** Solar Plexus (3rd) **ELEMENT** Earth **PHYSICAL** Increases life force, optimal functioning of organs and systems **EMOTIONAL** Releasing fear of judgment or conflict, finding inner freedom **SPIRITUAL** Provides energetic protection from negative influences

Amber is an organic material made up of fossilized natural botanic resins; it is a mixture of hydrocarbons with a hardness of 2 to 2.5. The word "Amber" comes from *ambar*, the Arabic word for ambergris, a similarly colored material discharged from the sperm whale and used in making perfumes. Amber varies in color from yellow to brown or reddish brown, and is often transparent.

Many stones help us to connect with Light, but Amber brings us to Warmth. The energies of Amber are very solar, and they have the quality of creating a comfortable sense of warmth, health and well-being in the wearer. Amber is recommended to be worn or carried by anyone recovering from illness or injury, because its warm and nurturing energies put us in touch with our own essential strength and security. It is excellent for convalescence, because it warms the inner being and activates the life force, as well as one's emotional desire for wellness. It helps one to see the path to recovery and have the courage and confidence to follow it.

Amber can also spur one's innate capacity to manifest prosperity. To amplify this potential, I recommend using it with prosperity stones such as Tsavorite, Yellow Sapphire and Moldavite. Pairing Amber with Moldavite is also helpful for bringing positive and successful inner transformation. In addition, Amber works especially well when combined with Jet, facilitating purification, health and protection from negativity.

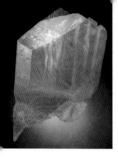

AMBLYGONITE

KEY WORDS Calm power of the will, manifestation of creative ideas **CHAKRAS** Solar Plexus (3rd) **ELEMENT** Fire **PHYSICAL** Soothing and restorative to the digestive system and bowels **EMOTIONAL** Overcoming anxiety, establishing a calm, optimistic outlook **SPIRITUAL** Finding the courage to express oneself creatively, discovering and fulfilling one's life purpose

AMBLYGONITE is a lithium sodium aluminum phosphate mineral with a hardness of 5.5 to 6. It is usually a pale yellow color, but is sometimes greenish yellow or lilac.

Amblygonite is an excellent stone for bringing one's emotional body into balance for the liberation of one's innate creative energies. Many individuals feel called to do creative work in artistic fields, such as writing, music, dance and so forth, but are hindered by blockages that stem from the emotional areas. One may feel inadequate to manifest one's dreams, or perhaps a past wound or trauma has created a fixation that blocks one's progress. Wearing, carrying or meditating with Amblygonite can assist one in finding the peace and inner clarity necessary to do one's unique work of self-expression. Amblygonite can help ignite the creative spark, moving one forward on the path to the fulfillment of one's higher purpose. It is both a soother and an energizer, calming the emotions while awakening the creative mind.

Because it activates creativity, Amblygonite can also help to manifest in this world the images one pictures in the etheric. It can help one do the necessary work to make one's dreams come true. To enhance this, Amblygonite can be combined with Phenacite, which has great power to assist in bringing the imagined into reality.

AMEGREEN

KEY WORDS Mind/Heart integration, spiritual connection, compassion, psychic ability, emotional healing
CHAKRAS Heart (4th), Crown (7th), Etheric (8th–14th)
ELEMENT Earth, Wind **PHYSICAL** Supports overall healing, recovery from injury, is beneficial to the heart
EMOTIONAL Releasing emotional wounds, learning to trust and love **SPIRITUAL** Facilitates connecting with Divine Love

AMEGREEN is a combination of purple Amethyst and Prasiolite (Green Amethyst) with a hardness of 7. The stones come from Africa, and the crystals often grow in conjunction with white Quartz.

There is a wonderful softness and lightness about the energies of Amegreen. The Amethyst brings in the Purple Ray of purification and stimulates the crown chakra. The Prasiolite soothes the emotions and balances the energies of the heart chakra. The white Quartz that connects them emanates the pure white Divine Light energy. Amegreen provides a wellspring of emotional support, helping one to heal past wounds or simply to lift the veil of sorrow or depression.

Wearing or carrying Amegreen helps one integrate the mind and heart. It allows for the creativity and inspiration of the mind to be guided by the heart's wisdom. It opens one's consciousness to the influence of the higher energies of the Divine. It helps one give and receive both spiritual and human love. It assists in lifting oneself out of the doldrums and making a new effort in one's life.

Amegreen works well with Moldavite, which brings the active energy of transformation into union with Amegreen's harmonious flow. Combining Amegreen with Petalite, Azeztulite or Phenacite can serve to emphasize one's connection to higher spiritual realms.

AMETHYST

KEY WORDS Protection, purification, Divine connection, release of addictions **CHAKRAS** Third Eye (6th), Crown (7th), Etheric (8th–14th) **ELEMENT** Wind **PHYSICAL** Overcoming addictions, tinnitus, nerve disorders, aids oxygenation of the blood **EMOTIONAL** Helps clear negative or addictive emotional patterns **SPIRITUAL** Facilitates conscious connection with Spirit Guides, Angels and Source

AMETHYST is a member of the Quartz family with a trigonal crystal system and a hardness of 7. Its color, which varies from pale to deep purple, is derived from the combination of trace amounts of iron and aluminum. Amethyst crystals and gem rough are found in Brazil, Bolivia, Mexico, Africa, Canada, Russia, the USA and Europe.

Amethyst is a stone of spiritual protection and purification. It can be an aid to curbing overindulgence and giving up bad habits. It can be used to assist one in quitting smoking, drinking or drug use. It stimulates the crown chakra and is an aid to meditation, helping one to still one's thoughts and move into higher states of consciousness. It can clear one's energy field of negative influences and attachments, and can thereby facilitate the creation of an energetic "shield"—a field of spiritual Light around the body that wards off the negativity in one's environment.

Amethyst can bring the feeling that one is surrounded and protected by a "bubble of Light." If one is ill, placing an Amethyst specimen in one's room can help keep one's healing space clear. Wearing Amethyst maintains the inner space of one's body and energy field in a state of balance and well-being. For spiritual protection, Amethyst works especially well when combined with Moldavite. The spiritual connection provided by Amethyst can be enhanced by Azeztulite, Phenacite, Scolecite and Natrolite.

AMETRINE

KEY WORDS Mental and spiritual clarity, decisiveness
CHAKRAS Solar Plexus (3rd), Crown (7th)
ELEMENT Wind, Fire **PHYSICAL** Stimulates
metabolism and digestion, enhances brain function
EMOTIONAL Aids in overcoming fear and insecurity,
finding one's own power **SPIRITUAL** Facilitates attuning
to Divine inspiration and acting on inner guidance

Ametrine is a combination of Amethyst and Citrine—a member of the Quartz family with a hexagonal (trigonal) crystal system and a hardness of 7. Natural Ametrine is found in Brazil, Uruguay and Bolivia.

Ametrine is a harmonious blend of Amethyst and Citrine energies. It is stimulating to the crown chakra, protective to one's auric field, purifying to one's personal energies and uplifting to the spirit. It can aid greatly in letting go of bad habits and addictions. It is a stone for enhancing mental clarity, creativity and will. It brings one's spirituality into harmony with the mind, often catalyzing a profound flow of new ideas and insights. It is beneficial to keep Ametrine at one's desk or beside one's computer, or wherever else one sits to do the mental side of work. The Ametrine will help the mind stay clear, creative, energetic and on task. Those trying to lose weight or break other self-defeating habits are also advised to work with Ametrine, in this case as a jewelry piece or pocket stone, keeping its energies within one's auric field.

Ametrine combines well with all other members of the Quartz family, as well as Sugilite, Golden Labradorite, Yellow Sapphire, Lilac Lepidolite, Phenacite and Azeztulite. Combining Ametrine with Moldavite multiplies its effects manyfold, as its transformational energies activate all the chakras and focus upon manifestation of the will and advancement of one's spiritual evolution.

AMULET STONE

KEY WORDS Positive energy, slow and steady healing, clearing negativity **CHAKRAS** All **ELEMENT** Earth **PHYSICAL** Supports all organs and systems, ideal for recovery from illness **EMOTIONAL** Helps quell anxiety, tension; dispels bad moods, bad dreams **SPIRITUAL** Assists in finding natural harmony with oneself and the Earth

Amulet stone is a type of Rhyolite, a silica-rich mineral with a hardness of about 7. It is from central Australia. The Aborigines call the stones "Uluru's children," after the sacred site now known Ayer's Rock.

Amulet Stones offer a special kind of vibrational "protection." It is not that they repel negativity, but that they vibrate so positively that there is no resonance with negative people or situations. These stones emanate such good-natured currents that they can clear one of a bad mood just by holding one, and they make one feel so comfortable that fear and stress seem long gone and forgotten. Amulet Stones are attuned to the natural harmony of the Earth. They can aid in regulating healthy sleep patterns and in dispelling bad dreams. They are excellent stones for children, because their currents are stable and comforting. In healing, the effects are slow and steady, rather than dramatic. The stones tend to encourage the body to find its own natural equilibrium. They are ideal for people who are convalescing after the crisis of an illness or injury is past. Amulet Stones calm emotional instability, anxiety and/or depression. They support harmonious relationship within the self, as well as with other creatures, nature and the Earth.

Amulet Stones harmonize with almost all other stones. They can help one adjust more easily to high-vibration stones such as Azeztulite, Anandalite, Phenacite, Herderite and Isis Calcite. With Moldavite, they enhance one's process of positive self-transformation.

ANANDALITE

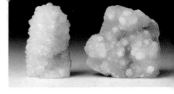

KEY WORDS Kundalini awakening, enlightenment, genius, creativity **CHAKRAS** All
ELEMENT Storm **PHYSICAL** Stimulates and
clears meridian system, fills the cells with Light **EMOTIONAL** Dissolves negative
patterns, rekindles one's natural joy **SPIRITUAL** Stimulates latent psychospiritual
capacities, awakens genius

Aنان NANDALITE is a type of druzy Quartz, a silicon dioxide with a hexagonal
crystal system and a hardness of 7. It forms in many shapes, including
"stalactites," and some pieces display multicolored reflections from the crystal surfaces (Rainbow Anandalite). It is found in India.

Anandalite is the premier stone for awakening the *kundalini*, the "Serpent
Fire" energy lying dormant around the base of the spine. For thousands of years
practitioners have prescribed kundalini awakening as the path to enlightenment, calling it the energy of genius and evolution. Anandalite stimulates and
moves the kundalini in a way that is both powerful and safe. The simplest
method is to ask a friend to take a pair of Anandalite stones and move them
slowly up the front and back of one's body, beginning at the root chakra,
all the way to the Soul Star above the Crown. Virtually all crystal-sensitive
people who have tried this have experienced a powerful, pleasant movement
and alignment of energies throughout the entire chakra column. Often the
currents are felt initially as heat, then joy, and finally as Light. Anandalite
stimulates spiritual awakening. It awakens latent capacities, psychic abilities,
past-life memories and creative inspirations. In healing, it can clear blockages
in the chakras and meridian system, and it fills the cells with spiritual Light,
dispelling destructive patterns and activating one's Divine blueprint.

Anandalite works marvelously with all types of Azeztulite, as well as
Danburite. Tibetan Tektite can strengthen its kundalini energies.

ANDALUSITE

KEY WORDS Cleansing, comforting, protective, friendly **CHAKRAS** Root (1st), Third Eye (6th) **ELEMENT** Storm **PHYSICAL** Acts as an overall strengthener of one's constitution **EMOTIONAL** Provides replenishment of the emotional body, psychic protection **SPIRITUAL** Provides connection with Divine realms, protection of one's energy field

ANDALUSITE is an aluminum silicate mineral with a hardness of 7.5. It is named after Andalusia in Spain, where it has been found. Its crystal system is orthorhombic. Its color is most often brown and/or green, and in gems the colors can vary when viewed from different angles.

Andalusites are ancient stones, and they carry in their crystalline structure the very heartbeat of the Earth. When they are held in the hand, one can feel a slow, deep pulsation, which seems very friendly and comforting. This is an excellent stone for helping sensitive people feel at home and safe here on Earth. It offers psychic protection, grounding, an infusion of life force and a sense of contentment and well-being. Andalusite can be used to strengthen and energize any chakra and to repair holes in the auric field. It carries the etheric pattern of wholeness for the body, especially the teeth and skeletal system. The friendliness of this stone makes it ideal for those trying to overcome feelings of loneliness, isolation, depression, anxiety and various fears. It is recommended as a protection stone for those traveling or working in areas of danger or negativity. Andalusite works well with Lemurian Seed Crystals, Shaman Stones, Jet, Sugilite and Moldavite. It will also adapt itself to almost any other stone. The feeling of good-natured friendliness and generosity emanating from these stones is remarkable and unique.

ANGEL AURA QUARTZ

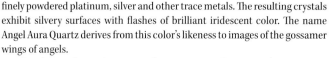

KEY WORDS Upliftment, peace, serenity, expanded awareness
CHAKRAS Crown (7th), Etheric (8th–14th) **ELEMENT** Wind
PHYSICAL Aids in releasing stress; helps with muscle cramps,
indigestion **EMOTIONAL** Ideal for calming, purifying and
uplifting the emotional body **SPIRITUAL** Facilitates reaching
deeper states in meditation, connecting with Angels

Angel aura quartz is produced when clear Quartz
points or clusters go through a special treatment process in which their surfaces are bonded with vaporized or
finely powdered platinum, silver and other trace metals. The resulting crystals
exhibit silvery surfaces with flashes of brilliant iridescent color. The name
Angel Aura Quartz derives from this color's likeness to images of the gossamer
wings of angels.

Angel Aura Quartz is a stone of attunement to beauty, and it can assist
one in remembering to pay attention to the beauty surrounding one, in both
Nature and Spirit. Wearing Angel Aura Quartz helps one to be a beacon of
inner beauty, peace and spiritual awareness. Meditating with these stones,
one can easily move beyond the body and go to one's "inner temple." This is a
place of purification and rest in which one's angelic guides are present, ready
to help one release stress and move into deep peace.

Remembrance of past incarnations, insights into one's spiritual purpose,
the ability to channel higher knowledge, and the opportunity to commune
with loving spiritual entities are among the possibilities available through
working with Angel Aura Quartz. And all of these things take place in a
"bubble" of peace, tranquility and contentment.

Angel Aura Quartz harmonizes well with Aqua Aura Quartz, Danburite,
Petalite, Seraphinite, Oregon Opal, Alexandrite and Kunzite.

ANGEL WING BLUE ANHYDRITE

KEY WORDS: cleansing; purification; angelic connection
CHAKRAS Throat (5th), Third Eye (6th), Crown (7th)
ELEMENT Wind **PHYSICAL** Stimulates energetic cleansing in healing, supports skeletal system and joints
EMOTIONAL Enhances compassion, forgiveness, communication **SPIRITUAL** Deepens meditation and prayer, aids in communing with angels

ANGEL WING BLUE ANHYDRITE is a calcium sulfate min-eral with an orthorhombic crystal system and a hardness of 3.5. These crystal clusters, which often form in fan-shaped sprays reminiscent of wings, are found in Mexico. Their color is the same soft blue as Angelite.

Angel Wing Blue Anhydrite is one of the most powerful "soft" energy stones in the mineral kingdom. It is ideal for clearing blocks, erasing implants, soothing all sorts of disharmony and providing a conduit of strength through which one can reconnect with Source. In meditation, this stone can provide the experience of "flight." For those who are "angels in human form"—those who have taken on a human incarnation in order to assist in the planetary transformation of consciousness—Angel Wing Blue Anhydrite can facilitate a deep remembrance of one's true identity.

Angel Wing Blue Anhydrite harmonizes with Azeztulite, Petalite, Danburite, Diamond and all types of Azeztulite. All of these stones have connections with the Angelic realm. In addition, combining Seraphinite with Angel Wing Blue Anhydrite can help one "call down" the angelic energies for healing purposes. Combining Angel Wing Blue Anhydrite with Oregon Opal can aid in healing and rebuilding a wounded emotional body. Adding Alexandrite can increase one's ability to see and remove limiting implants and "crystallized" emotional blocks.

ANGELITE (Blue Anhydrite)

KEY WORDS Angelic communication, serenity, expanded awareness   **CHAKRAS** Throat (5th), Third Eye (6th), Crown (7th)   **ELEMENT** Wind   **PHYSICAL** Supports bone density and health; helps with arthritis, healing fractures   **EMOTIONAL** Encourages clear and compassionate communication   **SPIRITUAL** Facilitates angelic communication, developing spiritual gifts

ANGELITE is the name commonly given to a form of blue Anhydrite found in Peru. It is a calcium sulfate mineral with an orthorhombic crystal system and a hardness of 3.5. It has a soft blue color and tends to form in nodules with white exteriors.

Angelite can act as the anchoring talisman for the energies of one's guardian angels, guides and other friends in Spirit. Carrying, wearing, holding or being near an Angelite stone provides one with a focal point of connection for receiving love, guidance and help from the invisible ones who surround us on the higher planes. The stones themselves seem to emanate serenity and benevolence, and these are the energies being constantly broadcast through them to assist us.

Communication and communion with beings in higher dimensions are Angelite's special gifts, making these stones useful to those wishing to develop powers of psychic attunement, channeling, mediumship, clairvoyance and spiritual healing. Angelite can assist one in receiving spiritual guidance for oneself and others. It can help one remain lucid in the dream state and remember the guidance received in dreams. Angelite can help one tune into memories of past lives and to the Akashic records. It can assist one in understanding and interpreting the symbolic content of dreams and inner visions. In meditation, Angelite can facilitate moving into peaceful inner states of expanded awareness.

APACHE TEARS

KEY WORDS Grounding, protection, psychic attunement, emotional healing
CHAKRAS Root (1st), Sexual/Creative (2nd), Heart (4th)   **ELEMENT** Earth, Fire
PHYSICAL Supports strength and stamina, boosts immune system
EMOTIONAL Clears negative thought patterns, heals emotional wounds
SPIRITUAL Appreciation of physical life, protection from negative forces

A PACHE TEARS are a variety of Obsidian, a silica-rich, glassy volcanic rock with a water content of less than one percent. Their hardness is 5 to 5.5. Apache tears are native to Mexico and the Southwest of the USA. Apache Tears are roundish, about ½ inch to one inch in diameter, and are usually semitransparent and black-brown in color.

Apache Tears can be used for grounding and for protection from negative energies. They link easily with one's emotional body and can be used to cleanse and heal old wounds or emotional baggage one may be carrying from the past, whether in this life or a previous one. Apache Tears facilitate processing and release of frozen emotional patterns, especially those held below one's level of awareness. Meditation with Apache Tears can open the floodgates of grief, allowing cleansing and release of feelings of woundedness or victimization. Apache Tears are excellent talismans of protection from all sorts of negative forces. They raise one's level of psychic attunement so that one can "feel" the approach of threatening persons, situations or energies. They can be used to cleanse one's auric field and etheric body of astral parasites, or one's own self-inflicted limitations and burdens.

Apache Tears ally themselves with grounding and protective stones such as Smoky Quartz, Black Tourmaline, Aegirine, Red Garnet and Healer's Gold, as well as Moldavite, Tibetan Tektite and Libyan Gold Tektite.

APATITE, BLUE

KEY WORDS Psychic activation, access to knowledge
CHAKRAS Third Eye (6th) **ELEMENT** Wind
PHYSICAL Helps calm headaches, overcome vertigo,
improve eyesight **EMOTIONAL** Uplifting one's mood,
overcoming acrophobia **SPIRITUAL** Aids exploration of
past lives, lucid dreaming, dream recall

B LUE APATITE is a calcium phosphate mineral with a hardness of 5. Its crystal system is hexagonal (trigonal). It is found in Madagascar and Sri Lanka. Its rich shades of tropical blue make it a popular stone for jewelry and ornaments.

Blue Apatite is a cleansing influence on the auric field, especially in the mental body—the vibratory level associated with psychic perception and paranormal abilities. It is stimulating to visionary states and is a good stone to keep in one's pillowcase for lucid dreaming and astral travel. Blue Apatite can enhance one's experience of "vertical vision," in which one is able to see multiple levels of consciousness operating harmoniously and simultaneously. It is a stone of inspiration, capable of making one more susceptible to the "aha experience" in which one has an instant of understanding which crystallizes the answer to long-standing problems or questions. Its vibration attracts the "blue beings" of the supernal regions—whether they be ETs, guides or godlike entities such as Krishna—and it allows one to commune with them.

Blue Apatite aids in recovering past-life memories and information from ancient civilizations. It is an excellent stone to use in combination with "record keeper" crystals. For purpose of prophetic work, it can be used with Trigonic Quartz crystals.

APATITE, GOLDEN

KEY WORDS Creation, clarity, confidence, manifestation
CHAKRAS Solar Plexus (3rd) **ELEMENT** Fire
PHYSICAL Stimulating metabolism and endocrine
system, weight loss **EMOTIONAL** Enhancing self-
confidence and charisma, hope and passion
SPIRITUAL Aids manifesting prosperity and one's
passions and dreams

GOLDEN APATITE is a calcium phosphate mineral with a hardness of 5. Its crystal system is hexagonal (trigonal). It is found in Mexico.

Golden Apatite is one of the purest crystals of the Yellow Ray, the vibration of mental clarity, strength of will and manifestation. It is a solar stone, and therefore male in tone. It can help either men or women strengthen the male side of the personality. It assists one in developing assertiveness and confidence in all situations. Golden Apatite is also a stone of learning, and it can enhance one's capacity for taking in and digesting new information—especially information which helps in manifesting one's strongest desires. If one is unclear about what one really wants out of life in general, or any specific aspect of life, meditation with Golden Apatite can bring both the needed insight and the strength of purpose to make it so.

Carrying or wearing Golden Apatite can increase the effect of one's will in social situations and can enhance personal charisma. It can assist in the manifestation of prosperity on all levels. It can help one find the courage to take risks and the clarity to know which risks to take. Golden Apatite can be a useful ally to anyone in a competitive situation, from sports to the corporate world.

Golden Apatite harmonizes with Golden Beryl, Libyan Gold Tektite, Golden Labradorite and Moldavite.

APATITE, GREEN

KEY WORDS Knowledge of the heart, relaxation, revitalization **CHAKRAS** Heart (4th), Throat (5th), Third Eye (6th) **ELEMENT** Water, Earth **PHYSICAL** Aids overall healing and refreshment, healing the heart **EMOTIONAL** Supports health of the emotional body, optimism, generosity **SPIRITUAL** Facilitates prosperity consciousness, abundance of health and happiness

GREEN APATITE is a calcium phosphate mineral with a hardness of 5. Its crystal system is hexagonal (trigonal). It is found in Madagascar and Sri Lanka. Its rich shades of green make it a popular stone for jewelry and ornaments.

Green Apatite is a wonderful tonic for frayed nerves and stress. Its energies are so soothing and cooling, one is reminded of the feeling of plunging into a pristine lake on a hot day. By blending the energies of the heart chakra, throat chakra and third eye, Green Apatite allows one to clearly communicate the balanced wisdom of the mind and heart, keeping one attuned so as not to overdo either one's logical or emotional side. This gemstone is ideal for those who wish to pursue a teaching or healing role in life, since it aids one in putting out energy while maintaining inner balance. Green Apatite can also assist one in communication with Nature spirits, as well as in channeling healing energies to the Earth. These gems harmonize with most others, especially Danburite, Phenacite, Azeztulite and Larimar. The first three are high-vibration stones and will elevate the states accessible via Green Apatite. With Larimar, communication and emotional balance are enhanced.

Green Apatite is quite "user-friendly," and most people will enjoy connecting with it. It is a stone of renewed hope, and it engenders optimism and courage.

APOPHYLLITE, CLEAR

KEY WORDS Interdimensional awareness
CHAKRAS Crown (7th), Third Eye (6th)
ELEMENT Wind, Earth   **PHYSICAL** Supports
infusion of spiritual Light, making the Light
Body physical   **EMOTIONAL** Aids in rediscovering
trust in the Divine after disillusionment   **SPIRITUAL** Facilitates interdimensional
travel, connecting with guides and angels

Cʟᴇᴀʀ ᴀᴘᴏᴘʜʏʟʟɪᴛᴇ is a hydrated potassium calcium silicate mineral with a tetragonal crystal system and a hardness of 5. The finest Clear Apophyllite crystals are found in India.

Clear Apophyllites excel at attuning one to the higher-frequency energies of the angelic and interdimensional domains. Indeed, these crystals can serve as windows into many other worlds, and those wishing to experience interdimensional travel will enjoy working with them.

Meditation is one of the chief ways of working with Clear Apophyllites. If one can imagine one's point of awareness moving into the interior of one of the Clear Apophyllite crystals, one will find, once "inside," that geometric corridors of Light lead off in all directions, and that one's consciousness can travel along these corridors to myriad realms of inner experience. Keeping one or more of the Clear Apophyllites in one's environment can provide an atmosphere of purity and spiritual presence in one's home, meditation area or work space.

One can use Clear Apophyllites to contact one's guardian angels and spirit guides, or to visit the higher angelic realms. They are useful for developing prophetic vision. Clear Apophyllite works synergistically with Azeztulite, Scolecite, Natrolite, Phenacite, Herderite, Brookite and Tibetan Tektite. Selenite in conjunction with Clear Apophyllite can open the pathway to conscious communion with the Higher Self.

APOPHYLLITE, GREEN

KEY WORDS Connection with Nature spirits
CHAKRAS Crown (7th), Third Eye (6th), Heart (4th)
ELEMENT Wind, Earth **PHYSICAL** Helps with
healing degenerative diseases, detoxifying the body
EMOTIONAL Encourages joy in the wonder of physical
life, finding hope and sweetness **SPIRITUAL** Facilitates
communication with Nature spirits, psychic opening

G REEN APOPHYLLITE is a hydrated potassium calcium silicate mineral with a tetragonal crystal system and a hardness of 5. Most Green Apophyllite is found in India.

Green Apophyllite crystals and clusters emanate a sweet energy that resonates with the abundant life force of the world of Nature. Meditation with them can open one's perception to seeing and interacting with Nature spirits, devas and even to telepathic communication with animals and plants. Just keeping one or more of these stones in one's indoor environment will infuse it with the refreshing energies of Nature. Carrying or wearing one will increase the flow of life force throughout one's whole being. These are ideal stones for those recovering from illness—invoking the energies of rebirth, healing and growth. Green Apophyllite can assist those who wish to work with Nature spirits in gardening or in restoring wild areas. It can assist one in animal communication, opening the psychic channel whereby one can interact with both individual animals and the collective minds of entire species. It can work similarly with plants and even other minerals.

Green Apophyllite resonates with Seriphos Green Quartz, Green Phantom Quartz, Seraphinite, Hiddenite and Fairy Wand Quartz. Dioptase, Ajoite and Emerald enhance Green Apophyllite's capacity to facilitate forgiveness and emotional healing.

AQUA AURA QUARTZ

KEY WORDS Calming and relaxing, connection with spiritual realms, enhanced communication, psychic protection **CHAKRAS** Throat (5th), Third Eye (6th) **ELEMENT** Water **PHYSICAL** Cooling fever, relieving stress, cleansing the auric field **EMOTIONAL** Calming anger, finding inner peace **SPIRITUAL** Aids channeling, communication of truth, creating prosperity

AQUA AURA QUARTZ is produced when clear Quartz points or clusters go through a special treatment process in which their surfaces are bonded with vaporized or finely powdered pure gold. The resulting crystals exhibit vivid blue surfaces with subtle flashes of iridescent rainbow colors.

Aqua Aura Quartz is highly stimulating to the throat chakra, enhancing one's ability to communicate inner truth. It also has a calming effect on the emotional body. Aqua Aura Quartz can be used to soothe anger, cool feverishness and release stress. It is a stone for enhancing one's access to the truth of the emotions and the inner portals of Spirit. It can be an aid in becoming a conscious channel for spiritual wisdom.

Aqua Aura Quartz has a very high and intense vibration. It can be used to activate all of the chakras. It can smooth and heal the auric field and release negativity from one's emotional, physical, etheric and astral bodies. Wearing Aqua Aura Quartz can help one to shine with one's inner beauty, to attract wealth and success, to bring forth esoteric wisdom, to relieve depression and anxiety, and to assist in creating an aura of peace and well-being in oneself and one's surroundings. It is a stone of spiritual elevation, that can help raise the vibration of humanity as we enter the next phase of evolution.

AQUAMARINE

KEY WORDS Cooling, soothing, enhancement of clear communication **CHAKRAS** Throat (5th), Heart (4th)
ELEMENT Water **PHYSICAL** Helps with sore throats and throat conditions, inflammatory illnesses **EMOTIONAL** Good for calming anger, relieving stress, expressing true emotions **SPIRITUAL** Speaking one's deepest truth, meeting the Divine Feminine

AQUAMARINE is a blue or blue-green variety of Beryl, a beryllium aluminum silicate with a hardness of 7.5 to 8. Its name, derived from the Latin meaning "water of the sea" is an apt description of the color and clarity of fine Aquamarine crystals.

Aquamarine facilitates calming and cooling, from anger to hot flashes, and they also activate the throat chakra, assisting in the clear communication of one's highest truth. They are stones of the Water element, bringing one in touch with the subconscious, the domains of Spirit and our deepest emotions. Their energy is as refreshing as a shower under a cool waterfall. It brings one to a relaxed, alert stage of consciousness in which one is fully aware of one's own store of knowledge, wisdom and feelings, and able to articulate them all with clarity and conviction.

For women, Aquamarine lends the courage and clarity to express one's inner knowing, and it enhances intuitive abilities. It is a doorway to communication with the Goddess, both within the self and in Her outer manifestations. For men, Aquamarine helps dispel emotional numbness and the difficulty men sometimes experience in communicating their feelings. It also calms frustration and helps one keep one's temper, even when provoked. Aquamarine connects to the Divine Feminine, the Source of life energies, and those who wish to know Her better can use this stone as a gateway.

ARAGONITE, BLUE

KEY WORDS Intuition, increased emotional perception and psychic ability
CHAKRAS Throat (5th), Heart (4th), Third Eye (6th) **ELEMENT** Wind, Water
PHYSICAL Aids respiratory issues, lung health, *prana yama*, breath work
EMOTIONAL Increases enjoyment of emotion, renewed zest for life
SPIRITUAL Facilitates enhancement of spiritual and psychic capacities

ARAGONITE is a calcium carbonate mineral with a hardness of 3.5 to 4. It occurs in various colors, including white, gray, reddish, yellow-green and blue. Blue Aragonites occur in numerous shapes, including stalactitic, and are turquoise colored. Most are found in China.

Blue Aragonites enhance all levels of emotional perception and intensify one's enjoyment of all emotional states. It relieves the fear which leads us to numb ourselves to the joys and sorrows of life, and brings a renewed zest and courage for experiencing all of one's feelings. It is not only a powerful intensifier of positive emotional states but is also of assistance in healing past and present emotional wounds. It allows one to embrace fully everything that life brings, making it easier to see the beauty and perfection of both triumph and tragedy, love and loss, as well as all states in between.

Just as it activates and improves the state of the emotional body, Blue Aragonite intensifies one's natural empathic and psychic abilities. This is of special importance to those who are healers, psychic readers, medical intuitives or body workers. Its vibrations are harmonious with the reiki energies. This is an excellent stone to use in body layouts for self-healing or activation of higher states of awareness.

Blue Aragonite combines well with Moldavite, Aquamarine, Owyhee Blue Opal, Larimar and Blue Topaz.

ARAGONITE, SPANISH

KEY WORDS Awareness of the living world, awakening higher awareness, attunement to the future stream, grounding heavenly energies on Earth **CHAKRAS** Third Eye (6th), Crown (7th), Etheric (8th–14th) **ELEMENT** Wind, Fire, Storm **PHYSICAL** Supports regeneration and rejuvenation of the cells and body **EMOTIONAL** Strengthens empathy, especially with animals **SPIRITUAL** Opens Crown for full energy infusion and Light Body activation

SPANISH ARAGONITE is a calcium carbonate with an orthorhombic crystal system and a hardness of 3.5 to 4. Its form is columnar and its colors are gray-green and purple. It is from Molina de Aragon, Spain.

Spanish Aragonite is the most highly energetic form of Aragonite. It powerfully stimulates the third eye and crown chakra and allows one to attune to the etheric chakras above the head. This facilitates connection with the higher-frequency domains such as the angelic realms. One of the strengths of Spanish Aragonite is its ability to help us connect empathically with animals. It is highly recommended for those working with animal communication. On a deeper level, Spanish Aragonite encourages one's capacity to link with the living world. Working with this stone in meditation or carrying it through the day can sensitize one's energy field to subtle currents operating beneath the surface. One recognizes one's own creating activity, and the creating activity of the world. Spanish Aragonite carries powerful life-force currents, which enter through the crown chakra, initiating the infusion of the Light Body into the physical form, as well as the regeneration of the organism.

Spanish Aragonote works well with Herderite, Natrolite, Phenacite and all the Azeztulites. Guardianite is a powerful ally to help ground the pro-found energies coming through Spanish Aragonite.

ARAGONITE, STAR CLUSTERS

KEY WORDS Balanced energies, emotional healing, strength, confidence **CHAKRAS** All **ELEMENT** Storm **PHYSICAL** Supports healing and regenerating bones, increased vitality and stamina **EMOTIONAL** Healing emotional wounds, aligning the self with love **SPIRITUAL** An ideal diagnostic aid in energy work, clears the auric field

ARAGONITE is a calcium carbonate mineral with a hardness of 3.5 to 4. It occurs in various colors, including white, gray, reddish, yellow-green and blue. Aragonite Star Clusters are reddish clusters of Aragonite crystals, and are found in Morocco.

Aragonite Star Clusters are powerful allies for the healing and balancing of the emotional body. They can assist in maintaining a center of serenity in trying circumstances and in discharging subconsciously held tensions relating to past emotional wounds. When such attachments have been cleared from the body and the auric field, Aragonite Star Clusters can facilitate a real adventure of exploration, wherein one may cruise the archives of one's soul history, recovering beneficial information for soul advancement. These stones can help one be consciously aware of imbalances within one's energy field or within the field of someone else who holds them. They are powerful diagnostic tools for crystal workers who do body layouts. Also, wearing an Aragonite Star Cluster can enhance one's feeling of emotional strength and confidence, allowing one to become a "human star" emanating love and compassion for others. They are wonderful tools for releasing pain and fear, and bringing more love into the world.

Aragonite Stars resonate with all Calcites, as well as Selenite, Celestite, Phenacite and Herkimer "Diamonds."

ASTARALINE

KEY WORDS Protecting and nourishing the Light Body, healing the cells **CHAKRAS** All **ELEMENT** Wind, Water **PHYSICAL** Supports healing of destructive habits on a cellular level **EMOTIONAL** Encourages comfort and joy in the transformation process **SPIRITUAL** Builds a "cocoon" for the Light Body, activates the Divine blueprint

Astaraline is a combination of Muscovite, Quartz and Cronstedtite. It is grayish pink or grayish yellow. It is found in Colorado, USA.

Astaraline is a very active stone. It resonates throughout the body, readily entering through the third eye and the heart chakra, and making itself felt throughout the body, even to the hands and feet. It fills the Liquid Crystal Body Matrix with a sense of well-being, as if one is being cradled in Light. As a stone of cellular consciousness, Astaraline can help those involved in self-healing to bring harmony and functional alignment to all of the bodily organs and systems. Its nourishing, coherent emanations encourage the cells to find the new path to existing in a state of grace, leaving behind the old habits of deterioration and degeneration. Astaraline amplifies the power of the Divine blueprint for the Body of Light, not as a separate vehicle for the ascension of the individual, but as the transformation of the gross body into one of radiant spiritual Light. It is as if the stones' currents form an inner cocoon of Light within which we can go through the metamorphosis into a new luminous Self. Astaraline stimulates the cells to produce more biophotons and it helps one consciously link with one's Higher Self. It is a fully awakened stone, having come forward to help with humanity's transition into beings of Light.

Astaraline harmonizes with all other stones. Azeztulites can amplify its Light Body awakening. Guardianite helps with protection.

ASTROPHYLLITE

KEY WORDS Self-knowledge, link with
one's Divine Blueprint **CHAKRAS** All
ELEMENT Storm **PHYSICAL** Assists in over-
coming addictions and self-destructive habits **EMOTIONAL** Aids in overcoming
depression and boredom, promotes the zest of self-discovery **SPIRITUAL** Inspires
realization of multidimensional self and life purpose

Astrophyllite is a complex mineral, a potassium, sodium, iron, manganese, titanium silicate with a hardness of 3.5. It forms in bladed crystals
which often occur in starbursts within its tan matrix rock. Its color is most
often a coppery bronze but can also be golden yellow.

Astrophyllite aids in navigating the twists and turns of travels beyond
the body—in and beyond the astral realm. It can help even in the often cha-
otic domain of dreams. It is both a spur to expanding consciousness and an
anchor to assist one in returning to "home base."

Astrophyllite can reveal the hidden pattern of one's Divine blueprint, or
life purpose. This may be revealed through an increase in synchronicities.
Astrophyllite is both a magnet for these synchronicities and an aid to being
more aware of their occurrence and meaning.

Being out of alignment with one's inner purpose can cause all sorts of
symptoms, such as boredom, depression, overeating, addictions and so forth.
Astrophyllite can aid one in shedding such states, as an amplifier of one's
latent interest in the deeper and more significant purposes of one's life. The
complex structures and flashing reflections of Astrophyllite resonate with its
deeper purpose—to shine a light on the mirror of consciousness, to illuminate the true self.

Astrophyllite harmonizes with Moldavite, Tibetan Tektite, Natrolite, Scolecite, Black Tourmaline, Smokey Quartz and Hematite.

AURALITE-23

KEY WORDS Union with Higher Self, inner purification, increased psychic sensitivity, visionary consciousness **CHAKRAS** All **ELEMENT** Storm **PHYSICAL** Initiates cellular purification, can dispel chronic problems **EMOTIONAL** Inspires the joy of meeting with one's Higher Self **SPIRITUAL** Enhances psychic ability, links one to the Magic Presence

Auralite-23 is the name given to a group of crystals from north of Lake Superior, Canada. They are primarily composed of amethyst, a silicon-dioxide mineral with a hardness of 7, and are said to contain as many as twenty-two other minerals.

Auralite-23 stimulates higher awareness and telepathic connection with one's guides and guardian spirits. It offers a direct and immediate link to what is called the "Magic Presence" in esoteric literature—the Higher Self beyond the everyday "I." The blessings offered by Auralite-23 include inner purification—the release of patterns of anxiety, resentment, judgment, depression and defeat. This facilitates an uplifting of one's spirit and an awakening to the potentialities for a new life, all the way into one's cellular consciousness. The body itself is awed and made reverent by the clearing of the veils of illusion and the dawning of the presence of one's Higher Self. Other effects can include an increase in psychic sensitivity, enhanced insight, disappearance of chronic physical problems, a balanced awakening of kundalini, spontaneous visions of future events, enhanced capacity for soul travel and lucid dreaming, and experiences with Angels.

Auralite-23 works most harmoniously with all forms of Azeztulite as well as Rosophia, Guardianite, Mystic Merlinite and Master Shamanite. Auralite-23 can be enhanced with the Azozeo super-activation process.

AVENTURINE, GREEN

KEY WORDS Vitality, growth, confidence
CHAKRAS Heart (4th) **ELEMENT** Water,
Earth **PHYSICAL** Supports general healing,
increase of life force, heart and circulation
EMOTIONAL Inspires optimism, self-confidence, peace amid difficulty
SPIRITUAL Brings good fortune and blessing, manifestation and prosperity

G REEN AVENTURINE is a member of the Quartz family, a silicon dioxide mineral with a hardness of 7. Its structure is hexagonal (trigonal) and is crypto-crystalline. Its name is derived from the Italian *a ventura*, a type of glass discovered around AD 1700. The color of Green Aventurine comes from microscopic Fuchsite particles.

Green Aventurine is a stone of optimism and zest for life. It helps one move forward with confidence into new situations, and even assists one in embracing such challenging issues as aging, illness and one's own mortality. It brings with it a feeling of lightness, even humor, as it assists one in dealing with the ups and downs of life. In emotional life, it allows one to look at the bright side of difficult issues. In healing, it instills life force and aids in rebuilding depleted energy reserves.

Green Aventurine can be a stone of "good luck" and is recommended for those who wish to manifest greater prosperity. It can assist in other situations where one's overt external actions do not control the outcome. It would be a good stone to carry to the racetrack, a tax audit or a first date.

Green Aventurine harmonizes with all members of the Quartz family, as well as Moldavite, Moonstone, Morganite and both Green and Pink Tourmaline. The Tourmalines can magnify Aventurine's heart chakra energies, making one prone to give and find love more easily.

AVENTURINE, BLUE

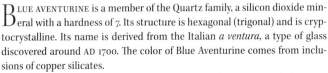

KEY WORDS Psychic attunement, self-discipline, inner strength **CHAKRAS** Third Eye (6th) **ELEMENT** Wind, Water
PHYSICAL Supports hormonal balance, respiration, circulation, healthy blood
EMOTIONAL Aids in achieving emotional maturity, self-discipline
SPIRITUAL Enhances psychic and intuitive capacities

Blue aventurine is a member of the Quartz family, a silicon dioxide mineral with a hardness of 7. Its structure is hexagonal (trigonal) and is cryptocrystalline. Its name is derived from the Italian *a ventura*, a type of glass discovered around AD 1700. The color of Blue Aventurine comes from inclusions of copper silicates.

Blue Aventurine is a stone of self-discipline and inner strength. It assists one in making clear decisions and sticking by them. It can be useful in initiating changes of problematic habits such as smoking, overeating, substance abuse and even traits such as selfishness and passive aggression. It can be useful for individuals with the "Peter Pan" syndrome of never wanting to grow up. Under the influence of Blue Aventurine, one may realize that adulthood is preferable to perpetual youth. As one works with Blue Aventurine, innate powers and sensitivities which had been blocked by inner disharmonies can begin to surface. Psychic and intuitive abilities, attunement to beneficial inner guidance, the capacity to empathically "read" others, and the knack for "tuning in" to information from the Akashic record are among the potentials which Blue Aventurine can help one realize.

Blue Aventurine harmonizes with other Aventurines, Amethyst, Clear Quartz, Citrine, Opal, Moldavite, Lapis, Sodalite, Phenacite, Azeztulite, Celestite, Herderite, Scolecite, Brookite, Natrolite and Datolite.

AVENTURINE, RED

KEY WORDS Discernment, determination, strength, creativity, sexuality **CHAKRAS** Root (1st), Sexual/Creative (2nd), Third Eye (6th) **ELEMENT** Earth, Fire **PHYSICAL** Supports the immune system, blood and liver **EMOTIONAL** Aids endurance, faith and perseverance through difficulty **SPIRITUAL** Facilitates insight, artistic inspiration, manifestation of visions

R‌ED AVENTURINE is a member of the Quartz family, a silicon dioxide mineral with a hardness of 7. Its structure is hexagonal (trigonal) and is crypto-crystalline. Its name is derived from the Italian *a ventura*, a type of glass discovered around AD 1700. The color of Red Aventurine comes from inclusions of Hematite.

Red Aventurine is a stone of vitality, creativity, sexuality, mental alertness and manifestation through action. It increases one's desire to take on and overcome the challenges of life, and it helps one find the determination to persevere. It increases the flow of life force, helping those with low vitality to get things done. Individuals recovering from illness can use it to aid in rebuilding their physical energies, as well as their confidence. It can help people with diminished sexual appetites find renewed excitement. Artists, writers and others who rely upon their creative capacities may discover that Red Aventurine assists them in finding new inspiration. Those who must work long hours with focused attention will find a powerful ally in Red Aventurine. And everyone who wishes to bring their desires into reality will take heart from Red Aventurine's ability to infuse one with confidence, faith and energy.

Red Aventurine harmonizes with Quartz, Ruby, Zincite, Phenacite, Golden Labradorite and Moldavite. If Red Aventurine makes one feel excessively powerful, Ajoite can temper any harshness.

AXINITE

KEY WORDS Grounding, endurance, vitality, inner exploration **CHAKRAS** Root (1st), Third Eye (6th) **ELEMENT** Storm **PHYSICAL** Supports general healing, vitality, energizing the body **EMOTIONAL** Aids conflict resolution, cooperation, inner harmony **SPIRITUAL** Brings awareness of other spiritual planes, past-life memory

$\mathbf{A}$XINITE is a borosilicate mineral with a hardness of 6.5 to 7. Its color is usually brown, although blue and violet specimens have also been found. Its crystal system is triclinic. Its name is derived from the similarity of its sharp-edged, wedge-shaped crystals to the form of an ax. It is found in France, Mexico, Russia and the USA.

Axinite emanates a very wholesome and helpful energy. It is clarifying to one's consciousness, harmonizing to one's emotions, expansive to one's awareness and balancing to one's physical energies. It is strongly grounding, and it helps one bring Earth energies up through one's feet and into one's whole body. It can be a powerful aid to one's endurance, and it is recommended for anyone who works long hours.

Axinite acts to allow the waking mind access to the subconscious and superconscious realms. It also helps one hold in memory the experiences of the spiritual planes. Axinite can be used to assist one in gaining conscious access to the morphic fields of knowledge accumulated by each species throughout time and space. Axinite can function as a "savant stone," facilitating direct mental access to knowledge, independent of any outside source.

Axinite harmonizes with Zincite, Moldavite, Herderite, Phenacite, Azeztulite, Beryllonite, Tremolite and Danburite. Axinite with Alexandrite can facilitate past-life recall.

AZEZTULITE (General Overview)

Azeztulite has one of the most unusual stories of any stone in this book. Chemically it is a variety of Quartz with a hexagonal (trigonal) crystal system and a hardness of 7. The original Azeztulite came from a find in North Carolina around 1970. Over thirty years later, a second occurrence was found in Vermont. More Azeztulites have since been discovered in South India, the Rocky Mountains and Vermont of the USA, northern India, and an island off the coast of Africa. There have been new finds in North Carolina, and the most recent Azeztulite discoveries are from New Zealand. All of these new forms carry Azeztulite frequencies, yet each has its own special qualities.

The original White Azeztulite discovery was predicted before it occurred. Naisha Ahsian reported having telepathically connected to an angelic group soul entity called Azez. They declared themselves to be servants of the Nameless Light of the Great Central Sun, and announced the activation of an earthly stone to carry the currents of the Nameless Light, for purposes of the spiritual awakening of humanity and the Earth. The stone was ultimately found, and it had exceptional energetic properties, including cellular regeneration and Light Body Activation. Azeztulite is what has come to be called an Awakened Quartz. Most recently, the Azozeo Super-Activation process was discovered, taking all Azeztulites which undergo it to a much higher vibrational level.

The Azez stated that they are etherically stationed at key vibrational points all over the Earth, and that our work with them, and with the Azeztulites, can awaken more and more Quartz around the Earth to carry the illuminating energies of the Great Central Sun, the Divine center of the Universe. Their ultimate goal is for all the Quartz on Earth to carry and manifest these high frequencies of spiritual enlightenment. They predicted the discovery of more forms of Azeztulite in different localities, and this has come about. (For more information, see *The Book of Stones* and *Stones of the New Consciousness*.)

AZEZTULITE, WHITE

KEY WORDS Receiving the Nameless Light, link with the Great Central Sun, cellular reattunement for healing and awakening **CHAKRAS** All (including the Etheric chakras 8th–14th) **ELEMENT** Storm **PHYSICAL** Initiates cellular regeneration, infusion of the body with spiritual Light **EMOTIONAL** Supports awakening to Universal Love, clearing the emotional body **SPIRITUAL** Inspires union with Divine Light, mutual awakening with the Earth

WHITE AZEZTULITE is the original type of Azeztulite found in North Carolina and Vermont. It is an opaque white or transparent Quartz with a hardness of 7. It is distinguished from other Quartz primarily by its powerful high vibrational currents.

White Azeztulite from Vermont and North Carolina carries one of the highest spiritual frequencies of any stone. Its currents of the Nameless Light from the Great Central Sun flow throughout the body, realigning the entire Liquid Crystal Body Matrix, encouraging cellular regeneration and healing. These stones stimulate all of the potentials of the Spiritual Human Being, the awakened beings we are destined to become. Through our connection with the currents of Azeztulite, we can channel Divine Light into the Earth for her healing and awakening. Meditation with White Azeztulite brings Light into one's consciousness, often beginning as scintillating sparks, evolving into the immersion of one's awareness in the Clear Light of the Divine. White Azeztulite quickens cellular consciousness as well, aiding in the development of the Mind of the Cells, a new center of awareness destined to work in cocreative partnership with us. It is a stone of Light Body awakening, of resurrection and Ascension. It is the key stone of the New Consciousness and can elevate the energies of all other stones.

AZEZTULITE, SANDA ROSA

KEY WORDS Healing, inner harmony, grounding spiritual Light in the body, purification, attunement with the soul of the Earth   **CHAKRAS** All (1st–7th) **ELEMENT** Storm, Earth   **PHYSICAL** Supports digestive system, harmonizes body systems and consciousness   **EMOTIONAL** Supports inner serenity, soothing the etheric body **SPIRITUAL** Enhances meditation and dreams, meeting spiritual beings

SANDA ROSA AZEZTULITE which was found in North Carolina where Azeztulite was first discovered, is different from the original Azeztulite in that it contains particles of Spessartite Garnet and Green Black Mica. It is primarily white with black and reddish veins and spots.

Sanda Rosa Azeztulite, perhaps because of its mica and garnet inclusions, is more grounded than other forms of Azeztulite, and is therefore easier for some highly sensitive people to work with. It works in a more body-oriented way than some other Azeztulites, harmonizing the Liquid Crystal Body Matrix and bringing various bodily systems into proper energetic alignment. It is very soothing to the etheric body and is particularly helpful to the digestive system.

Sanda Rosa Azeztulite stimulates the third eye and crown chakras in a way that allows one to see into very deep levels of meditative awareness. It is calming to the emotional body, and this benefits those who are working to quiet the mind. Sanda Rosa Azeztulite is a good stone to take into the realm of dreaming. It stimulates vivid images in the psyche in both meditative and sleep experiences, and it helps one remember dreams. It aids one in meeting high beings on the inner planes.

Sanda Rosa Azeztulite harmonizes with all Azeztulites, Moldavite, Circle Stones, Seraphinite, Tanzanite, Morganite and Seriphos Green Quartz.

AZEZTULITE, AMAZEZ

KEY WORDS Purification, healing, communication with spiritual beings, psychic capacities **CHAKRAS** Third Eye (6th) **ELEMENT** Storm **PHYSICAL** Promotes resonance with one's Divine Blueprint of health **EMOTIONAL** Frees one from negativity and negative attachments **SPIRITUAL** Enhances psychic capacities, stimulates the process of enlightenment.

AMAZEZ is an amethyst variety of Azeztulite, a silicon-dioxide mineral with a hardness of 7. It was discovered on an island off the southeastern coast of Africa.

Amazez is an ideal therapeutic stone for crystal practitioners. It can be used to bring spiritual aid to any weak or afflicted areas of the body. It can clear any gray areas from the auric field, and wake up the power of one's Divine Blueprint. It can dispel all types of negativity from the body and auric field—including implants and entities—and is powerful enough to be used as a tool in "psychic surgery."

Amazez can cleanse one's field in a way that makes possible conscious interaction with higher beings on many spiritual planes. The angels, and even the Azez themselves, can more readily approach one who has been purified by this stone. Amazez enhances all the psychic capacities, including clairvoyance, clairaudience, clairsentience, remote viewing, prophetic vision, psychic healing and many more. It can stimulate intuitive abilities, acting as a source of creative inspiration and instant knowing. It can powerfully activate the "Mouth of God" chakra near the top of the spine at the back of the head.

Amazez harmonizes with all Azeztulites, as well as Auralite-23, Purple Angeline, Violet Flame Opal, Guardianite, Phenacite, Danburite, Scolecite, Brookite, Natrolite, Merkabite Calcite and Nirvana Quartz.

AZEZTULITE, PINK

KEY WORDS Heart awareness, emotional healing, serenity, compassion
CHAKRAS Heart (4th), Third Eye (6th), Crown (7th), Etheric (8th–14th)
ELEMENT Storm, Water **PHYSICAL** Aids with soothing the heart, relieving stress **EMOTIONAL** Supports healing the emotional body and inner child
SPIRITUAL Facilitates soul retrieval, Ascension, empathic resonance

PINK AZEZTULITE was discovered in Colorado in 2008. It is a mixture of Quartz and Pink Dolomite, and is softer than other Azeztulites.

Pink Azeztulite resonates rapidly through the Liquid Crystal Body Matrix, and one senses tingling over the entire surface of one's skin, as though being gently touched by innumerable tiny hands. (These may indeed be the hands of the Azez!) Yet even with its tingles, Pink Azeztulite is a deeply soothing stone. As it awakens sensitivity, and as it sweeps through the liquid crystal body with the pattern of the Nameless Light, it also soothes the emotional body. It goes to the heart and seeds there the pattern of compassionate acceptance and love toward all aspects of oneself. It helps heal fragmentation caused by emotional wounding, and it deeply comforts the inner child.

Pink Azeztulite can aid in soul retrieval. It is an ideal stone for healers, facilitating a compassionate rapport between practitioner and client. It promotes empathy, and can help those who do intuitive readings to connect with the client's soul, and to read the client's Divine blueprint.

Pink Azeztulite facilitates a sweet, calm, serene, yet highly activated state of awareness. It clears all emotional blocks to the Ascension process and opens the heart to receive spiritual Light. It teaches the body that it is worthy of healing and regeneration. It harmonizes with heart stones such as Morganite, Rosophia, Rhodocrosite and Rose Quartz.

AZEZTULITE, CINNAZEZ
(CINNABAR AZEZTULITE)

KEY WORDS Consciousness expansion, brain stimulation, increased synchronicities, alchemical knowledge **CHAKRAS** All **ELEMENT** Storm **PHYSICAL** Stimulates nervous system **EMOTIONAL** Increases zest for life **SPIRITUAL** Access to inner realms

CINNAZEZ is a red, white and black mixture of quartz, cinnabar and zinc, recently discovered in New Zealand. Its vibrational qualities have earned it a place among the several types of New Zealand Azeztulites.

Cinnazez is a quickener of consciousness and an awakener of higher awareness. It can stimulate one's nervous system to actualize latent capacities of clairvoyance, telepathic communication, attunement to heavenly realms, and direct knowledge of Divine truth. It is felt as the solidified essence of the Philosopher's Stone, and it can help the body open to become a conduit of the Celestial Fire of the Great Central Sun.

Cinnazez stimulates the brain and central nervous system, increasing one's receptivity to fields of knowledge in the inner realms, including alchemical knowledge. It aids those who wish to access the Akashic Records. It makes one into an "attractor" of new knowledge and insights in the same way that a metal post attracts lightning. Cinnazez also stimulates the intelligence of the heart, and strengthens the neural networks through which the mind and heart communicate. Because it opens the channels of angelic and interdimensional communication, it is an ally for those seeking to understand the inner workings of the Universe. It can trigger an increase in synchronicities in one's life, and awareness of their meaning.

Cinnazez harmonizes with all Azeztulites, as well as Phenacite, Danburite, Cinnabar, Zincite, Spanish Aragonite, Herderite and Brookite.

AZEZTULITE, GOLDEN CRYSTALS

KEY WORDS Attunement to the Gold-White Light, Light Body awakening, time travel, accessing the Hall of [Akashic] Records, kindling the Sun of the Heart
CHAKRAS Heart (4th), Third Eye (6th), Crown (7th), Soul Star and Etheric (8th–14th) **ELEMENT** Storm **PHYSICAL** stimulation of the nervous system to new capacities **EMOTIONAL** empathic awareness, compassion, commitment to truth **SPIRITUAL** incarnation of the Divine, direct knowing, transformation

GOLDEN AZEZTULITE CRYSTALS were found in North Carolina in 2008. They are the only prismatically crystallized Azeztulites, except for some small, rare Vermont specimens. They vary from pale milky white to smoky brown, with various shades of golden Citrine, but are all called Golden Azeztulite because of their link to the Gold-White Ray. Golden Azeztulite crystals are important in their stimulation and awakening of the Light Body. In meditation, their currents can quickly fill the body and one's auric field with Gold-White Light. This energy can center in the heart chakra, kindling the Sun of the Heart, which is the incarnation of the Divine within the human.

Golden Azeztulite is aligned with the purpose of our evolution into spiritual human beings. It specifically is attuned to the unknown latent capacities of the brain/mind and nervous system, stimulating the prefrontal lobes of the brain very intensely and very precisely. It activates our capacity of direct knowing, simply by turning attention to a question or a subject, or toward the Hall of Records on the inner planes. Golden Azeztulite also activates latent capacities such as time travel, empathic awareness of others, and consciousness as interior Light. It harmonizes with Moldavite and all high vibration stones of Ascension.

AZEZTULITE, HONEY AND CREAM

KEY WORDS Inner Light and sweetness, pleasure, bliss and ecstasy, contact with the Azez, love, blessing, emotional healing, recovery from illness **CHAKRAS** All **ELEMENTS** Water, Wind, Earth **PHYSICAL** Supports recovery of vitality after illness **EMOTIONAL** Emotional healing, currents of sweetness **SPIRITUAL** Emanates love and spiritual blessing, offers comfort and sense of security

HONEY AND CREAM AZEZTULITES are found in remote rivers and ocean bays in New Zealand. Their name is derived from their brown-and-white coloration. Like other Azeztulites, they are a quartz with a hardness of 7.

Honey and Cream Azeztulite emanates currents of sweetness and spiritual Light. It is a very pleasurable sensation, stimulating one's higher capacities and filling one with soft, comforting vibrations. These stones generate love within every cell of the body. They combine power and love in a way that recalls Nature in her most fertile and lovely expressions. In sleep, they can waft you on a carpet of sweetness into the realm of dreams, which are often profoundly spiritual. One can even travel to the Great Central Sun, accompanied by the Azez themselves. These stones can aid one in entering the Activity of Blessing, an essential element of the New Consciousness

Honey and Cream Azeztulites are ideal allies for emotional healing. They can soothe and comfort one's inner child, and they can be used in soul-retrieval, providing a cocoon of loving currents within which one may "call home" any lost parts of one's original wholeness. They are ideal for recovering from exhaustion caused by stress or overwork. These stones especially support the adrenals and the parasympathetic nervous system. Honey and Cream Azeztulites resonate with all other Azeztulites, and the Synergy Twelve and Ascension Stones. (See Appendix II) They can be Azozeo super-activated.

AZEZTULITE, HIMALAYA GOLD

KEY WORDS Creative manifestation, cocreating with Sophia, kindling the Great Central Sun in the heart, filling the body with Gold Light **CHAKRAS** Heart (4th), Third Eye (6th), Crown (7th), Soul Star and Etheric (8th–14th) **ELEMENT** Storm **PHYSICAL** Energetically strengthens the visceral organs and systems **EMOTIONAL** Initiates ecstatic union with Sophia, Soul of the World **SPIRITUAL** Enhances one's capacities of creating, inner vision

Himalaya gold azeztulite was discovered in 2008, in northern India near the Himalaya mountains. Like other Azeztulites, it is a form of Quartz with a hardness of 7, in this case displaying a bright yellow color.

Himalaya Gold Azeztulite is one of the prime stones of creative manifestation through the will. It has a powerful resonance with the solar plexus chakra, stimulating one's capacity to bring one's visions into reality. This occurs because it also stimulates the Seat of Vision in the Third Eye, inspiring one with enlightened awareness of one's creative power.

Himalaya Gold Azeztulite kindles the resonant awakening of the Great Central Sun in the heart. The currents of all Azeztulites derive from this Source energy, and every human heart is potentially a holographic embodiment of this Divine Sun. This is the Christic energy, the Son of the Sun incarnating in the world through us. When we allow it fully, our awakened creative capacity joins with that of Sophia, Soul of the World, and we can ultimately be united with Her in shared cocreative consciousness, transforming the universe into a Cosmos of Love. Himalaya Gold Azeztulite also lends power to our personal intention, helping us manifest our desires through alignment with the Tao. These stones resonate with Rosophia and all high-vibration stones of Ascension.

AZEZTULITE, PINK FIRE

KEY WORDS Inner fire of Divine Love, High Heart activation, passionate self-identification with Love, emotional and physical self-healing **CHAKRAS** Heart (4th) and High Heart (between 4th and 5th)
ELEMENT Fire **PHYSICAL** Supports recovery from autoimmune illnesses, facilitates healing by filling the cells with the Light and Fire of Divine Love **EMOTIONAL** Highly beneficial for emotional healing **SPIRITUAL** Kindles inner fire of Divine Love, for both receiving and transmitting Love

P INK FIRE AZEZTULITE is colored by streaks of dark, brownish-red hematite. It is a super-activated type of Agnitite, a quartz with a hardness of 7.

Pink Fire Azeztulite is a stone of passion. It encourages one to love with great intensity, with no holding back. It triggers the potential to truly know that love is our foundation, our Life Force and the animating energy of the Universe. Pink Fire Azeztulite can teach the cells that love is the antidote to illness and even death. Thus it is ideal for those seeking to heal dysfunctions such as autoimmune disorders. It is useful for emotional self-healing as well, bringing an infusion of unconditional love into one's energy field, dissolving the lingering echoes of old wounds. It can trigger moments of exuberant joy, awakening one's desire to serve the flow of love as it rises to permeate and transform our world. This stone offers proof that evolutionary transformation through love is both essential and genuine—its own special energies were kindled through subjecting it to the Azozeo super-activation process.

Pink Fire Azeztulite pieces can be used to fill one's environment with powerful love energies. The stone can be worn to help keep oneself always connected to the currents of Divine Love. It works harmoniously with all other Azeztulites, as well as Azumar, Healerite, Rose Quartz, Morganite, Rhodonite, Rhodocrosite and Kunzite.

AZEZTULITE, RED FIRE

KEY WORDS Life Force, enthusiasm, vitality, power, passion, sexuality, etherization of the blood, intelligence, visionary experience, healing, longevity, alchemical transmutation **CHAKRAS** All **ELEMENT** Earth, Fire, Storm **PHYSICAL** Supports all parts of the body, especially blood, heart, lungs and brain **EMOTIONAL** Kindles enthusiasm, confidence, power, optimism, sexuality **SPIRITUAL** Stimulates intelligence, visionary experience, alchemical transformation of the self

Red Fire Azeztulite is an opaque, deep-red form of Azeztulite found only in New Zealand. It is chemically a type of quartz with a hardness of 7.

Red Fire Azeztulite is a stone of power and passion. It has an affinity with the blood, which carries its currents on enlightened energy to every cell in the body. This triggers an "inner rejoicing" that brings forth a surge of passion, confidence, optimism and power like a red fire within one's soul. This stone can be used to replenish one's strength, endurance and vitality. It can activate the energy centers linked to sexuality, and can even enhance the sexual currents between spiritual partners.

Red Fire Azeztulite stimulates the intelligence of brain, heart and body. It aids with solving problems and provides increased access to inspired ideas. It greatly enhances one's enthusiasm and energy for carrying one's visions forward into manifestation. It can be used to improve the quality and duration of one's physical life. As a stone of spiritual self-healing, Red Fire Azeztulite resonates beneficially with the heart, lungs and bloodstream as well as the brain. However, its vibrations can be utilized for any organ or bodily system.

Red Fire Azeztulite resonates well with all other Azeztulites, plus Master Shamanite, Phenacite, Danburite, Natrolite, Scolecite, Zincite, Crimson Cuprite, New Zealand Carnelian, Rosophia and Morganite.

SAURALITE
(AZEZTULITE, NEW ZEALAND)

KEY WORDS Realization of Divine purpose,
marriage of Heaven and Earth **CHAKRAS** All
ELEMENT Earth, Wind, Fire, Water,
Storm **PHYSICAL** Triggers bodily experience of ecstatic union of Earth with
Divine Light **EMOTIONAL** Heals grief, fear, pain and anxiety; brings a flood of joy
and ecstasy **SPIRITUAL** Awakens one fully to the Divine union with the Earth

SAURALITE (New Zealand Azeztulite) is a silicon dioxide with a hexagonal
crystal system and a hardness of 7. Its color is white and it occurs as crystal
points and/or geometrically inscribed masses. It's name is from the Sanskrit
saura, meaning the Divine Sun. It is found in New Zealand.

Sauralite vibrates with astonishing intensity, combining the Nameless
Light of the Great Central Sun with the living vitality of the Earth. New Zealand is one of the energetically clearest places on the planet, a place where
the Light of Heaven and the love of Earth are vibrantly intermingled, and
these stones are evidence of it. They carry the purpose of Azeztulite in its full
realization—the living Light of the Divine married to the density of matter.
In meditation, these stones literally draw the Light down through the crown
while they open the base chakra for the upwelling of Earth energies. They
allow one to become a living vessel for the manifestation of Divine purpose
on Earth, the spreading of Light and dissolving of fear, contraction and pain.
They are stones of physical enlightenment, making the body a place of ecstatic
celebration of union with the Divine. Sauralites are the most feminine Azeztulites, because the Earth's vitality is alive in them. These stones bring one to
the question, "Will you give up your old life for a new, unknown joy?"

Sauralite resonates with Rosophia, Anandalite, Tibetan Tektite, Astaraline, Guardianite and all other Azeztulites.

AZEZTULITE,
SATYALOKA CLEAR

KEY WORDS *Sat-chit-ananda*, truth, consciousness, bliss **CHAKRAS** All
ELEMENT Storm, Wind

PHYSICAL Initiates infusion of spiritual Light into the body
EMOTIONAL Inspires the awakening to Divine bliss
SPIRITUAL Facilitates intense expansion of consciousness, enlightenment

SATYALOKA AZEZTULITE was discovered in south India, near the Satyaloka Monastery. It is a transparent or translucent type of Quartz with a hardness of 7. The name Satyaloka means "place of truth." The area where it is found has been called the "crown chakra of the world."

Satyaloka Azeztulite opens the crown chakra with a tremendous flow of energy. Its energies pulse downward, clearing and activating each successive chakra. When placed upon the heart it produces a deep sense of reverence, an awareness of the presence of the Holy Silence. It has a direct resonance with the vastness of consciousness at the site of Origin. It opens a stream through which one may venture to the Source. Satyaloka Azeztulite vibrates to the frequency of enlightenment, and it is more intense in its currents than any other form of Azeztulite. It is a stone of pure White Light energy.

Satyaloka Azeztulite is resonant with the energies described in India's mystical traditions as *sat-chit-ananda*. *Sat* means truth, *chit* is consciousness and *ananda* is bliss, so this *sat-chit-ananda* is the quality of truth, consciousness and bliss as one whole pattern. Satyaloka Azeztulite can infuse this pattern into the entire Liquid Crystal Body Matrix. It is a stone of powerful spiritual dedication. It can guide in purification of one's energy bodies, of one's intention, will, even of one's love activities and energies. It resonates with Moldavite and all the Ascension stones.

AZEZTULITE, SATYALOKA ROSE

KEY WORDS Ascension of the Heart
CHAKRAS Heart (4th), Third Eye (6th),
Crown (7th)   **ELEMENT** Storm
PHYSICAL Stimulates cellular mind to
embrace the Heart's love and truth   **EMOTIONAL** Elevates and expands Heart
awareness—the power of love   **SPIRITUAL** Brings forth the Heart as the sovereign
center of one's being

ᏚATYALOKA ROSE AZEZTULITE is a silicon dioxide with a hexagonal crystal
system and a hardness of 7. The name Satyaloka means "place of truth."
Color ranges from pale pink to salmon. It is found in South India.

Satyaloka Rose Azeztulite carries the currents of Heart Ascension. Like
all the Satyaloka Azeztulites, its vibrations are intense and powerful. These
stones not only stimulate the heart chakra, they also encourage the heart to
"move" upward into the head. They awaken the Divine "I" of the heart and
lift it to its rightful throne in the center of the brain. When this occurs, one
thinks, speaks and acts out of the heart's wisdom. The mind and brain then
take their places as the servants of the heart. When this transformation is
fully realized, one can speak and act only in truth, because the heart knows
only truth. This shift affects the body as well, dissolving all falsehood and
self-negation in the mind of the cells. The cells vibrate with the heart's love
and truth, aligning themselves with the Light and Love emanated by the
Great Central Sun and the Ascended Heart.

To bring forth the fullness of this profound transformation, combining
Satyaloka Rose Azeztulite with Satyaloka Yellow Azeztulite is advised. Using
the Rose Azeztulite at the heart and the Yellow Azeztulite at the third eye, the
circuit of Light and Heart Ascension can be created and energized.

AZEZTULITE, SATYALOKA YELLOW

KEY WORDS Enlightenment, Ascension, acceleration of one's evolution

CHAKRAS Solar Plexus (3rd), Third Eye (6th)

ELEMENT Storm **PHYSICAL** Aids the body in assimilating and integrating spiritual Light **EMOTIONAL** Encourages one to seek and savor the thrill of transformation **SPIRITUAL** Inspires awareness of and enthusiasm for spiritual awakening

SATYALOKA YELLOW AZEZTULITE is a silicon dioxide with a hexagonal crystal system and a hardness of 7. The name Satyaloka means "place of truth." These bright yellow stones are found in South India.

Satyaloka Yellow Azeztulite powerfully stimulates the third eye chakra. Its currents move very deep into the brain, bringing intense and pleasurable sensations. It can feel as though it is "pulling" one's consciousness upwards! The power of Satyaloka Yellow Azeztulite is the power of evolutionary change. It is programmed for the awakening of humanity and the Earth to a higher level of spiritual awareness, and its energy of awakening carries extraordinary force. Satyaloka Yellow Azeztulites carry the currents of enlightenment. They have a strong enthusiasm for one to wake up and ascend! They seem to have a will of their own, focused on the rapid acceleration of our spiritual awakening. Satyaloka Yellow Azeztulite also stimulates one's will forces, helping align one's intention with Divine will. It aids in focusing one's energies to serve one's highest intention. These stones provide clarity and enhance purpose, as well as awakening the mind to perceive and embrace one's destiny.

Satyaloka Yellow Azeztulite works well with all the Ascension and Synergy stones. It harmonizes with Astaraline for building the Body of Light. Guardianite protects the Light Body within this process.

AZEZTULITE, BLACK

KEY WORDS Light within Darkness, complete transformation, memory of one's divinity, protection, infusion of Light, alchemical Philosopher's Stone **CHAKRAS** All **ELEMENTS** Earth, Wind, Storm **PHYSICAL** Supports treatment of autoimmune-type conditions **EMOTIONAL** Aids in releasing negative emotions, infuses one with spiritual joy **SPIRITUAL** Clears inner obstacles, fills the body with Light, protects, empowers and awakens

BLACK AZEZTULITE is a mixture of quartz and black calcite. It is found in Vermont, USA, alongside White Azeztulites. Its hardness varies from 3 to 7.

Black Azeztulite helps one attune to the Light within Darkness. It is a stone of the Midnight Sun. It is related to the huge black hole at the center of our galaxy, and represents the moment of the singularity or Zero Point, in which the laws of the universe become fluid and changeable, making it a powerful catalyst for spiritual transformation. When one attunes to Black Azeztulite, one can change literally anything about oneself, and can ultimately create profound changes in the outer world. Black Azeztulite brings Light and Power into one's entire energy system.

In spiritual self-healing, Black Azeztulite cleanses and clears one's body and energy field of negative energies, disharmonious attachments, psychic parasites, implants, and inappropriate karmic patterns. It can be used for conditions in which the body attacks itself. It offers power and protection to those who work with it. It aids in releasing emotional wounds. Its power is increased during eclipses and/or the new moon.

Black Azeztulite works synergistically with Master Shamanite, Obsidian, Black Jade, Black Tourmaline, Smoky Quartz, Guardianite, Z Stone, Prophecy Stone, Phenacite, Natrolite, Herderite, Brookite, Danburite and Petalite. It responds favorably when subjected to the Azozeo super-activation process.

AZUMAR

KEY WORDS Pleasure, serenity, ecstasy, truth, compassion, love **CHAKRAS** Heart (4th), Crown (7th) **ELEMENT** Water **PHYSICAL** Kindles bodily joy and rejuvenation **EMOTIONAL** Increases happiness and compassion **SPIRITUAL** Attunes to planetary consciousness and spiritual love

AZUMAR combines quartz, kaolinite and trace minerals such as copper silicates to form a vivid blue-green material of myriad shades and patterns. It was first found in Arizona, USA. Its name means "blue ocean."

Azumar's currents bring about a rejoicing in the body, as the cells assimilate its profoundly refreshing and rejuvenating energies. One often feels flooded with waves of pleasure, healing and power. Azumar can aid in dispelling anger, envy, fear and stress, replacing them with serenity, enthusiasm, confidence and the feeling of being enveloped within an atmosphere of love. This brings a peaceful clarity of consciousness.

Azumar demonstrates that life itself is a flow of ecstasy, and that when one is in tune with the truth of life, one is in a state of rapturous joy. When one meditates with it, one discovers that its surging pulsations move one toward more profound happiness and more intense pleasure.

Azumar allows one to penetrate to the heart of matters, and enhances the ability to eloquently express one's deepest truth. It is a stone of compassion, engendering one's innate capacity to understand and care for others. It is an Earth Spirit stone, allowing one to feel and harmonize with planetary consciousness. It aids in attuning to whales, dolphins and devic beings.

Azumar harmonizes perfectly with Healerite, and works synergistically with all Azeztulites, Sugilite, Moldavite, Aquamarine, Azurite, Larimar, Lithium Light, Rathbunite, Phenacite, Herderite, Danburite and Petalite.

AZURITE

KEY WORDS Insight, vision, intuition, intellect   **CHAKRAS** Third Eye (6th), Crown (7th)   **ELEMENT** Wind   **PHYSICAL** Helps with migraines, tinnitus, vertigo, overall brain health
EMOTIONAL Supports insight into emotions, inspires emotional growth   **SPIRITUAL** Initiates inner visions, intuitive leaps of spiritual understanding

AZURITE is a copper carbonate mineral with a hardness of 3.5 to 4. Its name is derived from its deep azure blue color. Its crystal system is monoclinic. It is found in Australia, China, Chile, Russia and the USA.

Azurite powerfully stimulates the third eye chakra. It is a stone of inner vision and can be used for the enhancement of dreams and the development of psychic powers. It can stimulate intellect as well as intuition, and can aid the assimilation and retention of new information and ideas. Azurite can also facilitate the agility of mind required to make conceptual leaps and reach new insights. Azurite can strengthen the astral and etheric bodies, making one less vulnerable to psychic attack or attachments. It can be used to seal "holes" in the aura, thus alleviating tendencies to succumb to fatigue. It stimulates all the mind centers, nourishing within the self a keen interest in all aspects of one's life and function in society. It is an excellent antidote to boredom, since it opens one's inner eye to a wide array of connections and possibilities. It is a stone of synthesis, whereby the discovery of new commonalities and links between different ideas leads to higher levels of understanding of life and the world.

Azurite blends well with Malachite, Cuprite, Chrysocolla, Turquoise, Rainbow Moonstone, Sunstone, Red Aventurine, Carnelian, Azeztulite, Phenacite, Brookite, Natrolite, Scolecite and Moldavite.

BARITE

KEY WORDS Inner vision, energetic alignment, interdimensional travel
CHAKRAS Third Eye (6th), Crown (7th)
ELEMENT Storm **PHYSICAL** Supports balanced brain chemistry, supports function of brain cells
EMOTIONAL Encourages releasing fear, taking joy in spiritual exploration
SPIRITUAL Facilitates interdimensional travel, dream work, meditative Ascension

BARITE is a barium sulfate crystal with an orthorhombic crystal system and a hardness of 3 to 3.5. Most often it is colorless, white, light blue, green, yellowish or reddish brown. Barite is found abundantly in England, Romania and the USA.

Barite provides a smooth, clear connection to the higher worlds, aiding the inward journeyer in discovering the many mansions of the spiritual realms. It is a stone of interdimensional travel, allowing those who meditate or dream with it to use their journeys to enrich earthly life. It assists one in maintaining contact with the higher self. For exploratory dream work, one is encouraged to place a Barite crystal or rosette in the pillowcase or to tape a small one to the forehead. Either application will open the third eye and crown chakras to the high-frequency domains with which Barite resonates. One should record one's dreams for at least a month. Working with Barite in dreams can give one a stunningly beautiful symbolic picture of how inner spiritual patterns are unfolding for oneself. Meditation with Barite can allow one to experience a temporary "ascension" into the higher worlds. Upon these inner journeys, one may encounter angels, spirit guides, and even the archetypal entities referred to as "gods" in ancient times. One may see divine landscapes of breathtaking beauty and geometric corridors of fantastic lattices of Light. Barite works well with all Ascension Stones.

BENITOITE

KEY WORDS Channeling, psychic abilities, increase in synchronicity **CHAKRAS** Third Eye (6th) **ELEMENT** Wind **PHYSICAL** Supports brain activation, accessing information in the connective tissues **EMOTIONAL** Inspires the euphoric joy of expanded awareness **SPIRITUAL** Facilitates interdimensional travel, paranormal capacities

BENITOITE is a barium titanium silicate mineral with a hexagonal (trigonal) crystal system and a hardness of 6 to 6.5. It is named after its only occurrence, in San Benito county, California. Benitoite crystals are light to dark blue and they vary from opaque to fully transparent.

Benitoite facilitates travel to the astral, subtle and causal planes and can help one maintain stability of consciousness when out of the body. It helps open the doors for enhancement of all types of paranormal abilities, and it increases one's awareness of the meaningful synchronicities that are constantly happening around us. It is said by some clairvoyant seers that one's angelic guardians are involved in arranging the synchronicities which facilitate one's spiritual growth. Meditation with Benitoite can facilitate the process by which one can enter into conscious communication with these angelic guides. One can request synchronistic "messages" confirming the communication. The events of one's life can turn into a kind of living puzzle or game in which one may, to a degree, consciously steer one's evolutionary path.

The fact that Benitoite is found in conjunction with Natrolite is no coincidence either. Natrolite is among the most powerful activators of the third eye and crown chakra and the transpersonal chakras above the head. Such energy works perfectly in harmony with Benitoite's native ability to activate the higher senses.

BERYLLONITE

KEY WORDS Light in darkness, Divine purpose, joy
CHAKRAS Heart (4th), Third Eye (6th), Crown (7th)
ELEMENT Storm   **PHYSICAL** Supports healing through alignment with spiritual truth   **EMOTIONAL** Aids release from depression and grief through spiritual insight
SPIRITUAL Enhances clairvoyance, linking with angels and inner guides

BERYLLONITE is a sodium beryllium phosphate mineral with a hardness of 5.5 to 6. It is usually colorless or white, sometimes a pale yellow. Its crystal system is hexagonal (trigonal). Crystals can be prismatic and usually have striations along the body.

Beryllonite is a stone which sends Light to pierce the veil and reveal the way in which the highest good is constantly manifesting, even in the midst of suffering. It can be a remedy to the "dark night of the soul." It strongly activates the third eye chakra, initiating visionary experiences and helping one to develop clairvoyant sight. This stone can aid one in seeing the blockages or imbalances which hold one back from full consciousness and realization of one's spiritual destiny. It can provide the validation one needs to believe in the help available from the higher planes, by making it possible for one to see one's guides and angels. On deeper levels, Beryllonite also energizes the heart and crown chakras and is a powerful aid to consciousness expansion.

Beryllonite combines synergistically with Brookite, Phenacite, Herderite, Petalite, Danburite, Natrolite, Scolecite and Azeztulite—all stones of the highest vibrational levels. Combining Beryllonite with Moldavite will accelerate its effects and will assist in attracting synchronous experiences. Beryllonite also harmonizes with Aquamarine, Emerald, Heliodor, Goethite and Morganite.

BIXBITE (Red Beryl)

KEY WORDS Vitality, courage, love, self-esteem, passion
CHAKRAS Root (1st), Heart (4th) **ELEMENT** Earth
PHYSICAL Revitalizes the body's constitution, increases life
force **EMOTIONAL** Helps awaken passion, compassion
courage and loyalty **SPIRITUAL** Supports centering oneself
in the heart, making deep commitments

BIXBITE is a member of the Beryl family, a beryllium aluminum silicate mineral with a hexagonal crystal system and a hardness of 7.5 to 8. It was discovered in Colorado, USA, in the 1980s and is the rarest of the beryls. Its raspberry color comes from manganese.

Bixbite stimulates courage, passion, physical vitality, strength of purpose and a dynamic personality. Yet it does these things while helping one remain centered in the heart, compassionate toward others and oneself, and loving in one's actions. This stone skillfully blends the energies of the heart and root chakras, helping one draw life force from the earth and enhancing emotional bonds with the world and other people.

For healers, Bixbite can be a very useful tool. Placed at the first and fourth chakras, it can help revitalize clients who are fatigued, stressed or convalescing. As it opens the heart chakra, repressed wounds may come to the surface for healing and release. Bixbite can be excellent for enhancement of love relationships, bringing the hearts of individuals into vibrational harmony. It can help stir the fires of passion and can assist one in finding the courage to make deep emotional commitments. A stone of courage, Bixbite stimulates and harmonizes the root and heart chakras. It strengthens loyalty and camaraderie, as well as self-confidence and groundedness. Bixbite harmonizes with Ruby, Morganite, Dioptase, Kunzite, Emerald, Rhodocrosite, Aquamarine and Heliodor.

BLACK PHANTOM QUARTZ

KEY WORDS Inner Light; releasing self-judgment; reclaiming soul fragments, courage and resolve; increased self-awareness

CHAKRAS All **ELEMENT** Storm **PHYSICAL** Helps with bone health, overcoming illnesses related to repressed Shadow material **EMOTIONAL** Encourages self-acceptance, self-love, love of others, release of judgment **SPIRITUAL** Facilitates soul retrieval, release of past-life fixations, inner clarity

BLACK PHANTOM QUARTZ is a silicon dioxide mineral with a hardness of 7. Its crystal system is hexagonal (trigonal). It grows in prismatic crystals and is characterized by inclusions of carbon or manganese

Black Phantom Quartz is useful for seeing and integrating one's personal Shadow. Such work also reunites the missing or "lost" parts of the soul, healing the psyche and bringing a deeper sense of wholeness. Using Black Phantom Quartz in meditation, prayer or dream work can assist in opening the inner doors so this material can be experienced, understood and released. Through the light it sheds upon the dark areas of the self, it quiets the inner "judge." It fosters self-acceptance and self-love, making it possible to offer unconditional love to others. If past-life patterns feed into one's psychological limitations in this life, Black Phantom Quartz can be used to help recall and release them. They are ideal tools for honing in on the particular lives which are relevant to one's difficulties in the present incarnation.

To enhance visionary experiences, combine Black Phantom Quartz with Herkimer "Diamonds" and/or Phenacite. Black Phantoms harmonize well with Moldavite, which accelerates the inner processes of transformation. Natrolite, Scolecite, Danburite, Petalite and Azeztulite can help one to focus on the spiritual openings initiated by working with these crystals.

BLOODSTONE

KEY WORDS Strength, courage, purification, vitality
CHAKRAS Root (1st)   **ELEMENT** Earth   **PHYSICAL** Aids
detoxification, blood purification; liver and endocrine
system   **EMOTIONAL** Inspires courage to face illness and
mortality, altruism, zest for life   **SPIRITUAL** Facilitates
dispelling negative energies, entering Christ consciousness

BLOODSTONE is a variety of opaque chalcedony with a hardness of 6.5 to 7.
It is dark green with red spots and blotches. In the Middle Ages, the red
spots in Bloodstone were thought to be spots of Christ's blood, and magical
powers were attributed to the stones. Bloodstone deposits have been found
in India, China, Brazil, Australia and the USA.

Bloodstone is a great purifier, a healing tool for dispelling negative influences from the auric field and bringing one's subtle energies into wholeness
and balance. It grounds one fully in the body, for the enhancement of one's
strength, determination and courage. It increases vitality, and can aid one in
facing physical mortality. It is a good talisman for those who are ill, even if
curing the illness is not possible, because of its power to let one look unflinch-
ingly at the truth. Bloodstone is a stone of noble sacrifice, and it can offer
courage and solace. It can elicit the highest, most altruistic character traits in
whoever carries or uses it. At its most effective, it stimulates the urge toward
Christ consciousness.

Bloodstone strengthens the root chakra, increasing one's zest for living
and endurance in physical activity. It supports blood purification and purging
the body of toxins. Bloodstone works harmoniously with Cuprite, Smoky
Quartz, Zincite, Black Tourmaline, Jet and Obsidian. For connection with the
vibrations of Christ consciousness, one may combine Bloodstone with Imperial Topaz and/or Golden Azeztulite.

BRAZILIANITE

KEY WORDS Creativity, manifestation, inner cleansing, empowerment of the will, Atlantean connection
CHAKRAS Sexual/Creative (2nd), Solar Plexus (3rd)
ELEMENT Wind, Fire **PHYSICAL** Aids in purifying the visceral organs, strengthening digestion
EMOTIONAL Enhances self-confidence, commitment to self-fulfillment **SPIRITUAL** Facilitates regaining the gifts of Atlantis, creative manifestation

BRAZILIANITE is a sodium aluminum phosphate with a monoclinic crystal system and a hardness of 5.5. Its color is yellow to yellow-green, and it forms prismatic crystals. It is found in Brazil and the USA.

Brazilianite carries the vibrational energy of the ancient civilization of Atlantis and is associated with the creative power of directed and focused will, which was instrumental in many of the astounding accomplishments of the beings who dwelt there. Whether Atlantis actually existed on the material plane of the Earth or was in a higher-frequency domain, the stone Brazilianite serves as a conduit for what one might call "the Atlantean energies." These energies can assist one in extraordinary acts of creativity and manifestation.

Brazilianite can amplify the potency of one's will. The will is primarily expressed through the solar plexus, or third chakra, and Brazilianite strongly magnifies third-chakra energies. Brazilianite's message is that one should "go for it." However, one is cautioned to be conscious and benevolent in directing the profound power of the focused will. Brazilianite's energies combine synergistically with Golden Labradorite, Heliodor, Datolite, Citrine, Scapolite and Golden Apatite. Moldavite is particularly recommended with Brazilianite, because of its power to accelerate one's evolutionary progress and its attunement to the highest good.

BROOKITE

KEY WORDS Higher-chakra awakening and alignment, interdimensional communication
CHAKRAS Third Eye (6th), Crown (7th), Etheric (8th–14th) ELEMENT Storm
PHYSICAL Supports integrating higher frequencies into the body
EMOTIONAL Encourages calm, stable self-awareness in expanded states
SPIRITUAL Facilitates interdimensional exploration, meeting beings of higher realms

BROOKITE is a titanium oxide crystal with an orthorhombic crystal system and a hardness of 5.5 to 6. It occurs, rarely, as an inclusion in Quartz and more commonly as squarish charcoal-colored crystals under ½ inch in size. It is found in England, France and in Arkansas, USA.

Brookite is one of the primary power stones for expansion of awareness beyond the physical body. It is a powerful activator of the sixth and seventh chakras and the etheric chakras above the head. It can align all the upper chakras with the rest of one's energy body, allowing one to explore the subtle realms with a highly sensitive and stable awareness.

Brookite enables one to reach an expanded state where one can communicate and commune with beings on the higher vibrational levels. It teaches one the nature of the higher levels of consciousness vibration. It can help one gain the "cosmic perspective" that allows one to see even unpleasant situations as beneficial to growth. It is inspirational and energizing, assisting one in overcoming old patterns and moving ahead to greater inner development.

Brookite combines well with high-vibration stones such as Phenacite, Azeztulite, Danburite, Herderite, Seraphinite, Natrolite, Scolecite, Tibetan Tektite, Satyaloka Azeztulite, Petalite, Tanzanite, Elestial Calcite and Moldavite. For grounding, use Zincite or Black Tourmaline.

BUMBLEBEE "JASPER"

KEY WORDS Inspiration, intensity, creative manifestation, adventure **CHAKRA** Solar Plexus (3rd) **ELEMENT** Fire **PHYSICAL** Supports intestines, liver and kidneys **EMOTIONAL** Infuses passion with sense of purpose, inspires courage and adventurousness **SPIRITUAL** Aids in becoming aware of one's destiny, and finding the courage and strength to pursue it

BUMBLEBEE "JASPER" is not a true jasper. It is actually a sedimentary rock containing sulfur, manganese oxides, the arsenic-sulfide minerals realgar and orpiment, and calcium carbonate. It is found in Australia.

Bumblebee "Jasper" resonates strongly with the second (sexual/creative) and third (solar plexus) chakras. It brings inspiration and intensity to the realm of one's creative manifestation. It is a powerful aid for melding passion and purpose together for the unfolding of one's destiny, and it can help one persist and overcome obstacles.

Bumblebee "Jasper" is a stone of adventure. It stimulates one's mental acuity, so one is more able to notice and seize opportunities. These stones can increase the level of activation of the complex of neurons in the gut, making it possible to more readily be aware of one's "gut feelings," or instincts. It stimulates courage, assertiveness, endurance and concentration. If worn, it can increase mental clarity and sharpness, inspiration and manifestation.

In spiritual self-healing, Bumblebee "Jasper" can help energetically cleanse and clear the intestinal tract, liver and kidneys. In emotional self-healing, it is an antidote to fear, indecisiveness and hesitation. In spiritual evolution, it sets one upon the path of one's highest destiny.

Bumblebee "Jasper" harmonizes with Moldavite, Phenacite, Heliodor, Libyan Gold Tektite, Apatite, Tibetan Tektite, Anandalite and Azeztulite.

BUSTAMITE

KEY WORDS Playfulness, joy, vitality, sexuality, creativity, dreams, initiation **CHAKRAS** Root (1st), Sexual/Creative (2nd) **ELEMENT** Fire **PHYSICAL** Supports sexual organs, digestive system, endocrine system **EMOTIONAL** Encourages enjoyment of physical life, playfulness in relationships **SPIRITUAL** Inspires awareness of one's unity with the All

BUSTAMITE is a calcium manganese silicate with a triclinic crystal system and a hardness of 6. Its color is light red to brownish red. It is found in South Africa and in New Jersey, USA.

Bustamite clears and opens the root chakra, allowing for greater vitality and enjoyment of physical life. It reminds one to appreciate simply living as a human animal on a planet rich and diverse with life. Wearing or meditating with Bustamite activates one's ability to dissolve the artificial barriers between one's "self" and the rest of the living Universe. It allows one to see the astonishing intertwinement of all things and to joyfully participate as a conscious aspect of All-That-Is. Bustamite stimulates one's creative and sexual energies as well. Carrying or wearing Bustamite during creative work or play can bring greater inspiration and fertility to one's endeavors. The same can also happen in times of sexual intimacy. Bustamite can also increase the vividness of dreams. It can assist one in making progress in meditation and can facilitate initiation experiences on the higher planes. Spirit guides and angelic beings seem to enjoy this energy, and it is easier for one to make contact with them while using these stones.

Bustamite works with Strombolite for humor and play and Rhodocrosite for healing the inner child. It also harmonizes with Lapis, Rhodonite, Brazilianite, Heliodor, Golden Labradorite and Phenacite.

CACOXENITE

KEY WORDS Alignment with the Divine plan, spiritual cleansing and purification, regeneration of the body **CHAKRAS** Solar Plexus (3rd), Third Eye (6th), Crown (7th) **ELEMENT** Wind **PHYSICAL** Aids with clearing digestive issues, "new" DNA strand activation **EMOTIONAL** Encourages surrender to the Divine, diffusing ego fixation **SPIRITUAL** Facilitates acceleration of spiritual evolution, grounding spiritual Light

CACOXENITE are stones with the power to assist in one's spiritual evolution and in raising the vibration of one's physical self. The reprogramming of the cells to continually renew themselves and resist the aging process, as well as the activation of the "new" strands of the genetic spiral, are both applications for which Cacoxenite is well suited. These processes may be initiated consciously through meditation and dream work, but they can also happen quite unconsciously through simply wearing or carrying the Cacoxenite stone.

Allied with Phenacite, Danburite, Azeztulite, Scolecite, Natrolite or Herderite, or a combination of these stones, Cacoxenite can powerfully activate the third eye and crown chakras for inner visionary experience and for interdimensional communication and connection to Spirit. Pairing Cacoxenite with Brookite, or using it with Brookite and other high-vibration stones, will open the transpersonal chakras above the head and facilitate conscious travel beyond the physical body. Moldavite and Cacoxenite make the strongest pair for raising cellular vibrations and accelerating one's evolutionary path. In body layouts and daily wear, Cacoxenite works to attract and ground the highest spiritual Light. If one wishes to utilize Cacoxenite as an adjunct to healing and/or regenerating the body, Sugilite and Seraphinite will aid in this process.

CALCITE, CLEAR
(Iceland Spar)

KEY WORDS Insight, clarity, manifestation, forgiveness **CHAKRAS** All **ELEMENTS** Fire, Wind **PHYSICAL** Stimulates metabolism and energy flow through the aura **EMOTIONAL** Encourages forgiveness, releasing anger, resentment, arrogance and envy **SPIRITUAL** Facilitates creating inner clarity, initiating multilevel awareness

CLEAR CALCITE is a calcium carbonate mineral with a rhombohedral crystal system and a hardness of 3. It is a colorless, transparent variety, also known as optical Calcite. It was originally discovered in Iceland but can also be found in Mexico and other localities.

Clear Calcite is the Calcite most akin to clear Quartz. Both stones can be programmed to amplify the effect of one's intent, helping to bring that intent into the physical world. In addition, this stone is excellent for those in need of an "attitude adjustment." It helps one see clearly to the roots within the self of problems causing symptoms of anger, resentment, envy and/or arrogance, especially if accompanied by flare-ups of temper. With such insights, one can more easily forgive oneself and others for past actions and move toward the higher good. Also, the double-refractive nature of Clear Calcite allows those who use the stone in meditation to achieve a multilevel awareness, which allows one to hold paradoxical or contradictory ideas within the mind without taking one side or the other. This is especially useful, since it seems that reality is paradoxical in its very essence, and those who wish to understand it must embrace paradox.

All types of Calcite work well with one another, but Clear Calcite also harmonizes with Moldavite, Phenacite, Scolecite and Danburite. Its capacity to initiate higher awareness is greatly aided by Azeztulite.

CALCITE, BLUE

KEY WORDS Psychic ability, astral travel, soothing the emotional body **CHAKRAS** Throat (5th), Third Eye (6th) **ELEMENT** Fire, Air **PHYSICAL** Helps with throat problems, laryngitis, lungs and respiratory issues **EMOTIONAL** Soothes and protects the emotional body **SPIRITUAL** Facilitates access to the creative unconscious, inspired self-expression

Blue Calcite is a calcium carbonate mineral with a rhombohedral crystal system and a hardness of 3. It is found abundantly in Mexico, but some specimens with deep color have been found in South Africa.

Blue Calcite is one of the most soothing stones to the emotional body. It softens the impact of psychic stimuli, allowing those who are energetically sensitive to relax, protected from the bombardment of other people's thoughts and emotional energies. It provides a "cocoon" of gentle blue spiritual Light which gradually wraps itself around the auric field of those who hold or carry it. This field enables one to float gently out of the body, either into the dream state or the domain of astral travel. In astral journeys, Blue Calcite can screen out negative or unpleasant energies.

Blue Calcite stimulates one's access to inspiration. It opens the inner avenue for conscious exploration of the unconscious realms, from which many of one's most creative ideas spring. Blue Calcite also enhances the vividness and symbolic content of dreams and one's ability to recall and integrate them. Blue Calcite's stimulation of the throat chakra enables one to better express the insights one receives from inner explorations, in words, music or art.

Blue Calcite's protective quality is magnified by Moldavite. It works with Herderite and Brookite for consciousness expansion, and Aquamarine, Blue Chalcedony and Blue Lace Agate for communication.

CALCITE, GREEN

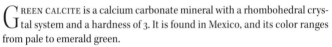

KEY WORDS Relaxation, emotional balance, release of stress and resentment, connection with the heart
CHAKRAS Heart (4th) **ELEMENT** Fire, Water
PHYSICAL Supports heart and artery health, rejuvenation, clearing bodily stress **EMOTIONAL** Cools and soothes anger, relieves emotional stress **SPIRITUAL** Inspires compassion and altruism, helps one connect with Nature spirits

G REEN CALCITE is a calcium carbonate mineral with a rhombohedral crystal system and a hardness of 3. It is found in Mexico, and its color ranges from pale to emerald green.

Green Calcite's energy is refreshing to the etheric body. It is cooling to the "hot" emotions such as anger and irritability, it nurtures positive traits like compassion and altruism, and it clears the heart chakra of stress and other types of unhealthy psychic debris. It assists one in being more attuned to Nature and the spirits of plants and animals. Green Calcite helps one direct the attention of the mind to the urgings of the heart, assisting one in listening to and acting on what the heart knows.

Green Calcite can improve the quality of meditations, helping to still the incessant voice of the thinking mind, allowing one to experience wordless awareness. Sleeping with Green Calcite can make dreams more pleasant. Carrying or wearing it can make one feel clear and relaxed amid the stresses of daily life. Green Calcite harmonizes with all other Calcites, as well as Green Apophyllite, Chrysoprase, Petalite and Lepidolite. Green Apophyllite accentuates Green Calcite's affinity for Nature spirits and its gentle focus on the heart. The other stones work with Green Calcite to facilitate deep relaxation and the release of stress. Those using Green Calcite in healing may increase its efficacy by adding Seraphinite.

CALCITE, ORANGE

KEY WORDS Creativity, sexuality, playfulness, confidence, innovation **CHAKRAS** Sexual/Creative (2nd), Solar Plexus (3rd) **ELEMENT** Fire **PHYSICAL** Aids sexual enjoyment, hormonal balance, metabolic health **EMOTIONAL** Helps heal wounds related to sexuality, creativity and will **SPIRITUAL** Instills greater energy for creative work, helps to spiritualize sexuality

ORANGE CALCITE is a calcium carbonate mineral with a rhombohedral crystal system and a hardness of 3. It is found in Mexico, and its color ranges from pale to vivid orange, with some white inclusions.

Orange Calcite helps one mobilize one's energies and resources for all types of activities, especially those involving creativity and/or sexuality. It is ideal for those who are looking for new and innovative strategies for dealing with long-standing problems or stalled projects. Orange Calcite gets the energy moving and encourages one to see old dilemmas in new ways, so that the solution is right before one's eyes. Orange Calcite can be used for healing emotional issues related to wounds to one's sexuality, creativity and/or will. It can be an ally for those working to recover from childhood experiences of shame and even deep issues like sexual abuse. Orange Calcite invigorates playfulness and encourages confidence. It can be a catalyst for inspiration and even a kind of mineral aphrodisiac. It will affect different people in different ways, according to their needs and receptivity.

Orange Calcite harmonizes with Carnelian, Golden Labradorite, Citrine, Heliodor and all other Calcites. Carnelian emphasizes the stimulation of sexual/creative energies. For issues of physical vitality, Cuprite can offer valuable aid. In situations requiring insight and/or a magnification of Orange Calcite's energies, Selenite is recommended.

CALCITE, HONEY

KEY WORDS Clarity of insight and action, confidence, persistence, intellectual power **CHAKRAS** Root (1st), Solar Plexus (3rd), Third Eye (6th) **ELEMENT** Fire, Wind **PHYSICAL** Supports strength and stamina, helps conserve physical energy **EMOTIONAL** Aids in maintaining emotional stability through difficulty **SPIRITUAL** Inspires perseverance in spiritual practices, fulfilling one's commitments

HONEY CALCITE is a calcium carbonate mineral with a rhombohedral crystal system and a hardness of 3. It is found in Mexico, and its color ranges from pale to deep brown, with a degree of transparency.

Honey Calcite assists in bringing about that unique combination of mental clarity, focused energy and groundedness necessary to successfully complete complex tasks or long-term projects. It activates the root chakra, solar plexus and third eye, harmonizing and unifying their energies. It stimulates the intellect, making it possible for one to analyze challenges and see the most efficient solutions. It is one of the best stones for all types of work situations requiring full attention and persistence over the long haul. It can help one overcome drowsiness, allowing one to stay alert during jobs that require long hours. At the same time, it facilitates a state of relaxation, so that one's work does not result in stress.

Honey Calcite combines well with Moldavite, which can guide one to work that suits one's higher purpose. With Heliodor and Phenacite, Honey Calcite can be applied to manifesting of one's dreams through using one's will and intellect.

Honey Calcite harmonizes with Natrolite and Scolecite for progress in meditation, with Cuprite for physical stamina, and with Celestite for conscious traveling in the higher realms.

CALCITE, PINK TRANSPARENT

KEY WORDS Emotional healing, compassion and joy
CHAKRAS Heart (4th) **ELEMENT** Fire, Water
PHYSICAL Aids with stress-related digestive problems, strengthens kidneys **EMOTIONAL** Encourages loving kindness, awakens the heart to joy **SPIRITUAL** Facilitates communion with Kwan Yin, inspires compassion

PINK TRANSPARENT CALCITE is a calcium carbonate mineral with a rhombohedral crystal system and a hardness of 3. It is found in Mexico, and its color ranges from salmon pink to yellowish pink.

Transparent Pink Calcite is a stone of deep compassion, and it generates this energy in those who work with it. It also facilitates the state of non-judgmental acceptance and unconditional love. This stone connects to the energy of Kwan Yin, Bodhisattva of Compassion. One may use Transparent Pink Calcite in meditation and ritual to consciously connect with Kwan Yin. Sometimes, in such meditations, one will feel Her unexpected joyful opening of the heart, filling the physical and energetic bodies with love. Looking into the interior of one of these gem-like Pink Calcites can bring one into a state of rapturous appreciation of the beauty of existence. This in turn can kindle the flame of joy in one's own heart. For those drawn to such an experience, meditation with one of these stones, imagining the crystal moving into the chest and merging with one's own heart, is highly recommended.

Transparent Pink Calcite harmonizes with Pink Tourmaline, Rosophia, Rose Quartz, Morganite and Kunzite. Combining it with Pink Azeztulite and Satyaloka Rose Azeztulite takes the awakened heart energy to its highest expression. Phenacite, Danburite, Amethyst and Lilac Lepidolite enhance its linking of the Self to the higher realms of Spirit.

CALCITE, PINK OPAQUE

KEY WORDS Well-being, wholeness, health, empathy
and connection with the "mind of the heart"
CHAKRAS Heart (4th) **ELEMENT** Fire
PHYSICAL Supports healing of heart and circulatory
system, aids cellular nutrition and tissue regeneration
EMOTIONAL Helps clear destructive emotional fixations, helps calm hysteria
and despair **SPIRITUAL** Facilitates attunement of one's heart to Divine Love

PINK OPAQUE CALCITE is a calcium carbonate mineral with a rhombohedral crystal system and a hardness of 3. It is found in Peru and Bulgaria, and its color ranges from pale to vivid pink.

Opaque Pink Calcite can be used to enhance and stabilize the heart's field and make one more perceptive of the energies of everything in one's environment. Because the heart knows without words, one's consciousness through the heart field can take the form of empathic identification with whatever one perceives. In other words, through the heart, we "become what we behold." Such perception is one of the deep joys of life and is not to be missed.

Opaque Pink Calcite is a stone of empathy. It is helpful for those who do "absent healing" work, because it assists in attuning to the energy fields of others, even if they are not present. It can be used to dispel arguments and stubbornness in oneself and others, aiding one in seeing the other's point of view as if it were one's own. Opaque Pink Calcite harmonizes with other heart stones, such as Rose Quartz, Morganite, Kunzite and Moldavite, as well as all other Calcites. Using it in conjunction with Transparent Pink Calcite, one can enhance the full spectrum of the heart's physical and nonphysical aspects. Pairing this stone with Moldavite will amplify and accelerate its effects.

CALCITE, RED

KEY WORDS Vitality, sensory awareness, clarity **CHAKRAS** Root (1st), Crown (7th) **ELEMENT** Fire, Earth **PHYSICAL** Supports reproductive health, bone growth and density
EMOTIONAL Inspires the courage to be passionate, enthusiastic for life
SPIRITUAL Facilitates being spiritually present in the physical world

R ED CALCITE is a calcium carbonate mineral with a rhombohedral crystal system and a hardness of 3. It is found in Mexico, and its color ranges from pale to vivid red.

Red Calcite is a stone of "soft vitality," in that it energizes the base chakra and brings in additional *prana,* or life-force energy, yet it does so in a subtle way that is very easy to accept, and it brings no "jolts" or dis-comforts with it. These stones also link the base chakra with the crown, bridging the frequent gap between physical existence and spiritual life. Red Calcite helps one appreciate the wonders of physical life and the ecstasies of sense-perception. It can dispel the half-sleep of "normal" consciousness and help restore the sense of wonder which full awareness brings. It allows one to learn to give complete attention to the senses whenever one desires to do so. This can engender shutting down the inner dialog of the brain and giving one the experience of wordless consciousness. Meditation outdoors with Red Calcite is recommended for facilitating this experience.

Red Calcite works well with Cuprite, Ruby and Red Garnet for enhancement of life-force energies. For grounding, Hematite, Smoky Quartz, Black Andradite Garnet and/or Black Tourmaline are recommended. Celestite can bring an uplifting feeling to Red Calcite's energies. This stone also harmonizes with all other varieties of Calcite.

CALCITE, STELLAR BEAM

KEY WORDS Divine will, manifestation, interdimensional travel, access to higher knowledge **CHAKRAS** Solar Plexus (3rd), Third Eye (6th), Crown (7th), Etheric (8th–14th) **ELEMENT** Fire, Storm **PHYSICAL** Aids in attuning the body to carry higher vibrational energies **EMOTIONAL** Helps dispel negative thoughts, opens one to higher awareness **SPIRITUAL** Facilitates attuning to ancient wisdom, past lives and ET intelligence

STELLAR BEAM CALCITE is a calcium carbonate mineral with a scaleno-hedral form and a hardness of 3. Some of the best specimens come from Tennessee, USA. Most are a golden brown color.

Stellar Beam Calcites are very powerful for stimulating the third eye and crown chakras, and they align these chakras with the higher etheric body, making possible an ascension into higher realms of consciousness. They stimulate remembrance of the individual's experiences in the pre-birth state of full immersion in Spirit, and they assist in the recollection of past lives. Stellar Beam Calcites can also help one establish contact with extraterrestrial intelligences in meditation or dreams. They can facilitate inner travel through corridors of sacred geometric forms, through which one can gain access to the Hall of the Akashic Records. Atlantis, Lemuria and ancient Egypt are among the civilizations whose spiritual secrets can be found with these tools. Skilled travelers can also attune to the morphic fields of an almost unlimited range of information, especially those existing in the history of the Earth.

Stellar Beam Calcite harmonizes with Merkabite Calcite, Azeztulite, Phenacite, Natrolite, Herderite, Petalite, Scolecite, Clear Apophyllite, Celestite and Danburite.

CALCITE, MERKABITE

KEY WORDS Consciousness expansion, interdimensional travel, ascension, access to higher knowledge
CHAKRAS Third Eye (6th), Crown (7th), Etheric (8th–14th)
ELEMENT Fire, Storm   **PHYSICAL** Stimulates nervous system, awakens untapped brain capacities
EMOTIONAL Encourages one to release anxieties and trust in Spirit   **SPIRITUAL** Facilitates interdimensonal travel though the Light Body

MERKABITE CALCITE is named after the fabled Merkabah vehicle of Light mentioned in kabbalistic texts, for it opens many doorways to inner realms. When it is held to the third eye, one can feel a great rush of energy, like an interior wind, blowing through the upper chakras and out the top of the head. Allowing this energy to move through and aligning oneself with it, one can be transported, in definite stages, upward through each of the seven Light Body chakras above the head. If there are blockages to this, Merkabite will assist one in gently removing whatever congestion exists in the etheric body and the upper chakras. If one's blockages exist below the fifth chakra, however, it might be useful to wear or hold a powerful stone such as Moldavite to clear things out on the lower levels. Merkabite Calcite appears not to connect with the body below the fifth chakra, at least not for clearing. However, it can help bring about the full integration of the Light Body with the physical once all the chakras are clear.

Merkabite Calcite works synergistically with Stellar Beam Calcite, Moldavite, Phenacite, Azeztulite, Danburite, Scolecite, Natrolite, Seraphinite, Ajoite, Fulgurite and most of the high-frequency stones. For those who need grounding, Sugilite, Charoite or Amethyst is suggested.

CALCITE, ELESTIAL ANGEL

KEY WORDS Angelic communication, music of the spheres, link to the psychoid realm, visionary experience **CHAKRAS** Heart (4th), Third Eye (6th) **ELEMENTS** Wind, Storm **PHYSICAL** Supports central nervous system, can be used to dissolve energetic blockages and relieve headaches
EMOTIONAL Can bring joy and rapture by linking to higher beings **SPIRITUAL** Stimulates communion and communication with angels and other spiritual beings

ELESTIAL ANGEL CALCITES are clear-to-white calcite crystals found in Arizona, USA. They are characterized by a very "wrinkly" surface texture, with tiny fissures. They are calcium-carbonate crystals with a hardness of 3.

Elestial Angel Calcites are among the most high-vibration, high-intensity calcite crystals. They can stimulate activation of an energetic circuit between heart and mind. Placing them at the temples and/or third eye can trigger spiritual activation of the prefrontal lobes of the brain, facilitating angelic communication and other latent capacities. These stones stimulate one's ability to hear the "music of the spheres"—the astonishing harmonies of the "singing" of angelic beings. They also enhance communication with spirit guides, extraterrestrials, devas and other spiritual beings such as the archetypes. Elestial Angel Calcites can be used to relieve headaches and to vibrationally support the central nervous system. They stimulate the areas of the brain linked to vision, and can help one have more vivid inner visions of spiritual realities.

Elestial Angel Calcites combine well with Moldavite, Phenacite, Herderite and/or any variety of Azeztulite. They stones resonate well with the super-activated Azozeo Azeztulites. They also harmonize with Clear Apophyllite, Celestite, Green Apophyllite and Seriphos Green Quartz.

CARNELIAN

KEY WORDS Courage, vitality, sexuality, confidence, action **CHAKRAS** Root (1st), Sexual/Creative (2nd), Solar Plexus (3rd) **ELEMENT** Fire **PHYSICAL** Supports strength, vitality, sexuality, detoxing from alcohol or drugs **EMOTIONAL** Increases one's courage and enthusiasm **SPIRITUAL** Aids in overcoming hesitation, finding courage to grow spiritually

CARNELIAN is an orange-colored variety of Chalcedony with a hardness of 7. Its name is derived from its resemblance in color to the Kornel type of cherry. Carnelian's color can vary from pale orange to deep red-orange. Carnelians are found in India, Brazil and Uruguay.

Carnelian activates the first, second and third chakras, bringing an influx of life force, sexual and creative energies, and assertive will. It is a powerful aid to those who wish to build their confidence, courage, passion and power. Carnelian is a stone of physical vitality and energy, and can act spiritually to help one regain one's strength after illness or injury. Carrying or wearing it can aid in awakening the vital energies of the three lower chakras, increasing zest for living and the willingness to take the risks inherent in all strong actions.

Carnelian blends its energies well with all other varieties of Quartz, Jasper and Chalcedony. Combining it with Rose Quartz, Blue Lace Agate, Blue Quartz and Amethyst can bring about the harmonious activation of all seven chakras in the body. If extra grounding is needed, Smoky Quartz can be added at the root chakra. For higher vibrational activation, activating the Soul Star and etheric chakras, a clear Quartz laser wand can be employed. To go further, adding Moldavite at the heart chakra, Phenacite at the third eye, and Danburite or Petalite at the crown will bring all the energies up to a higher octave.

CASSITERITE

KEY WORDS Manifestation and destruction, birth and death, initiation, navigating the liminal threshold
CHAKRAS Root (1st), Sexual/Creative (2nd), Solar Plexus (3rd) **ELEMENT** Storm **PHYSICAL** Supports shamanic healing, rallying the body to handle serious illness
EMOTIONAL Helps overcome fear of death or of entering the other world **SPIRITUAL** Facilitates shamanic journeying, channeling, mediumship

CASSITERITE is a tin oxide mineral with a tetragonal crystal system and a hardness of 6 to 7. Its name is derived from the Greek word for tin. It has been found in Australia, Bolivia, Mexico, England and Namibia.

Cassiterite connects one's consciousness with the deep Source. It is a stone of initiation, and its vibration is that of the threshold, the liminal space between worlds. This trait makes it ideal for shamans, mediums, channelers and all those who work in the "other world." It facilitates the shifts of consciousness which make such inner journeys possible.

Cassiterite stimulates the lower chakras—root, sexual/creative and solar plexus—as well as the Earthstar below the body and the Soul Star and etheric chakras above the head. It is unique in that it works on the lowest bodily chakras as well as the transpersonal chakras. This is necessary for its purpose as a stone of initiatory gateways. In spite of its heavy-duty nature, Cassiterite is a stone of optimism and humor. It helps one recognize that even the deepest travails of life are but momentary stations on the path of the soul.

Cassiterite harmonizes with Zincite and Cuprite. If one is in need of extra *prana,* or life-force energies, Cuprite is preferable. If one wishes to rouse the sexual/creative fires, Zincite is the best possible ally.

CATHEDRAL QUARTZ

KEY WORDS Access to spiritual information, multidimensional awareness **CHAKRAS** Third Eye (6th), Crown (7th), Etheric (8th–14th) **ELEMENT** Storm, Wind **PHYSICAL** Aids in recalling past civilization information for healing the body **EMOTIONAL** Supports overcoming fears of entering expanded consciousness **SPIRITUAL** Facilitates accessing stored information from the spiritual domains

CATHEDRAL QUARTZ is a variety of Quartz, a silicon dioxide mineral with a hexagonal crystal system and a hardness of 7. Cathedral Quartz is so named because of small points embedded in the main crystal body, reminding one of the turrets of an ancient castle or cathedral. Cathedral Quartz is found in Africa, Russia, Switzerland and Madagascar.

Cathedral Quartz crystals are among the richest of the information-bearing stones in the mineral kingdom. They have been programmed by spirit entities to make it possible for humans to access the necessary knowledge for raising their vibrational frequencies and evolving into the next level of existence. Among other things, these stones act as repositories of knowledge of the energetic structures of the higher dimensions. Through working with them, one can develop the clairvoyant vision necessary to create an internal map of the astral, subtle, causal, devic, angelic and other realms. The ultimate benefit of such efforts is to allow humans to develop multidimensional awareness.

Cathedral Quartz can be used with any other stone, as well as with herbs, oils, sound and various frequencies of Light. With all of these, the crystals are capable of opening the inner doors to deeper knowledge. When placed on light boxes which pulsate with different colors at different speeds, Cathedral Quartz can catalyze one's entry into multidimensional consciousness.

CAVANSITE

KEY WORDS Clairvoyance and clairaudience, access to Akashic records, enhanced communication, consciousness **CHAKRAS** Third Eye (6th), Crown (7th) **ELEMENT** Wind **PHYSICAL** Aids with clearing headaches and stress-induced maladies **EMOTIONAL** Encourages inner peace, courage, gentleness **SPIRITUAL** Enhances psychic capacities, channeling and ESP

CAVANSITE is a hydrous calcium vanadium oxide silicate with a hardness of 3 to 4. Cavansite's color ranges from blue to bluish-green. The finest specimens are from its famous location in Poona, India.

Cavansite is a stone of the purest Blue Ray vibrations. It unites the energies of the fifth and sixth chakras—the throat and the third eye—facilitating clear insight and articulate communication. Thus Cavansite is a stone of inner truth. It opens one's mind to direct comprehension and allows one to be a clear receiver for higher truth. Cavansite can assist those who channel spiritual information, or who wish to do so. It can aid one in all areas of intuition, including psychic abilities such as mediumship, psychokinesis, psychometry, remote viewing, etc. It can help one to step aside and let one's truth flow freely, without the interference of thought or doubt. Cavansite is soothing to the emotions and calming to frayed nerves. It helps one find the courage and the gentleness to speak the words that must be said, without inflicting blame or shame. It is an excellent stone to carry or wear in difficult situations in which one wishes to avoid conflict without sacrificing truth.

Cavansite and Stilbite together can be an opening and healing combination of truth, love and peace. It can open the doors of perception while increasing one's attunement with the realm of the heart.

CELESTITE

KEY WORDS Angelic communication, access to higher dimensions, serenity **CHAKRAS** Third Eye (6th), Crown (7th), Etheric (8th–14th) **ELEMENT** Wind **PHYSICAL** Aids in clearing negative attachments, overcoming infections **EMOTIONAL** Helps one dispel fear and paranoia, calms the emotional body **SPIRITUAL** Enhances inner vision and intuition, elevates one's awareness

CELESTITE (also known as Celestine) is a strontium sulfate mineral with an orthorhombic crystal system and a hardness of 3 to 3.5. It forms both tabular and prismatic crystals. The main location it's found is Madagascar, but a significant deposit was found in Ohio in 1996.

Celestite offers a gentle, uplifting energy which can raise and expand one's awareness into the higher realms. It is one of the most effective stones for accessing the angelic realm and can facilitate communication between oneself and one's guardian angels or angelic guides. It stimulates the third eye and crown chakras and the etheric chakras above the head. It is a soft stone both physically and energetically. As it elevates one's awareness, Celestite makes one feel as if one is floating on a cloud rather than zooming in a rocket.

Madagascar's Blue-gray Celestite comes primarily in clusters, and it is ideal for placement in one's bedroom, healing room or meditation space, as an environmental cleanser and source of soft, positive energies. Its vibrations radiate in all directions, making it wonderful to have around, although it is somewhat less useful for healing or meditation work that requires focus on specific chakras or meridian points. For these applications, single crystals of Ohio Celestite are much preferred. When used with Ascension stones, Celestites will amplify the other stones' energies and bring vibrational elevation and balance to the blend.

CERUSSITE

KEY WORDS Alchemical transformation of self, evolutionary change **CHAKRAS** Root (1st), Crown (7th) **ELEMENT** Storm **PHYSICAL** Facilitates alchemical transformation of the body **EMOTIONAL** Encourages equanimity through change, embracing spiritual desires **SPIRITUAL** Initiates the transformation from the human to Divine self

CERUSSITE is a lead carbonate mineral with an orthorhombic crystal system and a hardness of 3.5. It often forms crystals, which are colorless, gray or brown. Cerussite crystals have been found in the Czech Republic, Sardinia, Austria, Scotland, Namibia and the USA.

Cerussite is a stone of inner alchemy. It works to transform the human persona into a living manifestation of the Divine. For those spiritual pioneers who desire self-transformation, Cerussite can be a useful tool. It stimulates the energies of the root chakra and links them to the crown chakra. It builds a vibrational spiral up through the spinal column, energizing each of the chakras along the way. In so doing, it creates a pattern of realignment which reverberates through all levels of one's being, offering one the opportunity to choose to restructure one's life at a higher level of spiritual functioning. It can assist those going through unexpected transitions—in health, relationships or self-awareness—to find the most appropriate new pattern for their life.

Cerussite links with Azeztulite, Petalite, Scolecite and Natrolite, all of which stimulate the crown chakra, opening one's consciousness to awareness of the Divine. Zincite, Black Andradite Garnet, Sphalerite and Galena can provide additional grounded support to Cerussite's purpose. Celestite can take the newly awakened energies brought to awareness by Cerussite and raise them beyond the level of the physical body.

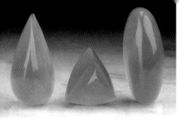

CHALCEDONY, BLUE

KEY WORDS Calm, balance, centeredness, inner knowledge **CHAKRAS** Throat (5th), Third Eye (6th) **ELEMENT** Water **PHYSICAL** Aids with issues of the throat and larynx, voice problems **EMOTIONAL** Encourages release of inhibitions, clear communication of truth **SPIRITUAL** Enhances telepathy, past-life recall, spiritual counseling

BLUE CHALCEDONY is a silicon dioxide mineral with a hardness of 7. It differs from Jasper in that the Quartz is arranged in fibrous layers rather than the sugar-like grains found in Jasper. Blue Chalcedony is found in India, Brazil, Turkey and the USA.

When there is a need for softness in the auric field, at times when stresses mount and one's center begins to wobble, Blue Chalcedony can restore calm and balance. Because it is a strong representative of the Blue Ray, associated with the throat and third eye chakras, Blue Chalcedony affects the mind on many levels. It stimulates telepathy and all types of communications with the invisible realms. It helps one speak things which are below one's normal conscious awareness and is thus a good stone for those in therapy and an excellent tool for those engaged in counseling others. Because it connects to the subconscious, Blue Chalcedony can also assist in the remembrance of past lives, and its orientation toward inner healing means that the memories recovered with Blue Chalcedony will be those most relevant to what is needed for one's progress and growth.

Blue Chalcedony harmonizes with Purple Chalcedony, Chrysoprase, Owyhee Blue Opal, Oregon Opal, Alexandrite, Petalite, Lapis and Ajoite. Alexandrite and Oregon Opal can assist Blue Chalcedony in recovering memories of past lives.

CHALCEDONY, PURPLE

KEY WORDS Awakening of psychic abilities, aura cleansing, purification, union with the Higher Self **CHAKRAS** Third Eye (6th), Crown (7th) **ELEMENT** Wind **PHYSICAL** Supports higher brain functions, heals nerve damage
EMOTIONAL Helps clear negative emotional attachments from past lives
SPIRITUAL Facilitates awakening psychic capacities, attuning to the Higher Self

PURPLE CHALCEDONY is a silicon dioxide mineral with a hardness of 7. It differs from Jasper in that the Quartz is arranged in fibrous layers rather than the sugar-like grains found in Jasper. Purple Chalcedony is found in Mexico, Brazil, Turkey and the USA.

The psychic energies softly touched by Blue Chalcedony can be fully activated by Purple Chalcedony. One's capacities for clairvoyance, clairaudience, clairsentience, psychometry, channeling, prescience and prophecy—as well as access to the Akashic records and knowledge of ancient civilizations—are all stimulated through work with this stone.

Purple Chalcedony is a pure stone of the Violet Ray. It is a powerful influence for purifying and cleansing the auric field, and for providing psychic protection. Negative attachments from this life, or even many past lives, can be severed by calling forth the purifying energies of these stones. It is strongly associated with the energies of St. Germaine and with what is known as the Magic Presence—the interlocking of one's everyday identity with the Higher Self through a ray of Violet Light. The Violet Ray (or Violet Flame) radiated by Purple Chalcedony is also useful for those who wish to attract their spiritual twin, or soul mate. Purple Chalcedony harmonizes with Moldavite, Blue Chalcedony, Amethyst, Sugilite, Charoite, Phenacite, Lilac Lepidolite and Gel Lithium Silica.

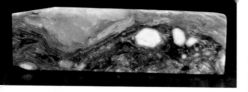

CHAROITE

KEY WORDS Revealing one's path of service, purging inner negativity, protection, healing **CHAKRAS** Third Eye (6th), Crown (7th), Soul Star (8th), Solar Plexus (3rd), Root (1st), Earthstar (below the feet) **ELEMENT** Wind **PHYSICAL** Aids in overcoming illnesses caused by past-life attachments **EMOTIONAL** Helps one to dispel nightmares, overcoming fears, unconditional love **SPIRITUAL** Initiates psychic protection, etheric purification, more synchronicities

CHAROITE is known for its powerful emanation of the Purple Ray. It can therefore be used to purify and cleanse one's etheric body, releasing disharmonies and dispelling negativity. It can protect one from psychic attack and dispel the tendency to have bad dreams. It facilitates the release of unconscious fears, serving as a catalyst for the healing and transmutation of old patterns of imbalance. It can help one access past-life memories and integrate the lessons of past-life experience. For those suffering from difficult-to-diagnose maladies that have their roots in internalized negativity or fear, Charoite can be a powerful aid. It can help one merge the heart and crown chakra energies, allowing for deeper spiritual insights in an inner climate of unconditional love.

Working with Charoite can increase the likelihood of synchronicities in one's life. If one learns to notice these and the messages they imply, one can move through life as if guided by a golden thread, and the pathless path of one's highest potential will be revealed.

Charoite blends its energies synergistically with Moldavite, Phenacite, Seraphinite, Petalite, Amethyst, Kunzite and Blue Apatite. For those using Charoite as protection from negative energies, Sugilite, Jet, Black Tourmaline and Smoky Quartz are all good allies.

CHLORITE
PHANTOM CRYSTALS

KEY WORDS Self-healing, linking with Earth and Nature spirits **CHAKRAS** Heart (4th), Third Eye (6th) **ELEMENT** Storm, Earth **PHYSICAL** Initiates energetic cleansing of the body, facilitates psychic surgery **EMOTIONAL** Encourages making a heart connection with Nature and the Earth **SPIRITUAL** Instills conscious relationship with Nature spirits and the Earth

CHLORITE PHANTOM CRYSTALS are Quartz crystals with a hexagonal crystal system and a hardness of 7. They are formed when a deposit of Chlorite occurs on the termination of a Quartz crystal, and is then covered by later growth of the Quartz, leaving a green "phantom" impression.

Chlorite Phantom Crystals are excellent sources of connection with the realm of the Nature spirits. Meditation with Chlorite Phantom Crystals can facilitate communication and energy exchange with plant spirits, as well as devas, fairies and other beings. Chlorite Phantoms resonate to the heartbeat of the Earth, and they can help one learn to ground one's energies and emotions in the Earth. We live in symbiosis with the Earth, each depending on the other. Just as human beings are physically nourished by the Earth, the Soul of the Earth can only be fully realized through the consciousness of human beings. Chlorite Phantoms resonate with a remarkably clear version of pure Earth energy. Meditation with them can facilitate conscious contact with Her. Use of these stones in planetary healing will also be most efficacious.

Chlorite Phantoms harmonize with Seraphinite, Charoite, Moldavite and Seriphos Green Quartz. Using Danburite with Chlorite Phantoms assists in making a clearer inner link with Nature spirits. Bringing in Phenacite enhances the visionary qualities of these experiences.

CHRYSANTHEMUM STONE

KEY WORDS Grounding, prosperity, discovering and achieving the soul's purpose **CHAKRAS** All **ELEMENT** Earth **PHYSICAL** Helps with women's issues with reproductive organs and tissues **EMOTIONAL** Inspires courage, embracing one's true potential **SPIRITUAL** Facilitates following the soul's longing, calling in helpful serendipities

CHRYSANTHEMUM STONE is a black and white rock made up of gypsum clay, dolomite and limestone, with internal crystals of Calcite, Feldspar, Celestite or Andalusite, in flower-like patterns. They were discovered in Japan, and are also found in Canada, China and the USA.

Chrysanthemum Stone can act as a catalyst for activating the dormant capacities that lie within individuals. If one has always wanted to do something—write, dance, climb a mountain, start a business—Chrysanthemum Stone offers energetic support for finding the courage and opportunities to live one's dreams. If one doesn't yet even know one's dream, sleeping or meditating with this stone can help one receive the inner message that makes clear the nature of one's neglected purpose.

These auspicious stones offer even more. They are magnets for positive synchronicities—the sorts of things some people call "luck." When we embark on the road of our soul's longing, the very act of turning in that direction can give the Universe the cue it needs to help us. Chrysanthemum Stone, like other talismans of good fortune, seems to draw such welcome turns of fate.

For one's destiny path, Chrysanthemum Stone combines well with Moldavite or Seraphinite. For enhancement of the vitality to follow one's deepest desires, Cuprite, Zincite and Carnelian are recommended.

CHRYSOBERYL

KEY WORDS Alignment of the will with the heart, abundance, prophetic vision **CHAKRAS** Solar Plexus (3rd), Heart (4th) **ELEMENTS** Wind, Water **PHYSICAL** Energetically supports heart, kidneys and bloodstream **EMOTIONAL** Encourages generosity and altruism **SPIRITUAL** Instills power through gentleness, prosperity, generosity, prophecy

CHRYSOBERYL is a beryllium aluminum oxide with an orthorhombic crystal system and a hardness of 8.5. Its yellow, green or brown colors are caused by small amounts of iron or chromium. It is found in Brazil, Sri Lanka, Burma, Madagascar and Russia.

Chrysoberyl assists us in merging and unifying the energies of the solar plexus and the heart, bringing empowerment of the will, under the guidance of the heart's compassionate wisdom. It can shift the vibration of one's energy field to enhance one's ability to act powerfully from a place of gentleness. It assists one in persevering in altruistic projects, such as those that help to heal and preserve Nature or that benefit other humans in need. Chrysoberyl's energy also concerns the creation of prosperity through generosity. In this Universe of infinite abundance, we are more like valves through which energies flow than we are like containers in which things accumulate. Like priming a pump, we open our valve and start the flow by giving—and the receiving will then follow. Chrysoberyl can help us set up the vibrational conditions which are ideal for this flow.

Catseye Chrysoberyl facilitates the gift of prophecy.

Chrysoberyl's altruistic energies are enhanced by combining it with Charoite, Morganite, Kunzite, Emerald and/or Rose Quartz. Its ability to magnetize prosperity is strengthened by Phenacite and Tsavorite.

CHRYSOCOLLA

KEY WORDS Communication, expression of the sacred, goddess energies, gentleness and power
CHAKRAS Throat (5th), Heart (4th), Root (1st)
ELEMENT Water **PHYSICAL** Supports adrenals and thyroid, aids with stress-related illnesses **EMOTIONAL** Aids with calming, release of stress and anxiety
SPIRITUAL Facilitates expressing inner wisdom, linking with the Earth's awareness

CHRYSOCOLLA is a hydrous copper silicate with an amorphous crystal system and a hardness of 2 to 4. The color is green, blue or blue-green. Deposits have been found in Chile, Zaire, Russia and the USA.

Chrysocolla is a stone of empowerment of the feminine energies, in both women and men. It is a stone of the Goddess, and those who resonate with Chrysocolla will likely feel her ancient and enduring energies rising within themselves. It stimulates the throat chakra for clear communication of one's inner wisdom. It can even be an aid to learning what that wisdom actually is. Those who have been surprised by hearing oneself speak a thought more profound than that which one had in mind will understand this. The process of formulating and speaking one's ideas can reveal one's innate wisdom. Wearing Chrysocolla, especially near the throat chakra, can facilitate these and other gifts of expression.

Chrysocolla is closely attuned to the vibrations of the Earth and can facilitate one's empathic connection with the Earth's consciousness. In addition to activating the throat chakra, it can harmonize and balance the heart chakra and can link both heart and throat chakras with the base chakra, for greater life force and physical vitality.

Chrysocolla harmonizes with Larimar, Aquamarine, Ajoite, Malachite, Azurite, Lapis and Shattuckite. Azeztulite raises its vibration.

CHRYSOPRASE

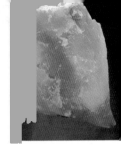

KEY WORDS Growth, compassion, connection with Nature, forgiveness, altruism **CHAKRAS** Heart (4th), Solar Plexus (3rd) **ELEMENT** Water **PHYSICAL** Supports general health, regeneration, youthfulness, vitality
EMOTIONAL Encourages love and trust, release of fear-based emotions **SPIRITUAL** Aids in connecting with Divine Love, Nature spirits, Soul of the Earth

CHRYSOPRASE is a green Chalcedony, a member of the Quartz group with a hexagonal crystal system and a hardness of 7. Chrysoprase was used as a gemstone in ancient Greece as far back as 400 BC. It has been found in Australia, Brazil, Madagascar, South Africa and Russia.

Chrysoprase is a lovely stone of the pure Green Ray, and as such it is a stone of the heart. It can link one to the domain of Nature spirits. Wearing or meditating with these stones can facilitate a deep heart connection with the spirit of the Earth, as well as devas and other Earth-spirit entities. Chrysoprase helps one remain centered in the heart, providing the courage to face difficult or threatening situations with steadfast resolve and truth-centered compassion. These stones give strength to the emotional heart and offer energetic support to the physical heart.

Chrysoprase also activates the solar plexus chakra, seat of the will. It helps blend one's personal will with the urgings of the heart, uniting one's individual desires with the heart's higher longing for the good of all. Chrysoprase harmonizes with Ajoite, Danburite, Lepidolite, Amblygonite, Phenacite, Azeztulite, Kunzite and Morganite. Kunzite and Morganite bring forth the loving aspects of the heart. Phenacite and Azeztulite open inner vision. Lepidolite and Amblygonite emphasize the relaxing and stress-relieving properties of Chrysoprase.

CINNABAR

KEY WORDS Alchemy, magic, transformation, insight, manifestation, wealth, mental agility
CHAKRAS Root (1st), Sexual/Creative (2nd), Third Eye (6th) **ELEMENT** Fire
PHYSICAL Energetically supports clearing toxins, overcoming infections
EMOTIONAL Helps one release anger and resentment, face truth courageously
SPIRITUAL Facilitates perceiving the Divine pattern, alchemical transformation

CINNABAR is a mercury sulfide mineral with a trigonal crystal system and a hardness of 2 to 2.5. Its color is vermilion red. It forms around volcanic vents and hot springs. Cinnabar sometimes forms in conjunction with Quartz, and Cinnabar Quartz is the most beneficial form of Cinnabar for metaphysical use.

Cinnabar Quartz stones are talismans of the alchemical transformation—the full manifestation of one's spiritual blueprint, the fulfillment of the Divine pattern we carry within. This requires burning away the dross of one's imperfections and refining what remains into the pure essence of the Higher Self.

In addition to the first two chakras, Cinnabar Quartz stimulates the third eye, making for greater insight and the ability to see visions of the potential future. It helps one ground one's visions in physical reality as well. This makes it an ideal stone for creative people as well as business owners, both of whom can use it to actualize their dreams and create prosperity. It can balance and remove blockages in one's energy body.

Cinnabar Quartz is the stone of the Magician archetype. The Magician acts as a conscious conduit between the spiritual and material worlds. If one feels a kinship to the Magician archetype, Cinnabar Quartz can assist one in creatively directing subtle energies into manifestation.

CIRCLE STONE

KEY WORDS Attunement to Earth's consciousness, awakening of dormant capacities, cocreative union with the World Soul
CHAKRAS Third Eye (6th), Crown (7th)
ELEMENT Storm   **PHYSICAL** Stimulates full brain activation and awakening body intelligence   **EMOTIONAL** Inspires exhilaration and passionate devotion to World Soul   **SPIRITUAL** Awakens many latent capacities; co-creative union with Sophia

Circle STONE is the name given to pieces of Flint that have been gathered from within the crop circle formations in England. Flint is a sedimentary rock composed entirely of silica.

Circle Stones share with the Azeztulites the unique property of being "awakened stones," which have received their vibrational patterns recently, through the intervention of higher intelligence. In the case of Circle Stones, the awakening of each group of stones occurs when a crop circle is formed. People who find them attest that the stones embody the remarkable energies of the Crop Circle itself. Circle Stones are evolutionary triggers. They stimulate the entire brain and activate latent capacities such as clairvoyance, prescience, access to "instant knowing" (clairsentience) and awareness of the Earth's consciousness. They help one attune to the Time Stream of the Future, and they awaken our potential for cocreating the world in partnership with the World Soul. When one meditates with Circle Stones, one can literally feel Her urging one to awaken and take up this path of our highest destiny.

Circle Stones work harmoniously with Rosophia for communicating with Sophia (the World Soul) and experiencing Her love. Herderite and Azeztulite aid Circle Stone's quickening of our evolution. Guardianite helps to ground and integrate the powerful potentials awakened by Circle Stone.

CITRINE

KEY WORDS Manifestation, personal will, mental clarity, creativity **CHAKRAS** Root (1st), Sexual/Creative (2nd), Solar Plexus (3rd) **ELEMENT** Fire **PHYSICAL** Energetically supports digestion, metabolism, weight loss **EMOTIONAL** Stimulates optimism, playfulness, decisiveness in difficult situations **SPIRITUAL** Enhances creative imagination, manifestation through the will

C ITRINE is a silicon dioxide mineral, a member of the Quartz group with a hexagonal crystal system and a hardness of 7. Its yellow pigmentation is derived from iron. The name Citrine comes from the French word *citron*, meaning lemon. Citrine deposits have been found in Brazil, Africa, Madagascar, Spain, Russia, France, Scotland and the USA.

Citrine opens the inner doors to increased clarity of thought, enhanced creativity and magnified powers of will and manifestation. It is one of the premier stones for the second chakra and is capable of awakening the powers of creative imagination. It helps one turn toward the time stream from the future, opening the self beyond what has been into the realm of what can be. Citrine, in both natural and heated forms, stimulates imagination through three portals—the second, third and sixth chakras. The vibratory resonance of Citrine activates and harmonizes these three energy centers, all of which are necessary to the process of creative imagination. Citrine activates the thinking process and enhances mental clarity, as well as the visionary function through which inner images appear. Through the second chakra, Citrine stimulates the creative function, the wellspring from which new potentials are born. Through the third chakra, Citrine generates the human dynamo of personal will. Citrine works synergistically with Heliodor, Golden Labradorite, Imperial Topaz, Zincite, Orange Calcite and Carnelian.

CLINOCHLORE

KEY WORDS Healing, vitality, love, Divine blueprint of well-being, angelic communication
CHAKRAS Heart (4th) **ELEMENT** Storm, Earth
PHYSICAL Aids in attuning to the Divine pattern of health **EMOTIONAL** Supports joyful link with the higher realms **SPIRITUAL** Facilitates connecting with spirit guides and angels

CLINOCHLORE is a magnesium iron aluminum silicate with a hardness of 2 to 2.5. Its colors include green, white, yellowish, colorless or purple. There is notable chemical variety in the Clinochlore minerals, which include such species as Seraphinite, Cookeite and Kammererite.

Clinochlore minerals are among the strongest for bringing healing and well-being to the physical body through alignment with the Divine blueprint. These stones are attuned to the archetypal patterns through which living entities, including human beings, are physically expressed. When one works with one's intention focused on linking to the pattern of perfect health, the stones provide a "window" through which one may resonate with this pattern. This energetic resonance makes an imprint upon one's etheric body, which then translates the pattern into the physical form. Clinochlore assists in communicating with angelic beings and spirit guides. Its vibrational pattern provides a window into these domains similar to the one used for healing resonance.

Clinochlore harmonizes for healing purposes with stones such as Sugilite, Emerald, Amethyst and Charoite. For spiritual upliftment, Petalite, Danburite, Phenacite, Brookite and Azeztulite can be most helpful. For emotional healing, Lilac Lepidolite, Lithium Quartz, Amblygonite and Rhodochrosite are beneficial allies.

COROMANDEL STONEWOOD

KEY WORDS Awareness of Earth's ancient memories, time travel to the past, Lemurian consciousness, receptivity, link to the Earth's heartbeat, telomere protection, longevity **CHAKRAS** All, especially Root (1st) **ELEMENT** Earth **PHYSICAL** Enhances vitality, supports the telomeres for increased longevity **EMOTIONAL** Facilitates inner peace, contentment, and ecstatic resonance with the Earth's heartbeat **SPIRITUAL** Facilitates entrainment with the Earth's heartbeat, aids one in recalling and identifying with Lemurian consciousness

Coromandel stonewood is a rich brown petrified wood from New Zealand's Coromandel Peninsula. It is a silicon dioxide with a hardness of 7.

Coromandel Stonewood carries deep memories of the ancient Earth. It carries the memories of New Zealand's Lemurian history, as well as the Lemurian qualities of deep intuition, empathy and bodily knowing. It encourages one to envision the potential for a Lemurian revival in the world today, and suggests that the New Consciousness for which humanity is destined is one of empathic rapport. It enhances one's receptivity to the subtle vibrational currents of the Earth, including the Earth's heartbeat. With these stones, one can learn to fall into ecstatic resonance with that heartbeat! It permeates one's being on all levels—spiritual, mental, emotional and physical.

Coromandel Stonewood emanates a curative vitality that is placid, slow-moving and long-lasting. It is ideal for aiding recovery from chronic conditions. These stones vibrationally benefit the telomeres on one's DNA, helping to preserve cellular memory and support longevity.

Coromandel Stonewood harmonizes well with all types of Jasper, as well as Revelation Stone, Sauralite Azeztulite, Cinnazez, New Zealand Carnelian, Empowerite and Sanda Rosa Azeztulite.

COVELLITE

KEY WORDS Psychic abilities, inner vision, transformation, bridging the higher and lower worlds
CHAKRAS All **ELEMENT** Storm
PHYSICAL Helps one overcome illnesses based in negative past fixations **EMOTIONAL** Inspires courage to take the journey through one's inner depths
SPIRITUAL Facilitates making the evolutionary leap to awakened consciousness

COVELLITE is a copper sulfide mineral with a hexagonal crystal system and a hardness of 1.5 to 2. Its color is deep blue to black, usually with a play of gold or deep red on its surfaces. Covellite has been found in Montana, USA, as well as in Italy and Peru.

Covellite connects strongly with physical reality and Earth energies and at the same time carries much of the higher spectrum of vibrations from the etheric planes. It makes an energetic bridge between worlds, and it can be an important ally for anyone attempting the evolutionary leap to the next level of being. Covellite is also a facilitator of the deep journey into the self and can be of great assistance in bringing the unconscious Shadow side into one's awareness. This is where the energy necessary for fully awakened consciousness has been frozen—in old traumas, losses, shame and fear. Those who work with Covellite in meditation or dreaming may find themselves unearthing and reliving memories of old traumas, losses, shame and fear. This can facilitate a healing release.

Covellite harmonizes with Nuummite for added emphasis on the deep journey. Adding Azeztulite helps one "carry a Light into dark places." Phenacite or Cinnabar Quartz can bring forth additional powers of insight for understanding the symbols and ideas that emerge from the depths of the unconscious.

CREEDITE

KEY WORDS Expansion of awareness, attuning to spiritual information **CHAKRAS** Third Eye (6th), Crown (7th), Etheric (8th–14th) **ELEMENT** Storm **PHYSICAL** Reveals the etheric body for diagnosis of imbalances **EMOTIONAL** Helps one govern the emotional body from a higher perspective **SPIRITUAL** Facilitates great expansion of awareness in the spiritual realms

CREEDITE occurs in white, colorless, orange and sometimes purple crystals. The orange Creedites often form in porcupine-like balls that bristle with spiny crystals going out in all directions. Creedite is a rare mineral, and the best specimens come primarily from Mexico.

Creedite quickly and powerfully activates the third eye and crown chakras and those above. There is a vivid sense of expansion of one's field of awareness and a euphoria that feels like a floating upliftment. Over time, one senses a deepening of the energy, moving down to the heart. Creedite is an access-key stone. It can assist one in attuning to the Akashic records, "opening the files" in record keeper crystals, understanding the messages of spirit guides, interpreting oracles such as the tarot, and channeling the messages of spirit beings. It can help meditators make the quantum leap to higher domains of consciousness, clearing any blockages in the higher chakras. Creedite is a stone of the angelic realm, and it can help one manifest spiritual Light in one's everyday life.

Creedite resonates well with Azeztulite, Scolecite, Phenacite, Natrolite, Clear Apophyllite and/or Herderite. Jet and Black Tourmaline can help one purify one's energy field and stay grounded. Combining Carnelian, Orange Calcite, Zincite or Amber with orange Creedite will enhance one's creative energies. Creedite and Moldavite work together to bring one experiences of spiritual awakening and transformation.

CRIMSON CUPRITE

KEY WORDS Life force, vitality, physical energy, courage, healing, Divine feminine, etherization of the blood   **CHAKRAS** Root (1st), Sexual/Creative (2nd) **ELEMENT** Earth   **PHYSICAL** Triggers an infusion of life force, aids most organs and systems **EMOTIONAL** Instills passion and vitality, assuages anxiety and fear **SPIRITUAL** Links one with the Earth Goddess, stimulates transformation

CRIMSON CUPRITE is a copper oxide mineral with a hexoctahedral crystal system and a hardness of 3.5 to 4. It is bright red, sometimes with blue inclusions of Chrysocolla. It is from a single find in Mexico.

Crimson Cuprite is a profoundly helpful stone for those working on healing issues, irrational anxieties or fears around one's mortality. It offers pure first-chakra energy, and its abundant flow of *prana* is a boon to anyone whose first chakra is closed or weak. Meditation with Crimson may be instrumental in awakening the kundalini energies. As a stone of *prana*, it offers vibrational support for healing lung dysfunctions, circulation difficulties, prostate or lower-bowel issues or problems with the sexual organs. Crimson Cuprite is a stone of feminine power, and it activates the feminine archetype of the Earth goddess. Women who wish to find their own connection to Her are advised to wear, sleep or meditate with it, and to imagine their own base chakra with a red root extending deep into the Earth. Crimson Cuprite can also be a stone of alchemy, and it resonates with the archetypes of the Magician and the High Priestess. Just as copper conducts electricity, Crimson Cuprite carries divine energies from the inner world to their manifestation in the outer world.

Crimson Cuprite harmonizes with Ruby, Master Shamanite, Mystic Merlinite and Rosophia. The Azeztulites elevate its energy. Guardianite amplifies is power, strengthening and protecting the body.

CROCOITE

KEY WORDS Physical vitality, wisdom of the heart, communion with the Divine, passion, love, enlightenment **CHAKRAS** Root (1st), Heart (4th), Crown (7th) **ELEMENT** Storm **PHYSICAL** Supports reproductive systems **EMOTIONAL** Kindles love and passion **SPIRITUAL** Enhances creativity, kundalini activation

CROCOITE is a lead chromate mineral with a monoclinic crystal system and a hardness of 2.5 to 3. Crocoite's color is red or red-orange, and sometimes yellow. The best known deposits are in Tasmania, Australia, but it has also been found in the Ural Mountains of Russia.

Crocoite is a beneficial stone for making breakthroughs, especially for those whose most passionate pursuit is the realization of enlightenment. This stone activates a harmonic, triune vibration of the crown, heart and root chakras, opening the kundalini channel and moving one's core energies through it. This powerful opening can catalyze all sorts of quantum leaps in one's consciousness, dispelling old blockages and allowing the full expression of one's spiritual self through the physical body. Crocoite can stimulate passion, love and spiritual awareness all at once.

For couples, the vibrations of Crocoite are highly conducive to tantric love making practices, which rouse these same energies. Keeping a Crocoite cluster in the bedroom can infuse the area with blissful waves of ecstatic engagement. Crocoite stimulates all types of creative fertility, and is an excellent stone for artists, writers and musicians.

Crocoite works well when combined with Azeztulite, Herderite, Natrolite and/or Phenacite. For fertility, creativity and sexuality, Zincite, Orange Calcite and/or Carnelian are most helpful.

CRYOLITE

KEY WORDS Intelligence of the heart, future stream, Divine purpose, surrender, liberation, integrity, spiritual truth
CHAKRAS All (1st–7th), Soul Star (8th)　**ELEMENT** Storm　**PHYSICAL** Supports neurological health, strengthens heart/brain links　**EMOTIONAL** Awakens inner joy and peace through heart awareness　**SPIRITUAL** Facilitates expansion of consciousness into heart/brain partnership

CRYOLITE is a sodium aluminum fluoride mineral with a monoclinic crystal system and a hardness of 2.5 to 3. Most Cryolite has been found at the Ivigtut site on Greenland's west coast. It has been found in Colorado, USA; Quebec, Canada; and at Miask, Russia.

The energies of Cryolite focus directly on the most needed component of human evolution at this time—the awakening of our awareness to the intelligence of the heart, and the partnering of the most evolved areas of the brain with that intelligence. Cryolite powerfully stimulates the third eye, as well as the entire pre frontal cortex of the brain. It also stimulates the heart and crown chakras, linking them with the third eye and facilitating inner vision. Further, it opens the channels through which the holographic knowing of the heart and its language of silent understanding can be received and comprehended by the conscious mind. It also switches on dormant capacities in the "silent areas" of the brain. The emotional tone of Cryolite is one of peace and quiet joy.

It encourages an inner surrender that is actually a release into liberation, as one realizes that oneself and the Divine purpose are one and the same.

Cryolite is a excellent stone to use in combination with Hollandite Quartz. Moldavite, Phenacite, Natrolite, Scolecite, Herderite, Azeztulite and Petalite can aid in further activating the High Brain.

CUPRITE

KEY WORDS Life force, vitality, physical energy, courage, healing, Divine feminine
CHAKRAS Root (1st), Sexual/Creative (2nd)
ELEMENT Earth   **PHYSICAL** Supports lungs, circulation, bowels, prostate, sexual organs   **EMOTIONAL** Aids in overcoming fears linked to physical survival   **SPIRITUAL** Stimulates ones's awakening to kundalini, alchemy, Goddess energies

CUPRITE is a copper oxide mineral with a hardness of 3.5 to 4. The color is red, ranging from brownish or blackish to pure crimson. Cuprite has been found in the Congo, Namibia and in Bisbee, Arizona, USA.

Cuprite is helpful for physical domain problems linked with the root chakra—healing issues, irrational anxieties, fears around mortality, unconscious terror connected to past traumas. It emanates pure first-chakra energy, and its abundant flow of *prana* is a boon to anyone whose first chakra may be closed or weak. Meditation with Cuprite can activate the first chakra and may be instrumental in awakening the kundalini energies. This can be especially helpful to people who feel that they are "low energy" types for Cuprite emanates a wellspring of vitality. It offers vibrational support for healing lung dysfunctions, circulation difficulties, prostate or lower-bowel issues or problems with the sexual organs.

Cuprite is a stone of feminine power, and it activates the feminine archetype of the Earth goddess. It is also a stone of fertility on all levels—helpful to those who wish to conceive, and to those who want to birth their creative projects into the world. Cuprite can also be a stone of alchemy, and it resonates with the archetypes of the Magician and the High Priestess. Zincite and Tibetan Tektite can be used to augment the powerful life-force energies awakened by working with Cuprite.

DANBURITE

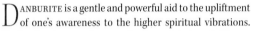

KEY WORDS Angelic communication, channeling, interdimensional travel, peace, freedom from stress   **CHAKRAS** Heart (4th), Crown (7th), Etheric (8th–14th)   **ELEMENT** Wind
PHYSICAL Supports recovery from stress-related illnesses
EMOTIONAL Aids in finding inner peace, calming worries and fears   **SPIRITUAL** Facilitates interdimensional travel, angelic communication

DANBURITE is a gentle and powerful aid to the upliftment of one's awareness to the higher spiritual vibrations. Danburite clears and opens the crown chakra, linking and harmonizing it with the heart. It activates and integrates the transpersonal and etheric chakras above the head, all the way up to the fourteenth chakra. This allows one to move in consciousness into the angelic domain, with which Danburite has a special resonance. It also facilitates interdimensional travel and communication with spiritual entities other than angels.

Danburite is excellent for those who need to release stress and worry. It soothes the heart and sends it the message that all is well. Holding a Danburite in each hand can be a very calming experience and a boon to meditation. Those who have difficulty sleeping are advised to hold a Danburite in the hand or place one in the pillowcase to bring peace to the subconscious self. Danburite has a way of calming down the mind chatter that can create a cycle of stress.

Danburite is one of the Synergy Twelve stones (including Moldavite, Phenacite, Tanzanite, Azeztulite, Petalite, Herderite, Tibetan Tektite, Brookite, Natrolite, Scolecite and Satyaloka Azeztulite). It harmonizes with Lilac Lepidolite, Amblygonite and Lithium Quartz (for stress relief) and Merkabite and Elestial Calcite (for interdimensional travel).

DARWINITE

KEY WORDS Heart awareness, loving relationship, linking heart and brain, kinship with all life, holographic consciousness, gestation of the New Human Being **CHAKRAS** Heart (4th), Third Eye (6th), Crown (7th) **ELEMENT** Storm **PHYSICAL** Supports the brain, corpus callosum and heart, engenders energetic links between the brain hemispheres **EMOTIONAL** Entrains with heart to stimulate a consciousness of love, removes fear from the emotional body **SPIRITUAL** Quickens spiritual evolution, awakens spiritual capacities

Darwinite is a glassy meteoric material similar to Moldavite and other Tektites. It is found around in a one-kilometer crater southeast of Mount Darwin in Tasmania, Australia. It is grayish-green and often translucent.

Darwinite is a stone of loving relationship with the world and all beings. It teaches that everything is love, and that we experience that reality by meeting each moment of life with action based on love. It stimulates the brain and heart, triggering the awakening of new spiritual capacities. They offer vibrational support to the unification of the hemispheres of the brain, and can catalyze increased connectivity in the brain through the corpus callosum.

Darwinite stimulates the prototypal pattern of the New Human Being—the next phase of evolution. It can be used to remove fear from the emotional body and the cellular consciousness. It quickens the vibratory rate of the etheric body, so that we can keep pace with the accelerating vibrations of the Earth. Darwinite stimulates insight, and the capacity to "make all things new" through attunement with what is arising from the spiritual realms.

Darwinite resonates well with Moldavite, Libyan Gold Tektite and Tibetan Tektite, Himalaya Gold Azeztulite, Sunset Gold Selenite, all of the Synergy Twelve Stones and Ascension Seven stones. It works well with Azozeo super-activated stones.

DATOLITE

KEY WORDS Connection with the higher worlds, retrieval of lost information, mental power, spiritual awareness **CHAKRAS** Solar Plexus (3rd), Heart (4th), Third Eye (6th), Crown (7th), Etheric (8th–14th) **ELEMENT** Water, Wind **PHYSICAL** Supports and soothes the nervous system **EMOTIONAL** Helps one overcome grief and depression, encourages optimism **SPIRITUAL** Activates subtle vision and multidimensional awareness

DATOLITE is a calcium borosilicate with a monoclinic crystal system and a hardness of 5 to 5.5. It can be colorless, white, pale yellow or pale green. Many of the best Datolite specimens come from Russia.

Datolites are strong crystals for the third eye, crown and etheric chakras. They open one's subtle vision, allowing one to see auras, as well as beings in the astral, causal and subtle domains. Nature spirits, angels, guides, non-physical teachers, healers and helpers all become visible and available for communication. The fast-pulsing energies of Datolite increase the vibration of one's energy field so one can consciously experience one's own spiritual body, using it to explore the many higher dimensions surrounding us. These stones can retrieve lost memories of childhood, past lives and even the Akashic record of humanity's ancient history. They can enhance the accuracy of one's memory and sharpen all mental abilities. They especially aid in developing mathematical intelligence but also improve linguistic learning, memorization, analysis of systems, abstract geometries and other applications of the mind.

Datolite works very well with the high-vibration stones Phenacite, Natrolite, Scolecite, Danburite and Azeztulite, as well as Heliodor, Lapis, Cinnabar Quartz, Calcite, Fluorite, Pyrite and Axinite.

DIAMOND

KEY WORDS Intensity, radiance, sovereignty
CHAKRAS Heart (4th), Third Eye (6th),
Crown (7th), Etheric (8th–14th)
ELEMENT Storm

PHYSICAL Activates prefrontal lobes, magnifies effects of other stones
EMOTIONAL Intensifies emotional states, helps "burn through" old issues
SPIRITUAL Facilitates awakening higher capacities, entering visionary states

Diamond is a cubic crystal of pure carbon with a hardness of 10—the hardest of all substances. However, Diamonds are often colorless, but can be yellow, brown, blue, pink, green, orange or red. For centuries they have been said to provide spiritual protection, as well as such qualities as victory, courage, faithfulness, purity and enhancement of love.

Diamond can assist one in activating the prefrontal lobes of the brain, the seat of most paranormal abilities and visionary consciousness. Diamond crystals are transducers which can make the high-frequency vibrational energies of the spirit realms more available to the conscious self. They can accelerate one's evolution and open the doors to psychic powers. In meditation, Diamond crystals can facilitate the entry into visionary states. Worn in everyday life, they can intensify one's ability to focus consciousness on manifesting one's goals and dreams. Intensity is a key word for Diamond. It works on the emotional body to amplify the power of any emotional state. Therefore, one should be vigilant about wearing Diamonds and should usually remove them if one is in a bad frame of mind. However, they can be used therapeutically to intensify and "burn through" underlying emotional issues.

Diamond crystals can enhance and magnify the energies of high-vibration stones such as Moldavite, Phenacite, Azeztulite, Herderite, Celestite, Libyan Gold Tektite, Tibetan Tektite and many others.

DIASPORE

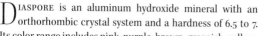

KEY WORDS Adaptability, mental enhancement, meditative exploration **CHAKRAS** Solar Plexus (3rd), Heart (4th), Third Eye (6th) **ELEMENT** Wind **PHYSICAL** Supports recovery from brain damage and brain diseases **EMOTIONAL** Aids in relieving stress, "letting go," attuning to Divine will **SPIRITUAL** Enhances meditation, communication with higher beings

DIASPORE is an aluminum hydroxide mineral with an orthorhombic crystal system and a hardness of 6.5 to 7. Its color range includes pink, purple, brown, greenish, yellow, white, colorless and gray. A discovery of Diaspore crystals in Turkey in the 1990s sparked great interest in Diaspore's use as a gem and as a metaphysical stone.

Diaspore assists in developing the strength of adaptability in life. It stimulates willingness—the release of one's personal desires in order to be in accord with Divine will. Diaspore predisposes the user to find the path of flow rather than forcing one's way through situations. It is therefore useful in relieving stress, developing relationships that work, finding one's best niche in job and career areas, and working in partnership with spiritual beings from the higher planes.

Diaspore stimulates areas of the mind which enhance one's ability to see different points of view on all issues and ideas. In meditation, Diaspore helps one find and maintain the state of "beginner's mind." It opens new areas of consciousness, and it also keeps one from falling into patterns of expectation and judgment. Those who do readings or channeling will find that Diaspore brings back the sense of surprise, wonder and delight in the unexpected insights one receives.

Diaspore harmonizes with Kunzite, Aquamarine, Peridot, Natrolite, Scolecite, Phenacite, Azeztulite, Danburite and Moldavite.

DIOPSIDE

KEY WORDS Connection with the Earth, opening the heart, healing, balance, subtle perception **CHAKRAS** Heart (4th), Root (1st), Earthstar (below the feet) **ELEMENT** Earth **PHYSICAL** Supports tissue regeneration, recovery of strength, reproductive organs **EMOTIONAL** Aids with relaxation, release of stress, embrace of physical life **SPIRITUAL** Facilitates communion with Earth, grounding, geomancy, love

DIOPSIDE is a calcium magnesium silicate with a monoclinic crystal system and a hardness of 5.5 to 6. Its color can be white, light green, dark green, reddish brown, yellowish brown, gray or black. Diopside are found in China, India and the USA.

Diopside varies in its energy, according to its color, and the two most important types are black and green. Black Diopside resonates with the root chakra, and it helps one establish a firm grounding in the Earth. This is a stone for improving one's physical well-being through energetic resonance with the "heartbeat" of the planet. Because it helps focus consciousness downward into the ground, it is excellent for dowsers, assisting one in developing the intuitive feeling for what is hidden below one's feet. Black Diopside is a wonderful stone for geomancy. Those who work with ley lines will find their perceptions enhanced by Black Diopside.

Green Diopside sends its energies along the entire chakric column, from the top of the skull to the tailbone. It charges and activates the heart, root and earthstar chakras. It is oriented toward balancing and healing, and can bring all the chakras into alignment, sending the Green Ray of healing throughout the body and auric field. It can be particularly balancing for females in the area of the reproductive organs. In the heart chakra, Green Diopside supports one's ability to give and receive love.

DIOPTASE

KEY WORDS Forgiveness, compassion, release
of karmic patterns, prosperity
CHAKRAS Heart (4th)   **ELEMENT** Water
PHYSICAL Supports healing of the heart and
of illness caused by emotional trauma
EMOTIONAL Helps one forgive past abuses;
supports joy, peace and compassion
SPIRITUAL Instills freedom from karmic bonds, full heart-centeredness

DIOPTASE is a hydrous copper silicate mineral with a hexagonal crystal
system and a hardness of 5. The color is emerald green to deep bluish
green. It is found in Chile, Namibia, Russia and the USA.

Dioptase is a powerful ally for awakening loving compassion and for healing emotional pain. It lends strength to the emotional heart through the power
of compassion. It supports the physical heart through its constant message
of serenity and well-being. It awakens the spiritual heart through its high-
frequency vibrational pattern, which resonates with the "high heart" chakra
just above the physical heart. Through these channels it stimulates forgiveness and the healing of old inner wounds.

Dioptase is useful for the attainment of past-life insights and for the activation of one's higher purpose. It opens our inner eyes to recognize repetitive
karmic patterns, releasing our attachment to them, and moving forward with
renewed energy. The vibration of Dioptase is wholesome and fresh, and it can
help clear the auric field of disharmony. It can also be used for creating abundance and prosperity. As one of the purest stones of the Green Ray, it attracts
wealth and all good things which can make our physical lives more pleasant.

Dioptase harmonizes with Malachite, Azurite, Cuprite, Turquoise, Danburite, Scolecite, Herderite, Brookite, Phenacite and Azeztulite.

DOLOMITE

KEY WORDS Centeredness, calm, balance, moderation, grounding **CHAKRAS** All **ELEMENT** Earth **PHYSICAL** Supports bone health and detoxification, gets one "in the body" **EMOTIONAL** Lessens emotional extremes, supports calm centeredness **SPIRITUAL** Stone of the "middle way," helps one avoid spiritual extremes

Dolomite is a calcium magnesium carbonate with a rhombohedral crystal system and a hardness of 3.5 to 4. The color ranges through white, gray, greenish, brownish and pinkish. Dolomite crystals have been found in Spain, Italy, India, Great Britain, Switzerland and Namibia.

Dolomite is excellent for achieving calm, centeredness and balance. Holding a piece of Dolomite, one's auric field naturally fills in any gaps, purges itself of negative energies, pulls in any overextended plumes and goes into its optimal form. Dolomite acts like a "reset" button on one's emotions as well. It softens negative emotions and reins in excessive passions. It takes the allure away from unrealistic fantasies, without detracting from one's enthusiasm for one's true purpose. Dolomite is a good stone to place in the environment and can provide a beneficial influence around children. It can help counteract moodiness and other symptoms of "raging hormones." With smaller children, it supports an environmental ambience of calm and security which may reduce the likelihood of nightmares, tantrums and other emotional extremes.

Dolomite can provide a useful "home base" for grounding and centering. It is a good stone to hold after a crystal body layout, a past-life regression, rebirthing, breathwork or other transformational practice.

Dolomite harmonizes with almost every type of stone, though its influence is one of moderation.

DREAM QUARTZ

KEY WORDS Dream enhancement, astral travel, contact with guides, release of stress **CHAKRAS** Third Eye (6th), Crown (7th), Soul Star (8th) **ELEMENT** Storm, Earth, Water **PHYSICAL** Supports healthy weight loss, psychic protection for the body **EMOTIONAL** Aids with inner peace, emotional healing via dreams, past-life recall **SPIRITUAL** Stimulates visionary awareness, lucid dreaming, enhanced psychic abilities

DREAM QUARTZ is the metaphysical name given to Quartz crystals with Epidote inclusions. It is a silicon dioxide crystal with a hexagonal crystal system and a hardness of 7. Its color is a milky green. Dream Quartz comes from crystal mines in Colombia.

Dream Quartz emanates a soft, soothing energy, conducive to states of deep meditation and lucid dreaming. These stones can help bring peace to the heart and relaxation to the body and mind. It helps one enter the inner gateways to visionary experience and interdimensional travel. Dream Quartz can facilitate contact with spirit guides and can be an aid to the development of psychic abilities and channeling.

Dream Quartz can help one remember dreams, and can enhance their spiritual quality. It allows one to more clearly envision and manifest one's dreams for the kind of life one wishes to create. It can aid in recalling past-life memories and breaking patterns from the past which may still be governing one's life. Past-life exploration with Dream Quartz can also help one remember skills and talents one possessed before, but which may now lie dormant in the unconscious. Dream Quartz harmonizes well with Moldavite and Herkimer "Diamonds," both of which intensify vivid dream activity. Oregon Opal and Alexandrite increase recall of past lives.

DUMORTIERITE

KEY WORDS Divine inspiration,
psychic ability, inner guidance, enhanced
learning capacity, mental discipline
CHAKRAS Third Eye (6th)
ELEMENT Wind **PHYSICAL** Supports
neural functioning and clarity of consciousness **EMOTIONAL** Enhances
emotional intelligence and empathy **SPIRITUAL** Stimulates psychic abilities,
prophetic vision, spiritual insight

Dumortierite is an aluminum borate silicate with an orthorhombic crystal system and a hardness of 7. Its colors include dark blue, violet blue and red-brown. It can be found in Brazil, Sri Lanka, Madagascar, Canada, Poland, France, Namibia and the USA.

Dumortierite opens the doors of insight, activating the third eye chakra and assisting one in making the mental leaps necessary for transcending difficulties and solving problems. It enhances all mental abilities—linguistic, mathematical, abstract, etc.—as well as "emotional intelligence." It activates the latent psychic abilities and stimulates clairvoyance, clairaudience and clairsentience. In gifted individuals, it can instill the gift of prophetic vision. It can even facilitate the building of skills in psychometry and psychokinesis. Dumortierite is a strong stone of mental discipline and is capable of enhancing one's willpower in regard to learning. It aids in memory retention and in the mental manipulation of concepts necessary to bring forward a new synthesis of ideas. Because of its stimulation of mental and psychic powers, Dumortierite is ideal for those who work in areas such as astrology and tarot.

Dumortierite harmonizes with Blue Sapphire for mental discipline, with Lapis Lazuli and Lazulite for psychic ability, with Phenacite for inner vision and with Azeztulite for spiritual awakening.

EISEN QUARTZ

KEY WORDS Vitality, creativity, optimism, playfulness, humor, eroticism, insight, self-confidence, spiritual freedom
CHAKRAS Root (1st), Sexual/Creative (2nd), Solar Plexus (3rd) **ELEMENTS** Fire, Wind, Earth **PHYSICAL** Supports the immune system, sexual organs and digestive system **EMOTIONAL** Can be a remedy for discouragement or "stuck" emotions **SPIRITUAL** Stimulates creative inspirations, sexual energies, spiritual freedom; encourages taking the risks that lead to creative and/or romantic fulfillment

Eisen QUARTZ is a yellow, red, orange or brown quartz, colored by inclusions of iron compounds. Its name derives from the German Eisenkiesel, meaning "iron pebble." It is a silicon dioxide with a hardness of 7.

Eisen Quartz is a stone of great vitality. It emanates an infusion of vitality, creativity and optimism, encouraging one to confidently embark on one's creative projects or visions. It strongly activates the second chakra, stimulating both creativity and eroticism. It can kindle romance, or fuel inspirations for writing, art, poetry, dance and other creative intentions. Eisen Quartz can trigger the "aha" moment of sudden insight that brings together disparate ideas into a new synthesis. In healing, Eisen Quartz supports the sexual organs, intestinal tract and spleen. It aids digestion and assimilation, stimulates the immune system, and can help one overcome fatigue and stress.

Eisen Quartz works to inspire and energize those who have become "stuck" and/or discouraged. It can be used to increase self-confidence, enhances one's awareness of one's spiritual freedom, and encourages one to take risks when they are necessary for following one's dreams.

Eisen Quartz works well with Phenacite, Cinnazez, and all types of Azeztulite. With Moldavite, it can trigger intense bursts of transformation!

ELESTIAL QUARTZ

KEY WORDS Energy infusion from the higher realms, Divine Love, angelic communication, grounding the Higher Self in earthly life
CHAKRAS All **ELEMENT** Earth **PHYSICAL** Supports skeletal system for healing broken or diseased bones **EMOTIONAL** Aids in receiving love, joy and well-being from the higher realms
SPIRITUAL Facilitates awakening to multidimensional communication, time travel

ELESTIAL QUARTZ is the name given to Quartz crystals with natural terminations on the faces and body of a layered or etched crystal. It is a silicon dioxide crystal with hexagonal crystal system and a hardness of 7, and is found in Brazil, Africa, Madagascar, Romania and the USA.

Elestial Quartz crystals are like switchboards linking multiple dimensions, times and levels of consciousness to one another. These crystals constantly emanate vibrations that remind us and reconnect us to the inner worlds of Spirit. They easily attune to the angelic domain. Through this Elestial connection, one may receive a "download" of cosmic love, which can infuse every cell in the body with joy and well-being. Elestials offer the wonder and joy of seeing the angelic realm through the inner eye and communing with its inhabitants through the heart.

Smoky Quartz Elestials are also known to lighten the heart, relieving the burden of sorrow. They can attune one to the Akashic records and to the eternal wisdom that permeates the Universe. They allow one's consciousness to travel freely through time and space, viewing probable futures as well as past events. Smoky Elestial crystals can help bring accord to personal relationships and can reveal underlying emotional fixations or blockages. Smoky Elestial Quartz can be combined with Moldavite for transformation, attunement and awakening.

EMERALD

KEY WORDS Love, compassion, healing, abundance
CHAKRAS Heart (4th)   **ELEMENT** Water
PHYSICAL Supports the heart, blood and circulatory
system   **EMOTIONAL** Opens the heart to love, forgiveness, compassion and trust   **SPIRITUAL** Facilitates the
awakening to Divine Love

EMERALD is a green variety of Beryl, a beryllium aluminum silicate mineral with a hexagonal crystal system and a hardness of 7.5 to 8. Emeralds have been found in Colombia, Brazil, Russia and Africa.

Emerald is the purest crystalline emanation of the Green Ray, and it is the stone which most purely represents the energy patterns of the activated heart chakra. It encourages one to live and act from the heart, offering unconditional love and compassion in one's daily life and relationships, opening one to receive love from others and clearing the channel for one's connection with Divine Love. It can help one stay centered in the heart's wisdom, and can aid in healing heartbreak.

Emerald is known as a stone of prosperity. Wearing Emerald helps attune one's vibrational pattern to the spectrum of abundance, allowing one to attract what one needs and desires. Emerald is also a stone of courage. It helps one move forward on the "path with heart," regardless of any threats or dangers which seem to threaten one. Like Moldavite, Emerald is associated in legend with the fabled Stone of the Holy Grail.

Emerald works in harmony with Moldavite and with other heart stones such as Dioptase, Aventurine, Morganite, Kunzite, Rhodochrosite and Rose Quartz. Tsavorite can enhance Emerald's effectiveness as a prosperity stone. Lepidolite and Emerald soothe the emotional body. Emerald also aligns with Aquamarine, Heliodor, Goshenite and Bixbite.

EPIDOTE

KEY WORDS Release of negativity, embracing positive patterns, attraction of what one emanates **CHAKRAS** All **ELEMENT** Earth, Water **PHYSICAL** Supports dissolution of blockages in the body **EMOTIONAL** Helps one develop emotional generosity **SPIRITUAL** Aids one in creating through the Law of Attraction

EPIDOTE is an iron aluminum silicate with a monoclinic crystal system and a hardness of 6 to 7. Its color can be black, dark green or yellow green. Epidote crystals have been found in Austria, Pakistan, Mexico, Norway, Mozambique and the USA.

Epidote tends to bring one more of what one already has, in accordance with one's highest good. For example, if one is filled with love and generosity, working with Epidote will bring more of these traits into one's life. If, on the other hand, one is filled with negative thoughts, jealousy and intolerance, Epidote will greatly increase the supply of those!

When used consciously and programmed to enhance desired outcomes, Epidote can be a very powerful tool. It can be used to create abundance and prosperity, to attract new loving relationships, to catalyze the creative process, etc. Yet one must always contain at least the seed of what one is trying to attract. If one desires prosperity (generosity from the Universe), one must act generously. If one wants love, one must be loving, and so forth. Epidote does not provide a free ride, yet it can be of great aid to those prepared to give a little of what they wish to receive.

Epidote combines with Moldavite to accelerate its magnetization processes. It also harmonizes with Seraphinite, Tsavorite, Azeztulite, Herkimer "Diamonds" and Phenacite.

EMPOWERITE

KEY WORDS Confidence, strength, personal power, courage, self-awareness, will, commitment **CHAKRAS** Root (1st), Sexual/Creative (2nd), Solar Plexus (3rd), Third Eye (6th) **ELEMENTS** Earth, Storm **PHYSICAL** Supports the visceral organs, hands, feet and shoulders, facilitates efforts to increase muscle and bone strength **EMOTIONAL** Inspires release of self-doubt and inner turmoil, encourages commitment to one's path **SPIRITUAL** Enhances confidence and awareness of one's power, stimulates the soul's full incarnation

EMPOWERITE is a highly silicated form of chert rock from New Zealand, a cryptocrystalline quartz with a hardness of 7, similar to flint.

Empowerite is a stone of confidence, strength and personal power. It is tremendously potent for grounding one's energies in the Earth, and for receiving and storing the Earth's Life Force. Those who feel disconnected from the Earth will find that Empowerite can completely dispel this disorientation. It helps the soul commit to full incarnation in the body. Empowerite relieves hesitation and indecision, enhances willpower, inspires courage, stimulates practicality and encourages one to act with resolve. It helps a erase fear and self-doubt, and enables full focus of intention. Empowerite's influence can strengthen the digestive system and intestines. It supports the liver and gall bladder as well as the hands, feet and shoulders. It is useful in bodybuilding and for strengthening the muscles and skeleton. It is highly recommended for anyone convalescing after an illness or injury, and for those who wish to put the psychological effects of grief or trauma behind them.

Empowerite harmonizes with Hypersthene, Smoky Quartz and Crimson Cuprite. It works with Auralite-23 for purifying and repairing the etheric body. With Moldavite, it can facilitate spiritual evolution and transformation.

EUCLASE

KEY WORDS Transformation of negativity, integrity, truthfulness, clarity, intuition, spiritual commitment **CHAKRAS** Heart (4th), Throat (5th), Third Eye (6th) **ELEMENT** Wind **PHYSICAL** Supports eyesight, mental function, proper speech **EMOTIONAL** Encourages compassion, commitment to truth **SPIRITUAL** Initiates clairsentience, spiritual integrity, access to inner guidance

EUCLASE is a beryllium aluminum silicate with a monoclinic crystal system and a hardness of 7.5. Its color is blue to blue green, and it is found in Brazil, Zimbabwe, Tanzania and Russia.

Euclase is a stone of inner clarity and strength of self. It encourages impeccability and opens one's eyes to the sea of everyday deceptions in which we live. It helps one clear the air of hidden agendas and unhealthy tacit agreements. Yet it works not through righteous anger, but through compassionate, persistent adherence to the truth.

Euclase's effects focus on heart and throat chakras. The heart is the place where truth and compassion reside, and the throat is the place from which these qualities emerge through our communication. The fact that Euclase also stimulates the third eye means that one can clearly "see" the truth it reveals. The third eye enhancement offered by Euclase also assists clairvoyants and other intuitives in their work. Euclase seems also to have the effect of increasing the frequency of synchronicities in one's life, and it encourages one to recognize them as messages from Spirit.

Euclase harmonizes well with natural Blue Topaz, Blue and Green Tourmalines, Apatite, Moldavite and Ajoite. For its use as an energetic cleanser and balancer, adding Black Tourmaline and/or Jet can enhance the effects.

EUDIALYTE

KEY WORDS Opening and following the heart, self-love, healing the emotional body **CHAKRAS** Heart (4th), Root (1st)
ELEMENT Earth, Water
PHYSICAL Supports overall health and vitality, increased life force
EMOTIONAL Facilitates fulfillment of the heart's desires, emotional healing
SPIRITUAL Encourages awakening to and following the wisdom of the heart

EUDIALYTE is a complex silicate mineral containing sodium, calcium, cerium, iron, manganese, yttrium and zirconium. Its crystal system is hexagonal, and its hardness is 5 to 5.5. Its color ranges from pink to red to reddish brown. It has been found in Greenland, Canada and Russia.

Eudialyte is a stone of the life force and the love force, combined to unify the heart's yearnings with one's physical life. Many of us feel our lives are dominated by the things we must do to survive—providing food, clothing, shelter and the maintenance of physical health for ourselves and our families. Sometimes this seems to come at the expense of fulfilling our most heartfelt wishes, the very things that provide emotional satisfaction that makes life more than just survival. Eudialyte's energies bring resonance and harmony to the parallel tracks of survival and fulfillment. It activates both the first and fourth chakras and brings them into alignment, and it evokes synchronicities which can bring together what we must do and what we dream of doing.

Eudialyte can be used in self-healing for repairing the emotional body and bringing in more vitality and life force. The black inclusions in Eudialyte purify its energies and provide psychic protection. Eudialyte harmonizes with Blue Scapolite for self-actualization, with Smithsonite and Lilac Lepidolite for emotional healing and with Ruby for life force.

FADEN QUARTZ

KEY WORDS Healing the etheric body and auric field, catalyzing physical healing **CHAKRAS** All **ELEMENT** Earth, Storm **PHYSICAL** Fadens are all-purpose, programmable healing stones **EMOTIONAL** Aids in healing the emotional body **SPIRITUAL** Facilitates spiritual healing, awareness of past and future Earth changes

FADEN QUARTZ is a silicon dioxide mineral with a hexagonal crystal system and a hardness of 7. It is distinguished from other Quartz crystals by the presence of a fuzzy white line running through the middle. Faden Quartz comes from Pakistan, Brazil and Arkansas, USA.

Faden Quartz is one of the premier healing stones of the Quartz family. Perhaps because the stones themselves were "injured" (broken and re-healed) during their growth process, they carry the pattern of healing very strongly within their natural programming. Thus, when one moves into resonance with one of these crystals, one's own capacity for healing is activated and/or reinforced. Faden Quartz crystals are highly programmable, making it possible to increase their potency as healing stones.

Faden Quartz is ideal for consciousness expansion and accessing any of the higher vibrational planes. It is also well suited for those who wish to attune to the inner movements of the Earth. The Fadens' experience of past earth changes makes them ideal tools for those who seek information on current and future physical and vibrational shifts. Faden Quartz can be charged to an even stronger activation by combining it with power stones such as Moldavite, Phenacite, Tanzanite, Danburite and Azeztulite. For healing purposes, Seraphinite and Sugilite are powerful amplifiers of the natural healing influence of Faden Quartz.

FAIRY WAND QUARTZ

KEY WORDS Attunement with fairy, devic and angelic realms, relaxation, inner peace **CHAKRAS** Heart (4th), Third Eye (6th), Crown (7th), Etheric (8th–14th) **ELEMENT** Water, Wind **PHYSICAL** Helps with balancing headaches, vertigo and vision issues **EMOTIONAL** Supports overcoming fear of judgment or the unknown **SPIRITUAL** Facilitates entering the fairy realm, interdimensional travel, creativity

Fairy Wand Quartz is the name given to a variety of Quartz crystals found in Mexico. They are silicon dioxide crystals with a hexagonal crystal system and a hardness of 7. The name is derived from the widely varying fanciful forms in which these crystals occur.

Fairy Wand Quartz crystals are keystones of interdimensional travel, assisting the user in moving freely into and out of many of the inner worlds, especially the fairy realm. This domain looks and feels much like Earth, except that it has no seasons, living on in a kind of eternal summer. Though this realm is bathed in beautiful light, there is no sun, and time as we think of it does not exist there. Traveling interdimensionally with Fairy Wand Quartz is done best through meditation, though it can also happen in dreams. In either situation, Dream Quartz can be an empowering aid. Fairy Wand Quartz stimulates the third eye and activates visionary consciousness. Holding it near the forehead, one can experience a "rush" through the geometric interdimensional corridors. In accessing the highest dimensions, pairing Fairy Wand Quartz with Phenacite can enhance the effect.

Fairy Wand Quartz also facilitates emotional healing, the release of traumatic fixations from the past, including past lives, and the activation and enhancement of creativity, especially in art and music.

FLINT

KEY WORDS Grounding the spiritual in the physical, creating structure and self-discipline, increasing honesty and practicality **CHAKRAS** All **ELEMENT** Earth **PHYSICAL** Helps with replenishment, grounding the Divine blueprint into the cells **EMOTIONAL** Soothes the emotional body, helps one release past wounds **SPIRITUAL** Stimulates psychic abilities, intuition, bringing spiritual Light into the body

F LINT is a sedimentary rock composed entirely of silica. It occurs as concretions, in band or nodule form, in limestones, especially chalk. Its color is usually black, brown or tan. Flakes of Flint were used by primitive peoples for making arrowheads, scrapers and other tools.

Flint grounds the etheric body more completely into the physical. This affects both consciousness and life force. It helps those with flighty or disorganized temperaments to get into their bodies and focus themselves in the physical world. It provides more life force by bringing the etheric body into alignment with the physical. Flint can affect one's intuitive and psychic abilities, enhancing the specificity and clarity of the information received. Flint is highly recommended for those who do readings, channeling, mediumship or other related work.

In healing work, Flint is a replenisher, grounding a great deal of spiritual Light into one's physical form. It strengthens the links between the root chakra and all the other chakras and the meridian system, allowing *prana* to move freely throughout all these channels. It enhances one's connection to the Earthstar chakra below the feet.

Flint's energies are magnified by Blue Sapphire, Iolite, Citrine, Hematite, Black Tourmaline and Aegirine. Prophecy Stone can be used to enhance Flint's strengthening of psychic abilities.

FLUORITE

KEY WORDS Mental enhancement and clarity, improved decision making, clearing the energy fields **CHAKRAS** All **ELEMENT** Wind **PHYSICAL** Supports brain chemistry, bones and teeth; helps overcome vertigo or dizziness **EMOTIONAL** Aids in dispelling confusion, dishonesty, anxiety about the future **SPIRITUAL** Helps with cleansing the astral body, enhancing mental capacities

FLUORITE is a calcium fluoride crystal with an octohedral growth pattern and a hardness of 4. Its colors include green, purple, white, yellow, red, pink and black. Fluorite deposits have been found in Germany, England, China, Argentina and the USA.

Fluorite can act as a "psychic vacuum cleaner," clearing the atmosphere of confusion, cluttered thoughts, negativity and astral contamination. It is balancing to the third eye and to mental energies in general. It can assist one in thinking clearly and in making subtle but important discriminations regarding the kinds of energies and people one will allow into one's world.

Purple Fluorite is ideal for purification and access of the mind to the domains of Spirit. Black Fluorite is the ultimate astral cleanser. Yellow Fluorite magnifies the mental powers and enhances intellectual ability. Green Fluorite can cleanse and heal the heart chakra. Pink Fluorite cleanses and heals the emotional body and works to activate the "high heart" chakra, or "seat of the soul." Blue Fluorite is good for the throat chakra, ensuring clear communication of one's ideas.

Fluorite harmonizes with Black Tourmaline, Smoky Quartz, Jet, Obsidian, Lapis, Iolite, Golden Labradorite, Heliodor, Emerald, Dioptase, Pink Tourmaline, Rose Quartz, Kunzite, Morganite and Calcite.

FULGURITE

KEY WORDS Manifestation of one's higher purpose, enhancement of prayer, kundalini awakening, purification, sudden awakening **CHAKRAS** All **ELEMENT** Storm **PHYSICAL** Supports blood flow, oxygenation, *prana* and life force **EMOTIONAL** Clears dysfunctional patterns in the emotional body **SPIRITUAL** Facilitates sudden spiritual awakening, amplification of prayers

Fulgurites are glassy tubes formed by lightning strikes on sand or other silica-rich soil. The heat is intense enough to vaporize the sand at the center of the strike and to melt the material around the edges.

Fulgurites are among the most powerful stones for manifesting one's visions through the power of prayer. The lightning energy, long believed to be the touch of the Divine, still resides in them, and they can act as magnifiers of one's intention, building resonance between oneself and the powers of the higher worlds. "Blowing one's prayers" through a Fulgurite tube is a powerful technique. Fulgurites have a strong, high-frequency vibration. Holding a Fulgurite, one may sense a vortex of energy whizzing through the chakras and the Light Body, purifying and cleansing the entire system. There may also be a strong arousal of the kundalini forces of creativity and inner power.

For interdimensional travel, Merkabite Calcite, Herderite, Scolecite, Phenacite or Natrolite can be added. Fulgurites have a tremendous affinity with Moldavite. The combination of these energies can bring about profound purification, transformation and awakening of evolutionary forces in the individual. Fulgurites also work well with Tibetan Tektites, Herderite, Azeztulite, Phenacite, Danburite and Brookite. For those who find Fulgurites too intense, Ajoite can soften the Storm.

GAIA STONE

KEY WORDS Connection with the Heart of the Earth, love and compassion, emotional healing, goddess energies **CHAKRAS** Heart (4th) **ELEMENT** Water **PHYSICAL** Supports healing of migraines and tension headaches, stress, gastric upsets **EMOTIONAL** Soothes the emotional body, supports restful sleep **SPIRITUAL** Links one with the Divine Feminine and the Heart of the Earth

GAIA STONE is the name given to a glassy material derived from the ash of the Mount St. Helens volcanic eruption of 1980. It is a deep green glassy material made by melting and enhancing the volcanic ash gathered from the eruption site.

Gaia stones are ideal for bringing one's heart into resonance with the heart of the Earth. They carry the heart chakra energy of the anima terra, the soul of the Earth. Gaia Stone promotes loving relationships between people. It is an ideal gift for one's romantic partner, as its energies promote the growth of love and intimacy. It can be used to heal tensions between parents and children, or between any estranged members of a family or friendship circle. Gaia Stone induces compassion and diffuses anger. It can assist one in negotiations where one must try to persuade an unsympathetic person to understand one's point of view.

Gaia Stones are Goddess stones, and one may use them to send and receive love to and from any aspect of the Divine Feminine. They can be used to heal and soothe the heart and to energize the emotional body.

Healers can use the stones on clients for heart-chakra activation and to bring harmony to all chakras. Gaia Stone harmonizes with Amethyst, Danburite, Azeztulite, Phenacite and all types of Quartz. For emotional healing, it works well with crystallized Rose Quartz and with Morganite.

GALENA

KEY WORDS Shamanic soul retrieval, alchemical self-transformation, past-life recall   **CHAKRAS** Root (1st)   **ELEMENT** Earth   **PHYSICAL** Supports recovery from infection, radiation, chemotherapy   **EMOTIONAL** Helps with soul retrieval, healing past-life issues   **SPIRITUAL** Facilitates shamanism, visionary experience, alchemical transformation

G ALENA is a lead sulfide mineral with acubic crystal system and a hardness of 2.5. Its color is metallic gray. Galena crystals have been found in Kansas, Missouri and Oklahoma in the USA.

Galena is a stone of the alchemical process of self-transformation. It can place within one's vibrational field the restless desire of the seeker, who will not cease until the journey to enlightenment is complete. Galena is also a powerful grounding stone, and it can carry the awareness of the meditator deep into the Earth. In fact, it is an ideal stone for taking one on the journey to the underworld, the necessary exploration for retrieving the lost parts of the soul. Those interested in shamanic work will find a ready ally in Galena, which tends downward into the depths, into the "other world" where shamans do much of their work. Those afflicted with ailments that are difficult to diagnose may find in Galena the tool which will offer the necessary insights for discovering the psycho-spiritual source of the problem and moving toward healing.

Galena can assist one in past-life regression work, functioning like an "inner radar" to guide one's visionary experience to the appropriate memories needed for seeing and healing the issues most important to the individual at that time. Galena harmonizes with Phenacite, Nuummite, Labradorite and Covellite.

GARNET, GROSSULAR

KEY WORDS Prosperity, health **CHAKRAS** Solar
Plexus (3rd), Heart (4th) **ELEMENT** Earth
PHYSICAL Supports vibrant, abundant health;
recovery after illness **EMOTIONAL** Helps one overcome financial anxiety and/or scarcity consciousness
SPIRITUAL Facilitates manifestation of prosperity,
zest for living

Grossular garnet is a calcium aluminum silicate mineral with a hardness of 7 to 7.5. Its name is derived from the Latin word for gooseberries, because of the likeness of the colors of the berries and certain light-green Grossular Garnets. Many Grossular Garnets are found in Africa.

Grossular Garnets are excellent natural grounders of abundant manifestation. Their vibrational pattern creates an eager confidence, a motivation to get down to business and make things happen. Paired with Moldavite, these would be unbeatable for bringing into reality one's rightful abundance and highest path of achievement in this world.

One Grossular Garnet of particular interest is Tsavorite. They are stones, not just of prosperity, but of wealth in all its positive aspects—financial, creative, emotional, artistic and even physical health, the foundation of true wealth. They are attuned to the pure Green Ray, and they rival Emerald in their power and beauty. Tsavorites can open and cleanse the heart chakra, enhance vitality, increase zest for living, induce feelings of charity and benevolence and help one to align with and bring about the heart's desires.

All types of Grossular Garnet harmonize with Aventurine, Green Jade, Emerald and Malachite. For directing their power of manifestation into spiritual areas, it is helpful to combine them with high-vibration stones such as Celestite, Azeztulite, Natrolite and Clear Apophyllite.

GARNET, SPESSARTINE

KEY WORDS Creativity, sexuality, attraction
CHAKRAS Root (1st), Sexual/Creative (2nd),
Solar Plexus (3rd) **ELEMENT** Earth, Fire
PHYSICAL Supports fertility and sexual
reproduction, endocrine system
EMOTIONAL Encourages optimism, confidence, daring and action
SPIRITUAL Enhances manifestation, creativity, charisma

SPESSARTINE GARNET is a manganese aluminum silicate with a hardness of 7 to 7.5 Its name derives from its discovery in Spessart, Germany. It is also found in Sri Lanka, Brazil, Madagascar, Sweden and the USA. Its characteristic color is yellowish orange.

Spessartite Garnet is a powerful stone of attraction. It can help one to "magnetize" a lover, a new job, a creative project or anything in which one's personal energy of attraction is a key factor. Spessartine Garnet helps clear one's auric field of disharmonious elements. It enhances charisma. It magnifies the vibrations of the second chakra, emphasizing creativity and sexuality. It also works on the solar plexus chakra, lending power to one's will. It pulls potential realities into manifestation. Because of its magnification of second chakra energies, it can increase fertility on any level, from getting pregnant to being inspired by a brilliant idea for a novel, poem, painting or other creative project. Spessartine Garnet gets things moving, and it is therefore a potent tool to be used carefully and skillfully, yet with a sense of enjoyment and fun.

Spessartine Garnet's energies are magnified by Russian Phenacite, Zincite, Orange Calcite, Carnelian, Heliodor and Golden Labradorite. Pairing Spessartine Garnet with Tsavorite creates a very powerful energy for financial prosperity. Combining it with Rose Quartz and Rhodolite Garnet, one can attract new love into one's life.

GARNET, RHODOLITE

KEY WORDS Emotional healing, self-worth, walking the spiritual path **CHAKRAS** Root (1st), Heart (4th), Crown (7th) **ELEMENT** Earth **PHYSICAL** Supports healing of physical issues rooted in emotional wounds **EMOTIONAL** Soothes and heals the emotional body **SPIRITUAL** Facilitates linking with one's guides and angels, attuning to the heart

RHODOLITE GARNET is a variety of Pyrope Garnet, a magnesium aluminum silicate with a hardness of 7 to 7.5. Its color varies from rose red to pale violet. Its name is derived from Greek words meaning "rose stone." It is found in Sri Lanka, Tanzania, Zambia, Brazil and the USA.

Rhodolite Garnet combines the energies of the base chakra, heart chakra and crown chakra, offering physical, emotional and spiritual support. Its gentle energies activate one's connection to inner guides and guardian angels, while they simultaneously put one in touch with the wordless voice of the heart's yearnings. In this way it creates an inner alignment that allows one to know clearly what steps to take on the spiritual path. Meanwhile the grounding influence of Rhodolite's connection with the base chakra aids in making and keeping the inner commitments to take one forward on that path.

Rhodolite Garnet offers emotional healing, particularly in the areas of guilt and shame. Those who were wounded in these ways may find that Rhodolite lightens and lifts the burdens of such memories. If the memories are not conscious, this may manifest as a lightening of one's overall mood and a sense of quiet happiness. Rhodolite Garnet strengthens the emotional body, making it easier to hear the call of Spirit and to walk the spiritual path. Azeztulite, especially Pink Azeztulite, can facilitate the spiritual healing supported by Rhodolite Garnet.

GARNET, ALMANDINE

KEY WORDS Strength, security   **CHAKRAS** Root (1st)
ELEMENT Earth   **PHYSICAL** Supports reproductive
organs, aids recuperation from injury
EMOTIONAL Dispels negativity, worry and panic;
helps one adhere to truth   **SPIRITUAL** Provides
grounding and protection, arouses kundalini energies

ALMANDINE GARNET is an iron aluminum silicate with a hardness of 7.5. Its name is derived from the town of Almandine in Asia Minor. It is found in Sri Lanka, India, Afghanistan, Brazil, Austria and the Czech Republic. Its color ranges from orange-red to purplish red.

Almandine Garnet is a stone of the ancient times in human history, when people were more intimately connected to the Earth, and when life was more physically demanding. It can vibrationally enhance one's vitality and endurance. It activates and strengthens the base chakra, our portal of connection to the physical world. It is excellent for those who are a bit ungrounded, or who lack energy. This is also a stone of tangible truth. If one tends to build "castles in the air," Almandine Garnet can assist one in manifesting a realistic version of them here on Earth.

Almandine Garnet is also a stone of psychic protection. Its relatively dense energies keep one strongly connected to the body, and when one is rooted in this way, it is more difficult for negative energies or entities to attach themselves. As a stone of the first chakra, Almandine Garnet can help arouse the energies of kundalini. For this, Tibetan Tektite can be a helpful ally. Once stimulated, the kundalini energies are stabilized and kept more grounded by Almandine Garnet's steady, slow vibrations. If one wishes additional grounding and protection, one is advised to combine Almandine Garnet with Black Andradite Garnet.

GARNET, BLACK ANDRADITE

KEY WORDS Grounding, protection, knowledge, creative power **CHAKRAS** Root (1st), Earthstar (below the feet) **ELEMENT** Earth **PHYSICAL** Protects the body from invasion by negative forces **EMOTIONAL** Aids in empowering the self, enhances confidence **SPIRITUAL** Helps one access elemental energies, "magical" powers, lost knowledge

BLACK ANDRADITE GARNET is a calcium iron silicate mineral with a cubic crystal system and a hardness of 6.5 to 7.5. It was named after the Portuguese mineralogist d'Andrada. It is also known as Melanite, a name derived from the Greek word for "black." It is a glossy black. Fine specimens have been found in Mexico and Greenland.

Black Andradite Garnet is a powerful grounding stone, which can also be used to kindle the magic and evoke the mysteries of the Earth. It can help one attune to elemental forces and engage their aid. One can meditate with this stone to penetrate the depths of the collective unconscious and to read the morphogenic fields of knowledge held not only by humanity but also by other intelligent species of this planet. It is a stone which connects with the nourishing darkness, and one can use it to enlist the aid of one's own secret wellsprings of power. It is ideal for tapping into one's life force, for arousing the creative fires of sexuality and for the empowerment and focus of the will. It aids one in establishing the dynamic grounding which is needed for those of high intention to actualize their visions.

The fiery energies of Zincite can enhance Black Andradite Garnet. For prosperity, Tsavorite and African Green Garnet aid the work. For creativity and sexuality, Spessartine Garnet, Carnelian and Zincite are helpful. For purification, add Black Tourmaline, Jet or Black Obsidian.

GARNET, UVAROVITE

KEY WORDS Overcoming poverty consciousness, manifesting abundance **CHAKRAS** Heart (4th), Solar Plexus (3rd) **ELEMENT** Earth **PHYSICAL** Benefits vitality, replenishment of soft tissues, hydration **EMOTIONAL** Supports knowing one has all one needs; inner peace, contentment **SPIRITUAL** Facilitates attuning to the infinite flow of Universal abundance

UVAROVITE GARNET is a calcium chromium silicate with a hardness of 7.5. It is found in Russia, Finland, Poland, India and the USA. Because of its deep green color, it is sometimes confused with Emerald. Uvarovite was named after a Russian statesman.

Uvarovite Garnet heals the feeling of insufficiency in all its aspects. Whether it is the sense of scarcity in finances or the lack of self-confidence, love, power, knowledge, vitality or anything else, Uvarovite can clear away the idea that it is not enough. It opens the heart, allowing one to see that one contains everything one truly needs. It brings a sense of peace and contentment, plus the knowledge that the Universe provides one with precisely what is required in any given moment—at least as far as the agenda of one's spiritual evolution is concerned. In seeing this, one learns to surrender to that agenda, healing the struggle to satisfy the lower desires, which are, after all, the source of the feelings of lack to begin with. Uvarovite gently leads one to this lesson, for as soon as the feelings of lack have been discharged, one is in the flow of Universal abundance. This flow, too, is enhanced by Uvarovite.

To magnify Uvarovite's transformative properties, using it with Moldavite is recommended. For manifestation of financial prosperity, combining both stones with Phenacite, and another prosperity stone such as Tsavorite or African Green Garnet, is ideal.

GARNET, RAINBOW

KEY WORDS Happiness, felicity, exuberance, playfulness, kindness, generosity, healing the Inner Child **CHAKRAS** Heart (4th) **ELEMENTS** Earth, Water **PHYSICAL** Supports the heart; brings life-affirming energies to the whole body **EMOTIONAL** Dissolves old negative emotions; gently and playfully healing to one's Inner Child **SPIRITUAL** Brings happiness, good humor and zest for life; helps one fully enjoy one's spiritual path

RAINBOW GARNET is a grossular Garnet from Africa, with an isometric crystal system and a hardness of 6.5 to 7. It is characterized by vivid shades of red, green and blue-green, and many specimens are bicolored.

Rainbow Garnet stimulates one's innate sense of playfulness, and can be deeply healing to one's Inner Child. It can bring important emotional healing to one's adult side, lightening the load of stress and dispelling one's attachment to worries, fears, angers and sorrows. It is a stone of good humor, and can bring out surprising wittiness, as well as kindness, generosity and cordiality. When one is meeting new people, a Rainbow Garnet can stimulate a more enjoyable encounter. It can help one see the bright side of difficult situations, allowing one to recognize that all things ultimately work toward the good. It is nourishing to the heart, emotionally and physically, because it promotes a state of light-heartedness. It resonate to the vibration of joy, and can help one learn to adopt joy as one's habitual mode of being.

Rainbow Garnets work well with Azeztulite, bringing together high spiritual energies in an atmosphere of pleasure and good humor. With Moldavite, they can help one relax and enjoy the process of transformation. When used with visionary stones such as Phenacite, they can facilitate the journey into realms of cosmic bliss.

GASPEITE

KEY WORDS Spiritual perception and expression, manifestation, emotional healing, weight control, digestion
CHAKRAS Earthstar (below the feet), Base (1st), Solar Plexus (3rd), Heart (4th) **ELEMENT** Earth
PHYSICAL Supports harmonious function of heart and digestive systems, supports management of diabetes
EMOTIONAL Instills joyful recognition of Spirit in the mundane, healing the inner child **SPIRITUAL** Facilitates integration of spiritual aspirations into daily life

GASPEITE is a nickel magnesium iron carbonate with a trigonal crystal system and a hardness of 3. Its name is derived from the location where it was first discovered—the Gaspe peninsula of Quebec, Canada. Its color is pale green to apple green, often with brownish inclusions. Its crystal system is trigonal. It is found in Canada and Australia.

Gaspeite's energy is about bringing the spiritual realms into expression in everyday life. It facilitates one's being able to "walk the talk" of one's spiritual aspirations without allowing old habits or patterns to take over. Gaspeite can help seekers to realize that the answers to their most burning questions are spread out all about their feet. It is also excellent for awakening and healing the inner child. Gaspeite blends the energies of the heart and solar plexus, yet it does so in a grounded, physical way. It promotes the health of the heart and digestive system, as well as the visceral organs, in a way that integrates their energies. Gaspeite can help those with poor appetites to enjoy food, and to eat the proper foods at the right times. It helps one to inwardly "hear" what sorts of foods the body and soul need and desire. This in itself can bring profound healings.

Gaspeite combines harmoniously with Pyromorphite, Tugtupite, Cryolite, Hiddenite, Amber, Turquoise, Jet and Sugilite.

GEL LITHIUM SILICA

KEY WORDS Calming, soothing, emotional serenity and stability, antidote to stress and negativity **CHAKRAS** All **ELEMENT** Water **PHYSICAL** Supports energetic balance, aids assimilation of medicines **EMOTIONAL** Soothing and healing to the emotional body, aids release of stress **SPIRITUAL** Facilitates embodying the Divine Feminine, projecting peace in the world

GEL LITHIUM SILICA is a rich magenta-colored form of Lepidolite, a potassium lithium aluminum silicate mineral with a monoclinic crystal system and a hardness of 2.5 to 3. It is found in New Mexico, USA.

Gel Lithium Silica carries the vibration of pure tranquillity and receptivity. It is the very embodiment of the *yin* energy, the power of the feminine. Gel Lithium Silica is highly recommended for meditation and prayer. These are excellent stones for eliminating stress. If a piece is placed beneath one's pillow, it can assist one in finding more peaceful sleep. Soaking with this mineral in a warm, sea-salted bath can also help one release tensions and find the deepest possible relaxation.

Gel Lithium Silica is a stone of peace, and it can assist one in spreading peace in the world. It is an excellent stone to be given as a gift, since one is giving the gift of tranquillity, serenity and sometimes even euphoria! It is also capable of doing this work undercover. Using Gel Lithium Silica to project peace clarifies and amplifies one's conscious benevolent intention and increases its effectiveness.

Other Lithium-based minerals such as Tourmaline and Amblygonite can amplify the energies of Gel Lithium Silica. Access to the highest vibrational planes can be brought about by combining Gel Lithium Silica with stones such as Phenacite, Azeztulite, Herderite, Danburite, Brookite and Selenite.

GEM SILICA

KEY WORDS Enhanced communication, connection with Goddess energies, clairvoyance, joy, peace **CHAKRAS** Throat (5th), Heart (4th), Third Eye (6th) **ELEMENT** Water, Wind **PHYSICAL** Supports heart and throat; healing emotionally based ailments **EMOTIONAL** Heals aura and emotional body, aids in communication **SPIRITUAL** Facilitates deep link with the Goddess; clairvoyance, prophecy, mediumship

GEM SILICA is silicated Chrysocolla, a combination of Chrysocolla and Quartz with a hardness of 6 to 7. It is a rare material which is found in small pockets of copper-bearing ores. Its color can vary from blue-green to deep turquoise blue.

Gem Silica is perhaps the finest stone in the mineral kingdom for energizing the throat chakra and bringing forth one's inner truth, with impeccability, clarity and eloquence. It also evokes the Goddess energies within those who use or carry it. Gem Silica can take one deeply into the spiritual realms, and it is also a stone of lightheartedness. It assists one in letting go of the many concerns that can weigh down the psyche, freeing the heart to soar into joy. It increases emotional discrimination, so one can focus on what truly matters in one's inner life and relationships. Gem Silica lends clarity to one's communication, and can enhance one's powers of inner vision. It is excellent for stimulating clairvoyance and even prophetic visions of the future, as well as spirit communication. It can heal energetic "holes" in the astral and etheric bodies, especially around the heart. It can support vibrational healing of the physical body, particularly in regard to problems with the heart and throat.

Gem Silica harmonizes with Chrysocolla, Chrysoprase, Turquoise, Ajoite, Azurite, Malachite, Azeztulite, Tibetan Black Quartz and Chlorite Phantoms.

GLENDONITE

KEY WORDS Precise stimulation of chakras and meridians, transmutation into the New Human Being and the Body of Light **CHAKRAS** All main chakras, secondary chakras and meridians **ELEMENT** Fire **PHYSICAL** Aids in relaxing and releasing stress, infuses the body with Light **EMOTIONAL** Instills awe and wonder at one's awakening **SPIRITUAL** Instills heart/brain integration and awakens Light Body consciousness

GLENDONITE is the name of a certain pseudomorph—Calcite that occurs after Ikaite crystals. Calcite is a calcium carbonate mineral with a rhombohedral crystal system and a hardness of 3. It comes from Russia.

The currents of Glendonite enter the brain, and they work very quickly to free the mind via their awakening of inner truth. Glendonite stimulates the third eye, crown chakra and Soul Star chakra above the head. It can help increase psychic capacities, make inner visions more vivid and open the doors to profound interior silence. Its influences can deepen meditative and dream experiences. It can help the mind become more aware of the activity and thought of the heart. Glendonite affects the brain and the thinking processes, increasing the influence of the right hemisphere. It quiets the inner dialog and opens the doors to the silent synthesis of ideas, emotions and perceptions. It increases feelings of spiritual awe and wonder. Glendonite can be used for calming headaches, relieving mental stress, overcoming insomnia, relaxing tense muscles and clearing blocked energies in the meridians. It can open and harmonize any of the chakras. It facilitates the process by which the new Body of Light is brought into being.

Glendonite works well with Satya Mani Quartz, Natrolite, Phenacite and Herderite, Merkabite Calcite and all types of Azeztulite.

GOETHITE

KEY WORDS Access to Akashic records, past-life recall, connection with Earth, healing through grief, enhanced soul life, artistic creativity **CHAKRAS** Root (1st), Sexual/Creative (2nd), Third Eye (6th) **ELEMENT** Earth **PHYSICAL** Supports the blood and bone marrow, blood oxygenation **EMOTIONAL** Helps energize or calm the emotion body to bring balance **SPIRITUAL** Aids recall of past-life information for fulfillment in this life

Goethite is an iron hydroxide mineral with an orthorhombic crystal system and a hardness of 5 to 5.5. Its color is blackish brown, yellowish brown or reddish brown. Fine Goethite crystals have been discovered in Cornwall, England, and Pikes Peak, Colorado.

Goethite is a stone for going deep within, for finding the link between the self and the Earth, facilitating the sensitization of oneself to the perceptions, emotions and energies of one's body and of the Earth. It is excellent for individuals dealing with grief. It takes one into awareness of one's wounds, which have often been pushed into the unconscious. Goethite facilitates the recovery of one's lost or repressed grief and the catharsis of healing and emotional rebirth that follows. Goethite stimulates the emotional body, making one more conscious of the entire spectrum of one's feelings. It assists in opening the heart, awakening one's compassion and love. It strengthens the creative aspect of the second chakra and is a powerful aid to artists and writers.

Nuummite can combine with Goethite to assist one in making inner journeys and in accessing the Akashic records. Alexandrite and Oregon Opal can also help with this. Smoky Quartz magnifies Goethite's grounding aspects. If one has difficulty "coming back up" from Goethite's tours of the depths, Danburite and Petalite are recommended.

GOLDEN HEALER QUARTZ

KEY WORDS Pure Golden Ray of spiritual Light, self-healing, Christ consciousness **CHAKRAS** All **ELEMENTS** Earth, Fire **PHYSICAL** Supports self-healing of the heart, lungs and circulatory system **EMOTIONAL** Helps one feel inner joy regardless of outer circumstances **SPIRITUAL** Aids in drawing the highest spiritual Light into oneself and the Earth; can initiate one's connection to Christ consciousness.

GOLDEN HEALER QUARTZ is a silicon-dioxide mineral with a hardness of 7. It is characterized by a rich yellow coating on part or all of its surfaces, caused by the presence of hematite. It has been found in Brazil and in Arkansas, USA.

Golden Healer Quartz crystals emanate profoundly powerful currents for the healing of the body and the expansion of consciousness. They emanate strong waves of pleasurable energy that permeate the entire body. They are linked to the Divine Messenger and are attuned to the purpose of cocreating the Earth as a Planet of Light. In their highest capacity, Golden Healers give access to Christ consciousness, enabling human beings to become the living vehicles for the Gold Christ Light to enter the world. These crystals resonate to the Great Central Sun, the source of the Golden Ray within the Universe.

In spiritual self-healing, Golden Healer Quartz supports all parts of the body through its infusion of spiritual Light. It resonates most readily with the heart, and can work as a catalyst for healing the heart, lungs and circulatory system.

Golden Healer Quartz resonates strongly with other stones of the Golden Ray, such as Himalaya Gold Azeztulite, Libyan Gold Tektite, Heliodor, Golden Azeztulite crystals, Satyaloka Yellow Azeztulite, Golden Apatite, Brazilianite and Agni Gold Danburite. It has a natural affinity to stones that have been super-activated through the Azozeo process.

GOLDEN LABRADORITE

KEY WORDS Right use of will, clarity, confidence, power, vitality, creativity, purposefulness, link with Great Central Sun   **CHAKRAS** Solar Plexus (3rd) **ELEMENT** Fire   **PHYSICAL** Aids detoxification; supports kidneys, gallbladder and spleen **EMOTIONAL** Enhances self-confidence, charisma and social skills   **SPIRITUAL** Helps one recognize and attain one's destined spiritual purpose

GOLDEN LABRADORITE is a variety of plagioclase feldspar with a triclinic crystal system and a hardness of 6 to 6.5. It is usually transparent and its color is a golden yellow. It is found in Oregon and Mexico.

Golden Labradorite is one of the best stones for working with the third chakra, enhancing inner strength, vitality, courage, clear thinking, endurance, mental activity, spiritual focus and purposefulness. It can help one see the Divine pattern in one's daily struggles. In dream work, it can assist one in consciously awakening in the higher planes and in bringing back important information. Golden Labradorite takes one into communion with the energies of our own sun, and with the Great Central Sun, the home and origin of consciousness in the Universe. This is Golden Labradorite's greatest gift. The Great Central Sun is the spiritual center of the Universe, existing in the etheric realm. It is constantly surrounded by multitudes of orbiting angels, and it is from this domain that the "music of the spheres" emanates. In meditation, one can follow the golden thread of this stone's energy into the holy realm.

Golden Labradorite harmonizes with all types of Labradorite, Spectrolite, Moonstone and Sunstone, as well as Zincite, Moldavite, Phenacite, Herderite, Scolecite and Natrolite. It resonate with all varieties of Azeztulite, which are deeply linked with the Great Central Sun.

GOSHENITE

KEY WORDS Mental stimulant, enhanced dreams, loyalty, truth, prayer, spiritual assistance **CHAKRAS** Third Eye (6th), Crown (7th), Etheric (8th–14th) **ELEMENT** Wind **PHYSICAL** Supports healing of headaches, insomnia, sinusitis, brain imbalances **EMOTIONAL** Encourages emotional health, enthusiasm, clarity **SPIRITUAL** Aids spiritual discernment, enhances the power of prayer

GOSHENITE is a colorless variety of Beryl, an aluminum beryllium silicate mineral with a hexagonal crystal system and a hardness of 7.5 to 8. It was named after a find in Goshen, Massachusetts. Goshenite is found in Brazil, Pakistan, Afghanistan, Southern Africa and the USA.

Goshenite clears and activates the crown chakra, opening the portals of Spirit. It stimulates the mental centers and enhances one's thinking abilities. It is particularly stimulating to mathematical intelligence. Goshenite is a stone of persistence, helping one retain the focus and determination to see things through to completion. It is also a stone of loyalty. Goshenite can also enhance the power of prayer, for help with health, spiritual growth or relationships. It aids in calling in one's angels, guides and friends in Spirit. It is a stone of truth, helping one to speak only truth and to see through deceptions.

To modify Goshenite's clear and dispassionate detachment, one might wish to employ Emerald or Morganite. Both of these stones, which are closely related to Goshenite, bring one to the heart's loving and forgiving qualities. Goshenite also resonates with other beryllium silicate minerals such as Aquamarine, Heliodor and Phenacite. Nuummite combines with Goshenite for clear perceptual journeys into the deep, hidden past. Azeztulite moves Goshenite's vision into the domain of one's highest possible future.

GREENSTONE (POUNAMU)

KEY WORDS Life Force, personal power, magic, vitality, longevity, self-loyalty and self-love, inner radiance **CHAKRAS** Heart (4th), Third Eye (6th) **ELEMENTS** Earth, Water, Fire **PHYSICAL** Supports the heart, lungs and circulatory system, offers great quantities of chi **EMOTIONAL** Inspires powerful self-loyalty and self-love **SPIRITUAL** Stimulates Life Force and power in oneself, aids in doing real magic, and can link one to spiritual helpers from ancient New Zealand

G REENSTONE is a name referring to certain green gemstones native to New Zealand including both nephrites and serpentines. The hardness can range from 3 to 7. The Maori people have long revered Greenstone, naming it Pounamu, "a stone of the wairua," the world of the spirit realm that surrounds all.

Greenstone is a stone of life, and emanates currents of strong Life Force energies. It is a stone of longevity, and can be used in healing work to implant the vibrations of vitality and program the body for long life. Greenstone is also a stone of power. Its currents easily enter one's energy field through the heart or the third eye, filling one's auric field with strength and vitality. It stimulates the emotions of courage, loyalty, passion and freedom, and brings to consciousness how important it is to honor each of them. It is a stone of magic, capable of transferring power to the one who carries it. Greenstone is linked to the ancient peoples of New Zealand, and enables one to call upon their spirits for aid.

In healing, Greenstone acts as a fountain of vitality, helping one overcome fatigue and stress. It supports the heart, lungs, and circulatory system. It can clear congested energies and purify the auric field. It helps one find the deep self-loyalty to release unhealthy relationships, bad habits, self-doubt, anxiety and/or depression. Greenstone can work in synergy with Moldavite, Crimson Cuprite, Tibetan Tektite, Empowerite, Revelation Stone and Sauralite Azeztulite.

GREEN TARALITE

KEY WORDS Flowing, friendly energies, connection with Green Tara, spiritual attunement of one's consciousness, out-of-body travel, healing and insight **CHAKRAS** Heart (4th), Third Eye (6th) **ELEMENTS** Earth, Water **PHYSICAL** Supports all types of circulation and flow within the body, can stimulate cells into a state of spiritual luminescence **EMOTIONAL** Engenders joy, compassion and friendliness **SPIRITUAL** Inspires inner union with qualities of the Divine Green Tara: peace, cooperation, energy, destiny, spirituality and Universal Unity, offers spiritual protection and removal of obstacles

GREEN TARALITE is the name given to a green variety of andesite discovered in New Zealand. It is a volcanic stone, an extrusive rock intermediate in composition between rhyolite and basalt.

Green Taralite is a stone of well-being, happiness and spiritual Light. It connects one's awareness to the cosmos, and helps one recognize oneself as a member of the entire Universe. It can enable one to enter vibrational resonance with Divine beings, including Green Tara herself. Tara is a Star Goddess who encompasses all of time and the spark of life.

Green Tara is the "Mother Earth"—a fierce Goddess who overcomes obstacles and saves us from dangers. Green Taralite provides the embodiment of these qualities. It supports all bodily systems that depend on flow, including the heart and circulatory system, lungs, lymphatic system, liver and digestive system. Green Taralite is an intensely feminine stone. In men, it invokes an enhanced awareness and appreciation of the Feminine Divine. In women, it can expand self-awareness to the level at which one recognizes oneself as both an individual and as an emanation of the Goddess.

Green Taralite harmonizes with almost all stones. It has strong resonance with Moldavite and all Azeztulites. It works well with the Azozeo energy.

GUARDIANITE

KEY WORDS Infusion of life force, grounding, strength, protection **CHAKRAS** All
ELEMENT Earth, Wind, Water, Fire, Storm
PHYSICAL Fills the Liquid Crystal Body Matrix with life force **EMOTIONAL** Encourages positive, uplifting emotional states
SPIRITUAL Simultaneously attunes to the Earth and the spiritual realms

GUARDIANITE is a complex material, composed of Aegirine, Feldspar, Nepheline, Analcime, Riebeckite-Arfvedsonite, Biotite, Olivine and Apatite. Its color is black on gray-white, and it is found in Oregon, USA.

Guardianite brings a deep and immediate grounding through the root chakra. It offers an instantaneous connection with the Earth and its upwelling life force. As Guardianite's currents flow into one's field, they permeate the Liquid Crystal Body Matrix with a humming vibration of well-being. Guardianite makes one feel happy, calm and safe. It nourishes the etheric and astral bodies, enhancing their integration with the physical self. The Aegirine and Riebeckite components give it a strong purifying and protective quality, while the Feldspar and Nepheline help one receive the nourishing life force energies of the Earth. The Biotite's influence is one of grounding and strengthening. The Apatite aids in cleansing the auric field, soothing the emotional body, enhancing mental clarity and strengthening the will. The Olivine promotes one's inner sense of well-being and instills a positive emotional attitude. Analcime's currents provide an uplifting link to the higher vibrational realms. With so many beneficial minerals combined in a single stone, it is as if a team of angels has come together to provide the ideal combination of protective, purifying, balancing, strengthening and uplifting energies to aid human beings through these times of transformation.

HALITE, BLUE

KEY WORDS Cleansing, purification, psychic clearing, activating psychic abilities **CHAKRAS** All **ELEMENT** Earth **PHYSICAL** Supports inner cleansing, lymphatic and circulatory systems **EMOTIONAL** Aids in clearing unhealthy attachments, instills euphoria **SPIRITUAL** Encourages a state of enlightened compassion

BLUE HALITE is a sodium chloride crystal with a cubic crystal system and a hardness of 2 to 2.5. It is formed by the evaporation of salt water. It comes from the salt mines of Poland.

Blue Halite activates the third eye and crown chakras, unifying them with the Soul Star chakra above the head. Its colors—deep blue, violet and clear white—are the colors associated with those energy centers, and Blue Halite is the only mineral which displays all three of them together. The effect of this triple activation is an enhancement of psychic ability, a purification of one's energy field, and an elevation of one's awareness to higher spiritual levels. It helps one achieve a crystalline clarity of thought and a completely balanced flow of Light Body energies. It opens the pathways to communication with spirit guides and inner teachers, and it aids one in the verbal expression of spiritual truth.

Blue Halite is an instant cleanser for the etheric body and can "sweep up" any amount of psychic debris. It can also be used to cleanse and clear other crystals, simply by placing them in contact with Blue Halite for a few hours. Blue Halite itself can be cleansed and charged by placing it in bright sunlight for a day. It harmonizes well with Lilac Lepidolite, Pink Halite, Pink Lazurine, Scolecite, Natrolite, Merkabite Calcite, Elestial Calcite, Tibetan Tektite and all types of Phenacite.

HALITE, PINK

KEY WORDS Emotional cleansing, inner clarity, opening the heart, self-love **CHAKRAS** All **ELEMENT** Earth **PHYSICAL** Helps clear the body of emotionally related imbalances **EMOTIONAL** Encourages dispelling negativity, bringing joy, enhancing self-love **SPIRITUAL** Facilitates opening to higher awareness by clearing one's consciousness

PINK HALITE is a sodium chloride crystal with a cubic crystal system and a hardness of 2 to 2.5. It is formed by the evaporation of salt water. It comes from the salt mines of Poland.

Pink Halite is an excellent stone for manifesting self-love—not only to experience feelings of self-love, but also to take action to do the things that self-love implies. This is because Pink Halite blends the energies of the heart and solar plexus—the chakras of love and will.

Pink Halite is a stone of clarity. Its presence tends to dissolve foggy thinking, confusion, deception and doubt. It can really "clear the air" in many ways! It is recommended that those who work in environments of negativity or indirect communication keep a piece of Pink Halite on the desk or on one's person. Its energy will help one express oneself straightforwardly and will assist in seeing through to the truth in all types of interactions. Bathing in water in which Pink Halite is dissolved is a lovely and therapeutic experience. It is even superior to the sea-salt cleansing baths which many people use to clear and replenish their energies. Only a small amount of the Pink Halite is required to produce a full etheric cleansing, and a single stone may be used repeatedly, until it is completely dissolved.

Pink Halite harmonizes with the heart stones Rosophia, Morganite and Rose Quartz, as well as the high-vibration stones Phenacite and Azeztulite.

HANKSITE

KEY WORDS Purification, dissolving of blockages, cleansing of toxic energies, a "stone of truth"
CHAKRAS All **ELEMENT** Earth
PHYSICAL Supports body in eradicating toxins, dispelling water retention **EMOTIONAL** Aids in clearing anger and resentment from emotional body
SPIRITUAL Clears all types of disharmony, stimulates the Light Body

Hanksite is a potassium sulfate mineral with a hexagonal crystal system and a hardness of 3 to 3.5. It can be colorless, gray or pale yellow. Hanksite is found in boron-rich salt lakes of California.

Hanksite harmonizes quickly and easily with the human energy field, bringing a clearing and purifying influence to all the chakras. It strongly stimulates the third eye and can facilitate visionary states. It can be used to cleanse the energies of any other stone or crystal and works similarly to clear the room where it is kept of any disharmonious energies. Hanksite's clarifying energies extend to the mental body as well. It is a "stone of truth," assisting one in dispelling lies or illusions coming from others, or even from oneself. It helps one get to the essence of all issues and keeps one's awareness aligned with reality. In more advanced use, and in conjunction with powerful stones such as Moldavite, Libyan Gold Tektite and Heliodor, Hanksite can assist one in taking strong action on behalf of truth.

Hanksite combines synergistically with Pink Halite, Blue Halite, Moldavite, Heliodor, Libyan Gold Tektite, Tibetan Tektite, Golden Labradorite, Lapis Lazuli and most types of Quartz. Its energies empower and are empowered by Satyaloka Azeztulite and the original White Azeztulite. It can be used with Phenacite to activate visionary states.

HEALERITE

KEY WORDS Broad-spectrum healing, rejuvenation, longevity, joy, expansiveness, generosity, intimacy, heart-centered awareness, planetary healing **CHAKRAS** Solar Plexus (3rd), Heart (4th), Third Eye (6th) **ELEMENTS** Earth, Water **PHYSICAL** Supports all levels of the body, activates appropriate immune response, fills the body with Life Force for healing, rejuvenation, longevity **EMOTIONAL** Initiates states of joy and inner harmony **SPIRITUAL** Supports spiritual awakening and development, increases vitality, expands awareness

HEALERITE is a magnesium-silicate mineral with a hardness of 2.5 to 4. It is a lime-green color and is found in the Northwest USA.

Healerite emanates profound healing energies, working on multiple levels to restructure misaligned chakras, meridians and systems in the organic and etheric bodies, bringing a great beneficial infusion of subtle matter-energy. Its currents carry emanations of well-being to body and soul. It resonates with the heart, solar plexus and third eye chakras, facilitating an elevation and alignment of one's entire vibrational field. It stimulates the harmonious accord of awareness, love and will, empowering one to manifest these fully.

Healerite energizes the Liquid Crystal Body Matrix, creating revitalization on the cellular level, harmonizing with the Divine Blueprint of the holistic perfection of the body. Emotionally, Healerite encourages joy, expansiveness, generosity, intimacy and heart-centered awareness. It facilitates the recollection of past lives, for learning the lessons that allow one to correct dysfunctional patterns. On the spiritual level, Healerite is a stone of planetary healing, helping to dispel the ill effects of war, pollution, deforestation or environmental exploitation.

Healerite works harmoniously with Shungite, Moldavite, Phenacite, Golden Labradorite, Seraphinite and Azeztulites, including Azozeo stones.

HEALER'S GOLD

KEY WORDS Healing, grounding of high-frequency energies in the body, energetic harmony and balance **CHAKRAS** All **ELEMENT** Earth **PHYSICAL** Supports physical healing, blood oxygenation, overall vitality **EMOTIONAL** Helps one achieve inner balance and self-confidence **SPIRITUAL** Grounds high energies in the body, aids manifestation of desires

Healer's Gold is the name given to a combination of Pyrite and Magnetite mined in Arizona. Pyrite is an iron sulfide mineral with a hardness of 6 to 6.5. Magnetite is an iron oxide mineral with a hardness of 5.5 to 6.5. Both minerals have cubic crystal structures.

Healer's Gold emanates a powerful, positive energy. It harmonizes the astral, subtle and causal bodies and aligns them correctly with the physical. It is balancing to the male and female aspects of the self. It activates weak or lazy chakras and enhances the flow of subtle energies throughout the meridian system. It helps people with low energy and eliminates passivity. In healing sessions, Healer's Gold brings about a synergy in which both practitioner and client are likely to feel a marked increase in their energy levels both during and after a session.

Healer's Gold can be used on any chakra. This stone is a source of *prana*, as well as an integrative balancer of all one's energy systems. Healer's Gold promotes a positive outlook and facilitates the initiation of new creative projects. Wearing Healer's Gold can create an overall sense of well-being, comfort in the body, confidence in oneself, acceptance of others and balance on all levels. Healer's Gold harmonizes with Moldavite, which can speed and strengthen its effects. It also works in synergy with Seraphinite, Sugilite, Aegirine, Smoky Quartz, Carnelian, Phenacite and Black Tourmaline.

HELIODOR

KEY WORDS Activation of mind and will   **CHAKRAS** Solar Plexus (3rd)   **ELEMENT** Fire   **PHYSICAL** Supports digestion and assimilation, healing gastric disorders   **EMOTIONAL** Brings possibility, hope and vitality to the emotional body
SPIRITUAL Aids in achieving the highest spiritual aspirations

HELIODOR is a golden yellow variety of Beryl, a beryllium aluminum silicate mineral with a hexagonal crystal system and a hardness of 7.5 to 8. Its name is derived from Greek words meaning "gift of the Sun." It is found in Brazil, Pakistan, Afghanistan, Madagascar and Namibia.

Heliodor is a potent ally for the development of personal power through the activation of the mind and the appropriate use of will. It helps one focus at the solar plexus—the chakra through which one can channel spiritual energies into physical reality. It emphasizes the qualities of assertiveness, self-confidence, physical and mental strength, manifestation, discrimination, benevolence and power. Heliodor is a stone of higher consciousness and physical well-being. It can bring us more abundant awareness and more vibrant life. Heliodor can revitalize one when one's energies are low. It can help one rediscover one's sense of purpose and assist one in finding the willpower to move forward with one's mission in life. It hones the intellect from the inside out, creating vibrational alignment of the mental centers in the etheric body. Heliodor also links the personal will to Divine Will and Christ consciousness. It can activate in us the traits we associate with the Christed One—spiritual love, fully awakened awareness, clairvoyance, the power of transmutation and ultimately the vibrational quantum leap called Ascension. For those deeply committed to spiritual development, Heliodor can assist one in aligning and merging with this Divine pattern.

HEMATITE

KEY WORDS Grounding, manifestation, making the spiritual physical **CHAKRAS** Root (1st)
ELEMENT Earth **PHYSICAL** Supports the blood; protects the body's fields from toxic energies
EMOTIONAL Encourages a solid sense of self; aids in self-forgiveness **SPIRITUAL** Helps one believe in one's dreams and bring them into manifestation

HEMATITE is an iron oxide mineral with a hexagonal crystal system and a hardness of 5 to 6. Its name is derived from the Greek word for blood, a reference to its color in powdered form. Most Hematite in the marketplace is tumbled or polished, with a metallic gray color.

Hematite is among the most effective stones for grounding oneself in the body and the physical world. It can counteract spaciness and confusion, helping one to see practical concerns and move forward with useful action. Hematite can be used to balance the auric field and align the chakras. It pulls stray energies down through the meridian system to the root chakra.

Manifestation is one of the most commons problems for spiritually oriented people. Many do not realize that it is not enough to travel to the higher realms and experience expanded awareness. One goal, perhaps the primary one, of human evolution, is to bring the energies of the etheric realms into manifestation here in the physical plane. Hematite is an ideal tool in this work. Carrying or wearing Hematite can assist one in bringing one's dreams and aspirations into reality and in learning the difference between a true vision and a fantasy. Hematite harmonizes with other grounding stones, as well as Herkimer Quartz "Diamonds," Moldavite and Libyan Gold Tektite. It helps to ground the currents of high-vibration stones such as Azeztulite, Herderite and Phenacite.

HEMATITE, RAINBOW

KEY WORDS Increasing bodily crystalline coherence, repairing one's magnetic field, healing autoimmune disorders, spiritual protection, Vibrational Ascension, Unchained Power **CHAKRAS** Root (1st), Third Eye (6th), Crown (7th) **ELEMENTS** Earth, Storm **PHYSICAL** Supports recovery from anemia and autoimmune illnesses such as multiple sclerosis and post-polio syndrome **EMOTIONAL** Increases one's sense of well-being, empowerment and spiritual confidence **SPIRITUAL** Provides spiritual protection, enhances personal power, stimulates the activation of the Rainbow Body of Light, facilitates communication with Stone Beings

RAINBOW HEMATITE is a mixture of hematite and goethite. Its shale-like plates display a multicolored iridescence on the surfaces, which is the inspiration for the name. It is found in Brazil and in Arizona, USA.

Rainbow Hematites can energetically initiate increased crystal ordering of the blood. Greater crystalline coherence can lead to enhancement of consciousness and activation of latent capacities such as psychic ability and awareness beyond the body. Rainbow Hematites can be used to repair one's magnetic field. This makes one feel more powerful, alert, and more available to subtle energies and expanded consciousness. It makes one feel more grounded, clear-headed and in tune with the Earth. In spiritual self-healing, Rainbow Hematite can be used to help rectify issues such as anemia, as well as autoimmune illnesses such as multiple sclerosis and post-polio syndrome. It can help one strengthen the muscles through exercise. On subtle levels, it is a powerful stone of spiritual protection. In its highest manifestation, it can facilitate Vibrational Ascension and manifestation of Unchained Power.

Unchained Power is the capacity to act on the material world through consciousness alone. For this purpose, using Rainbow Hematite with Phenacite and Azozeo Azeztulites can be of great help.

HEMIMORPHITE

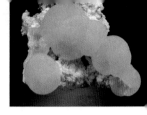

KEY WORDS Light activation, aura balancing, emotional healing and communication, empathy, joy, channeling and mediumship **CHAKRAS** Heart (4th), Throat (5th), Third Eye (6th), Crown (7th), Etheric (8th–14th) **ELEMENT** Storm **PHYSICAL** Supports proper hormonal balance **EMOTIONAL** Soothes emotional body, encourages forgiveness and compassion **SPIRITUAL** Aids attunement to higher spiritual frequencies, opens upper chakras

HEMIMORPHITE is a hydrous zinc silicate with an orthorhombic crystal pattern and a hardness of 4.5 to 5. Hemimorphite can form as crystals, botryoidal or stalactitic forms, or as coatings. Hemimorphite deposits are found in Algeria, Italy, Greece, Mexico and Namibia.

Hemimorphite manifests the energy of well-being, bringing balance to the auric field, dissolving and dispelling dark spots of negativity or weakness. It positively affects the emotional body, bringing in a vibration of joy which does not deny life's unavoidable incidents of grief and sorrow. In fact, Hemimorphite's energy tends to blend joy and sorrow into a single flow of compassionate emotional involvement and empathy, for oneself and others. It enables the emotional body to freely interpenetrate the mind and body, so this unimpeded flow is fully established.

Blue Hemimorphite enhances the communication of the truth of one's feelings and can aid in healing dysfunctional relationships. It facilitates the inner growth through which one can learn to communicate with souls who have "passed over." It can enable some individuals to become mediums or channels, and its vibration seems to attract spirit guides and angelic beings. Hemimorphite combines synergistically with Smithsonite, Andalusite, Pyrite, Aragonite and Calcite.

HERDERITE

KEY WORDS Evolution, activation of latent capacities, awakening the higher brain functions, discovering the Light Body
CHAKRAS Third Eye (6th), Crown (7th), Soul Star (8th), Transpersonal (9th) **ELEMENT** Storm **PHYSICAL** Supports balanced and increased brain function, recommended for headaches **EMOTIONAL** Helps one view emotional situations with higher perspective
SPIRITUAL Activates latent spiritual and psychic capacities of the brain

HERDERITE is a calcium beryllium phosphate with a monoclinic crystal system and a hardness of 5 to 5.5. It can be colorless, pale yellow, green, brownish, gray and sometimes lavender. Herderites are rare crystals, found most abundantly in Brazil and Africa.

Herderite is one of the preeminent stones for awakening and charging the upper chakras of the body and fully connecting one's conscious awareness to the higher dimensions linked to the chakras above the head in the etheric body. All varieties of Herderite share this trait, and they are incredibly powerful tools for interdimensional travel, communication with spirit guides and Light beings and embracing enlightened awareness as a full-time state of being. Herderite initiates growth in consciousness. It opens the third eye and crown chakras, as well as the first two etheric chakras, expanding one's sense of self. In fact, with Herderite, one can experience oneself as an energy field that exists far beyond the confines of the physical body. Herderites can kindle direct spiritual vision. The effect will vary with the sensitivity and preparedness of the individual, but the inner opening will be felt almost universally.

Herderite resonates powerfully with the other Synergy 12 stones: Moldavite, Phenacite, Tanzanite, Danburite, Azeztulite, Tibetan Tektite, Brookite, Satyaloka Quartz, Natrolite, Scolecite and Petalite, and also with Merkabite Calcite, Elestial Calcite and Cinnabar Quartz.

HERKIMER QUARTZ "DIAMOND"

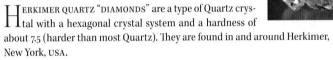

KEY WORDS Dreams, visions, purification, spiritualization of physical life **CHAKRAS** Third Eye (6th), Crown (7th) **ELEMENT** Storm **PHYSICAL** Supports general health, physical stamina and energy level **EMOTIONAL** Aids in clearing the emotional body and removing negative attachments **SPIRITUAL** Facilitates dream work, astral travel, time travel, dimensional shifting

Herkimer Quartz "diamonds" are a type of Quartz crystal with a hexagonal crystal system and a hardness of about 7.5 (harder than most Quartz). They are found in and around Herkimer, New York, USA.

These crystals are manifestations of pure, solidified spiritual Light. They emanate a high, harmonious energy that positively "sings" on the upper levels of the Quartz vibrational spectrum. Herkimers are ideal for body layouts, dream work, meditation pieces, jewelry, templates, energy tools or just about any other application. They not only broadcast their own energies—they can also pick up and magnify the frequencies of other stones. Herkimers emanate the brightest crystal Light, and they help purify one's energy field and attune one to the white Light of the Divine essence. Wearing Herkimer "Diamonds" can give one the grace of a constant, almost subliminal connection to the higher spiritual domains. Angels are drawn to the pure etheric radiance emanated by these stones, and Herkimers can therefore be used as aids for those who wish to communicate or commune with the angels. They are also ideal stones for lucid dreaming and other types of dream work.

Herkimers have a special affinity for Moldavite, and they also work harmoniously with Herderite, Satya Loka Quartz, Phenacite, Natrolite, Scolecite, Celestite, Danburite and all varieties of Azeztulite.

HEULANDITE, GREEN

KEY WORDS Dreams, visions, interdimensional travel, access to past civilizations, emotional healing **CHAKRAS** Heart (4th), Third Eye (6th), Crown (7th) **ELEMENT** Wind **PHYSICAL** Supports brain evolution and awakening of latent capacities **EMOTIONAL** Aids in reaching a state of calm, elevated awareness **SPIRITUAL** Helps in reaching deep meditative states and inner silence

Heulandite is a member of the Zeolite family, a sodium calcium aluminum silicate mineral with a monoclinic crystal system and a hardness of 3.5 to 4. It can be colorless, pink, red, green, yellow, gray or white. The most abundant deposits of Heulandite crystals are in India. The most popular types of Heulandite for metaphysical use are the White Heulandite and Green Heulandite from India.

The distinctions between Green and White Heulandite are in part a matter of focus. Green Heulandite is a stone of the heart, and it helps one to attune with the heart of the Earth. It helps one attain the natural state of the awakened heart—vibrating in resonance with the hearts of the Earth, the sun, the galaxy and the Universe, all in harmonic unison. Green Heulandite facilitates this resonance, helping one find the right energetic frequency. Green Heulandite also enhances "emotional intelligence" and can facilitate emotional healing through the awakening of compassion. It calms nervousness and alleviates fear. It calls forth courage and determination and is an aid to those working to overcome setbacks of all types.

Green Heulandite harmonizes well with Prasiolite (Green Amethyst), Green Apophyllite, Green and Pink Tourmaline, Morganite, Ajoite, Kunzite and other stones of the heart.

HEULANDITE, WHITE

KEY WORDS Dreams, visions, interdimensional travel, access to past civilizations, emotional healing **CHAKRAS** Heart (4th), Third Eye (6th), Crown (7th)
ELEMENT Wind **PHYSICAL** Supports brain evolution and awakening of latent capacities **EMOTIONAL** Aids in reaching a state of calm, elevated awareness
SPIRITUAL Helps in reaching deep meditative states and inner silence

HEULANDITE is a member of the Zeolite family, a sodium calcium aluminum silicate mineral with a monoclinic crystal system and a hardness of 3.5 to 4. It can be colorless, pink, red, green, yellow, gray or white. The most abundant deposits of Heulandite crystals are in India. The most popular types of Heulandite for metaphysical use are the White Heulandite and Green Heulandite from India.

Using White Heulandite in meditation, one may journey inwardly to many of the ancient civilizations of Earth's past—to Egypt, Babylon, even Lemuria and Atlantis. This stone seems to attune to the Akashic records in a very visual way. It can help one recover past-life memories, especially those having to do with psychological problems and blockages. This can be invaluable for spiritual self-healing. These stones have a special capacity for awakening dormant or latent subtle sensing capacities.

White Heulandite will work very well in combination with Lemurian Seed Crystals and/or Aqua Lemuria, especially for journeying to the interdimensional memory and consciousness of ancient Lemuria. Herkimer "Diamonds" will assist those intending to attune to the Atlantean vibration. Stones such as Natrolite will offer a greater multiplicity of access choices for interdimensional travel. Other recommended stones include Apophyllite, Merkabite Calcite, Phenacite and Satyaloka Quartz.

HIDDENITE

KEY WORDS Interpersonal love, heart healing, rediscovering the joy of relationships   **CHAKRAS** Heart (4th)   **ELEMENT** Water   **PHYSICAL** Supports the heart and hormonal systems
EMOTIONAL Stimulates the emotional body, encourages joy, bliss and love
SPIRITUAL Teaches the spiritual lessons of gratitude and abundance

Hiddenite is a yellow-green or emerald green variety of Spodumene, a lithium aluminum silicate mineral with a monoclinic crystal system and a hardness of 6 to 7. Hiddenite derives its name from W. E. Hidden, who discovered the stone in 1879 in North Carolina, USA. The most important deposits are in Brazil, Madagascar, Burma and the USA.

Hiddenite vibrates to the true chord of the spontaneously loving heart, attuned to the future yet unconcerned about future consequences. It teaches, through the feelings it generates in the self, that loving is its own reward, and that getting what one wants through manipulation sours the grapes. This is a very liberating state, and one which would change the entire human world into a paradise if it were universally practiced. Hiddenite's message is simple— even if love and loss go hand in hand, loving is still the best, the only thing to do. Those who are ready to reclaim their ability to love with their whole hearts are recommended to wear or carry Hiddenite. Spreading Hiddenite in all directions is good for one's relationships and good for the world.

Hiddenite works synergistically with all heart stones, such as Ajoite, Kunzite, Morganite, Rose Quartz, Pink and Green Tourmaline, Aventurine, Pink Calcite, Emerald, Rhodonite, Rhodochrosite and many others. When combined with interdimensional stones like Phenacite, Herderite or Natrolite, it allows one to ascend meditation to the realms of Universal love.

HOLLANDITE QUARTZ

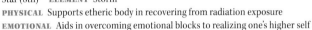

KEY WORDS Path of destiny, Higher Self, regeneration, spiritual insight, increased Light **CHAKRAS** All (1st–7th), Soul Star (8th) **ELEMENT** Storm
PHYSICAL Supports etheric body in recovering from radiation exposure
EMOTIONAL Aids in overcoming emotional blocks to realizing one's higher self
SPIRITUAL Facilitates the activation of one's higher spiritual capacities.

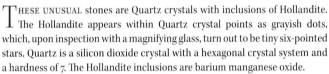

THESE UNUSUAL stones are Quartz crystals with inclusions of Hollandite. The Hollandite appears within Quartz crystal points as grayish dots, which, upon inspection with a magnifying glass, turn out to be tiny six-pointed stars. Quartz is a silicon dioxide crystal with a hexagonal crystal system and a hardness of 7. The Hollandite inclusions are barium manganese oxide.

The tiny stars of Hollandite within these Quartz crystals can act as keys for the awakening and activation of one's true self. Such activations can occur on cognitive, emotional, physical and even cellular levels. For example, meditation with a Hollandite Quartz can bring "memories from the future" concerning whom one is destined to become. On the physical level, carrying or wearing a Hollandite Quartz can activate the template of one's ideal form. If one's body is out of alignment with one's true identity, it may change, patterning itself in resonance with the newly claimed selfhood. For many, such shifts can appear as improvements in health and appearance, including weight loss, enhanced strength and stamina, relaxation of facial lines, clearing of the eyes and numerous other regenerative phenomena.

Hollandite Quartz harmonizes with Moldavite, Herderite, Natrolite, Phenacite and Cryolite, all of which enhance its capacity to bring forth one's ideal physical, emotional and spiritual self.

HYPERSTHENE

KEY WORDS Self-knowledge through visionary awareness, receiving understanding through connecting with morphic fields, self-healing through visualization, accepting one's shadow **CHAKRA** Third Eye (6th) **ELEMENT** Wind **PHYSICAL** Aids in the process of self-healing through creative visualization **EMOTIONAL** Brings awareness of one's shadow side into consciousness, aids emotional healing through understanding and self-acceptance **SPIRITUAL** Enhances psychic vision, increases spiritual awareness and intuitive understanding through resonance with morphic fields of knowledge

Hypersthene is a magnesium-iron silicate with a hardness of 5.5 to 6. It is related to Labradorite and other feldspars. It is dark-gray, black or brown. It has been found in America, Europe, Asia, Australia and New Zealand.

Hypersthene is a stone of psychic vision, and can reveal insights to help one solve problems. It is also a stone of magic, aiding those who wish to manifest their intentions by implanting their patterns into higher morphic fields, where they are received and from which responses will come.

Hypersthene can be used to promote the healing process through creative visualizations. Using Hypersthene's capacities to enhance vision and magnify intention, the results of visualization therapy can be greatly improved. In the emotional realm, Hypersthene helps one understand, accept and heal one's shadow side. Using this stone in meditation helps one to inwardly see and accept the judged and disregarded parts of one's nature, expanding one's conscious self-awareness and bringing one into a state of wholeness.

Hypersthene combines synergistically with Labradorite, Golden Labradorite, Spectrolite, Phenacite, Danburite and Moldavite. With Azozeo super-activated Azeztulites, Hypersthene lends a vivid visionary quality to the experience of spiritual awakening and transformation.

INFINITE

KEY WORDS Healing and protecting the auric field, activating kundalini, sensitivity to subtle energies **CHAKRAS** Root (1st), Sexual/Creative (2nd), Solar Plexus (3rd), Heart (4th) **ELEMENT** Earth **PHYSICAL** Helps the cells and DNA remain stable when exposed to electromagnetic or energetic pollution **EMOTIONAL** Encourages self-confidence and independence **SPIRITUAL** Clears the aura of habitual negative patterns

INFINITE is the trade name for a variety of green or gray-green Serpentine from South Africa, a magnesium silicate mineral with a monoclinic crystal system and a hardness of 3 to 4.

Infinite is an excellent stone for healing the etheric body. A "hole" or energy leak in the etheric body can bring about feelings of fatigue, depression and depletion. Etheric wounds or holes can allow psychic vampires to attach themselves to one's field, further depleting one's sources of emotional, mental and physical vitality. Infinite's vibration replenishes the etheric body and helps to seal the holes. In healthy individuals, Infinite can assist in raising one's vibration to higher frequencies. This is an excellent stone for the gradual activation of the kundalini channel. Meditation with Infinite, coupled with visualization of a benevolent white fire rising through the spine, can greatly facilitate this process.

Infinite can assist one in connecting with the energies of Nature. It is a good stone to bring along for outdoor meditations, as it can help one to see devic spirits, fairies and the spirits associated with waterfalls, mountains, canyons or other power spots.

Infinite is a stone of geomancy. It can heighten one's sensitivity to ley lines, the "dragon currents" of the Earth's meridian system. It can assist in all types of dowsing and can increase the potency of reiki and other types of energetic healing.

IOLITE

KEY WORDS Inner vision, shamanic journeying, healing of old wounds, soul retrieval
CHAKRAS Third Eye (6th)   **ELEMENT** Wind
PHYSICAL Supports healing of the eyes, memory problems, sleep issues   **EMOTIONAL** Encourages calm and resourcefulness in difficult situations   **SPIRITUAL** Facilitates visionary experience in meditation

IOLITE is a magnesium aluminum silicate mineral with an orthorhombic crystal structure and a hardness of 7 to 7.5. The name Iolite comes from the stone's violet color. The most important Iolite deposits are in Brazil, Madagascar, Burma, India and Sri Lanka.

Iolite offers to take one on the inner path to the deep self. It is an excellent stone to use in shamanic journeying. It assists by increasing the vividness and detail of inner visions and by calling up symbols from deep in the psyche that will illuminate the issues one must face for continued growth. It increases one's capacity to move into areas of old fear, teaching one that the exploration of one's wounds is the most direct path to healing. Iolite is also a stone of inner treasures. It helps one to move to the depths of one's unconscious and to uncover the lost parts of oneself. It is an excellent aid for exploring past lives and their karmic lessons. Iolite assists in blending normal conscious thinking with intuitive knowing. It aids in strengthening the energetic links between the brain and the heart. Wearing Iolite can help awaken and sustain one's psychic gifts. It is an excellent stone for astrologers, tarot readers, mediums and other intuitive channelers of inner information.

Iolite harmonizes with Lapis, Amethyst, Tanzanite, Lazulite, Azurite and other stones of the Indigo/Violet Ray. Scolecite spiritualizes its energies to a higher level. Hematite and other grounding stones will aid in grounding and integrating the lessons Iolite brings forward.

IOLITE-SUNSTONE

KEY WORDS Artistic inspiration, productive action, physical vitality, enhanced intuitive abilities   **CHAKRAS** Sexual/Creative (2nd), Solar Plexus (3rd), Third Eye (6th)   **ELEMENT** Wind, Fire **PHYSICAL** Stimulates endocrine system, aids in weight loss **EMOTIONAL** Aids self-confidence in social situations, public speaking   **SPIRITUAL** Enhances intuition, communication with guides and spirits

IOLITE-SUNSTONE is a naturally occurring combination of Iolite and Sunstone. Iolite is a magnesium aluminum silicate mineral with an orthorhombic crystal system and a hardness of 7. Sunstone is an oligioclase feldspar mineral with a triclinic crystal system and a hardness of 6. Iolite-Sunstone comes from a single find in India.

Iolite-Sunstone combines the properties of Iolite and Sunstone to create new energetic effects. Iolite is a stone of inner vision, stimulating the third eye, enhancing psychic abilities, kindling the gift of prophecy, increasing sensitivity to all types of subtle energies. It is also a stone of self-discipline, enabling one to make and follow concrete plans for the attainment of one's aims. Sunstone emanates the vibrations of courage and leadership. It enhances one's innate capacity to take responsibility for stepping forward in difficult situations and risking one's safety for the good of the collective. It stimulates the second and third chakras, seats of creativity and will. In addition to their individual properties, Iolite and Sunstone unite the vision of the third eye with the will-to-action of the solar plexus, making it possible to move quite powerfully for the actualization of one's dreams. It also enables one to travel interdimensionally without losing one's sense of self and purpose.

For interdimensional travel, combine with Phenacite and Herderite. For manifesting dreams, use with Tsavorite Garnet and Hematite.

JADE, GREEN

KEY WORDS Health, abundance **CHAKRAS** Heart (4th)
ELEMENT Earth **PHYSICAL** A spiritual aid to
strengthen the heart and overall health
EMOTIONAL Supports the emotional body in opening
to joy **SPIRITUAL** Encourages enjoying life without
becoming too attached to the material world

Jade is a name shared by two distinctly different minerals—Nephrite, a calcium magnesium silicate, and Jadeite, a sodium aluminum silicate. Nephrite has a hardness of 6 and Jadeite has a hardness of 6.5 to 7. Both have monoclinic crystal systems and are very tough stones, a trait caused by their finely interlocked and strongly bonded crystal structures.

Green Jade is a stone with a heart of healing, and a stone for healing the heart. Its energies are so strong and steady, one feels a flow of well-being and balance almost immediately upon touching them. These are good stones to wear during sleep, both for their harmonious and nourishing vibrations and for their beneficial effect upon one's dream life. Green Jade fosters wholesome and steady growth of one's *chi*, or life-force energies. It is recommended that one try wearing or carrying Green Jade when hiking, gardening or relaxing out of doors, because it draws upon the Earth's life force and imbues one's auric field with that energy. When one cannot be outside, Green Jade can help one carry the signature of Nature into even the most artificial environments.

Green Jade can harmonize and balance the heart chakra, aiding in both emotional and physical well-being. It can be used to attract abundance and prosperity and to broadcast peace and loving-kindness to all those in one's surroundings. It is a stone of abundance and can help to attract wealth and all kinds of prosperity.

JADE, PURPLE

KEY WORDS Humor, spiritual knowledge and attunement
CHAKRAS Crown (7th), Third Eye (6th), Earthstar (below the feet)
ELEMENT Earth **PHYSICAL** Aids in soothing the nervous
system and alleviating symptoms brought on by stress
EMOTIONAL Protects emotional bodies of sensitive people from
energy pathologies of others **SPIRITUAL** Helps regulate the
auric field, enhances dreams and visions

JADE is a name shared by two distinctly different minerals—
Nephrite, a calcium magnesium silicate, and Jadeite, a sodium
aluminum silicate. Nephrite has a hardness of 6 and Jadeite has a hardness of
6.5 to 7. Both have monoclinic crystal systems and are very tough stones, a trait
caused by their finely interlocked and strongly bonded crystal structures.

This stone fills one with mirth and happiness. Purple Jade is excellent for
purifying one's aura and dispelling any negative attitudes that hold one back
from experiencing the spontaneous joy of life. There is a lot of humor evoked
by this gemstone, and it also enhances one's appreciation of the perfection
of Divine order in all things. Purple Jade is an asset when worn or carried by
almost anyone, especially those who need to "lighten up" and relax into the
flow of life. Purple Jade can also aid one in letting go of self-imposed limitations and in maintaining one's awareness that the abundance of the Universe
is available to oneself.

Combining Purple Jade with Moldavite amplifies its potential for advancing one's prosperity, as well as one's appreciation of cosmic humor. Danburite, Azeztulite or Phenacite with Purple Jade can bring joy into one's experience of the higher dimensions, and easier access to them. Purple Jade is very
friendly, both with other stones and with our human energies. It offers an
experience of the truth of one's essential joy.

JADE, BLACK

KEY WORDS Protection, clearing negativity

CHAKRAS All   **ELEMENT** Earth

PHYSICAL Supports the body in protecting itself from illness, infection, parasites; especially recommended when traveling   **EMOTIONAL** Aids insight into and healing of darker parts of the self

SPIRITUAL Good for psychic protection, integration of one's Shadow side

JADE is a name shared by two distinctly different minerals—Nephrite, a calcium magnesium silicate, and Jadeite, a sodium aluminum silicate. Nephrite has a hardness of 6 and Jadeite has a hardness of 6.5 to 7. Both have monoclinic crystal systems and are very tough stones, a trait caused by their finely interlocked and strongly bonded crystal structures.

Black Jade is a stone that acts like an etheric "bodyguard" when it is worn or carried, emanating strong energies which clear one's aura of any vulnerability to attachments by negative forces or entities. It is as though the stone makes one "invisible" to such beings, including energy vampires and people who are projecting anger and aggression. Black Jade can also shield one from morphogenic fields of negative energy, such as the fear and violence projected through the media. It is an especially helpful ally in times of war or world crisis, when one wishes not to be swept up in the negative mass consciousness.

Looking inward, Black Jade can assist in "cleaning house" and ridding oneself of fear, anger, doubt, hatred and other destructive emotions. It allows the unconscious to open and release the traumatic memories which are often the roots of such feelings. Meditation with Black Jade can initiate deep inner voyages, and it is particularly useful for those doing soul retrieval and shamanic journeys, helping one go into the depths and return to a higher state of consciousness.

JADE, RED

KEY WORDS Courage, action **CHAKRAS** Root (1st),
Solar Plexus (3rd), Earthstar (below the feet)
ELEMENT Earth **PHYSICAL** Stimulates and
invigorates all bodily systems, increases *chi*
EMOTIONAL Encourages fortitude in overcoming
difficulties **SPIRITUAL** Enhances life force and
connection to Earth through the root chakra

JADE is a name shared by two distinctly different minerals—Nephrite, a calcium magnesium silicate, and Jadeite, a sodium aluminum silicate. Nephrite has a hardness of 6 and Jadeite has a hardness of 6.5 to 7. Both have monoclinic crystal systems and are very tough stones, a trait caused by their finely interlocked and strongly bonded crystal structures.

For gentle souls who have difficulty asserting themselves, Red Jade brings forward the energy of the warrior. It is a stone of individual power and will, helping one put aside fear, worry, doubt and the "anxiety of the threshold." This last malady is like the hesitation one might feel at the top of the diving board or the doorway of the office of one's boss. Red Jade dispels the fear that holds one back, urging one to take the plunge and let the chips fall where they may. It is a stone of action which says, "Don't just stand there—do something!" And with the help of Red Jade in the pocket or around the neck, we follow that impulse.

Fortunately, Red Jade also emanates a balancing vibration of wisdom which helps keep one from acting rashly. Nonetheless, its mode is that of the active solution, not one of quiet waiting.

Red Jade is an excellent talisman for those studying martial arts or training for athletic performances. It supports an increase in one's physical vitality, increases the flow of *prana,* stimulates creativity and sexual energy.

JADE, LAVENDER

KEY WORDS High spiritual attunement, compassion, serenity **CHAKRAS** Crown (7th), Heart (4th) **ELEMENT** Earth **PHYSICAL** Eases stress and brings the physical body into harmony with one's spiritual blueprint **EMOTIONAL** Encourages a state of serenity and benevolence **SPIRITUAL** Aids in attuning to the angelic realms, and to Kwan Yin

JADE is a name shared by two distinctly different minerals— Nephrite, a calcium magnesium silicate, and Jadeite, a sodium aluminum silicate. Nephrite has a hardness of 6 and Jadeite has a hardness of 6.5 to 7. Both have monoclinic crystal systems and are very tough stones, a trait caused by their finely interlocked and strongly bonded crystal structures.

Angelic beings hover around Lavender Jade like hummingbirds around a flowering bush. The energy it emanates is of the highest etheric spectrum, and it provides spiritual nourishment to all who touch or even gaze upon it. It can help one to harmonically attune to Kwan Yin, the bodhisattva of compassion, and to orient oneself toward loving and charitable actions in the world. Lavender Jade is a stone of the Violet Ray of spiritual purification, and it is a wonderful companion to take on retreats. In meditation, it can enhance the visionary state and gently help one enter the space of "no thought." It allows one to release cynicism and suppressed anger and to embrace an attitude of serene acceptance.

In much the same way that it turns the mind toward purification and compassion, meditation with Lavender Jade can enhance intuition, empathy and all varieties of psychic ability. It is much more attuned toward the higher angelic realms than to the astral plane.

Lavender Jade harmonizes with Kunite, Morganite, Hiddenite, Astaraline, Magnetite, Sugilite and all types of Jade.

JADE, BLUE

KEY WORDS Spiritual knowledge, clear thinking, discrimination **CHAKRAS** Third Eye (6th), Crown (7th) **ELEMENT** Earth, Wind **PHYSICAL** Assists in calming inflammation, swelling, arthritic conditions, asthma and bronchial conditions **EMOTIONAL** Soothes the emotional body; can assist in maintaining an objective, calm demeanor during stressful situations **SPIRITUAL** Provides activation of higher vibrations and grounding of excess energies, aids smoother transition during initiatory experiences

J ADE is a name shared by two distinctly different minerals—Nephrite, a calcium magnesium silicate, and Jadeite, a sodium aluminum silicate. Nephrite has a hardness of 6 and Jadeite has a hardness of 6.5 to 7. Both have monoclinic crystal systems and are very tough stones, a trait caused by their finely interlocked and strongly bonded crystal structures.

Blue Jade can calm the mind, allowing one to keep a cool head in stressful situations. It is a "philosopher's stone," enhancing one's capacity to see the world from a higher vantage point and to avoid losing oneself in the petty dramas of life. It enhances mental abilities of both sides of the brain, benefiting one's capacity for rational thought as well as creative intuition. Blue Jade helps one to hear the inner voices of one's spirit guides and of one's own heart and to make clear choices in light of the wisdom revealed. It stimulates psychic abilities and spiritual sensitivity. It is highly recommended for those who wish to be mediums, because it enhances both openness and discrimination, so one not only hears the voice within, but also considers its words carefully.

Blue Jade combines harmoniously with Blue Kyanite, Blue Sapphire, Indicolite Tourmaline, Phenacite and White Azeztulite.

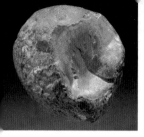

JASPER, RED

KEY WORDS Physical strength and vitality, stabilization of one's energies **CHAKRAS** Root (1st), Sexual/Creative (2nd) **ELEMENT** Earth
PHYSICAL Enhances strength and energy, encourages recovery from physical weakness due to illness, useful in generating muscle tissue, can enhance effects of exercise, supports the circulatory and respiratory systems **EMOTIONAL** Aids in releasing attachment to negative emotional or sexual experiences
SPIRITUAL Stimulates root chakra, supports rising of the kundalini energy

RED JASPER is a microcrystalline variety of Quartz, a silicon dioxide mineral with a hexagonal crystal system and a hardness of 6.5 to 7. The name Jasper is derived from a Greek word meaning "spotted stone." Jaspers can include up to 20% foreign materials, which account for its wide variety of colors and patterns. Red Jasper is found in Brazil, the USA and other countries.

Red Jasper can help enhance one's endurance and stamina and can work over time to increase the amount of *chi,* or life force, in one's energetic field. It strengthens the root chakra and deepens one's connection to the Earth. It enhances memory, especially of dreams or other inner experiences. Its vibrational pattern is so stable that it tends to stabilize one's own energies if one wears or carries it or keeps it in the environment. Such stabilization can lead to good health, balanced emotions, truthful expression and just actions. This stone has a kind of down-to-earth nobility that simply rubs off on the owner. Red Jasper does its work gradually, but it offers the advantage that the gains one makes are more permanent than those achieved with different stones or other methods.

JASPER, RAINFOREST

KEY WORDS Earth-healing, connection with Nature, joy in life **CHAKRAS** All **ELEMENT** Earth **PHYSICAL** Spiritually supports liver health and detoxification of the body **EMOTIONAL** Supports renewed hope, invigoration and energy, aids in overcoming grief or depression **SPIRITUAL** Facilitates deep connection with Nature, aids in connecting with Nature spirits and devic beings

JASPER is a microcrystalline variety of Quartz, a silicon dioxide mineral with a hexagonal crystal system and a hardness of 6.5 to 7. The name Jasper is derived from a Greek word meaning "spotted stone." Jaspers can include up to 20% foreign materials, which account for its wide variety of colors and patterns. Rainforest Jasper is found in Brazil and South Africa.

Rainforest Jasper offers a key to one's heart connection to Nature and one's impulse to work toward planetary healing. It awakens the awareness that we as creatures are not separated from the world of animals, plants—or minerals. With this awareness comes a delicious sense of joy. Once this joy has been kindled, an awareness of the precarious position of life on Earth comes at the same time. And these two experiences work together to help one commit to action on behalf of the preservation and support of life. Rainforest Jasper also works to align one with the balance of one's natural, perfected pattern as a living organism. This can bring needed balance to the body and can assist one in treating the body better. It supports the release of habits such as overeating, drinking, smoking or other practices that destroy the body. At the same time, the desire for good nutrition, exercise and time spent in Nature can increase.

JASPER, MOOK

KEY WORDS Earth-healing, connection with Nature, joy in life
CHAKRAS All **ELEMENT** Earth
PHYSICAL Spiritually supports liver health and detoxification of the body **EMOTIONAL** Encourages renewed hope, invigoration and energy, aids in overcoming grief or depression
SPIRITUAL Facilitates deep connection with Nature, aids in connecting with Nature spirits and devic beings

MOOK JASPER is a microcrystalline variety of Quartz, a silicon dioxide mineral with a hexagonal crystal system and a hardness of 6.5 to 7. The name Jasper is derived from a Greek word meaning "spotted stone." Jaspers can include up to 20% foreign materials, which account for its wide variety of colors and patterns. Mook Jasper is found in Australia.

Mook Jasper assists one in reclaiming one's latent capacity to feel the electromagnetic energy currents of the Earth and to use them in conjunction with one's own energies to maximize the effects of one's will and personal power. Mook Jasper reawakens the ability to simply "know" the right direction to take, in physical or nonphysical travel. It emanates the energy of animal knowing, or instinct, and it allows one to find the threads of one's own instinctual capacities. It is a beneficial stone for those interested in practicing animal communication, and it helps one to find rapport with the spirits of the ancestors. Mook Jasper can clear and activate the third eye and the solar plexus chakra, and align them with the root chakra, allowing for the intuitive perception of the patterns of Earth energies and life force, as they pulse through our world and ourselves.

Mook Jasper's effects are quickened and intensified by Moldavite.

JASPER, FANCY

KEY WORDS Grounding mental energies; discipline and perseverance; slow, steady healing **CHAKRAS** All **ELEMENT** Earth **PHYSICAL** Aids in overcoming insomnia and other sleep disorders, supports general health **EMOTIONAL** Helps calm fear or worry caused by overactive mental energies **SPIRITUAL** Helps to ground and organize the mind, aids in solving problems

FANCY JASPER is a microcrystalline variety of Quartz, a silicon dioxide mineral with a hexagonal crystal system and a hardness of 6.5 to 7. The name Jasper is derived from a Greek word meaning "spotted stone." Jaspers can include up to 20% foreign materials, which account for its wide variety of colors and patterns. Fancy Jasper exhibits a wide variety of colors. It is found primarily in India.

Fancy Jasper performs the task of helping one attend to the mundane details of life with efficiency and good humor. It grounds one firmly in the body and focuses the mental energies on dealing with whatever issues and duties are most significant at the time. It helps prevent procrastination and assists one in making coherent plans for the future. It encourages one's outlook on life by cutting difficulties and fears down to size. Fancy Jasper is a stone that helps one to "just deal with it," whatever "it" may be. It is also a good, slow healing stone. It works gradually but thoroughly to assist one in eliminating chronic problems in the body and the psyche. It resonates with all the chakras, not dramatically, but in a wholesome way that ultimately brings balance.

JASPER, PICTURE

KEY WORDS Inner journeying to sacred sites and ancient civilizations, connecting with Earth's consciousness   **CHAKRAS** Third Eye (6th), Root (1st)   **ELEMENT** Earth   **PHYSICAL** Energetically supports bone growth and healing   **EMOTIONAL** Helps one emotionally reconnect to the Earth and to the ancient knowledge of living in balance   **SPIRITUAL** Aids in attuning to power spots through Earth's electromagnetic field and energy systems, can help one link with distant places and times

P ICTURE JASPER is a microcrystalline variety of Quartz, a silicon dioxide mineral with a hexagonal crystal system and a hardness of 6.5 to 7. Its name is derived from the scenic quality of its tan and brown patterns. Picture Jasper is found primarily in the USA, especially in Oregon.

Picture Jasper can be used in meditation to merge with the consciousness of the Earth. This can be a fantastic experience of union with the energies of the Mother and all levels of the Goddess energies. Picture Jasper can also be used to find the ley lines of the Earth's meridian system. This can be helpful when deciding how to situate a house or other new construction, or where one can set up a crystal energy grid for maximum effect.

Picture Jasper can also facilitate other types of inner journeying. Using these stones, one can "travel" as a point of conscious awareness to the many power spots on the planet, and even through time to ancient civilizations. When journeying to power places, one can learn the nature and applications of the resident energies and draw upon them in one's everyday life. In the case of ancient civilizations, one can bring back knowledge of spiritual technologies for application in our present-day world.

JASPER, UNAKITE

KEY WORDS Healing, balance, release of bad habits, higher attunement, patient persistence **CHAKRAS** All, especially Heart (4th) **ELEMENT** Earth **PHYSICAL** Offers spiritual energetic support in the treatment of cancers or heart disease, promotes the growth of healthy tissue, can also be useful in recovery from injury **EMOTIONAL** Assists one in truly releasing negative emotions and the habitual thought patterns that give rise to them **SPIRITUAL** Raises the vibration of the physical and emotional bodies by helping release disharmonious emotional patterns and the lower emotional frequencies

UNAKITE JASPER is a microcrystalline variety of Quartz, a silicon dioxide mineral with a hexagonal crystal system and a hardness of 6.5 to 7. It is known for its lovely pink and green patterns. Unakite Jasper is found in Brazil, South Africa and other countries.

Unakite embodies Jasper's quality of slow-moving beneficial influence. It facilitates the gradual elimination of bad habits, especially those of overeating and overconsumption of alcohol. It helps one unearth and release the bonds of old emotional wounds in a way that avoids shock and trauma. It supports the purging, over a period of one to two years, of many toxic energies and substances from the cellular level of the body. It brings all the nonphysical bodies into eventual alignment with the physical body and with one another, creating the opportunity for attunement with the higher worlds. Unakite teaches patience and persistence and reminds one that anything worth having is worth waiting for. Unakite is a stone for true spiritual seekers who wish to hold steadfast to their chosen path.

JET

KEY WORDS Protection, purification, grounding **CHAKRAS** Base (1st), for grounding; All, for purification **ELEMENT** Earth **PHYSICAL** Provides spiritual protection of the body, heals energy leaks in the aura, aids in energetic cleansing of liver and kidneys **EMOTIONAL** Clears the energy field of negative emotional attachments **SPIRITUAL** Facilitates entering and exploring the inner void of creation

J ET is a black or dark brown variety of coal called lignite. It is a combination of carbon plus hydrocarbon compounds with a hardness of 3 to 4. Jet was formed by the lithification of submerged driftwood in sea-floor mud. It is found in England, Poland, Australia, Russia, the USA and other countries.

Jet can be an aid in the activation of the powers of magic and interaction with the forces of the elements. It assists in raising one's *shakti* and allows some of that fiery energy to be directed by the will. It helps one to draw upon Earth energies and to channel that powerful flow.

Jet is a neutralizer of negative energies, clearing one's field of disharmonious vibrations. It offers psychic protection in astral travel or spiritual mediumship. A necklace or pendant of Jet makes a powerful amulet for the purification of one's aura and protection from negative influences. A small bowl of Jet pieces is ideal for clearing crystals, gems and jewelry. Jet and Amber together in a body layout or jewelry combination create a circuit of healing energy.

For psychic protection and purification, Jet can be combined with Black Tourmaline, Aegirine, Smoky Quartz and/or Black Andradite Garnet. For raising the *shakti*, Serpentine and/or Tibetan Tektite make powerful allies. For healing, Jet be combined with Amber, Seraphinite and Sugilite. Moldavite and Jet facilitate powerful spiritual transformation.

KUNZITE

KEY WORDS Divine Love, emotional healing, activation of the heart's knowing   **CHAKRAS** Heart (4th)   **ELEMENT** Water   **PHYSICAL** Eases stress and supports the parasympathetic nervous system   **EMOTIONAL** Aids one in becoming receptive to love and energy   **SPIRITUAL** Connects one to the energy of Divine Love underlying all of creation

KUNZITE is the pink-to-violet form of Spodumene, a lithium aluminum silicate with a monoclinic crystal system and a hardness of 6 to 7. It forms as prismatic crystals with vertical striations. The main deposits of Kunzite are in Pakistan, Afghanistan, Brazil, Madagascar and California, USA.

Kunzite opens the heart to the energies of love—self-love, interpersonal love, love for humanity, animals, plants, minerals—all that is. Most importantly, Kunzite is a conduit from one's heart to the vibration of Divine Love. Through embracing all the other types of love, one is preparing to consciously receive Divine Love, and when that occurs, the immediate, inevitable response is love for the Divine. Meditating with Kunzite can facilitate profound experiences of Universal Love. Carrying or wearing the stone helps one move through one's day with kindness, gentleness and serenity. Kunzite can activate the silent voice of the heart, opening a wordless communion between one's mental and emotional aspects. It can awaken the heart and encourage it to communicate more intimately with the mind. If one is willing to listen and follow the quiet urging of the heart, one's life and world will benefit greatly.

Kunzite harmonizes with Hiddenite, Moldavite, Morganite, Rose Quartz, Ajoite, Emerald and Pink Tourmaline. Phenacite, Azeztulite, Scolecite and Natrolite can open the doors to the spiritual realms of Divine Love with which Kunzite resonates.

KAURILITE

KEY WORDS Link with Nature, longevity, purification, self-healing, love, wisdom, majesty, patience, humor **CHAKRAS** All **ELEMENT** Earth
PHYSICAL Supports the blood, lymph and immune systems; supports enhanced vitality and longevity **EMOTIONAL** Inspires good humor and a sense of well-being **SPIRITUAL** Emanates love, wisdom, majesty, patience and humor; renews one's energy field; stimulates connection with Nature spirits; facilitates access to the akashic records, especially to ancient Lemuria

KAURILITE is a petrified resin from New Zealand's ancient Kauri trees. It looks similar to Amber, but is actually a type of copal. It exudes a refreshing scent when briskly rubbed.

Kaurilite carries a tremendous amount of Life Force, bringing an infusion of prana into one's auric field and Liquid Crystal Body Matrix. The Kauri Being is naturally friendly to humans, and one can feel that. Love is simply in the nature of the Kauri Being, as are wisdom, majesty, patience and humor. When one aligns with Kaurilite, one resonates with all of these qualities.

Kaurilite can work metaphysically to enhance one's physical, mental and emotional vitality. It is beneficial for all self-healing practices, lending energetic support to the immune system, blood and lymph systems. Carrying or wearing Kaurilite can renew one's energy field and bring a wholesome sense of well-being. It works spiritually as an enhancer of longevity, and offers a direct connection with the consciousness of Nature. It aids in communicating with Nature spirits and devas. It can stimulate access to wide areas of the akashic records, especially those linked to ancient Lemuria. Kaurilite helps one to inwardly hear the voice of Wisdom and converse with the Soul of Nature.

Kaurilite works well with Sauralite Azeztulite, Red Fire Azeztulite, Vortexite, Vitalite, Empowerite, Revelation Stone, Healerite, Azumar and Jet.

KYANITE, BLACK

KEY WORDS Balance, grounding, energizing, time travel, soul retrieval **CHAKRAS** All, especially Root (1st) **ELEMENT** Storm **PHYSICAL** Balances the meridian system, promotes energy flow **EMOTIONAL** Aids in healing emotional issues caused by lost soul parts **SPIRITUAL** Supports awakening of interdimensional consciousness

BLACK KYANITE is an aluminum silicate mineral with a triclinic crystal system and a hardness varying from 4.5 to 7, depending on the axis. It occurs primarily in Brazil.

Black Kyanite can clear blocked energies in any chakra and can replenish the meridian system. It is both grounding and energizing, increasing one's vibrational frequencies without taking one out of the body. It is useful in energetic healing, because it clears imbalances and brings forth an unhindered flow throughout one's various systems.

Black Kyanite can take one back to past lives and forward to probable futures. It teaches one to experience interdimensional consciousness without losing one's connection to Earth. It lends intensity and vividness to shamanic journeys, and it helps shamanic healers attune to the soul-based issues of their clients, seeing clearly the inner work needed for healing and soul retrieval.

Black Kyanite combines synergistically with Nuummite. Both are powerful, dynamic stones that help one plumb the depths of the subconscious world and to return to this world with fresh insights. For shamanic journeying it combines well with Shaman Stone and Master Shamanite. For balancing the meridian system, Healers Gold can be a helpful ally. Black Kyanite also works well in combination with Black Tourmaline, Ajoite, Azeztulite and Tibetan Tektite.

KYANITE, BLUE

KEY WORDS Inner bridges, psychic ability, past-life recall, telepathy, empathy **CHAKRAS** All, especially Third Eye (6th) **ELEMENT** Storm **PHYSICAL** Supports healing of severed nerves and other neurological problems **EMOTIONAL** Aids in dissolving repeating dysfunctional emotional patterns **SPIRITUAL** Stimulates the third eye and psychic abilities

B LUE KYANITE is an aluminum silicate mineral with a triclinic crystal system and a hardness varying from 4.5 to 7, depending on the axis. It occurs in Brazil, South Africa, Burma, Kenya Mexico and the USA.

Blue Kyanites have a high vibration and create very rapid transfers of energy. They open the psychic channels and activate the mind centers, accentuating one's mental capacities and enhancing one's ability to "download" information from higher sources. They can make telepathic communication between individuals easier, especially if both parties are using them. If one chooses to sleep with Blue Kyanite, the process of lucid dreaming will be greatly stimulated.

Blue Kyanite can link the physical, astral and causal bodies, catalyzing full consciousness in waking, dreaming and dreamless sleep. One must work at this, but it is well worth it when the goal is achieved.

Blue Kyanites can be combined with Green Kyanite to bring their energies into resonance with the heart center. Using both stones together, one can channel the high-frequency vibrations into self-healing and other beneficial pursuits. Green Kyanite can also keep Blue Kyanite's psychic openings centered in the heart, protecting the self from using enhanced psychic abilities as an excuse for an ego trip. Blue Kyanite harmonizes with all other Kyanite, as well as Moldavite, Phenacite and Azeztulite.

KYANITE, GREEN

KEY WORDS Psychically connecting with
Nature   **CHAKRAS** All, especially Heart (4th)
ELEMENT Storm   **PHYSICAL** Supports
enhanced vitality through connection with Nature
EMOTIONAL Aids in experiencing the natural joy of
life in its essence   **SPIRITUAL** Facilitates interdimensional travel to Devic, astral and causal realms

G REEN KYANITE is an aluminum silicate mineral with a triclinic crystal
system and a hardness varying from 4.5 to 7, depending on the axis. It
occurs primarily in Brazil.

Green Kyanites can create a bridge between oneself and the dynamic balance of Nature. It helps one to feel the ever-moving, perfect flowing balance
of the Tao, the life force of the Universe.

Green Kyanite connects one with the truth of the heart. It can aid in dis-
cerning truth in one's environment, whether one is listening to the TV news
or to a friend or family member. If someone is or is not speaking from their
heart, one will know it. This stone also helps one live from the heart's truth.
This is very rewarding, because being in the heart's truth means one is not
looking outward for answers.

Green Kyanite can open the portals to inner domains. First and most
easily one can enter the realm of the Nature spirits and devas. With a bit more
experience and willingness to let go, one can reach the causal plane, where
the archetypes exist and where the great patterns of events are shaped before
they manifest in our world. Even astral travel to other planets is possible.
Green Kyanite can powerfully enhance dream life and can facilitate getting
into the lucid dream state. For this, it should be placed in the pillowcase or
taped to the third eye. Moldavite can be added to enhance these effects.

KYANITE, INDIGO

KEY WORDS Spiritual awakening, astral travel, lucid dreaming, inner vision   **CHAKRAS** All, especially Third Eye (6th) and Crown (7th)   **ELEMENT** Storm   **PHYSICAL** Supports spiritual healing of brain imbalances   **EMOTIONAL** Helps dispel confusion and anxiety   **SPIRITUAL** Stimulates the energies of spiritual awakening

INDIGO KYANITE is an aluminum silicate mineral with a triclinic crystal system and a hardness varying from 4.5 to 7, depending on the axis. It occurs primarily in South Africa.

Indigo Kyanite emanates energies that move deeply into the mind centers, stimulating the pineal gland and activating latent psychic abilities. When the pineal gland is fully awakened, it can trigger complete crown chakra activation and states of *satori*.

One can use Indigo Kyanite to enter the state of lucid dreaming by wearing one to bed or placing it in the pillowcase. Astral travel while in the lucid state is also greatly aided by the energy of Indigo Kyanite. When one needs penetrating vision to see the truth in a situation, or when confusion and uncertainty must be dispelled, Indigo Kyanite can help. Meditation with this stone can enhance inner clarity and can stimulate fresh insights into difficult situations. Indigo Kyanite also inspires loyalty and fair treatment of one's fellow humans. It can help one work through disagreements and disputes and can aid in repairing damaged relationships. It can help one reconnect with one's dreams and treasured aspirations, giving one the clear vision necessary to make them real.

Indigo Kyanite harmonizes with all Kyanites, as well as Phenacite, Herderite and all the Azeztulites. Satyaloka Azeztulite can aid Indigo Kyanite with pineal gland awakening.

KYANITE, ORANGE

KEY WORDS Creativity, sexuality, physical
evolutionary change, manifestation, clearing the
second chakra **CHAKRAS** Sexual/Creative (2nd)
ELEMENT Fire **PHYSICAL** Supports the sexual
organs, aids the beneficial transformation of DNA **EMOTIONAL** Clears old issues
of sexual abuse or other mistreatment from the past, including past lives
SPIRITUAL Awakens the vast power of creativity, and the joys of sacred sexuality

ORANGE KYANITE is an aluminum-silicate mineral from Tanzania with a
triclinic crystal system and a hardness varying from 4.5 to 7. Its orange
color is due to the presence of small amounts of manganese.

Orange Kyanite crystals can facilitatethe transformation of high etheric
energies into the liquid crystal of the body's DNA, helping one produce evolutionary changes during one's lifetime. The catalytic potential of these stones
is awesome. They are among the most powerful aids for manifestation.

Orange Kyanite can activate the awesome power of the second chakra,
seat of our sexual and creative energies. It can clear the second chakra of
negative energies and/or attachments, from this life or past lives. When
one's physical, emotional, astral and etheric bodies are cleared at the second
chakra, one's capacity to create can truly blossom. This clearing can also
open one sexually in a healthy way, and allows one to explore and enjoy one's
sexuality in joyful and creative ways. Orange Kyanite also stimulates the first
and third chakras, bringing an enhancement of Life Force and a strengthening of one's ability to use the will creatively. This is potentially one of Orange
Kyanite's greatest gifts, because it allows us to enter into cocreation with the
Soul of the World.

Orange Kyanite works synergistically with Moldavite, Zincite, Phenacite,
Satyaloka Rose Azeztulite, Cuprite, New Zealand Carnelian and all Kyanites.

LABRADORITE

KEY WORDS Magic, protection
CHAKRAS All **ELEMENT** Wind
PHYSICAL Amplifies the effects of healing prayers and affirmations **EMOTIONAL** Aids in doing "inner work" to root out old negative patterns **SPIRITUAL** Enhances psychic abilities; increases capacity to perceive with the inner eye; useful for magic, ritual and psychic protection

LABRADORITE is a plagioclase feldspar with a triclinic crystal structure and a hardness of 6 to 6.5. It is treasured for its remarkable play of color (labradorescence), which shows vivid flashes of green, blue, gold, orange, red and sometimes violet. It is found mostly in Canada and Madagascar.

Labradorite is the gemstone of magic, and it awakens in those who carry or wear it the mental and intuitive abilities which include but are not limited to clairvoyance, telepathy, astral travel, prophecy, psychic reading, access to Akashic records, past-life recall, communication with higher guides and spirits. It enhances "coincidence control"—the practice of increasing the observed degree of synchronicity and serendipity in one's life. It is an inter-dimensional stone, emanating an energy which helps one to consciously pierce the veil between our waking world and the many domains and planes of inner awareness. It is a gemstone of adventure, for it offers one the chance to embark upon a multitude of voyages in the inner realms, as well as increasing one's power to magically affect the outer world. Placed on the third eye in meditation, Labradorite can facilitate visionary experiences of the future, the past, and the many inner domains of time and timelessness.

Labradorite harmonizes with Moonstone, Sunstone, Spectrolite and Golden Labradorite. It also has an affinity for Moldavite, with which it stimulates the magical transformation of oneself to the Higher Self.

LAPIS LAZULI

KEY WORDS Inner vision, truthful communication, royal virtues   **CHAKRAS** Third Eye (6th), Throat (5th)
ELEMENT Wind   **PHYSICAL** Aids in seeing the karmic or psychological roots of illness   **EMOTIONAL** Helps in recognizing and dissolving emotional pathologies
SPIRITUAL Enhances telepathy, past-life recall, visionary awareness; deepens meditation

LAPIS LAZULI is a sodium aluminum silicate with an isometric crystal system and a hardness of 5 to 6. In Latin, the name means "blue stone." The finest Lapis Lazuli comes from Afghanistan.

Lapis was used to entomb and decorate the Pharaohs of ancient Egypt. As a stone of royalty and spirituality, it was unsurpassed. It still carries the vibration of the inner King or Queen that lies buried in each of us. Lapis activates the psychic centers at the third eye, facilitating enhanced intuition and access to spiritual guidance. It is a stone of visionary awareness, bringing new information to the mind in images rather than words. It enhances intellectual ability, making one a better learner and teacher. It is a stone of truth and a stimulating influence to the throat chakra. Lapis is a stone of initiation as well—a catalyst for a mystical journey to higher awareness. Lapis is often particularly attractive to individuals with past-life connections to ancient Egypt, and meditating with the stone can assist them in recovering memories of those past lives, aiding evolution in the current incarnation.

Lapis Lazuli works well with Moldavite, Alexandrite, Oregon Opal, Turquoise, Rhodochrosite, Sugilite, Chrysoprase, Pietersite, Rhodonite and Larimar. Guardianite aids by providing protection in the inner realms.

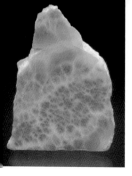

LARIMAR

KEY WORDS Calming, cooling, soothing to the emotional body, enhanced communication, feminine power, connection with goddess energies **CHAKRAS** Third Eye (6th), Throat (5th) **ELEMENT** Water, Fire **PHYSICAL** Aids spiritual healing of throat issues and stress-related illness **EMOTIONAL** Promotes serenity, relaxation and strength of emotional self **SPIRITUAL** Enhances one's link to the Divine Feminine, aids in freeing oneself from unhealthy attachments

LARIMAR is a form of blue Pectolite, a sodium calcium silicate mineral with a hardness of 4.5 to 5. It displays dramatic patterns of blue, blue-green and white. It is found on the island of Hispaniola, in the Caribbean Sea.

Larimar is a stone of tremendous benefit to the throat chakra, providing the power of clear communication and the emotional strength and stability that enable one to speak from the heart. It is a stone of feminine power, allowing one to access the Divine Feminine within. It supports a state of confident well-being and relaxed knowledge of one's capacities. It soothes the emotional body, releasing stress and tension. Larimar can cool hot tempers and guide excess passion into peace. It can be used to diminish the frequency and intensity of hot flashes and is a useful antidote when kundalini energies are overactive. In meditation, Larimar can help one see and release oneself from unhealthy inner bonds to people or principles which do not serve one's highest good. It opens the pathway to the "divine stair of ascension," upon which one leaves behind any obsolete past commitments. Placing Larimar stones in one's environment facilitates a pleasant, serene atmosphere.

Larimar works harmoniously with nearly all other stones, especially Lapis Lazuli, Azeztulite, Moldavite, Turquoise and Chrysocolla.

LAZULITE

KEY WORDS Psychic abilities, mental focus and discipline, enhancing transcendent brain function   **CHAKRAS** Third Eye (6th)
ELEMENT Wind   **PHYSICAL** Helps one in overcoming headaches, migraines and eye strain   **EMOTIONAL** Facilitates alternate-life exploration and can aid in dissolving patterns from other lifetimes   **SPIRITUAL** Stimulates the mind to resonate at higher frequencies, can assist in attuning to other dimensions, enhances dream recall

L AZULITE is a magnesium iron aluminum phosphate with a monoclinic crystal system and a hardness of 5 to 6. The color ranges from rich azure to pale blue, and sometimes greenish blue. Lazulite occurs in Brazil, India, Madagascar, Austria, Sweden and the USA.

Lazulite emanates the pure Indigo Ray and is highly stimulating to the third eye chakra. It can be used to activate all the psychic abilities, including clairvoyance, clairaudience, clairsentience, psychometry, mediumship, prophetic vision, channeling, remote viewing, telepathy, psychokinesis and other forms of ESP. Lazulite also works to bring about greater focus and self-discipline in one's mental pursuits. It is an excellent stone for students and professionals with heavy work loads. It can spark inspirational insights in creative people. Lazulite emanates a vibration which supports peak brain functioning, and its energies are resonant with hemispheric balance and exceptional coherence in the brain. It is a good stone to carry or wear to keep the "cobwebs of age" at bay, as it aids in preserving and increasing memory.

Lazulite harmonizes with Iolite, Lapis Lazuli, the lab-grown Siberian Blue Quartz, Sodalite and Azurite. Phenacite, Natrolite, Scolecite, Danburite, Herderite, Brookite and Azeztulite assist in its stimulation of the higher brain capacities and the awakening of psychic awareness.

LEMURIAN AQUATINE CALCITE

KEY WORDS Dream awareness, emotional healing, access to world memory, communication with whales and dolphins **CHAKRAS** Heart (4th) **ELEMENT** Water **PHYSICAL** Balances and replenishes the Liquid Crystal Body Matrix **EMOTIONAL** Nourishes the emotional body and emotional intelligence **SPIRITUAL** Enhances intuition, telepathy; allows one to atune to Lemuria

L EMURIAN AQUATINE CALCITE is a calcium carbonate mineral with a trigonal crystal system and a hardness of 3. It is a deep blue-green Calcite from a remote region of Argentina.

Lemurian Aquatine Calcite gets its name from its affinity to the element of water, and to the water-oriented civilization of Lemuria. Whether a physical or etheric place, Lemuria was a realm of the watery qualities—intuition, dreaming, feeling and visionary consciousness. Lemurian Aquatine Calcite deeply nourishes the emotional body. It is a strong antidote to stress, fear, worry and anxiety about the future. It soothes and replenishes the etheric body. It enhances dream life and facilitates lucid dreaming. It is ideal for opening up one's capacity for recalling past lives, ancient knowledge and tuning in to the morphic fields of the Earth's past. Those who wish to communicate with whales and dolphins can be aided by Lemurian Aquatine Calcite's capacity to enhance telepathic abilities. It increases conscious sensitivity through one's energy field. It helps increase awareness of spirit guides and angelic guardians, and allows for easier communication.

Lemurian Aquatine Calcite works well with Lemurian Seed Crystals, Lemurian Jade, Merkabite Calcite, Azeztulite, Rosophia, Satyaloka Rose Azeztulite and Pink Azeztulite.

LEMURIAN LIGHT CRYSTAL

KEY WORDS Inner Light, visionary experiences, activation of brain capacities, enhanced crystalline coherence, links to Lemuria **CHAKRAS** Third Eye (6th), Crown (7th), Mouth of God, and the whole brain **ELEMENTS** Wind, Storm **PHYSICAL** Supports the brain and central nervous system, may aid in overcoming brain dysfunctions
EMOTIONAL Offers the experience of expanded consciousness as pure pleasure
SPIRITUAL Stimulates visionary experience, triggers the Mouth of God energy point

L EMURIAN LIGHT CRYSTAL is the name given to a group of high-quality quartz crystal points from Colombia. Their composition is silicon dioxide with a hardness of 7, often water-clear and with unusually shiny surfaces.

Lemurian Light crystals aid meditation and visionary experience. They can open the "Mouth of God" energy point at the back of the skull, initiating powerful mystical awakening s. They allow one to see visions of ancient Lemuria and experience Lemurian consciousness. Lemurian Light Crystals are deeply soothing and quieting to one's consciousness, even as they awaken the inner Light. They can help one enter quickly and deeply into meditative states, releasing stress and opening the mind to receive inner guidance and inspiration. They can stimulate the organization of one's Liquid Crystal Body Matrix, enhancing one's capacities for many varieties of expanded awareness.

In spiritual self-healing, Lemurian Light Crystals can be used to support the brain and central nervous system. They may be useful in working with Alzheimer's disease or other types of dementia.

Lemurian Light Crystals work well with Moldavite, Rosophia, Natrolite, Danburite, Agni Gold Danburite and all Azeztulites. With Mystic Merlinite or Black Merlinite they can aid integration of one's Light and Shadow sides. With Phenacite, one's capacity for visionary experiences is much enhanced.

LEMURIAN SEED CRYSTALS

KEY WORDS Connection with the Divine Feminine, unification with the soul, access to knowledge and wisdom of ancient Lemuria **CHAKRAS** Crown (7th), Soul Star (8th) **ELEMENT** Earth, Wind **PHYSICAL** Links one with the healing qualities of Lemurian awareness **EMOTIONAL** Supports overcoming spiritual loneliness and/or depression **SPIRITUAL** Awakens multiple gifts of empathic and intuitive consciousness

LEMURIAN SEED CRYSTALS are a special variety of clear Quartz, a silicon dioxide mineral with a hexagonal crystal system and a hardness of 7. They come from the Diamantina region of Brazil, and are iden-tified by the ladder-like grooves crossing the bodies of the crystals. On some crystals, there is a reddish pink tinge caused by a coating of iron oxide.

Lemurian Seeds can help one attain "Lemurian awareness"—the balancing, nurturing, loving, spiritual and sensuous consciousness that has been long lost by much of humanity. The response to these crystals is often so emotional and so laden with love that one feels them as a balm to the soul. Lemurian Seeds can benefit just about everyone. Most people need the heart opening and emotional/spiritual healing they offer. Healers can use these crystals to bring such experiences to their clients.

Lemurian Seed Crystals emanate a decidedly *yin,* or feminine, energy. They harmonize wonderfully with stones such as Gem Silica, Larimar, Celestite, Azeztulite, Satyaloka Quartz, Petalite, Morganite, Rose Quartz and Kunzite. Moldavite can catalyze their activation to the highest spiritual level. They are strongly energized by Herkimer "Diamonds", Siberian Blue Quartz and Merkabite Calcite.

LEPIDOCROCITE

KEY WORDS Emotional healing, release of self-destructive patterns, love and empathy, soul retrieval, creative inspiration and communication **CHAKRAS** Heart (4th) **ELEMENT** Fire, Water **PHYSICAL** Supports the blood, heart, lungs, endocrine system and reproductive health **EMOTIONAL** Exerts powerful influence for emotional balance and healing **SPIRITUAL** Aids soul retrieval, psychic protection, attuning to Divine Love

L EPIDOCROCITE is an iron hydroxide mineral with an orthorhombic crystal system and a hardness of 5. Its color is reddish brown to deep red. In Madagascar, Quartz crystals have been discovered that have "phantom" inclusions of Lepidocrocite near the terminations.

Lepidocrocite is a stone of energetic alignment, bringing into proper relationship and harmony all aspects of one's astral, subtle and etheric bodies and the chakra system of the body. It can help to heal "holes" in the auric field which have been caused by drug or alcohol abuse or by negative attachments and entities. It offers psychic protection, surrounding one with an "egg" of gold-white Light. Lepidocrocite supports the emotional body, helping one tap into Divine Love to assist in healing old wounds. It aids in processing grief and relieving depression. It can help one retrieve soul fragments which have been left behind at traumatic moments in one's life. Lepidocrocite facilitates communication—verbal, empathic, telepathic, emotional, mathematical, musical and artistic. Lepidocrocite emanates love, and it can open one's heart chakra. It is excellent for helping romantic partners communicate deeply.

Lepidocrocite harmonizes with Rose Quartz, Kunzite, Morganite, Rhodochrosite, Ajoite, Larimar, Aquamarine, Siberian Blue Quartz, Lapis and Iolite. Satyaloka Rose Azeztulite increases its emotional healing effects.

LEPIDOLITE

KEY WORDS Emotional healing and balance, purification, serenity, relaxation, stress relief **CHAKRAS** All, especially Heart (4th) and Third Eye (6th) **ELEMENT** Water **PHYSICAL** Spiritually aids recovery from insomnia and stress-related disorders **EMOTIONAL** Supports emotional balance and helps dispel worry **SPIRITUAL** Inspires serenity, aids spiritual purification, deepens meditation

Lepidolite is a potassium lithium aluminum silicate with a monoclinic crystal system and a hardness of 2.5 to 3. Its color is most often pink, purplish or lavender. Lepidolite has been found in Africa, Brazil, Greenland and the USA.

Lepidolite is effective in calming frayed nerves, helping one to release stress and worry, and setting one on the path of willing acceptance. Lepidolite not only brings calm to stormy emotional seas, it also provides an energy of enlightened awareness that keeps one "on the beam" so one can handle the situation in the highest way. Lepidolite is a stone of serenity. It encourages one to respond to hostility without putting up defenses, to find the path of harmonious action and to see problems as opportunities to learn. Lepidolite is also a stone of spiritual purification, and meditation with it can clear blocked energies in any of the chakras and throughout the meridian system. It can dispel negative thoughts and remove negative emotional attachments.

Lepidolite harmonizes with other lithium-bearing minerals, such as Tourmaline, Kunzite, Petalite and Amblygonite. Its higher spiritual energies can be augmented by Phenacite, Azeztulite, Natrolite, Scolecite, Elestial Calcite and Merkabite Calcite. Its property of serenity can be further activated by Lemurian Seed Crystals and Aqua Lemuria.

LIBYAN GOLD TEKTITE

KEY WORDS Confidence, mental acuity, psychic protection, access to Akashic records, manifestation, realization of personal potential **CHAKRAS** All, especially Solar Plexus (3rd) and Sexual/Creative (2nd) **ELEMENT** Fire, Storm **PHYSICAL** Supports spiritual healing of stomach and digestive issues **EMOTIONAL** Aids in overcoming shyness and approaching life playfully **SPIRITUAL** Helps one access akashic records, aids creative manifestation through the will

LIBYAN GOLD TEKTITE is a glassy yellow material with an amorphous crystal system and a hardness of 5 to 6. It is found in Libya and Egypt. In ancient Egypt, the funerary necklace of King Tutankhamen contained a carved scarab made from a Libyan Gold Tektite.

Libyan Gold Tektites carry remarkable energies for enhancing the strength of one's will, one's ability to create, and one's power of manifestation. Libyan Gold Tektites can be powerful access keys to the Akashic records. They can aid in recovering the ties of the early Egyptian civilizations to the influence of extraterrestrial entities. They can link one with the energies of Isis and Osiris, the mythic figures said to have given birth to civilization. Meditation and ritual performed with Libyan Gold Tektite will be strongly enhanced, particularly for realizing desired outcomes in the material world. If one feels that one has yet to realize one's full potential, working with these stones is highly recommended. Combining them with Moldavite is ideal for the achievement of self-transformation to one's highest calling. Adding Tibetan Tektite will greatly speed the process of manifestation of one's goals. Using all three together can facilitate rapid transformation, under the guidance of one's higher Will. Libyan Gold Tektite links with Yellow Sapphire for creating financial abundance. Phenacite aids in manifesting one's spiritual visions.

LILAC LEPIDOLITE

KEY WORDS Soothing the emotional body, relieving stress, enhancing meditation, peace, serenity, love, Divine connection **CHAKRAS** All, especially Heart (4th) and Crown (7th) **ELEMENT** Storm, Water **PHYSICAL** Assists harmonious functioning of bodily organs and systems **EMOTIONAL** Aids in releasing stress and embracing serenity and love **SPIRITUAL** Activates one's link to the Divine Presence or Higher Self

L ILAC LEPIDOLITE is a potassium lithium aluminum silicate with a hardness of 2.5 to 3. Its color is a rich lavender, with some translucence. This variety of Lepidolite has been found only in Zimbabwe, Africa.

Lilac Lepidolite blends the Pink Ray of the Heart with the Violet Flame of Purification and spiritual awakening. It activates one's conscious connection to the Higher Self and assists one in maintaining that link. Wearing or carrying Lilac Lepidolite can facilitate development of one's awareness of the Divine Presence and can help one to become a conscious co-creator with that Presence. When this occurs, the number of positive synchronicities in one's life goes up dramatically. Lilac Lepidolite enhances feelings of peace, serenity and love, making it ideal for releasing stress, calming frayed nerves and simply letting go. It is recommended for those wishing to recover from grief or depression and for anyone undergoing a difficult time, such as an illness, marital breakup, career shift or other personal challenge,

Lilac Lepidolite harmonizes with Azeztulite, Morganite, Tourmaline, Gel Lithium Silica, Amblygonite, Lithium Quartz, Smithsonite and Seraphinite.

LITHIUM LIGHT

KEY WORDS Serenity, peace, comfort and relaxation within the process of spiritual unfoldment, Light Body activation, conscious link with the Divine **CHAKRAS** All **ELEMENT** Water **PHYSICAL** Facilitates self-healing through relief of stress and comfortable expansion of awareness, supports digestive system **EMOTIONAL** Emanates, aids mood stabilization and release of stress; can trigger euphoria **SPIRITUAL** Provides comfort, relaxation in spiritual transformation, stimulates Light Body activation, ecstatic rapture and visions of the Divine realms

L ITHIUM LIGHT is composed of lepidolite, quartz and iron silicate. It was discovered in Colorado. Its color ranges from gray to yellow and/or pink.

Lithium Light is powerful for elevating consciousness. Its soft currents, build in intensity until one feels wrapped in spiritual Light, a deeply comforting and relaxing glow. It is ideal for those undergoing a period of spiritual transformation because its presence builds a vibrational field of safety, pleasure, comfort, joy and healing relaxation. This sense of comfort is very helpful during Light Body activation, which is a full metamorphosis. In meditation, Lithium Light can lead to states of ecstatic rapture and visions of the Divine realms. It can even initiate states of recognition of one's true Divine self.

In spiritual self-healing, Lithium Light is recommended for mood stabilization, calming nervousness and releasing stress. It supports the heart and nervous system. It can aid in calming digestive issues brought on by anxiety. Bathing with Lithium Light stones is spiritually and physically therapeutic.

Lithium Light stones harmonize with Tourmaline, Sugilite, Petalite, Amblygonite, Lepidolite and other lithium-based stones. They work well with Sauralite Azeztulite, Honey and Cream Azeztulite, Phenacite, Herderite and Clear Apophyllite.

LITHIUM QUARTZ

KEY WORDS Inner peace, release from stress and negative attachments, aura healing, harmonizing relationships **CHAKRAS** All **ELEMENT** Storm, Water **PHYSICAL** Supports the body in overcoming stress and depression **EMOTIONAL** Fills the emotional body with calm, peaceful, loving energy **SPIRITUAL** Facilitates meditation by calming the mind and opening the heart

L ITHIUM QUARTZ is a silicon dioxide mineral with a hexagonal crystal system and a hardness of 7. It occurs as prismatic Quartz crystals with inclusions of lavender or pinkish gray material. The included material is lithium-bearing. It has been found in Madagascar and Brazil.

Upon holding a Lithium Quartz crystal, one may feel gentle yet powerful energies moving through one's body. The heart chakra will open, followed by a wave of pleasant euphoria. In the next moment, the third eye is stimulated, and one feels rhythmic pulsations of positive energy flowing into all the mind centers. These crystals are surprisingly strong, given the usually gentle energies of other Lithium minerals. They can be used to activate any chakra, and will enhance the depth of meditation as well as the quality of one's inner visions. Their vibration is one of profound healing, emotional peace, release from tension and awakening of the Higher Self. This makes it an ideal meditation stone. Also, wearing Lithium Quartz will bring the user into a more continuous state of connection to his or her own higher mind and heart. "Planting" these crystals in gardens will provide positive stimulation of growth and an invitation for the participation of the devas and Nature spirits.

Lithium Quartz harmonizes with Kunzite, Tourmaline, Amblygonite, Lepidolite and all other Lithium minerals.

MAGENTA FLUORITE

KEY WORDS Thought of the heart, inner truth, emotional healing, pineal gland, higher awareness, Divine nectar
CHAKRAS Heart (4th) , Third Eye (6th), crown (7th)
ELEMENT Wind, Water, **PHYSICAL** Activates deep brain centers, supports neural links with heart
EMOTIONAL Healing emotional body, encouraging forgiveness, entering states of ecstasy **SPIRITUAL** Initiates leaps of awareness and union with the Divine

MAGENTA FLUORITE forms as rich red-purple clusters on a white matrix rock. It has a hardness of 4 and is found in Mexico.

Magenta Fluorite is a stone of the heart, allowing one to become consciously aware of the heart's thought, desires and knowledge. It is a stone of inner truth, enhancing clarity and bringing emotional concerns into a state of peaceful understanding. It is a highly spiritual stone, linking the energies of the heart and crown chakras and opening one to higher awareness. Magenta Fluorite is a stone of emotional healing. It encourages forgiveness--of oneself and others, for whatever wounds have been caused.

In meditation, Magenta Fluorite stimulates the pineal gland in the center of the brain, encouraging the secretion of its Divine nectar. When this occurs, one can easily enter a state of ecstasy. For this purpose, I recommend holding a Magenta Fluorite in one's hands, with the eyes open, gazing at the stone. Imagine the rich color flooding your mind and finally permeating the center of the brain. Magenta Fluorite is also helpful in clearing the emotional body. It aids one in dispelling emotional confusion, and in knowing which choices are best for the good of all.

Magenta Fluorite works well in with Lepidolite, as well as Rhodocrosite, Madagascar Rose Quartz, Rosophia and Pink Tourmaline.

MAGNESITE

KEY WORDS Awakening the higher sensibilities, opening to inner vision, truth and bliss, listening to the heart **CHAKRAS** Third Eye (6th), Crown (7th) **ELEMENT** Storm **PHYSICAL** Aids the body in releasing tension; benefits bowels, muscle tension, stress-related issues **EMOTIONAL** Promotes joy and emotional harmony, relief from stress **SPIRITUAL** Opens one to transcendent spiritual experiences

M AGNESITE is a magnesium carbonate mineral with a rhombohedral crystal system and a hardness of 3 to 4. Magnesite is frequently white, but can also occur in shades of gray, yellow or brown. Crystalline specimens of Magnesite have been found in Minas Gerais, Brazil.

Magnesite is one of the most powerful stones for activating the third eye and crown chakras. Placing one of these stones upon the forehead and closing the eyes, one can expect to feel a rhythmic pulsing energy, becoming stronger as the minutes pass. This is the beginning of the activation of the eye of inner vision in the prefrontal lobes of the brain. If one receives the full experience of this opening, the crown chakra blooms into the "thousand-petaled lotus," and this experience indeed feels like a flower suddenly opening at the top of the head.

Magnesite can help one in the process of self-reflection and can clarify inner seeing. It is something of a "truth detector" when one is doing inner work, and it can help one to see through the unconscious blinders that may keep one in a state of confusion. Among Magnesite's mystical properties is the awakening of the mind to communication with the heart. Magnesite doesn't activate the heart chakra, but it does stimulate the part of the brain/mind which can hear and respond to the heart's "voice." This listening to the heart is the beginning of true wisdom.

MAGNETITE

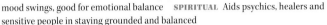

KEY WORDS Alignment of subtle energies with the body, grounding, balancing polarities, awakening hidden potentials **CHAKRAS** All **ELEMENT** Earth **PHYSICAL** Supports the blood, liver, bone marrow; clears the meridians **EMOTIONAL** Helps prevent mood swings, good for emotional balance **SPIRITUAL** Aids psychics, healers and sensitive people in staying grounded and balanced

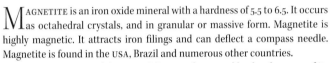

Magnetite is an iron oxide mineral with a hardness of 5.5 to 6.5. It occurs as octahedral crystals, and in granular or massive form. Magnetite is highly magnetic. It attracts iron filings and can deflect a compass needle. Magnetite is found in the USA, Brazil and numerous other countries.

Magnetite is one of the essential stones for crystal healers because of its many uses in aligning the currents of the auric field and the multiple levels of the energy body. It is excellent for balancing polarities—male and female, physical and spiritual, left and right hemispheres of the brain and a multitude of others. Its natural magnetism occurs as a symmetrical field, which, through resonance, brings one's own energy fields into like configuration. One can receive Magnetite's beneficial energies by simply sitting and holding one of the stones in each hand. This will affect one's entire auric field, moving it toward symmetrical balance, and the energy running through the meridian system initiates hemispheric balance in the brain. When this happens, hidden potentials begin to surface. Persons who are rational and linear in their thought will find their intuitive side awakening. Others who are intuitive but not practical may find themselves getting organized. These are merely examples, but this sort of rebalancing is available to those who work with Magnetite.

Magnetite harmonizes with and enhances the effects of virtually all other stones.

MAGNIFIER QUARTZ

KEY WORDS Vibrational amplification of stones, vitamins, water, energy tools, etc. **CHAKRAS** All **ELEMENTS** Wind, Storm **PHYSICAL** Amplifies the effects of healing stones and substances **EMOTIONAL** Amplifies all emotional states, so one is encouraged to use it in states of happiness, gratitude, love and peace **SPIRITUAL** Enhances the energetic effects of all stones, as well as other tools or substances used to further one's spiritual evolution

MAGNIFIER QUARTZ is a class of small, clear quartz crystals from Madagascar. They are silicon-dioxide minerals with a hardness of 7.

Magnifier Quartz got its name because it is a powerful enhancer of the energies of almost all other stones. This makes it invaluable for constructing crystal tools, and for stone grids and body layouts. The crystals can be added to wands, carried in medicine bags, placed with stones in one's environment, put on healing altars, included in elixirs, or any other application where one wishes to increase the power of stones and/or one's intention. Magnifier Quartz is a catalyst for all sorts of synergies, and can be dispensed to members of groups to enhance cooperation and inspire creative visions. Placing the stones in one's cabinets and refrigerator can enhance the Life Force and the energetic nutritional value of foods. Affixing Magnifier Quartz to water bottles is a way of empowering the water to be of maximum benefit. Putting these crystals inside a hat or headband can enhance one's mental processes. Magnifier Quartz can be one of the best abundance-enhancement stones. One might, for example, attach one of these crystals to one's checkbook.

Magnifier Quartz harmonizes with virtually all other minerals. Combining it with high-vibration stones like Phenacite, Moldavite or Azeztulites can strengthen its effects, and may help to accelerate one's spiritual evolution.

MALACHITE

KEY WORDS Enlightened leadership, creativity, confidence, protection, a healed heart **CHAKRAS** Solar Plexus (3rd), Heart (4th) **ELEMENT** Fire
PHYSICAL Increases vitality; supports tissue repair and recovery from illness; recommended for inflammation, arthritis, digestion, detoxification **EMOTIONAL** Aids in building self-confidence and emotional clarity **SPIRITUAL** Facilitates psychic protection, manifestation; enhances will forces

MALACHITE is a copper carbonate mineral with a monoclinic crystal system and a hardness of 3.5 to 4. Its name comes from the Greek word for its color, *malache* (mallow). Good Malachite is found in Russia and Africa.

Malachite is one of the most important stones for protection from negative energies. It permeates the auric field with positive vibrations and strengthens the natural energetic "shell" which can screen out hostile forces, and it activates the "psychic radar" with which one feels the presence of danger. It even accentuates the sort of protection in which synchronicities seem to conspire to keep one safe. Malachite emanates the healthiest energy pattern for the heart. It assists one in maintaining emotional balance, and it offers an enhanced ability to see and avoid one's own emotional pitfalls. The solar plexus chakra is stimulated by Malachite, enhancing one's willpower. In the presence of Malachite, it is easier to refuse temptations. Malachite instills confidence and responsibility and is useful in making spiritual progress through right action.

Malachite harmonizes with Tiger Eye for physical energy and protection, and with Morganite for balancing the heart chakra. It also works easily with other copper-based minerals such as Azurite, Turquoise, Shattuckite, Chrysocolla and Ajoite.

MANI STONE

KEY WORDS Forgiveness, inclusion, regeneration of hope, unity with the Higher Self, soul retrieval, rejuvenation, metanoia **CHAKRA** Heart (4th) **ELEMENTS** Earth, Water, Storm **PHYSICAL** Facilitates rejuvenation of the body through emotional and spiritual healing **EMOTIONAL** Helps heal emotional pathology created by self-judgment and fragmentation, encourages forgiveness and reconciliation **SPIRITUAL** Helps one reintegrate the fragmented self, allowing for spiritual wholeness and union with the Higher Self and the Divine

MANI STONE is a black-and-white jasper from the American Southwest. It is a microcrystalline variety of quartz with a hardness of 7. It was named Mani Stone after the third-century mystic teacher Mani.

The energies of Mani Stone encourage forgiveness, inclusion and the regeneration of hope. These energies go first to the core of the self, revealing wounds and fragmentation brought on by shame and self-judgment. Mani Stone dissolves these dysfunctional patterns and facilitates the process by which we bring our "lost parts" out of exile and back into ourselves. It is thus an excellent stone helper for doing Soul Retrieval work. As one recovers one's wholeness, one's sense of compassion for others is increased, and one can be effective in helping them on the path of self-forgiveness and wholeness.

As Mani Stone facilitates unity of self and union with the Higher Self, it is a stone of mystical awakening. It can even kindle metanoia, in which in which one's personal identity merges with the Divine. In metanoia, one is free to fly to spiritual heights or descend to the deepest corridors of the heart. In both places, one will discover the loving face of the Divine Self smiling to oneself, mirror-to-mirror.

Mani Stone works in synergy with Rosophia, Brookite, Shaman Stones, the original black-and-white Merlinite and Black Merlinite.

MANIFEST LIGHT CRYSTALS

KEY WORDS Kundalini awakening, stimulation of Inner Light, awakening the Light Body, manifestation of one's intentions **CHAKRAS** All, especially Crown (7th) and Root (1st) **ELEMENTS** Fire, Storm, Earth **PHYSICAL** Fills the body with chi, increasing vitality and longevity **EMOTIONAL** Stimulates the emotional body, bringing a feeling of pleasant expansion **SPIRITUAL** Helps one awaken and direct kundalini energies, balances polarized energies, aids in manifestation

MANIFEST LIGHT CRYSTALS are Brazilian quartz crystals with tiny "floating" inclusions of silver-gray hematite. They are made of a silicon-dioxide mineral with a hardness of 7. They may be either clear or smoky quartz.

Manifest Light Crystals are ideal for initiating Light Body activation, and for keeping the Light Body anchored and integrated with the physical body. They trigger a safe and subtle activation of kundalini energies, and are ideal for initiating new levels of spiritual growth. They enhance health and well-being by bathing the interior of the physical body with pure spiritual Light. They can help to ground those with overactive upper chakras, or stimulate sluggish energy systems. They can be used for uniting and reconciling all types of polarities, and are ideal for use in Polarity therapy. They emanate a great deal of Life Force.

Manifest Light Crystals, as their name implies, are excellent catalysts for manifesting anything one wishes to bring forth. One has only to "program" the crystal with a visual image of one's intention, and then hold the stone again while repeating the visualization. Bringing in the emotions of pleasure and gratitude while doing the visualization enhances the effect.

Manifest Light Crystals work synergistically with Moldavite, Cinnazez and all Azeztulites, including Azozeo activated stones. The grounding influence is strengthened by Hematite, and Phenacite aids Light Body activation.

MARCASITE

KEY WORDS Physical vitality, spirituality in physical life, balancing energetic polarities **CHAKRAS** Root (1st), Sexual/Creative (2nd), Solar Plexus (3rd), Earthstar (below the feet) **ELEMENT** Storm **PHYSICAL** Energetically supports recovery from bacterial infection, skin eruptions, fungal overgrowth and infections; can assist in weight loss **EMOTIONAL** Promotes clear emotional boundaries, claiming one's power **SPIRITUAL** Encourages self-direction and taking steps to realize one's goals

MARCASITE is an iron sulfide mineral with an orthorhombic crystal system and a hardness of 6 to 6.5. It is chemically identical to Pyrite, but it is lighter in color, with different crystal growth habits.

Marcasite enables one to see the interpenetration of the spiritual and physical worlds. It allows one to see how physical events mirror spiritual archetypal patterns, and it give clues in regard to the actions one can take to resonate with the spiritual patterns one wishes to embrace. On another level, it assists one in "walking the talk" of spirituality in one's everyday life. Marcasite helps balance polarities in the energy system. It clears the auric field of disharmonious influences and helps cut attachments to others with whom one may have unhealthy relationships.

Through these three lowest chakras, Marcasite works to optimize one's life force and courage, sexual energy, creativity, willpower and mental clarity. When these chakras are charged and balanced, the heart and the upper chakras have much more energy to work with and one discovers new enthusiasm for all one one's pursuits, inward and outward.

Marcasite blends synergistically with Pyrite, Hematite, Lodestone, Cuprite, Zincite, Malachite, Morganite, Phenacite, Natrolite and Scolecite.

MASTER SHAMANITE

KEY WORDS Linking the physical and spiritual realms, inner purification, spiritual protection, shamanic journeying, transformation to the Diamond Self **CHAKRAS** All **ELEMENT** Storm **PHYSICAL** Purifies the blood and cells of negative energetic attachments **EMOTIONAL** Lends courage and resolve for facing difficult circumstances **SPIRITUAL** Increases psychic sensitivity, aids in spirit communication, encourages one to be a spiritual warrior

M ASTER SHAMANITE is a carbon-rich form of Calcite, a calcium carbonate mineral with a rhombohedral crystal system and a hardness of 3. It is found in a remote mountainous area of Colorado.

Master Shamanite can be useful for initiating shamanic journeys, and it can help one connect inwardly with power animals and spirit guides. It is a Stone of the Ancestors, aiding in communication with spiritual elders and guides on the other side, as well as loved ones who have passed. It is a stone of those who wish to walk between the worlds and to heal others through soul retrieval. It can help dispel the fear of death through bringing one to a clear experience that death is not the end.

Master Shamanite resonates with the heart and third eye chakras, and it can activate a synergy of their energies to open the crown. It offers spiritual protection to those who wear or carry it. If one wishes to be a "Warrior of Light," Master Shamanite can be a powerful ally.

Master Shamanite resonates synergistically with Moldavite, Larimar, Shaman Stones, Nuummite, Cryolite, Azeztulite, Sanda Rosa Azeztulite, Lemurian Aquatine Calcite and Merkabite Calcite. Strontianite combines beneficially with Master Shamanite for inner journeyers who find themselves assailed by negative forces.

MERLINITE

KEY WORDS Magic, intuition, connection with elemental energies, past-life recall, psychic openings, mediumship **CHAKRAS** Solar Plexus (3rd), Third Eye (6th) **ELEMENT** Storm **PHYSICAL** Supports recovery from headaches and heart problems **EMOTIONAL** Encourages one's sense of adventure and inner freedom **SPIRITUAL** Opens intuitive capacities for magic and spiritual attunement

MERLINITE is a naturally occurring combination of Quartz and Psilomelane, with a hardness of 6 to 7. Some Merlinite occurs in rocky chunks, with mixed areas of white Quartz and black Psilomelane. Others are dark Psilomelane coated with sparkling druzy Quartz crystals.

Merlinite can part the veils between the visible and invisible worlds, opening the doors to deeper intuitive abilities. It can assist in contacting souls of the deceased who wish to give messages to the living.

Merlinite is an aid to learning all types of magic. It opens the psychic channels for higher guidance. It helps one grasp the interrelations between astrology, tarot, numerology and other occult sciences. It facilitates prophetic visions, and it attracts frequent synchronicities. It opens one to serve as a channel for manifestation of the creative forces of the higher planes. Merlinite allows one to call upon the elemental forces for aid in one's pursuits and ambitions. It can also be a potent catalyst for past-life recall. It evokes the realm of dreams and imagination and makes the recollections of past incarnations much more vivid than they might otherwise be. It activates the "inner radar" that makes certain that one's past-life experiences are the ones most relevant to one's current needs.

Merlinite harmonizes with Moldavite, Obsidian, Amethyst and Sugilite. Phenacite or any of the Azeztulites can raise it to higher vibrational levels.

MERLINITE, BLACK

KEY WORDS Link to the deep Unconscious, lucid dreaming, meditation, shamanic journeying, spirit communication, divination, prophetic vision **CHAKRAS** All, especially Third Eye (6th) and Root (1st) **ELEMENTS** Earth, Wind, Fire **PHYSICAL** Supports all organs and systems involved in bodily purification and elimination of wastes **EMOTIONAL** Quiets spiritual fears by teaching one that the Unconscious is part of oneself **SPIRITUAL** Facilitates access to the deep Unconscious

BLACK MERLINITE is a variety of pure psilomelane, a barium-manganese hydroxide with a monoclinic crystal system and a hardness of 5 to 6. It is composed of swirling bands of dark-gray and black. It was found in Mexico.

Black Merlinite is a stone of the deep Unconscious. It is an excellent stone for lucid dreaming, and it facilitates meditation, allowing one to "go deep" very readily. It offers a direct conduit to the Silence—the still point at the center of all things. It is useful in facilitating shamanic journeying, spirit communication, divination and prophetic vision. It teaches one to befriend one's inner darkness, recognizing that everything experienced inwardly is a part of oneself. Black Merlinite can help one meet and reintegrate one's rejected or lost parts, facilitating wholeness. In spiritual self-healing, Black Merlinite offers vibrational support to the liver, kidneys, bowels and other organs concerned with purification and elimination of waste products.

Black Merlinite is amplified by Moldavite, which raises its vibration. It also harmonizes with Obsidian, Amethyst and Sugilite. With Azozeo super-activated White Azeztulite, the Light of the pure White Ray merges with the Dark Ray, bringing a powerful union of energies. When fully integrated, the elemental power conveyed by Black Merlinite can be transmuted into spiritual power. As always, one is advised to remain true to benevolent paths.

METAL, GOLD

KEY WORDS Solar energy, the archetypal male energy, creativity, confidence, vitality   **CHAKRAS** All, especially Root (1st), Sexual/Creative (2nd), Solar Plexus (3rd)   **ELEMENT** Earth   **PHYSICAL** Brings vitality and solar energies into the body   **EMOTIONAL** Encourages optimism, courage, nobility, determination and overall sense of well-being; dispels fear and negative emotions   **SPIRITUAL** Stimulates the positive activation of the lower chakras, ignites the solar heart, encourages joyful participation in life

GOLD is the metal of royalty and of the Divine Father energy. It is associated with the Sun, with fire, with the life force in its creative mode and with male energy. It is the metal of the outer self, the sunlit personality. Gold is the metal which most easily conducts electricity, and it is also the one best suited to be an all-purpose conductor of the subtle energies of stones. Although Gold is the best metal for energetically active jewelry, one must take into consideration the stones and individuals involved. Both vary widely in their energy patterns, so there are many cases in which other metals are to be preferred.

Gold revitalizes one's physical energies and magnifies the power of most gemstones. It supports openness and integrity and builds confidence in the wearer. In fairy tales, it symbolizes the successful completion of an inner process of growth and the reward for doing so. In its radiance, it also symbolizes the heavenly realms.

Gold conducts the subtle energies of most gemstones better than any other metal. It has a particular affinity for Moldavite, Lapis Lazuli, Diamond, Precious Opal, Oregon Opal, Golden Labradorite, Heliodor and the transparent gem forms of Azeztulite.

METAL, SILVER

KEY WORDS Lunar energy, the archetypal feminine energy, mystery, introversion, the unconscious **CHAKRAS** All
ELEMENT Earth **PHYSICAL** Helps cool excess body heat, aids women's hormonal balance, supports the body in over-coming viruses and bacteria, energetically supports the immune system **EMOTIONAL** Stimulates attunement to the intuitive, emotional side of the self; links both men and women to their feminine side; encourages emotional recep-tivity; strengthens empathy **SPIRITUAL** Stimulates one's connection to the Goddess, allows one to travel the astral realms, attunes one to the inner depths of the subconscious

SILVER is the metal of the Goddess, the Moon, the night, the secret, the mys-terious, the High Priestess, the female energy, the life force in its hidden aspect. Silver is second to Gold in its electrical conductivity, and it, too, harmo-nizes well with most gemstones. Where Gold emanates an extroverted energy, Silver is introverted. Where Gold engenders self-confidence, Silver encour-ages self-containment and inward reflection. Where Gold blazes with fiery Light, Silver is a mirror to the soul, the metal of moonlight.

Silver works best with stones that enhance psychic abilities and/or work to heal the emotional body. In fairy tales, Silver symbolizes the journey through the dark forest and the confrontation with mystery. It is the symbol of the unconscious realm, the world of the soul from which the archetypal patterns of life arise. It aids in lucid dreaming and journeying to past lives.

Silver is particularly attuned to Moonstone, Oregon Opal, Obsidian, Mal-achite and Rosophia.

METAL, PLATINUM

KEY WORDS Cosmic connection, interdimensional communication **CHAKRAS** All, especially Third Eye (6th), Crown (7th), Etheric (8th–14th) **ELEMENT** Storm **PHYSICAL** Stimulates the body's energy systems, emanates a powerful field of protection around the body **EMOTIONAL** Aids in governing the emotions and keeping the neutral inner observer awake as the center of one's Self **SPIRITUAL** Activates the higher chakras, stimulates communion and communication with the higher realms, aids in out-of-body travel

A S GOLD is personality and Silver is Soul, Platinum is Spirit. It is the stars, the androgynous angelic energy, the life force in its aspect of transformation. Platinum has the highest vibrational spectrum of any metal, and its resonance is best with stones attuned to the upper chakras of the body and the nonphysical chakras above the head. Where Gold and Silver are extroverted or introverted, Platinum is transcendent. It stimulates one's consciousness to aspire to the highest realms. It is linked not only to the angelic realm, but to the archetypal pattern of the Divine Human Being. It evokes the energy of enlightenment and archetype of the Star. It is a powerful antenna for attuning to one's "I am" Presence.

Platinum can enhance one's connection with angels and spirit guides. It carries the energy pattern of revelation. It works in the auric field to heal wounds to the soul which were fated or chosen for one's learning (or blessing) in this lifetime. The healing power of Platinum comes through the vehicle of enhanced awareness. It opens one to understanding the perfection of one's life challenges in the context of spiritual evolution. Platinum has a particular affinity for Phenacite and Azeztulite. It can enhance the transcendent qualities of both of these stones.

METAL, COPPER

KEY WORDS Channeling and grounding higher vibrations, conducting and enhancing stone energies **CHAKRAS** All **ELEMENT** Earth **PHYSICAL** Supports the blood, aids tissue repair, increases vitality **EMOTIONAL** Helps one gain spiritual perspective on emotional experiences **SPIRITUAL** Aids in manifesting spiritual energies in the material world

COPPER is the metal of channeling energies. It has the ability to ground and transfer a wide array of vibrational frequencies from the spiritual to the physical. It is the metal of the Magician. It crackles with electricity and fire, but the fire is not its own—it belongs to the higher realms. Copper is a conduit between Heaven and Earth, and it performs the essential task of providing the medium for manifestation of the invisible to the visible.

Copper can carry stone energies the way a copper wire carries electricity. Crystal grids can be enhanced by connecting the stones with Copper wire. A Quartz Laser Wand or other crystal can be intensified by wrapping a coil of copper wire around it. One of the most powerful and basic energy devices one can make is a copper pipe filled with stones and a crystal point at one or both ends. This is the simplest type of energy wand tool. Pyramids or geometric forms constructed from copper tubing filled with crystals make extremely high-energy meditation chambers. Copper encourages experimentation and invention. It resonates with the planet Uranus and its energy of revolutionary ideas and unexpected serendipitous change.

Copper bracelets, which have long been used for treating arthritis, work by opening the blocked energy flow of which the arthritic symptoms are a manifestation.

METAL, TITANIUM

KEY WORDS Power, action, higher awareness, bringing contradiction into synthesis **CHAKRAS** All **ELEMENT** Earth **PHYSICAL** Offers protection from electromagnetic fields generated by computers and electronic equipment, supports physical healing by invigorating one's energy field **EMOTIONAL** Instills a sense of protection and security, assuages fear, uplifting and reinforcing for the emotional body **SPIRITUAL** Stimulates energetic strength and purity, provides spiritual protection by increasing the power of one's vibrational field, inspires determination

Titanium is the metal of power and invincibility. It evokes the imagery of the giant, the warrior, the hero, the willing defender of all that is precious. It resonates to the energies of the planet Mars. It enhances one's physical vitality and brings more energy into the auric field. It can be a vibrational antidote to sluggishness and fatigue. It is a stone of action rather than reflection, of movement rather than meditation.

Titanium works especially well with high-energy stones such as Moldavite, Natrolite, Herderite, Zincite, Tibetan Tektite and Prophecy Stone. It is ideal for use in building Light tools. Titanium is also a metal of higher awareness, bringing one to the resolution of inner conflict and the synthesis of apparently contradictory thoughts. It is a friend of fabulous, impossible ideas and can bear the tension inherent in paradox. It is a metal of the New Consciousness that will be the norm after the great transformation of humanity takes place. Wearing or carrying Titanium plants a seed of that energy firmly in one's auric field.

METAL, NIOBIUM

KEY WORDS Activation of the Rainbow Body, communication with ETs and etheric entities
CHAKRAS All **ELEMENT** Earth
PHYSICAL Offers a neutral vibration which supports the currents of whatever stones one works with to heal and help the body **EMOTIONAL** Encourages impartiality in regard to emotional issues, helps one look dispassionately at one's emotional triggers and to avoid identifying with old emotional patterns **SPIRITUAL** Facilitates communication with all of the higher realms, aids in consciously accessing angelic guidance, ideal for recalling and understanding ET experiences

Niobium is such a wild metal, one wonders if it really belongs on Earth. It vibrates to the frequencies used by many of the extraterrestrial visitors and can help one move into their planes of consciousness. Those who have half-conscious memories of ET experiences can be aided by Niobium in bringing those occurrences into consciousness. This metal also helps one attune to the angelic domain, especially in regard to receiving guidance.

Niobium encourages one to see everything from a fresh perspective, and it helps one discern the magic one has overlooked right under one's nose. Niobium is a metal of the Rainbow Body, and adorning oneself with it can help align all the nonphysical forms of the self in such a way that the true Rainbow Body can take shape. This metal can harmonize with any stone, but Azeztulite and Phenacite are its favorites for dimension-hopping. Niobium is useful in making Light tools and crystal energy devices. It resonates to the mystical energies of the planet Neptune.

METEORITE, NICKEL-IRON

KEY WORDS Kundalini activation, inner vision, spiritual awakening, patience and persistence in regard to spiritual growth   **CHAKRAS** Root (1st), Solar Plexus (3rd), Third Eye (6th), Crown (7th)   **ELEMENT** Fire   **PHYSICAL** Enhances stamina and strength; supports blood and tissues   **EMOTIONAL** Supports emotional balance; protects and grounds the emotional body   **SPIRITUAL** Catalyzes spiritual transformation via kundalini awakening

Nickel-iron meteorites vibrate with an almost electrical intensity. They can activate the kundalini channel, bringing the usually dormant spiritual fire that exists in all human beings into full force. These stones conduct the currents of the stars, the Saura Agni of the Hindu vedas, the hidden energy that animates the Universe. When one stirs this energy, great awakenings and changes can occur. Yet the effect varies widely. Some people will feel nothing at all, because their vibratory rate is too low to resonate with these powerful Meteorites. Others will feel over stimulated and will want to get away from them. This may be because the emotional body is not prepared to tolerate the potential transformation these stones engender.

Nickel-Iron Meteorites stimulate the third eye and crown chakras. They act as catalysts for inner vision and spiritual awakening. Yet they also activate the root chakra and solar plexus, providing an anchor of grounding which is much needed in order to handle everything else they do. In addition, Nickel-Iron Meteorites stimulate the solar plexus, the chakra of action and will.

Nickel-Iron Meteorites harmonize with Anandalite, Moldavite, Libyan Gold Tektite and Tibetan Tektites, each of which resonates to enhance the awakening of the inner kundalini fire.

METEORITE, CHONDRITE

KEY WORDS Interdimensional and extraterrestrial communication, access to the Akashic records of the solar system
CHAKRAS Third Eye (6th), Crown (7th) **ELEMENT** Earth
PHYSICAL Supports the bones, blood and circulatory system **EMOTIONAL** Works to balance and stabilize the emotional body **SPIRITUAL** Helps one connect with ETs, aids interdimensional travel

CHONDRITES are stony Meteorites. They contain mostly Pyroxene and Olivine, and small amounts of Plagioclase Feldspar and Nickel-Iron. Their structure is composed of small spherical grains called chondrules.

Chondrite Meteorites vibrate at the frequencies most attuned to interdimensional communication with and among the ETs. As silica-based stones, Chondrites are programmable, and can be aligned with specific functions, such as opening one's telepathic channel or "traveling" interdimensionally to other stars and planets. They can be used to store information, especially esoteric knowledge relating to the "ladder of consciousness" upon which high-frequency energies are exchanged. Chondrites carry the spiritual records of this solar system. They chronicle the histories of etheric entities that existed on other planets, from Mercury to Saturn. Although these planets are unfit for physical life as we know it, those who travel there astrally, or who tap into their spiritual histories, discover that consciousness has always existed in the solar system. Meditation with Chondrite Meteorites can give one a first-hand experiences of these interplanetary subtle realms.

Chondrite Meteorites combine harmoniously with Herderite, Brookite, Danburite, Petalite, Amethyst and Sugilite. Moldavite can be used with Chondrite Meteorite to tap into interplanetary currents, extraterrestrial intelligences and visions of many realms of higher awareness.

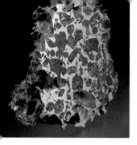

METEORITE, PALLASITE

KEY WORDS Union with the cosmic Overmind and fields of knowledge, interdimensional travel, prosperity, emotional stability **CHAKRAS** Heart (4th), Third Eye (6th) **ELEMENT** Earth **PHYSICAL** Supports the heart, aids blood purification, helps dispel unhealthy bacteria and viruses **EMOTIONAL** Instills emotional balance during spiritual experiences, helps overcome phobias **SPIRITUAL** Allows one to awaken to Cosmic Consciousness

PALLASITE METEORITES consist of a lattice of nickel-iron with pockets of yellow-green Olivine crystal. It stimulates the loving energies of the heart, along with the visionary capacities of the third eye. It opens the emotional gateway of the heart and the inner eye of expanded awareness, allowing one to experience the link between oneself and the cosmos.

In meditation with Pallasite, one's mind can move into an illuminated union with the cosmic Overmind, making it possible to tap into morphogenic fields of knowledge, whereby one can simply "ask and know" in a single instant. Through the heart connection, it is possible for one to move into ecstatic union with the heart of the cosmos, also known as the Great Central Sun. When both of these links are activated, one may feel that one's being extends throughout—and IS—the entire Universe.

Pallasite helps one release the fear of expanding consciousness beyond the body. It helps those who feel "stuck" in the body to let go and travel in the astral and other higher planes. It can calm the fear of flying and can assist those who suffer from agoraphobia. Pallasite can also assist one in manifesting prosperity and abundance in one's material life.

Pallasite harmonizes with Phenacite, Herkimer "Diamonds," Dioptase, Morganite, Emerald and/or Kunzite.

MOLDAVITE

KEY WORDS Transformation, rapid spiritual evolution, chakra activation, cleansing, protection, increased incidence of synchronicities **CHAKRAS** All, especially Heart (4th) and Third Eye (6th) **ELEMENT** Storm **PHYSICAL** Supports attunement of the body to its highest level of function **EMOTIONAL** Opens the heart, inspires one to fulfill one's highest destiny **SPIRITUAL** Catalyzes multiple and very powerful spiritual awakenings

MOLDAVITE is a member of the Tektite group, a glassy, deep green mixture of silicon dioxide, aluminum oxide and other metal oxides, with an amorphous crystal system and a hardness of 5.5 to 6. It is found only in the Bohemian plateau of the Czech Republic.

Moldavite has long been known as a sacred stone. It was found in altar amulets from 25,000 BCE, and has been linked in legend to the fabled Stone of the Holy Grail. It was believed in Czech folklore to guide one to one's destiny and to help one find and preserve true love.

In current times, Moldavite is known as a stone of rapid and powerful spiritual transformation. It can catalyze major priority shifts and even physical life changes. Its tendency is to attract all that relates to one's spiritual evolution and highest good, and to dissolve one's connections with whatever hinders that evolution. These can include changes in career, relationships, diet, health and personal goals, as well as inner awakenings, prophetic dreams, and visions of one's true destiny. Moldavite has often caused a sudden opening of the heart chakra, known as the "Moldavite flush." It can stimulate any chakra and it brings healing wherever it is needed in the body. Moldavite also has the capacity to disappear and reappear, displaying a Trickster quality.

Moldavite can energize the effects of many stones; it harmonizes especially well with Herkimer "Diamonds" and all types of Quartz.

MOLDAU QUARTZ

KEY WORDS Grounding spiritual Light in the body, appreciating and expressing beauty, heart awareness, grounding the vibrations of Moldavite **CHAKRAS** All, especially Heart (4th) and Third Eye (6th) **ELEMENT** Storm **PHYSICAL** Supports healing and transformation through infusion of Light **EMOTIONAL** Generates feelings of satisfaction and gratitude to Spirit **SPIRITUAL** Inspires an awakening to spiritual beauty and Wisdom

MOLDAU QUARTZ is a silicon dioxide mineral with a hexagonal crystal system and a hardness of 7. Its colors are white, gray, brown and rusty orange. It is found in the Moldavite fields of the Czech Republic.

Moldau Quartz has spent millions of years in the same soil where Moldavite is found. These stones have, in a sense, been "taught" by the presence of Moldavite. They are stones of the Earth that have been attuned to the frequencies of the higher worlds. In this, they hold the pattern we ourselves are reaching toward. The infusion of Light is the most important activity in the spiritual transformation now happening all over the world. Moldau Quartz is particularly helpful in this area. In meditation, one senses a distinct pull of Light energy into the body from above as one holds the stone over the heart. The heart itself resonates with Moldau Quartz more than most other varieties of Quartz. Moldau Quartz's vibration is a kind of synthesis of Moldavite and Azeztulite. Azeztulite is resonant with the highest spiritual realms, and Moldavite is deeply attuned to the Divine spark in our hearts. These realms are not truly separate, yet their vibrations are of different qualities. The bridge offered through Moldau Quartz allows one to incorporate much of Azeztulite's high frequencies with the heart-resonance characteristic of Moldavite. Moldau Quartz harmonizes with Moldavite and with all the Azeztulites.

MOLYBDENITE QUARTZ

KEY WORDS Balance, grounding, strength, centeredness, stability, vitality, endurance, loyalty, persistence, courage, resolve, health **CHAKRAS** All **ELEMENTS** Earth, Water **PHYSICAL** Holds the vibrational pattern of optimal function for the body, aids in detoxification **EMOTIONAL** Stabilizes the emotions, moderates fear, depression and anxiety **SPIRITUAL** Balances one's energies, engendering endurance and persistence in following one's goals

MOLYBDENITE QUARTZ is a quartz crystal from Peru, with inclusions of silver-gray molybdenum. The quartz component has a hardness of 7.

Molybdenite Quartz is a stone of harmonization. It brings a sense of stability and moderates feelings of depression, fear and anxiety, reminding one that trust is the way to freedom and that love is its own reward. It has the capacity to unify and balance the entire chakra column, producing a feeling of calm well-being. It are ideal for stimulating and balancing weak chakras, and for clearing etheric remnants of psychological or physical wounds. It can transmit the beneficial properties of molybdenum in repairing the auric field and/or performing "psychic surgery." Wearing or carrying Molybdenite Quartz supports one's strength, vitality and endurance. It carries the blueprint of optimal function for the body, and resonates with the "body consciousness." It is recommended for detoxification and maintenance of health.

Spiritually, Molybdenite Quartz speaks of holding one's clear intention until goals are met and changes are manifested. It engenders loyalty, persistence, courage, resolve and strength of will. It helps one hang onto hope in the midst of difficulty, and stay grounded and centered during the heights of success. It is in some ways an emblem of the Tao, the flowing water of life that modestly persists until all barriers are overcome.

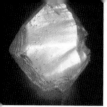

MOONSTONE

KEY WORDS Mystery, self-discovery, intuition, insight, dreams, the goddess **CHAKRAS** Third Eye (6th) and Crown (7th) **ELEMENT** Wind **PHYSICAL** Aids women in comfortable regulation of their menstrual cycles **EMOTIONAL** Encourages forbearance, calmness, patience, inner tranquility **SPIRITUAL** Stimulates inner reflection, attunement with Divine Feminine

Moonstone is a feldspar, a potassium aluminum silicate with a monoclinic crystal system and a hardness of 6 to 6.5. Moonstone was named after its blue-white sheen. It is found in Sri Lanka, Madagascar, Burma, Australia, India and the USA.

In India, Moonstone has always been a sacred stone, with a special significance for lovers. It was believed that placing Moonstone in their mouths when the moon was full would allow them to see their future. In Europe, Moonstone was said to reconcile estranged lovers and to cure sleeplessness.

Moonstone is the gem of the High Priestess, keeper of the feminine mysteries. In its reflected light we can project and thereby observe the hidden truths that reside in the depths of ourselves, out of the light of consciousness. Moonstone is a talisman for the inward journey, and meditation with it can take one deep into the self. What is revealed there is often recognized as the missing piece or pieces of the puzzle of one's life—parts of the soul that have been left behind or forgotten. Moonstone can also take one on a journey into past lives. It is an ideal stone to wear during past-life regression sessions. It can reveal to women their feminine power and their connection to the goddess. For men, it allows the expression of the feminine side, an important step on the path to wholeness.

Moonstone works synergistically with Ruby, stimulating the combination of love, intuitive awareness, courage and passion.

MOONSTONE, RAINBOW

KEY WORDS Optimism, vitality, inner peace, Rainbow Body of Light **CHAKRAS** All **ELEMENT** Wind **PHYSICAL** Supports the body in overcoming fatigue from depression **EMOTIONAL** Inspires enthusiasm, self-appreciation, joy **SPIRITUAL** Stimulates awakening of the Rainbow Body of Light

RAINBOW MOONSTONE is a feldspar, a potassium aluminum silicate with a monoclinic crystal system and a hardness of 6 to 6.5. It is found in India and is distinguished by its multicolored iridescence.

Rainbow Moonstones emanate great vitality, life force and exuberant joy. They offer the gifts of inner peace and harmony, emotional balance and strength, purification and transformation of negativity, as well as psychic protection. In addition, Rainbow Moonstone can facilitate the alignment and activation of all the chakras, while remaining grounded and centered. These powerful healers of the emotional body are recommended for those who suffer from stress or who carry old emotional wounds. Rainbow Moonstones promote a healthy optimism that can sustain one through dark times. They are stones of great Light, and they aid one in kindling the inner light of the heart. They can also facilitate activation of the Rainbow Body of Light, the spiritual vehicle by which our consciousness can travel throughout the many inner worlds.

Rainbow Moonstones are aligned with the energies of the Goddess, and they can help one successfully empower one's feminine aspect. Through its Goddess connection, one can also commune with the energies and spirits of Nature, from plant devas to galactic consciousness.

Rainbow Moonstone harmonizes well with all other types of Moonstone, as well as Sunstone, Labradorite, Black Jade, Amber, Golden Labradorite, Moldavite, Amethyst, Jet and Tibetan Tektite.

MORGANITE

KEY WORDS Divine Love and compassion **CHAKRAS** Heart (4th) **ELEMENT** Water **PHYSICAL** Supports the physical heart and its energy field **EMOTIONAL** Soothes the soul with Divine Love, helps overcome old sorrows **SPIRITUAL** Inspires rapturous merging with the all-pervasive Divine Love

MORGANITE is a pink, peach or purple/pink variety of Beryl, a beryllium aluminum silicate mineral with a hexagonal crystal system and a hardness of 7.5 to 8. It was named after financier and mineral collector J.P. Morgan. Deposits come from Brazil, Madagascar, Africa and the USA.

Morganite is attuned to the frequency of Divine Love. It opens the heart on a deeper level, making us aware of the huge ocean of cosmic love within which we all exist. It gives us the opportunity to surrender to the immense power of Divine Love and to let it show us our life path more clearly. Morganite can bring an immediate release of old pains and sorrow, and a sense of lightness, as though a burden has been lifted. Morganite brings in the frequency of Divine compassion. It powerfully facilitates emotional self-healing through an inner surrender which releases us from the pain to which we had been unconsciously clinging.

When one keeps Morganite on one's person for extended periods of time, there is a growth of confidence and power that comes from being constantly aware of one's connection to Divine Love. One can facilitate this process by holding a Morganite over the heart and "breathing in" Divine Love, then offering one's love out through the stone as one exhales. Through this practice, a circular flow of great sweetness and power can be established.

Morganite harmonizes with the other heart chakra stones such as Rose Quartz, Rhodochrosite, Rhodonite, Rosophia, Emerald, Tourmaline, etc., as well as Phenacite, Danburite, Petalite and Azeztulite.

MUSCOVITE

KEY WORDS Mental stimulation, inspiration, problem solving, attunement to the future, ESP, moderation of overly rapid spiritual awakening   **CHAKRAS** Third Eye (6th), Crown (7th)
ELEMENT Wind   **PHYSICAL** Soothes headaches, dizziness, etc., from too-rapid psychic awakening   **EMOTIONAL** Helps one see and dissolve unhealthy emotional attachments
SPIRITUAL Aids psychic opening, stimulates all mental energies

M USCOVITE is a potassium aluminum silicate with a monoclinic crystal system and a hardness of 2.5 to 4. Its color is often pink or grayish.

Muscovite is a stone of highly positive energies. It stimulates the mind, promoting clear and quick thinking, effective problem-solving and the synthesis of new ideas from old information. It is a stone of novelty, teaching one to try on unfamiliar frames of reference. Muscovite stimulates the higher capacities of the brain, leading one to embrace paradox, holding the tension of opposites without getting a brain cramp. Muscovite is a stone of inspiration, fostering the creation of new neural pathways and increasing the frequency of "aha!" moments. Muscovite assists one in attuning to the time stream of the future. It does this by allowing one's mental apparatus to rest comfortably in the state of indeterminacy. Muscovite stimulates the sixth and seventh chakras, activating the major mind centers. It supports the functions of intuition, telepathy, clairvoyance and other forms of ESP. It makes one receptive to information and suggestions from one's spirit guides. It assists one in embracing "bigger thoughts," allowing one to see the links between such diverse disciplines as art, music, philosophy and mathematics.

Muscovite harmonizes with Lepidolite for spiritual upliftment. Moldavite takes Muscovite's mental energies to a higher level. For visions and inspirations, Phenacite and Herkimer "Diamonds" are ideal allies.

MYSTIC MERLINITE

KEY WORDS Alignment of the chakra column, balancing and integrating polarities, claiming one's wholeness, creating through magic **CHAKRAS** All **ELEMENT** Fire, Earth **PHYSICAL** Supports recovery from spinal misalignments and joint problems **EMOTIONAL** Encourages one to reclaim exiled soul parts without judgment **SPIRITUAL** Aids elemental magic, integration of the Shadow, mystic union

MYSTIC MERLINITE is the name given to a unique mineral composed of Quartz, Feldspar and several trace minerals. Its color is a swirling blend of black and white. It was discovered in Madagascar.

Mystic Merlinite can part the veils between the visible and invisible worlds, opening the doors to deeper intuitive abilities. It can facilitate opening the dormant areas of the mind. It increases sensitivity to the communications of the subtle realms, allowing one to "talk" with plant and animal spirits, and devic entities. For those wishing to work with elemental energies for magical manifestation or awakening to mystical experiences, this stone can be a powerful ally. The black and white mixture of Mystic Merlinite symbolizes the Light and Shadow sides of the self, both of which one must embrace in the moment of inner awakening. One of Mystic Merlinite's key qualities is that of bringing the exiled parts of oneself back into the light of consciousness. This often difficult passage can lead to the true mystic union, which brings the self into wholeness and allows the unity of self and World.

Mystic Merlinite resonates with Master Shamanite, as well as all forms of Azeztulite, Black Tourmaline, Jet and Smoky Quartz. Its dream-enhancing qualities are encouraged by Lemurian Golden Opal. For attuning to the spiritual call of the unknown future, Mystic Merlinite can be combined with Circle Stones.

NATROLITE

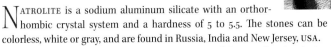

KEY WORDS Visionary experience, quantum leap to higher consciousness, brain evolution **CHAKRAS** Third Eye (6th), Crown (7th), Etheric (8th–14th) **ELEMENT** Storm **PHYSICAL** Supports spiri-tual healing of brain damage and dysfunction **EMOTION-AL** Aids emotional recovery from parasitic psychic attachments **SPIRITUAL** Stimulates expansion of consciousness and Ascension

Natrolite is a sodium aluminum silicate with an orthor-hombic crystal system and a hardness of 5 to 5.5. The stones can be colorless, white or gray, and are found in Russia, India and New Jersey, USA.

Natrolite is one of the two or three most powerful stones for stimulation of the third eye and crown chakras. It can actually cause the merging of these chakras into one huge energy center. Natrolite's energy moves beyond the confines of the physical body, activating one's conscious link with the eighth through fourteenth chakras above the head. These chakras are aligned with one's higher bodies, the astral and causal, as well as the Higher Self. Natrolite helps open the inner gateways to a myriad of inner realms, for one's exploration and enlightenment.

Natrolite provides psychic protection, making it impossible for negative entities or influences to penetrate one's auric field. Its pulsating vibrations can bring Light to any area of the body where energies are blocked. It can be used to clear the chakras and meridians and is useful in stimulating the nervous system to higher levels of sensitivity to the subtle spiritual energies that surround us. Natrolite is an Ascension stone, along with Herderite, Phenacite, Danburite, Azeztulite, Scolecite, Brookite, Phenacite and Satyaloka Quartz. This is the optimal group of stones for raising one's vibrational energies into resonance with the higher worlds. Natrolite is also one of the Synergy Twelve stones and works well with Tibetan Tektite, Moldavite and Tanzanite.

NEW ZEALAND CARNELIAN
(AZOZEO SUPER-ACTIVATED)

KEY WORDS Fire-element activation, cocreation, insights into destiny, transformation, visions of higher realms, passionate will, sexual path of tantra **CHAKRAS** All, especially Sexual/Creative (2nd), Third Eye (6th) **ELEMENT** Fire **PHYSICAL** Supports nervous system, sexual organs, blood flow, digestive system, immune system **EMOTIONAL** Brings passion into creative activities and love relationships, helps overcome hesitancy and fearfulness **SPIRITUAL** Stimulates spiritual awakening, creativity, courage, passion, power, accelerated evolution

NEW ZEALAND CARNELIAN is a silicon dioxide with a hardness of 7. Its color ranges from deep red-orange to pale yellow-white.

New Zealand Carnelian is highly receptive to the Azozeo super-activation process, which raises it to its true potential. As Azozeo Carnelian, it exhibits the capacity to kindle agni, the universal fire of creation, within one's body. It is a stone of initiation, and it reveals one's capacity for creation and cocreation with the Soul of the World. It also activates the heart's intelligence, which guides the creating process. It brings passion to one's will, allowing one to "burn through" roadblocks and past discouragement. It reminds us of our boldness and our power, and that the appropriate surrender of self into action is power. These stones activate the second chakra and can open the way to ecstatic tantric experiences on both the spiritual and physical levels. In self-healing, these stones support the nervous system, sexual organs, blood flow, digestive system and immune system. Emotionally, they dispel hesitancy and spiritual amnesia, reminding one of who and what one truly is.

New Zealand works well with all other Azozeo super-activated stones as well as Healerite, Azumar, Deva Quartz Green Phantoms and Anandalite.

NIRVANA QUARTZ

KEY WORDS Opening to the future, heart/brain synergy, inner rapture, destiny, evolution, trust, self-acceptance **CHAKRAS** All **ELEMENT** Storm **PHYSICAL** Helps dispel various physical symptoms of energy imbalances **EMOTIONAL** Expands emotional body into ecstatic union with the Divine **SPIRITUAL** Facilitates heart/brain synergy, *satori* and enlightenment

NIRVANA QUARTZ is the name given to a group of growth-interference Quartz crystals discovered in 2006 in the high Himalaya mountains of India. Like other Quartz, they are silicon dioxide crystals with a hexagonal crystal system and a hardness of 7.

Nirvana Quartz crystals resonate at the intersection of past and future time. These complex, almost unearthly crystals can aid us in the evolutionary transmutation which is our highest destiny. They can be conduits for currents of inner illumination that facilitate the incarnation of enlightenment. An aspect of this enlightenment is Nirvana Quartz's capacity to help us unite the consciousness of the brain and the heart, creating a feedback loop of joy, leading to inner Light and ecstasy. This rapturous state has earned this stone the name Nirvana Quartz. Its mission involves setting up the blueprint of post-human destiny—a way of being that is beyond the historic human limitations of fear, doubt and violence—living and creating each moment through utter, ongoing, trusting engagement with the fertile unknown which is the future. The beings expressing through these stones can be viewed as the angels of our potential, or as our future selves calling us into what we can be.

Nirvana Quartz Crystals work well with Moldavite, Phenacite, Herderite, Azeztulite, Satyaloka Quartz, Petalite and Danburite

NOVACULITE

KEY WORDS Infusion of subtle matter-energy, stimulation of enlightenment, discernment, cutting unhealthy ties to the past **CHAKRAS** Third Eye (6th), Crown (7th) **ELEMENTS** Wind, Storm **PHYSICAL** Frees blocked energies and cuts away negative attachments underlying physical ailments **EMOTIONAL** Facilitates freedom from the past, bringing zest for life and eagerness for learning and spiritual development **SPIRITUAL** Carries a stream of subtle matter-energy into the body, aiding the process of enlightenment

Novaculite is a microcrystalline variety of quartz with a hardness of 7. Its name derives from a Latin word meaning "razor" or "sharp knife." Novaculite powerfully stimulates the upper chakras. It acts as a conduit for the infusion of subtle matter-energy, or Celestial Fire, which changes and rapidly evolves the very cells and molecules of our bodies. This can activate one's latent capacities for spiritual powers, or siddhis. One can think of Novaculite as a sort of "guru stone," teaching our bodies how to reach enlightenment.

Novaculite is a stone of discrimination. Under its influence, one can greatly enhance one's discernment, intelligence and intuition. In energy work, one can use Novaculite to sever unhealthy emotional or karmic ties (sometimes called "cords"). Combining Novaculite with Quartz in a laser wand works especially well for this. In spiritual self-healing, Novaculite is an ideal stone for psychic surgery. It is particularly attuned to the heart and brain, and its currents can help clear the energies of the bloodstream, lymphatic system and nervous system.

Novaculite's power is enhanced by Moldavite, Shungite and all Azozeo super-activated stones. It aids healing when combined with Healerite or Seraphinite. It works with Cinnazez to be a useful ally for the nervous system.

NUUMMITE

KEY WORDS Personal magic, inner journeys, attuning to elemental forces, self-mastery   **CHAKRAS** Third Eye (6th), Solar Plexus (3rd), Root (1st)   **ELEMENT** Earth, Storm   **PHYSICAL** Helps calm and balance the nervous system   **EMOTIONAL** Encourages self-acceptance, recognition of inner strength   **SPIRITUAL** Aids in honoring one's depths and finding one's inner power

NUUMMITE is a combination of Anthophyllite and Gedrite with a hardness of about 6. It is composed of closely intergrown crystals which display flashes of iridescent colors. It is found only in Greenland.

Nuummites draw upon the fiery energies of the Earth's core, and they offer us the gift of inner power for self-mastery. It can take one on a journey into the depths of the psyche, to help one release energies trapped in the subconscious. It helps one recall and release fixated energies from childhood, birth and even past lives. It aids one's courage and determination to do the inner work that is necessary to be healed and whole. Nuummite may be used as a gazing stone, helping one move into altered states of consciousness. It is excellent for shamanic journeying. It can enhance clairvoyance and intuition; it can help one learn the language of the body and channel healing energies for oneself and others. It can assist one in attuning to the elemental forces of the Earth, so one may call upon them in times of need. It is a stone of personal magic that can increase the frequency of synchronicities and "good luck" in one's life. Nuummite can be a powerful meditation stone, opening the inner doors of self-discovery. It can be worn in jewelry to bring the dynamics of inner power, self-mastery, magic and manifestation into one's life.

Nummite harmonizes with Moldavite, Libyan Gold Tektite, Black Tourmaline, Amethyst, Labradorite, Sunstone and Moonstone.

OBSIDIAN, BLACK

KEY WORDS Psychic protection, grounding, cleansing of negativity, spirit communication   **CHAKRAS** Root (1st)   **ELEMENT** Earth   **PHYSICAL** Aids in healing issues caused by unprocessed Shadow material   **EMOTIONAL** Helps dispel self-judgment and self-sabotage   **SPIRITUAL** Facilitates psychic cleansing, grounding, protection, spirit communication

BLACK OBSIDIAN is a glassy, silica-rich volcanic rock with an amorphous structure and a hardness of 5 to 5.5. The name is derived from the name of the prominent ancient Roman, Obsius.

Black Obsidian powerfully eliminates negative energies in oneself and one's environment. It is like a psychic vacuum cleaner, cleansing the auric field of disharmony, negative attachments, astral "junk," as well as one's own anger, greed, fear, resentment, etc. It is a strong grounding stone, stimulating the root chakra to make its connection with the Earthstar chakra below the feet, and deep into the core of the Earth. It is useful for all types of scrying, including spirit communication. It is also a strong stone of spiritual protection. In addition, it helps bring one's own Shadow material out of exile, allowing it to be transmuted through the heart. It aids in recalling the exiled bits from the unconscious, even from past lives. This is a great aid to healing the body and the soul.

Black Obsidian harmonizes with Jet, Black Tourmaline and Smoky Quartz for grounding. Moldavite can raise Black Obsidian's vibration for self-transformation. Amber brings a healing influence. Alexandrite and Oregon Opal assist in using Black Obsidian to view past lives. High-vibration stones such as Phenacite, Scolecite, Natrolite and Azeztulite provide enhanced psychic abilities and a high spiritual focus to one's work with Black Obsidian.

OBSIDIAN, SNOWFLAKE

KEY WORDS Perseverance, insight, attunement to spiritual guidance, past-life recall, spirit communication **CHAKRAS** Root (1st), Third Eye (6th) **ELEMENT** Earth **PHYSICAL** Supports spiritual healing of cancer, encourages receptivity to healing **EMOTIONAL** Helps one dispel "victim consciousness," inspires belief in oneself **SPIRITUAL** Increases psychic sensitivity, past-life recall, awareness of synchronicities

SNOWFLAKE OBSIDIAN is a glassy, silica-rich volcanic rock with an amorphous structure and a hardness of 5 to 5.5. It is black with whitish spots. It is named after the prominent ancient Roman, Obsius.

Snowflake Obsidian enables one to make the best of a bad situation by clearing negative and self-defeating thoughts and inspiring one with new ideas that can improve one's condition. It grounds one's thinking, eliminating energy-draining fantasy. It increases one's psychic sensitivity, making one more able to notice meaningful synchronicities that can point the way to one's higher path. Meditating with Snowflake Obsidian can put one in touch with the world of souls, facilitating communication with lost loved ones. It also attunes one to memories of past lives or to forgotten events of the present life, focusing in on the recall of events that relate to present difficulties. In such recall lies the key to the insights that will allow one to overcome and release the problems.

Snowflake Obsidian works most synergistically with Magnesite, which enhances attunement with higher realms. Zincite strengthens the lower chakras, where imbalances may be exposed by working with Snowflake Obsidian. Lapis Lazuli, Iolite, Siberian Blue Quartz, Scolecite and Herderite assist in Snowflake Obsidian's enhancement of psychic ability.

OBSIDIAN, MAHOGANY

KEY WORDS Release from inner limitations, healing feelings of unworthiness **CHAKRAS** Root (1st), Sexual/Creative (2nd) **ELEMENT** Earth
PHYSICAL Energetically supports liver and kidney functions, aids in detoxification **EMOTIONAL** Facilitates healing unconsciously held shame, encourages self-love **SPIRITUAL** Ideal for psychic protection, clearing blockages, creativity

MAHOGANY OBSIDIAN is a glassy, silica-rich volcanic rock with an amorphous structure and a hardness of 5 to 5.5. It is black with reddish brown spots. It is named after the prominent ancient Roman, Obsius.

Mahogany Obsidian can help cleanse the second chakra of negative energies and residue from old wounds. Such fixations can block the flow of one's creative energies or create problems in the full expression of one's sexuality, so it is important work to make sure this chakra operates freely. Using Mahogany Obsidian in a body layout, between the first and second chakras, one can "draw out the poison" of unconscious memories of shame, humiliation or abuse, releasing them into the Light.

Mahogany Obsidian can remove negative psychic "implants" that hold one back in other areas. It is ideal for dispelling feelings of unworthiness that hold one back from fulfilling one's potential in work, love and spiritual awakening. Carrying or wearing Mahogany Obsidian shields one from psychic attack, whether it be from nonphysical entities or other people. It's a bit like having an etheric bodyguard!

Mahogany Obsidian works harmoniously with Tibetan Black Quartz, Sugilite and Black Tourmaline, in regard to providing psychic protection. Zincite helps in healing wounds to the second chakra. Bringing in Moldavite is useful in helping one move beyond past limitations.

OBSIDIAN, RAINBOW

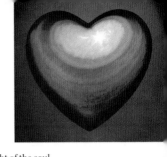

KEY WORDS Recovery from emotional wounds,
the deep journey through darkness into Light
CHAKRAS Root (1st)   **ELEMENT** Earth
PHYSICAL Facilitates removal of blocks and
attachments that can cause illness
EMOTIONAL Encourages optimism and hope,
supports the emotional body during dark times
SPIRITUAL Aids one in coming through the dark night of the soul

RAINBOW OBSIDIAN is a glassy, silica-rich volcanic rock with an amorphous structure and a hardness of 5 to 5.5. It is black with layers of iridescent color. It is named after the prominent ancient Roman, Obsius.

Rainbow Obsidian helps one take the downward journey to unexpected Light. For most human beings it is impossible to escape the prison of one's own wounded psyche without going down. This journey into the depths is as amazing as it is necessary. As one descends, one finds the forgotten pieces of oneself that have been left behind at each wounding. Reclaiming the parts and continuing downward, one may experience more emptiness and deeper darkness before suddenly bursting into Light at the very nadir of the descent. Often such journeys downward are precipitated by a crisis in one's outer life. However, meditation with Rainbow Obsidian can facilitate a more voluntary experience of the depths. Such chosen descents are usually of shorter duration than the ones brought about by crises, and they help one bring the soul closer to conscious awareness.

Rainbow Obsidian has an affinity for Rainbow Moonstone. Used together, one can maintain dual awareness, wherein a part of oneself remains in the lit world while another part takes the dark journey.

OBSIDIAN, PEACOCK

KEY WORDS Shamanic journeying, astral travel, psychic protection **CHAKRAS** Root (1st), Third Eye (6th) **ELEMENT** Earth **PHYSICAL** Helps with physical issues caused by holes in the auric field **EMOTIONAL** Inspires communion and celebration with spirit beings **SPIRITUAL** Facilitates shamanic journeying and spirit communication

Peacock obsidian is a glassy, silica-rich volcanic rock with an amorphous structure and a hardness of 5 to 5.5. It is black with swirls of iridescent color. It is named after the prominent ancient Roman, Obsius.

Peacock Obsidian's dance of iridescent colors opens the third eye to the inner world of visionary awareness. It is excellent for lucid dreaming, breath work, guided meditation and other practices of consciousness expansion. Like Rainbow Obsidian, it can show one the unexpected Light in darkness, but Peacock Obsidian is not exactly a stone of the depths. It is much more for entering the nearby planes of the astral, subtle and causal world. It is a tool for shamans and others who "walk between the worlds"—an ally for protection and clear-seeing, helping one to confidently negotiate the doorways between dimensions. Peacock Obsidian is also a stone that calls the worlds together for celebration. It is excellent for use in rituals and gatherings to which one wishes to call the ancestors, guides and helping spirits. In the other worlds, Peacock Obsidian's energies appear as undulating serpent-like patterns of vivid iridescent color, radiating in all directions from the physical stone. It draws the attention of spirit beings and attracts them. As such, it can be used when one calls upon deceased loved ones for spirit communication.

Peacock Obsidian works well with Moldavite, Shaman Stone, Prophecy Stone, Phenacite and Scolecite.

OBSIDIAN, GOLD SHEEN

KEY WORDS Healing abuse of power, activating the higher Will, enhanced manifestation **CHAKRAS** Root (1st), Solar Plexus (3rd) **ELEMENT** Earth **PHYSICAL** Supports the body in overcoming stomach and digestive issues **EMOTIONAL** Encourages self-confidence through self-knowledge **SPIRITUAL** Powerfully aids manifestation of Divine Will through oneself

GOLD SHEEN OBSIDIAN is a glassy, silica-rich volcanic rock with an amorphous structure and a hardness of 5 to 5.5. It is black with swirls of chatoyant gold. It is named after the ancient Roman, Obsius.

Gold Sheen Obsidian attunes one to the energy of the Great Central Sun through its cleansing and activation of the third chakra. The Great Central Sun could be called the Source for manifestation in the physical realm, and as such it emanates and maintains a thread of connection to the third chakra of each being in the Universe. The golden Light of the Great Central Sun is also reflected in the sparkling iridescent light of Gold Sheen Obsidian. These stones are ideal for clearing negative energies and purifying one's auric field, especially at the solar plexus. When one's channel is clear, all the way to Source, one's will is aligned with the Divine and one's power of manifestation is greatly enhanced. Gold Sheen Obsidian is useful in bringing forward one's hidden talents, and it can aid in achieving worldly success in their expression.

Gold Sheen Obsidian harmonizes well with Golden Labradorite, Heliodor, Amblygonite and Citrine, all stones of the Golden Ray. In linking one's consciousness to the Great Central Sun, Himalaya Gold Azeztulite, Satyaloka Yellow Azeztulite and North Carolina Golden Azeztulite are by far the most powerful aids. Moldavite enhances this stone's capacity to manifest one's truest and highest calling.

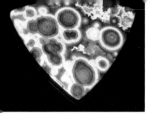

OCEAN JASPER

KEY WORDS Enjoyment of life, release of negativity and stress, relaxation, positive self-expression, physical and emotional healing   **CHAKRAS** Solar Plexus (3rd), Heart (4th), Throat (5th)   **ELEMENT** Earth
PHYSICAL Supports thyroid, adrenals, endocrine glands; aids tissue regeneration   **EMOTIONAL** Encourages high spirits, appreciation of the present moment   **SPIRITUAL** Brings clarity and centeredness, stimulates a positive attitude

OCEAN JASPER is an unusual Jasper variety found only in Madagascar. It is a silicon dioxide mineral with a hexagonal crystal system and a hardness of 6.5 to 7. Ocean Jasper's colors include vivid shades of white, green, pink, red and black. Its patterns are wild and indescribable.

Ocean Jasper is a stone of joy and high spirits. It opens one's awareness to the benevolent aspects of life and lifts one's mood. It stimulates the solar plexus, heart and throat chakras, conveying the urge to feel, speak and act positively. It supports the expression of love, and it helps one to realize what and whom one truly loves. It banishes complacency and the habit of taking one's loved ones, health, prosperity or security for granted. It brings consciousness to the present moment, relieving worry about the future or bitterness about the past. It allows for the release of stress and escapism, helping one to value the here and now. Ocean Jasper is helpful to those who suffer from depression or addictive behaviors by making them conscious of what they are doing and opening their eyes to a better reality. Using Ocean Jasper in meditation will help one let go of thoughts and become centered.

Ocean Jasper harmonizes with all types of Jasper and Quartz, as well as Amethyst, Sugilite and Charoite. Lepidolite and Amblygonite increase its relaxing influence. Strombolite can add humor to Ocean Jasper's high spirits.

ONYX

KEY WORDS Inner strength, focused attention, willpower, self-mastery, discipline, reason **CHAKRAS** Root (1st), Solar Plexus (3rd), Third Eye (6th) **ELEMENT** Earth **PHYSICAL** Aids in recovering strength and vitality after illness **EMOTIONAL** Exerts a calming influence, engenders confidence and power **SPIRITUAL** Encourages persistence, willpower; enhances mental ability

ONYX is a variety of Chalcedony, a member of the Quartz family with a hexagonal crystal system and a hardness of 7. Onyx is defined as a banded Chalcedony in which the lines of banding are parallel.

Onyx is a stone of inner strength. It enhances one's endurance and persistence, enabling one to carry even difficult and dreary tasks through to completion. It increases one's ability to maintain mental focus, allowing one to learn challenging new material and use well all that one has mastered. It energetically boosts the retention of memory and encourages attention to detail. Onyx is also a stone of physical strength. It assists one in containing one's energies rather than allowing them to dissipate. It helps one to gradually build up one's vitality. Onyx emanates the energy of self-mastery. It can help one to control, focus and direct the will, and this brings about a considerable increase in one's personal power. It assists one in learning that the most important control is self-control. Onyx cools and condenses excessive energies. It calms nervousness, quells anxiety, soothes hot tempers and brings reason to passion.

Onyx is a good grounding influence when one is meditating with high-energy stones. It works well with other stones by consolidating their energies. It helps one integrate spiritual insights. With Phenacite, Azeztulite and other visionary stones, it aids in grounding their benefits in the physical world.

OPAL, COMMON

KEY WORDS White: Purification, Pink: Emotional healing, Blue: Calming the mind, Brown and Black: Emotional protection **CHAKRAS** White: Crown (7th), Pink: Heart (4th), Blue: Throat and Third Eye (5th and 6th), Brown and Black: Root and Sexual: Creative (1st and 2nd) **ELEMENT** Earth, Water **PHYSICAL** All colors gently aid in various healing processes **EMOTIONAL** Works to support and heal the emotional body **SPIRITUAL** Opens one to Spirit through healing of wounds to the soul

C OMMON OPAL, a hydrated silica material with a hardness of 5.5 to 6.5, may be any of several different colors, but it is generally opaque and does not show any of the "fire" exhibited by precious Opal.

Common Opal vibrates at a lower frequency and gentler intensity than the transparent Opals and/or fiery Opals, and this enhances its calming and soothing effects on the emotional body. Common Opal in all of its colors is a stone of gentle energies. White Opal provides purification of one's energy field, cleansing and rebalancing the chakras of the etheric body and support for their connection to one's physical self. Pink Opal is for healing the emotions, especially those connected with subconsciously held pain. Blue Opal is an antidote to restless thoughts. If one tends to wake up at night with the mind racing, a Blue Opal in the pillowcase will help one sleep more peacefully. It can enhance the recollection of one's dreams, and can bring about more pleasant dream experiences. It assists one in communicating one's feelings. Brown and Black Common Opals are gentle catalysts to the physical healing process through their support of one's emotional body. They can aid in lifting depression through moderating the sense of isolation. They can help one receive more life force and creative energies through gently stimulating the first two chakras.

OPAL, WHITE PRECIOUS

KEY WORDS Intensification of emotions, purification
CHAKRAS All **ELEMENT** Water **PHYSICAL** Supports
healing through release of negative patterns, aids with skin
issues **EMOTIONAL** Powerfully stimulates emotional
clearing and healing **SPIRITUAL** Facilitates inner
cleansing that leads to link with the Higher Self

WHITE PRECIOUS OPAL, a hydrated silica material with a hardness of 5.5 to 6.5, is the best-known Opal and the most widely used in jewelry. Its milky background color sets off the multicolored fire in a very attractive way. The bulk of White Precious Opals come from Australia.

White Precious Opal carries a seed of the "holy fire," the intense spiritual energy that consumes the impure aspects of the self without necessarily "burning" us. The more willing we are to release our attachments to our angers, fears or other negative patterns, the better it can work. If we stubbornly hold on, of course, the release of even unhealthy energies can feel quite painful. White Precious Opal is an emotional amplifier—it can intensify both the positive and negative states. In each case, there is a benefit. With positive emotions, the reward is obvious. But with negative feelings, the magnification can make one fully aware of the destruction such indulgences can bring about—and this helps one agree to release them. White Precious Opal can be a warm, friendly teacher or a severe one. It all depends on what we bring with us to the experience.

White Precious Opal works well with all other kinds of Opal, amplifying their effects. It enhances the energies of Quartz, Amethyst, Citrine, Jaspers and Chalcedonies. With Lapis Lazuli, it can awaken the inner King or Queen. With Seriphos Green Quartz, it attunes one to goddess energies. With Zincite, it lends intensity to sexuality and creativity.

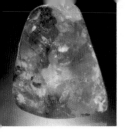

OPAL, BLACK PRECIOUS

KEY WORDS Manifestation of one's intention, amplification of emotions, revealing and releasing psychic wounds **CHAKRAS** Root (1st), Crown (7th) **ELEMENT** Storm **PHYSICAL** Supports healing (especially cysts or tumors) through release of past trauma **EMOTIONAL** Aids in release of one's deepest fears **SPIRITUAL** Supports one in finding the Light in the dark parts of the Self

Bʟᴀᴄᴋ ᴘʀᴇᴄɪᴏᴜꜱ ᴏᴘᴀʟ, a hydrated silica material with a hardness of 5.5 to 6.5, is a fiery opal with base color of black, dark gray or dark blue-gray. Most of it is found in Lightning Ridge, Australia.

Black Precious Opal is a stone of magic and mystery. It stimulates and links the root and crown chakras, assisting one in connecting one's highest spiritual aspirations with one's physical life. Black Precious Opal is a powerful magnifier of one's intention, especially if that intention carries an emotional charge. In fact, one is cautioned to make one's intentions conscious, because Black Precious Opal works so powerfully that one might manifest an outcome one does not consciously want! Black Precious Opal is excellent for those doing deep inner work. In meditation, it can take one into the roots of the psyche, allowing the release of traumatic memories of past experiences that may now be governing a part of one's life. These stones are useful in soul retrieval and past-life recall, and once again, they assist one in finding and releasing negative experiences that are holding one back.

Moldavite and/or Amethyst can be combined with Black Precious Opal for spiritual protection. Strombolite, Muscovite and Ocean Jasper will all help keep one's emotional and mental states in positive territory. Phenacite, Danburite and Azeztulite can help to assure the manifestation of one's highest spiritual potential.

OPAL, FIRE

KEY WORDS Passion, creativity **CHAKRAS** Sexual/Creative (2nd) **ELEMENT** Fire **PHYSICAL** Supports the reproductive systems, increases vitality and energy **EMOTIONAL** Encourages attitude of optimism, playfulness, zest for life **SPIRITUAL** Stimulates energies of creativity, passion, manifestation, sexuality

FIRE OPAL, a hydrated silica material with a hardness of 5.5 to 6.5, is named after its vivid orange color. It does not usually opalesce, but it is sometimes clear enough to make into faceted gems, and these can be strikingly beautiful. The largest sources of Fire Opal are in Mexico, but deposits have been found in Brazil, Guatemala, Honduras, Turkey, Australia and the USA.

Fire Opal is an awakener of passion. One's passion can be channeled in many directions, from the bodily desires to the spiritually sublime. Whatever one's choice, Fire Opal will enhance the intensity and the pleasure of the experience. In matters of sexuality, the Opal connection to the emotional body will help blend more love into the experience. In situations where shyness, fear or shame hold one back, Fire Opal will ease one's inhibitions and allow for greater enjoyment and less self-consciousness.

In the spiritual domain, Fire Opal can enhance the passionate pursuit of enlightenment. It can help engender the state in which many famous spiritual seekers in history have made the deity the goal of their love and longing. It has been said that in matters of spiritual growth, "It is the intensity of the longing that does the work." If one uses or wears Fire Opal during meditation and prayer, one may find the emotional intensity of the experience has been turned up several notches.

OPAL, OREGON

KEY WORDS Joy, self-expression, imagination
CHAKRAS Solar Plexus (3rd), Heart (4th), Crown (7th)
ELEMENT Fire   **PHYSICAL** Aids in healing through release of past-life issues, supports kidneys
EMOTIONAL Encourages dwelling in a state of joy, releasing past wounds   **SPIRITUAL** Facilitates discovery of past-life patterns that hold one back

OREGON OPAL, a hydrated silica material with a hardness of 5.5 to 6.5, is found only in Opal Butte, Oregon, USA. It was accidentally discovered there by a shepherd over 100 years ago. It is mostly transparent with a bluish tinge, but can be reddish or yellow. It rarely displays "fire."

Oregon Opal allows for the joyful experience and expression of the emotions and imagination. It encourages one to act upon one's desires in a loving way. Oregon Opal connects one to the joyful side of the emotional experience, while enabling one to integrate and release old wounds. Oregon Opal can be a key for unlocking the secrets of past lives. It also activates the "inner radar" which guides one to the life or lives one most needs to review in order to understand difficulties in the current life. This is especially true in instances in which one's present problems are echoes or repetitions of past-life patterns. Oregon Opal's energy of joyful acceptance allows one to comprehend and release such recurring issues and move forward in freedom and clarity.

Oregon Opal is related to the Fire element, and so encourages one to transmute any negativity one may encounter into useful energy. It is said that emotion is the doorway to spiritual experience and inner growth. For those who wish to enter it, Oregon Opal can be a key. It is also said that when we feel the most joy we are closest to truth. Oregon Opal can be a conduit to the truth of our essential joy.

OPAL, OWYHEE BLUE

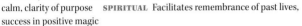

KEY WORDS Quiet strength, calm confidence, decisiveness, inner exploration, amplification of positive emotions, psychic protection **CHAKRAS** Throat (5th), Third Eye (6th), Solar Plexus (3rd) **ELEMENT** Water **PHYSICAL** Helps with throat issues, such as laryngitis, sore throat, thyroid **EMOTIONAL** Encourages self-confidence, calm, clarity of purpose **SPIRITUAL** Facilitates remembrance of past lives, success in positive magic

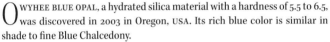

OWYHEE BLUE OPAL, a hydrated silica material with a hardness of 5.5 to 6.5, was discovered in 2003 in Oregon, USA. Its rich blue color is similar in shade to fine Blue Chalcedony.

Owyhee Blue Opal combines the pure Blue Ray of the throat chakra and third eye with subtle golden highlights, which activate the solar plexus. Thus they wed the powers of perception, expression and will, enabling the user to see, speak and act with clarity, authority and confidence. These stones are an antidote to indecisiveness, shyness, fear, powerlessness, confusion, inarticulateness and many other expressions of blocked energies. Owyhee Blue Opals are stones of calm, quiet strength, allowing one to choose words, action or inaction as the best means of achieving one's purpose. These are stones of deep memory, parting the veil separating one from awareness of past incarnations. They can also be used as talismans for all types of positive magic. Owyhee Blue Opal enhances one's experience of positive emotions but does not magnify negativity. In fact, this stone acts as a protection from psychic attack or the intrusion of astral energies and entities. In addition, it aids in lucid dreaming, shamanic journeying and communication with spirit beings.

Owyhee Blue Opal combines well with white Oregon Opal, Moldavite, Herderite, Black Precious Opal and Andean Pink and Blue Opals.

OPAL, LEMURIAN GOLDEN

KEY WORDS Integration of mental and emotional bodies, recalling Lemurian consciousness, dissolving inner walls and psychological boundaries **CHAKRAS** Crown (7th), Third Eye (6th), Heart (4th) **ELEMENT** Water, Air **PHYSICAL** Calms the body on a cellular level, aids stress relief **EMOTIONAL** Increases empathy, dispels loneliness, calms turbulent feelings **SPIRITUAL** Attunes one to Lemuria and gives access to its spiritual gifts

LEMURIAN GOLDEN OPAL is a hydrated silica material with a hardness of 5.5 to 6.5. The color is butterscotch yellow. These stones are found only in Madagascar.

Lemurian Golden Opal, more than any other stone, can take the inward journeyer back to the living memory of Lemuria in the Akashic records. One may see images of temples with round green domes, and semitransparent people. One may feel the air permeated by swirling currents of psychic impressions. Intuitive people meditating with Lemurian Golden Opal can do much fruitful inner research into the story of Lemuria, which can help us in these times. These stones can assist us in developing the inner capacities of telepathy, clairvoyance, empathy and prophecy that prevailed in Lemurian times. Lemurian Golden Opal allows one to relax and feel the flow of life, letting go of stress. It can aid in manifesting dreams, and it helps one move easily into deep states of meditation. It facilitates lucid dreaming and enhances memory of dreams. It can help one work spiritually to overcome sleep disorders. It instills calm and a pervasive sense of trust. Lemurian Golden Opal works well with Rosophia and Morganite. Lemurian Aquatine Calcite can enhance its deepening of psychic abilities and the memory of Lemuria. Oregon Opal enhances one's capacity to recall past lives, perhaps in ancient Lemuria.

OPAL, VIOLET FLAME

KEY WORDS Spiritual and energetic purification, emotional balance, angelic communication, link to the Violet Flame **CHAKRAS** All,
especially Crown (7th) **ELEMENTS** Water, Wind, Storm **PHYSICAL** Facilitates
release of stress, allowing the body to be guided by its innate wisdom **EMOTIONAL**
Brings emotional harmony to the cells and the etheric body **SPIRITUAL** Cleanses
and purifies etheric body and cellular energy matrix, enhances connection with
angelic beings, stimulates visionary experience

VIOLET FLAME OPAL is a purple-and-white Opal discovered in Mexico in
2011. It displays amazing and beautiful patterns of white with purple
ranging from pale lilac to indigo blue.

Violet Flame Opal soothes the emotional body, and brings tranquility to
the Liquid Crystal Body Matrix. It exerts an influence of healing to the stresses
that can linger in the cells and organs, allowing the body's inner wisdom to
prevail. It can spiritualize the emotions, transmuting them to higher forms
of feeling. It stimulates spiritual awareness and facilitates communication
with guardian angels and helping spirits. It activates the crown and third eye
chakras, initiating visionary experience. It can cleanse and purify the etheric
body and the cellular energy matrix. Its vibrations bring harmony to these
areas and dissolve negative attachments or inner constrictions. In meditation,
Violet Flame Opal has the capacity to call down the violet flame of spiritual
fire for purification, transformation and rebirth as a Spiritual Human.

Violet Flame Opal is enhanced in its effectiveness by the presence of
Moldavite, Azeztulite, Amethyst and especially Sauralite Azeztulite with
Amethyst. It also resonates powerfully with Auralite-23. Because of its own
high-frequency vibrations, Violet Flame Opal harmonizes readily with all
Azozeo super-activated stones.

PAKULITE

KEY WORDS Grounding at high energy, Life Force, creativity, personal power, sexual energies, youthfulness, intimate relationship with the Divine Feminine Earth **CHAKRAS** Root (1st), Sexual/Creative (2nd), Solar Plexus (3rd) **ELEMENTS** Earth, Fire **PHYSICAL** Supports the liver, kidneys, bladder and sexual organs **EMOTIONAL** Enhances one's optimism, humor, playfulness, self-confidence and eagerness for new adventures **SPIRITUAL** Arouses Life Force, creativity, will, persistence and personal power, facilitates relationship with the Spiritual Earth

PAKULITE is a spherulitic rhyolite found at Mount Paku, New Zealand. It is also called New Zealand Chrysanthemum Stone. Created by cooling lava, it is crystallized with radiating clusters of feldspars and quartz.

Pakulite is something of a sexy rock. It stimulates all three of the lower chakras, arousing one's Life Force energies, creativity and power. It can help artists find inspiration, and can benefit one's love relationship through its vibration of intimacy. It kindles the fires of will and persistence. It provides grounding at high levels of energy, and engenders a conscious, intimate relationship with Gaia. Pakulite stimulates youthfulness, vitality, optimism, humor, playfulness and eagerness for new adventures. It arouses a relaxed sense of self-confidence, and the desire to offer comradeship to others. In spiritual self-healing, Pakulite supports one's energy level, and boosts the immune system with an flood of vitality. It supports the liver, kidneys, bladder and sexual organs. For men, carrying or wearing a Pakulite can help dispel issues causing impotence. For women, it energetically protects the ovaries.

Pakulite vibrates harmoniously with Peridot, Amulet Stone, Moldavite, Phenacite, Revelation Stone, Empowerite, Sauralite Azeztulite, Honey and Cream Azeztulite, Moonlight Agate and New Zealand Carnelian.

PAPAGOITE

KEY WORDS Return to a state of grace, link with higher dimensions, transmutation of sorrow, crystallization of consciousness beyond the body **CHAKRAS** Third Eye (6th), Crown (7th), Etheric (8th–14th) **ELEMENT** Wind **PHYSICAL** Relief of pain from migraines, menstrual cramps, stress issues **EMOTIONAL** Aids with transmuting negative emotions into positive ones **SPIRITUAL** Stimulates the etheric body, awakens the Merkabah Vehicle

PAPAGOITE is a copper-based mineral with a rich blue color. It can occur in crusts or thin veins, or as an inclusion. Papagoite occurs as inclusions in Quartz crystals from Messina, South Africa.

Papagoites are stone of the inner Garden of Eden. When one holds a Papagoite crystal to the head, it is possible to enter a paradisal state. There is a great sense of expansion of awareness and a powerful joy and serenity pervading one's entire auric field. One feels complete and somehow far greater than in normal awareness. Just as its cousin Ajoite is known for transforming negative energy into positive, so Papagoite seems to transform sorrow into happiness. Papagoite also activates one's psychic abilities and facilitates such activities as out-of-body travel. It stimulates the third eye chakra and enhances all the intuitive capacities. If one continues to work with Papagoite, one will experience the opening of the crown chakra and ultimately its linkage to the nonphysical chakras in the etheric body. Papagoite assists one in building the Merkabah Vehicle of Light. Through this, oneness with All-That-Is can be experienced.

Papagoite works wonderfully with its cousin, Ajoite. It also harmonizes with Merkabite Calcite, Natrolite, Scolecite, Celestite, Satyaloka Azeztulite, White Azeztulite, Danburite, Herderite, Brookite, Tibetan Black Quartz and Lithium Quartz.

PERIDOT

KEY WORDS Increase prosperity, warmth, well-being **CHAKRAS** Solar Plexus (3rd), Heart (4th) **ELEMENT** Earth **PHYSICAL** Supports the heart and circulatory system, can be used to help one quit smoking **EMOTIONAL** Emanates sense of well-being, helps one feel worthy and happy **SPIRITUAL** Aids in creating abundance, quiets spiritual fear, inspires generosity

PERIDOT is a magnesium iron silicate with an orthorhombic crystal system and a hardness of 7. Its olive to lime green color is caused by iron. Major sources are Pakistan, Brazil, Australia and the USA.

Peridots are little green nuggets of positive power. Their vibration brings an inner sense of warmth and well-being, like sunshine on a spring day. Peridots help one activate and harmonize the third and fourth chakras, creating an integration of Love and Will. They can assist us in having the courage to act out our heart's desires, and to be generous to others, even as we pursue our individual destinies. Peridot is a stone of financial and spiritual abundance, and it can aid in attracting and creating our most important inner visions.

Peridot can be used to bless and energize one's work, whether it be tending one's garden, raising children, working as a healer, building a business or assisting others in such activities. It is a tool for helping to bring physical reality into alignment with one's inner truth. This includes success and abundance in one's career endeavors, if one is doing one's right work, and if one believes oneself to be deserving of success. Peridot can assist one in reestablishing a sense of self-worth if one is plagued by guilt or regret for past deeds. It quiets spiritual fears and allows one to move forward on one's evolutionary path. It supports one in taking responsibility and making amends for any suffering one may have caused.

PETALITE

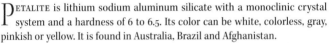

KEY WORDS Tranquillity, upliftment, expansion of
awareness, manifesting, the spiritual in the physical,
opening to the higher worlds   **CHAKRAS** Third
Eye (6th), Crown (7th), Etheric (8th–14th)
ELEMENT Wind   **PHYSICAL** Offers spiritual aid
for stress relief, lowering high blood pressure, calming hyperactivity and mania
EMOTIONAL Soothes the emotional body, supports healing of abuse issues
SPIRITUAL Ideal for attuning to higher dimensions, expanding awareness

PETALITE is lithium sodium aluminum silicate with a monoclinic crystal system and a hardness of 6 to 6.5. Its color can be white, colorless, gray, pinkish or yellow. It is found in Australia, Brazil and Afghanistan.

Petalite has a deep connection to the realm of Spirit. It can take one to a dimension of rest and healing, allowing one to bathe in the quiet bliss of the unencumbered spirit. Petalites are also stones of vision. They can open the inner eye to the many mansions of the higher dimensions, allowing the questing mind to discover multiple new horizons. Petalite can be used to enhance all the psychic powers, such as clairvoyance and telepathy, and to help one attune to the knowledge of one's *dharma*, or path of highest destiny. Petalite also has a grounding aspect that helps one stay connected to earthly life while one explores the inner dimensions it opens. Thus it is also a stone of manifestation, helping one bring to physical reality the exalted visions one finds as one journeys to the higher worlds. Healers are advised to wear Petalite during sessions with clients and to place Petalites on the client in appropriate places, as this will help to open spiritual channels of healing.

Petalite is one of the Synergy Twelve Stones. It also works harmoniously with Merkabite Calcite, Papagoite, Elestial Calcite, Ajoite, Lepidolite, Gel Lithium Silica, Tourmaine, Amblygonite and Morganite.

PETRIFIED WOOD

KEY WORDS Steady growth, a strong body, past-life recall, inner peace **CHAKRAS** Root (1st), Third Eye (6th) **ELEMENT** Earth
PHYSICAL Supports gradual increase of strength and vitality, aids the bones
EMOTIONAL Encourages inner peace, patience; helps heal ancestral issues
SPIRITUAL Opens visionary awareness of the deep past and past lives

Petrified wood is a member of the Quartz family, a silicon dioxide mineral with a hexagonal crystal system and a hardness of 6.5 to 7. In this material, the organic wood substance has been replaced by silicon.

Petrified Wood is a stone of patience, of slow, steady growth toward the goal of spiritual transformation. It is a good stone for gradually strengthening the body. It is recommended to be carried or worn by those who need greater stability in the spine or skeletal structure. It also instills strength of character and helps one live by one's ideals. It gives one a sense of peace during times of change. Petrified Wood assists in past-life recall. It is especially useful for grounding insights one gains from experiencing these memories. It helps one turn past weaknesses into new strengths, just as the perishable wood has evolved its form into that of immortal stone. Petrified Wood carries an imprint of the "recent" history (100 to 200 million years) of the Earth, and it can be utilized to view the Akashic records of this planet. Using Petrified Wood in conjunction with other stones attuned to the deep past (e.g., Nuummite), one can gain clear visions of previous civilizations and of times before humans.

Petrified Wood harmonizes with all members of the Quartz family, especially Agate, Jasper and Chalcedony. For physical vitality and strength, Bloodstone, Red Jasper, Onyx and Carnelian are ideal allies. For past-life recall, Oregon Opal, Owyhee Blue Opal and Alexandrite are highly recommended.

PIEMONTITE

KEY WORDS Intelligence of the heart, emotional healing, commitment to life, joy, purification of the blood and bodily tissues, Light Body activation **CHAKRA** Heart (4th) **ELEMENTS** Water, Earth, Wind **PHYSICAL** Supports the heart and circulatory system, aids in clearing the cells of toxic energies **EMOTIONAL** Dispels negative emotions, increases one's goodhearted enthusiasm for life **SPIRITUAL** Enhances consciousness of the heart, facilitates communion of mind and heart, helps heal and align one's energies, supports the formation of the Body of Light

PIEMONTITE is a sorosilicate mineral with a monoclinic crystal system and a hardness of 6 to 6.5. It was named after the Piemonte region of Italy. It is usually a dark-red color, and is often mixed with quartz or other minerals.

The currents of Piemontite move directly to the heart, filling it with strength, courage and a sense of purpose. These stones have the capacity to bring forth the heart's innate intelligence, helping one understand the heart's way of thinking. They can heal the heart of grief and rekindle one's commitment to life. Piemontite's heart-strengthening capacities can give rise to a great upwelling of joy. The vibrations of Piemontite are so life-affirming that they can shift the patterns within the Liquid Crystal Body Matrix, through the heart's influence on the blood as it passes through. Piemontite supports oxygenation of the body and stimulates the clearing-away of toxins. It is an ideal partner for those working to heal and align all the energetic levels of the self, ultimately creating the Body of Light. On more mundane levels, Piemontite's currents offer a dose of enthusiasm for our lives and relationships, increasing our sense of fun and helping us to remember the adventure of being human.

Piemontite works in synergy with Moldavite and Azeztulite, and with Astaraline, which provides an energetic cocoon for Piemontite's Light Body activation.

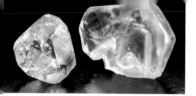

PHENACITE

KEY WORDS Third eye activation,
inner visions, awakening the Light Body,
interdimensional travel   **CHAKRAS** Third
Eye (6th), Crown (7th)   **ELEMENT** Storm

PHYSICAL Aids healing of nerve damage and nervous system disorders
EMOTIONAL Helps one find the courage to lead a spirit-centered life
SPIRITUAL Catalyzes multiple experiences of spiritual initiation

Phenacite is a beryllium silicate with a hexagonal crystal system and a hardness of 7.5 to 8. It varies greatly in form from one location to another. Phenacite has been found in Brazil, Madagascar, Mexico, Zimbabwe, Zambia, Norway, Russia, Tanzania, Switzerland and the USA.

Phenacites can activate one's third eye, crown chakra and inner-visioning capacities. They are highly beneficial for Light Body activation and are the best stones for interdimensional travel. They can give instant cleansing to the auric field, and can be used as conduits for communication with spirit guides, angelic beings and other entities of the higher domains. In working with Phenacites, one may undergo a series of initiatory experiences, each one serving as a platform from which to launch one's consciousness to a higher level. Phenacite is the supreme stone of the third eye chakra. Its pulsing energies are so strong they can be felt at the third eye, even by people not normally sensitive to crystal energies. It opens the interdimensional portals for inner journeying, allowing one's consciousness to plunge through unending corridors of sacred geometric forms. It can also be used to awaken the latent special capacities housed in the prefrontal lobes of the brain. This can sometimes bring spontaneous experiences of telepathy, psychokinesis, prophetic vision or remote viewing. Phenacite can raise the vibrational frequencies of almost any other stone.

PIETERSITE

KEY WORDS Insight, intuition, increased power of the will, precognition, interdimensional travel, self-transformation **CHAKRAS** Solar Plexus (3rd), Third Eye (6th) **ELEMENT** Storm **PHYSICAL** Increases mental and physical energies, enhances overall vitality **EMOTIONAL** Empowers the will and lends self-confidence and fearlessness **SPIRITUAL** Highly spiritually activating, catalyzes peak experiences, powerful aid to manifestation

PIETERSITE is a silicon dioxide mineral with a hexagonal crystal system and a hardness of 7. It has dramatic colors of gold, brown, gray, blue-gray and black. Pietersite is found in South Africa and China.

Pietersite creates a unified activation of the solar plexus and third eye chakras, engendering a powerful increase in the energy of the will and in one's intuitive capabilities. Under the influence of Pietersite, one's keen insights into the nature of situations lead to decisive actions. With Pietersite's gift of increased power, the likelihood is high that one will achieve one's aims. As Pietersite stimulates the third eye, one's vision expands into an awareness of the future. Readers of tarot or other oracles will find their vision sharper and their predictions more exact. Many users of Pietersite will feel an increase in the frequency of telepathic knowing. Pietersite is an excellent aid in interdimensional travel, because the empowered will can choose the direction of one's inner journeys. Pietersite enhances clarity of thought and encourages intuitive leaps. Sometimes the epiphanies seeded by Pietersite can lead to the state of *samadhi,* or spontaneous blissful enlightenment.

Pietersite harmonizes with Moldavite, Phenacite, Natrolite, Merkabite Calcite, Scolecite, Nuummite, Libyan Gold Tektite, Heliodor, Golden Labradorite, Tiger Eye, Moonstone, Sunstone and Labradorite.

PRASIOLITE
(GREEN AMETHYST)

KEY WORDS Awakening the heart, linking the lower and higher self, deep connection with Nature **CHAKRAS** Heart (4th), Crown (7th), Third Eye (6th), Solar Plexus (3rd) **ELEMENT** Earth **PHYSICAL** Supports the stomach and the heart, aids with digestive issues **EMOTIONAL** Facilitates the joy of seeing the Divine in oneself and others **SPIRITUAL** Initiates one's experience of the Higher Self

P RASIOLITE (Green Amethyst) is a silicon dioxide crystal with a hexagonal crystal system and a hardness of 7. Its name derives from the Greek word meaning "leek." It is found in Brazil and in Arizona, USA.

Prasiolite carries the energetic link between the heart and crown chakras, and it can be a catalyst for the identification with the spiritual Higher Self. Through purple Amethyst's association with the crown chakra and psychic protection, combined with Prasiolite's activation of the healing vibrations of the heart, there is the potential for a unifying experience in which one opens with full mind and heart to the experience of the Divine. Prasiolite assists in bringing spiritual ideals into expression in everyday life. It reminds one to love and bless others, seeing through their human foibles to the Divine essence within them. It is a stone of *namaste,* the recognition of the Divine spark within all beings. It helps one remain aware of this truth—a shift of focus which allows one to transcend the temptations of judgment and nega-tivity. In essence, it facilitates one's "walking the talk" of spirituality.

Combining Prasiolite with purple Amethyst amplifies one's connection to the higher spiritual realms. Prasiolite also harmonizes with Danburite, creating a link with the angelic domain and facilitating Light Body activation. Adding Moldavite increases the speed of spiritual transformation.

PREHNITE

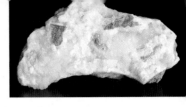

KEY WORDS Inner peace, union of the heart and the will, communication with non-physical beings **CHAKRAS** Solar Plexus (3rd), Heart (4th) **ELEMENT** Earth, Water
PHYSICAL Supports digestive, circulatory, lymphatic and urinary systems
EMOTIONAL Brings peaceful awareness, dispels worry and restlessness
SPIRITUAL Attunes one to higher dimensions through heart awareness

PREHNITE is a calcium aluminum silicate mineral with an orthorhombic crystal system and a hardness of 6 to 6.5. The color is usually yellow-green. Prehnite is found in Australia, China and New Jersey, USA.

Prehnite links the heart with the will, so one's power is used to carry out the prompting of the heart. One's actions take on the colorations of peace, and one's desires are in alignment with the highest good possible in each situation. Prehnite quiets restlessness, nervousness and worry. It helps one stay in the present moment and avoid the unhealthy use of the imagination (e.g., visualizing all the disastrous possible futures!). Prehnite reminds one of the existence of one's personal power at the same time it invokes the use of that power in the service of love. Prehnite aids in contact with beings from other dimensions. Using this stone in meditation, one can learn to "hear" the currents of angelic communication, the guidance of spirit beings or the song of one's own Higher Self. Prehnite can also help psychics and intuitive readers be more accurate in their predictions. Prehnite is a purifier for the energies of the digestive system, as well as the kidneys, adrenals, liver and gallbladder.

Prehnite harmonizes with Adamite, Jade, Smithsonite, Hemimorphite, Blue Aragonite, Libyan Gold Tektite, Heliodor, Emerald, Moldavite, Natrolite, Scolecite, Herderite, Lilac Lepidolite and all Azeztulites.

PROPHECY STONE

KEY WORDS Grounding spiritual Light in the physical self and the world, seeing prophetic visions **CHAKRAS** Soul Star (8th), Crown (7th), Third Eye (6th), Earthstar (below the feet) **ELEMENT** Earth **PHYSICAL** Clears the body of excess energy, removes energy blockages **EMOTIONAL** Allows one to feel the Earth's joy at receiving spiritual Light **SPIRITUAL** Aids one in Earth healing, stimulates capacity of prescience

Prophecy stone is a rare and odd stone found in the Sahara desert. It appears to be a concretion containing iron and other minerals. They were named by the man who discovered them, after he experienced what he termed a "prophetic vision" while meditating with one of them.

Prophecy Stones are perhaps the most powerful of all minerals for grounding Light energy in the physical body. When one holds one of these stones, a great deal of energy comes in through the crown chakra, filling the body all the way down through the soles of the feet. This grounding of spiritual Light can heal both oneself and the Earth, and is hugely important in these times.

True to its name, Prophecy Stone can catalyze visions of probable futures. To experience these, one must usually work with it in meditation regularly for some weeks, although sensitive individuals may receive the visions much sooner. Often, the initial experiences are fragmentary, though their vividness and completeness increases with practice.

Prophecy Stone harmonizes especially well with Moldavite and the Azeztulites, which can bring through even more Light energy. Shaman Stones, Master Shamanite and Nuummite help with grounding the energy. Herkimer "Diamonds" and Phenacite enhance its visionary traits.

PURPURITE

KEY WORDS Purification, initiation, freedom, insight, truth, power, sovereignty
CHAKRAS Crown (7th), Third Eye (6th)
ELEMENT Wind, Earth
PHYSICAL Supports the brain and nervous system, helps one bring more spiritual Light into the body **EMOTIONAL** Encourages the release of fear, stress and worry; helps one find spiritual certainty **SPIRITUAL** Links one with spirit guides, increases one's capacity to understand oracles

PURPURITE is a manganese iron phosphate with an orthorhombic crystal system and a hardness of 4.5 to 5. Purpurite's name is derived from its vivid purple color. The best specimens are found in Namibia.

Purpurite is one of the purest stones of the Violet Ray, offering purification of one's energy fields and meridians. It can activate the crown chakra, opening one to the spiritual realms. It emanates an energy of psychic protection, keeping one's auric field free of negative entities and attachments. Purpurite is a stone of initiation, helping one make a conscious connection with one's spirit guides and to hear their advice more clearly. It teaches one to love the unknown and to be at home in an indeterminate future. It helps one find the courage to leave behind one's familiar sense of self and to seek the spiritual promise of a greater identity. Purpurite is a stone of insight and truth. It helps one keep digging for the reality that underlies appearances. It allows those who utilize oracles such as the tarot or *I Ching* to more clearly understand their guidance. It reveals the deceptions of others, and it makes one incapable of consciously deceiving them. Purpurite is a stone of the "royal self," initiating within oneself the desire to claim one's power and use it wisely.

Purpurite harmonizes with Amethyst, Sugilite and Charoite, Lilac Lepidolite, Golden Labradorite and Heliodor.

PYRITE

KEY WORDS Masculine energy, manifestation, action, vitality, willpower, creativity, confidence
CHAKRAS Solar Plexus (3rd)
ELEMENT Earth   **PHYSICAL** Supports male reproductive health, aids in fighting infection   **EMOTIONAL** Encourages mastering fear and taking assertive action
SPIRITUAL Promotes positive attitude and strong resolve, banishes negativity

PYRITE is an iron sulfide mineral with a cubic or octahedral crystal system and a hardness of 6 to 6.5. Its name is derived from the Greek word for fire. Important deposits are in Italy, Spain and Peru.

Pyrite is excellent for increasing the power of the third chakra in both men and women. It imparts an immediate increase in vitality. It enhances willpower, assisting one in overcoming bad habits and establishing new patterns of health and positive energy. It aids one in overcoming anxiety and helps one establish a "can-do" attitude about whatever one has decided to attempt. It can screen out negative influences and give one the courage to banish them. Pyrite can be a helpful tool for balancing polarities and creating harmony within the auric field. Pyrite stimulates creativity in art, mathematics, sculpture, architecture, science and other disciplines. It feeds the qualities of ambition, commitment and persistence. It increases mental clarity and focus. It supports one in taking assertive action and developing the inner warrior for the benefit of the community. For men, it enhances masculinity and supports the sublime and enthusiastic expression of male eroticism.

Pyrite harmonizes with Zincite and Carnelian for male sexuality. Prehnite, Heliodor, Libyan Gold Tektite, Golden Labradorite and Citrine help Pyrite strengthen third chakra energies. For grounding purposes, Pyrite's ideal companion is Hematite.

PYROMORPHITE

KEY WORDS Enhanced digestion and assimilation, discharge of toxic substances and energies, blending love and will   **CHAKRAS** Solar Plexus (3rd), Heart (4th)
ELEMENT Earth   **PHYSICAL** Supports digestive system, liver, gallbladder, spleen, pancreas
EMOTIONAL Increases understanding of intuition, helps one tolerate ambient negativity without ill effects
SPIRITUAL Facilitates unification of heart (love) and solar plexus (will)

PYROMORPHITE is a lead phosphate mineral with a hexagonal crystal system and a hardness of 3.5 to 4. Its color is usually pea green. Good crystals are found in Germany, England, Australia and the USA.

Pyromorphite is a stone of the viscera. It can energetically support proper digestion and assimilation of food and maintenance of the proper flora in the intestinal tract. It vibrationally cleanses the large intestine, assisting in the elimination of waste products. Pyromorphite enhances the intuitive powers of the physical and etheric bodies, so one receives accurate "gut feelings" about other people and situations. It helps one digest and assimilate new information and energies on both mental and spiritual levels. It aids in eliminating bad habits and negative associations. It allows one to be more aware and appreciative of the body. Pyromorphite supports the liver, gallbladder, spleen and pancreas. On related psychological levels, it helps one calm anger and discharge negative thoughts. It allows one to tolerate a degree of toxicity among the people in one's environment without being detrimentally affected. Pyromorphite is a stone of the solar plexus and heart chakras. It aligns and blends love and will. It is powerful for the practice of benevolent magic.

Pyromorphite works harmoniously with Pyrite, Heliodor, Golden Labradorite, Doptase, Emerald, Morganite and Zincite.

QUARTZ, CLEAR

KEY WORDS Programmability, amplification of one's intention, magnification of ambient energies, clearing, cleansing, healing, memory   **CHAKRAS** All
ELEMENT Storm   **PHYSICAL** Offers support for the nervous system, can be programmed to assist in any type of healing   **EMOTIONAL** Can be used to intensify feelings and/or heal the emotional body
SPIRITUAL Enhances one's clarity, aids communication with spirit guides

C LEAR QUARTZ (aka Rock Crystal) is a silicon dioxide crystal with a hexagonal crystal system and a hardness of 7. It is among the most abundant of minerals, and is found on every continent.

Clear Quartz is by far the most versatile and multidimensional stone in the mineral realm. Three of its key properties are energy amplification, programmability and memory. Clear Quartz is also a stone of Light, bringing heightened spiritual awareness to whoever wears, carries or meditates with it. It provides a clear corridor for the higher vibrational frequencies of the realm of Spirit. Clear Quartz can be used to amplify the energies of other stones. It is the perfect base material for energy tools such as wands, staffs, templates, etc. Clear Quartz crystals are also ideal for making "energy grids"— patterned layouts of crystals on the ground or floor, within which one can sit or lie in order to receive the energies generated by the combination of the Quartz and the geometric form of the grid. Clear Quartz can be used for almost any metaphysical purpose, including healing, consciousness expansion, chakra opening, communication with guides, past-life recall, interdimensional travel, polarity balancing, enhancement of meditation and dreaming, attracting and sending love, generating prosperity, etc.

Clear Quartz beneficially harmonizes with all other stones.

RATHBUNITE

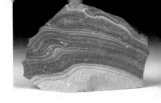

KEY WORDS Creative manifestation, fun and humor, developing psychic capacities, love, joy, pleasure and play **CHAKRAS** Solar Plexus (3rd), Heart (4th) **ELEMENTS** Earth, Water, Fire **PHYSICAL** Encourages production of endorphins, benefits the body through the positive mood it engenders **EMOTIONAL** Facilitates emotional healing, encourages playfulness and good humor **SPIRITUAL** Aids creative manifestation and development of psychic capacities, teaches lighthearted enjoyment of the spiritual path

RATHBUNITE is a type of jasper, a microcrystalline variety of quartz, with a hardness of 6.5 to 7. Its colors include reddish-brown, yellow, orange, white and gray in multi-looping stripes. It was discovered in Arizona, USA.

Rathbunite's currents are emotionally uplifting, stimulating the voice of the heart to speak from its wisdom. It enhances one's capacity to take on life's challenges with a buoyant spirit and good-natured determination. Its capacity to lift one's mood helps one to remember to see the humor in life, and it inspires wit and verbal play.

Rathbunite is a stone of creative manifestation. When placed on the solar plexus, it energizes that chakra, increasing one's capacity to focus the will to bring about a desired outcome. Rathbunite also stimulates the "sixth sense" and helps one develop latent psychic capacities.

Rathbunite's message is "Lighten up," which unexpectedly lifts one into the spiritual Light that the heart had been seeking all along. In essence, Rathbunite attunes one to love, joy, pleasure and play. If we truly embrace these qualities, we will move far along the path of enlightenment.

Rathbunite works well with Moldavite, Healerite, Azumar, Arkansas Golden Healers, Mani Stone, Revelation Stone, Empowerite and all forms of Azeztulite, including the Azozeo super-activated varieties.

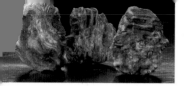

REDWOOD OPAL

KEY WORDS Emotional strength, confidence, vitality, perseverance, decisiveness, creativity, eroticism **CHAKRAS** Sexual/Creative (2nd), Solar Plexus (3rd) **ELEMENTS** Water, Fire **PHYSICAL** Supports the immune system; can increase overall energy and vitality **EMOTIONAL** Strengthens emotional body, enhances one's capacity to feel deeply without being discouraged by difficulties and sorrows; inspires confidence; encourages acceptance **SPIRITUAL** Aids in accepting ups and downs of life without disheartenment; stimulates creativity, eroticism, confidence and spiritual fortitude

Redwood Opal is the name given to a reddish-brown opal found in Mexico in 2011. It displays swirling layers of color and has a hardness of 5.5.

Redwood Opal strengthens the emotional body. It increases patience, and helps one to see things from a long-term perspective. Its strengthening of the emotional body enhances resilience to life's ups and downs, and allows one to bear grief and loss without being dragged into depression. It helps heal emotional wounds from the past, and enhances one's capacity to feel things deeply. It calms inner turbulence and brings confidence. In spiritual self-healing, Redwood Opal can be used to increase one's overall vitality and energy level. It supports the immune system, and aids one in dispelling physical problems brought on by discouragement or depression. It increases yang energies, enhancing decisiveness, inner strength and the capacity to persevere in the face of setbacks. It helps one to develop emotional endurance and forbearance. It increases erotic and creative energies. It is excellent for the first and second chakras, bringing forth powerful Life-Force energies that can be expressed through artistic endeavors, new projects or carnal love.

Redwood Opal resonates with New Zealand Carnelian, Violet Flame Opal, Owhyee Blue Opal, Vitalite and Vortexite.

REVELATION STONE

KEY WORDS Prophetic vision, psychic abilities, past-life recall, spirit communication, recovery of memory **CHAKRAS** Heart (4th), Third eye (6th) **ELEMENTS** Wind, Water, Storm **PHYSICAL** Steady healing influence to heart and brain; supports recovery of lost or suppressed memories **EMOTIONAL** Helps one to overcome fears about the future; the heart loves this stone! **SPIRITUAL** Stimulates visions of potential futures; enhances past-life recall and intuitive capacities, aids communication with departed souls; strengthens understanding between the heart and brain

REVELATION STONE is a multicolored microcrystalline quartz with a hardness of 7. It is found in remote areas of New Zealand.

Revelation Stone has a powerful resonance with the heart, and stimulates the heart's consciousness of the unfolding pattern of the future. It displays that awareness to the mind's eye as images or visions rather than words. The future one sees is not a precise, predetermined set of events, but a pattern of possibility—the potential future, or the blueprint for what may happen, depending on human choices. The pictures are readable, in much the same way one can read and decipher the I Ching or Tarot cards. It can stimulate one's innate capacity for prophetic vision by opening a channel of communication between heart awareness and mental consciousness. It is an excellent tool for anyone wishing to improve psychic capacities. It can bring vivid experiences of past-life recall, and it can enhance visionary experiences of the shamanic realms. In self-healing, it supports recovery of memories suppressed by trauma or amnesia. It also aids in releasing excessive worry or irrational fears about the future.

Revelation Stone resonates with Nirvana Quartz, Phenacite, Moldavite, New Zealand Carnelian, Vortexite and all varieties of Azeztulite.

RHODIZITE

KEY WORDS Magnification of the energies of other stones, increasing personal power and confidence **CHAKRAS** Solar Plexus (3rd) **ELEMENT** Storm **PHYSICAL** Strengthens other healing stones, supports the head and eyes **EMOTIONAL** Inspires optimism, enthusiasm, willingness to transform **SPIRITUAL** Enhances psychic ability, past-life recall, out-of-body travel

RHODIZITE is a complex borate mineral with a cubic crystal system and a hardness of 8.5. It can be colorless, white or yellow. Good quality crystals have been found in Russia and Madagascar.

Rhodizite crystals are usually small, but they vibrate with great power and intensity. They stimulate the solar plexus and are capable of increasing one's powers of will and manifestation. People carrying Rhodizite will experience a greater ability to make things happen, increasing one's self-confidence and further enhancing one's ability to manifest. Rhodizite increases the power of other stones as well. A good experiment is to try holding almost any stone until one feels its energies, getting a good sense of what the stone is doing. Next, put one or more Rhodizite crystals in the hand along with the other stone, then hold them together for a few moments. In most cases, one will experience a big increase in the power of the original stone. Rhodizite's amplification of energies can be especially helpful in healing applications. It can increase the effects of healing stones if it is touching them. Also, hands-on healers can increase the flow coming through them by using Rhodizite. Placing a Rhodizite crystal on the third eye chakra can enhance one's psychic abilities and awareness of inner guidance.

Rhodizite harmonizes with all other stones and nearly everything else. Be sure to use it only where you want the energies to intensify!

RHODOCROSITE

KEY WORDS Emotional healing, recovery of lost memories and forgotten gifts, self-love, compassion **CHAKRAS** Heart (4th), Solar Plexus (3rd) **ELEMENT** Fire, Water
PHYSICAL Helps with stress-related issues, heals the emotional body, repairs the aura **EMOTIONAL** Facilitates deep healing of inner child and past-life issues
SPIRITUAL Profound link with Love energy, enhances creativity, brings joy

RHODOCHROSITE is a manganese carbonate with a hexagonal crystal system and a hardness of 3.5 to 4. The most important deposit is in Argentina, where Rhodochrosite formed in the Incan silver mines.

Rhodochrosite is a stone of love, directed first toward the self for emotional healing. It assists in doing the necessary work of recovering, reliving and releasing the memories of one's emotional woundings. Rhodochrosite works vibrationally to support self-healing in these important areas. Through its energy of self-love and compassion for one's inner child, Rhodochrosite can be a valuable ally. It emanates currents of inner peace and self-forgiveness, allowing one to fully blossom.

Rhodochrosite can cleanse, soothe and heal the energy field around the heart. It can repair "holes" or damaged areas in the auric field, especially the emotional body. It can deepen meditations and past-life regressions. It is also a stone of joy. Taking a Rhodochrosite outdoors on a lovely day and allowing the beauty of Nature to enter one's senses, one can re-enter the sense of grace and magical happiness that are natural in the child who feels safe and loved.

Rhodochrosite harmonizes with the heart stones, including Rose Quartz, Pink Calcite, Rhodonite, Morganite, Emerald, Tsavorite Garnet and Rosophia. Moldavite can increase its intensity. It also works well with Phenacite, Alexandrite, Oregon Opal, Black Tourmaline and Jet.

RHODONITE

KEY WORDS Discovering and developing hidden talents, compassion, love, generosity, altruism **CHAKRAS** Heart (4th), Root (1st) **ELEMENT** Fire, Earth **PHYSICAL** Supports weight loss, detoxification and purification; good for liver and kidneys **EMOTIONAL** Encourages altruism and generosity, the joy of serving others **SPIRITUAL** Helps realize one's unique capacities and fulfill one's destiny

RHODONITE is a manganese metasilicate mineral with a triclinic crystal system and a hardness of 5.5 to 6.5. Its name derives from the Greek word meaning "rose red." It is now found in Sweden, Australia, India, Madagascar, Mexico, South Africa, Brazil, Canada and the USA.

Rhodonite promotes the energy of love. In this case, the love is more outer-directed than with stones such as Rhodochrosite. Rhodonite encourages using one's gifts and talents for the benefit of the community. The outer-directed love engendered by Rhodonite is one of altruism and generosity, using one's talents to bring gifts to others. This path of generosity often offers greater satisfaction than any amount of receiving what one wants. Rhodonite attracts the people and situations best suited for one's unique talents, and in so using them, one can experience fulfillment of the deep desire to love and be loved. Rhodonite can also enhance the depth, clarity and meaning of one's inner experiences, making it easier to understand the messages behind one's dreams and visions. It can provide a psychic link to the archetypal pattern of personal destiny, helping one remain "on the beam," for the fulfillment of one's highest aspirations.

Rhodonite harmonizes with most other heart stones, including Rosophia, Rose Quartz, Pink Calcite, Morganite and Emerald. It also works well with Phenacite, Scolecite, Natrolite, Herderite, Sugilite and Tibetan Black Quartz.

ROSE QUARTZ

KEY WORDS Love, gentleness, emotional healing, release of stress, uniting with the Divine
CHAKRAS Heart (4th) **ELEMENT** Water
PHYSICAL Supports the heart in healing from trauma and/or disease **EMOTIONAL** Aids in releasing past wounds, teaches trust and hope
SPIRITUAL Encourages spirituality of love, links one with the Great Mother

ROSE QUARTZ is a silicon dioxide crystal with a hexagonal crystal system and a hardness of 7. Its name is derived from its color. It is found in Brazil and Madagascar, as well as South Dakota in the USA.

Rose Quartz is the pure stone of love—for oneself, one's partner, children, family, friends, community, the Earth, the Universe and the Divine. Meditating with Rose Quartz brings an envelope of love around oneself and activates the heart chakra. Healing the heart of its wounds and reawakening its trust are among Rose Quartz's gifts. Its soothing vibrations are a balm to the emotions, and they calm and cleanse the entire auric field. It engenders the release of tension and stress, the dissolution of anger and resentment, the dispelling of fear and suspicion and the rebirth of hope and faith. Rose Quartz is one of the stones of the Great Mother. It links one's personal heart to the heart of the Earth and the Heart of the Universe. Its love vibrations can penetrate to the cellular level, reprogramming the cells for joy and longevity rather than despair and death. Rose Quartz can stimulate the crown, third eye and throat chakras, bringing them into harmony and unity with the heart. Even the lower chakras respond favorably to the abundance of love energy which flows from the heart under the influence of Rose Quartz.

Rose Quartz harmonizes with all stones. Moldavite activates Rose Quartz's capacity for spiritual awakening through the power of love.

ROSOPHIA

KEY WORDS The Love of Sophia, awakening of Heart Awareness, co-creating with the Divine, alchemical transmutation of self and world **CHAKRAS** Heart (4th) **ELEMENT** Earth **PHYSICAL** Supports healing of the heart, brings Love into the cells **EMOTIONAL** Powerfully awakens and deepens one's experience of Love **SPIRITUAL** Allows for co-creative ecstatic union with the Soul of the World

Rosophia is a mixture of reddish Feldspar, white Quartz and black Biotite discovered in the Rocky Mountains of the USA. The name is derived from "Rose of Sophia," meaning the "Heart of Wisdom."

Rosophia is the quintessential stone of the heart, putting one's individual heart into resonant union with the Heart of Sophia, the Divine Feminine Wisdom principle which underlies the beauty and harmony of the world. Holding this stone to the heart, one feels swirling currents of soothing love energy circulating within the chest. There is an immediate felt presence of the all-loving Feminine. Sleeping with a Rosophia stone near the heart will engender deeper and more peaceful sleep. Carrying or wearing a Rosophia can dispel depression and frustration, instilling the calm, loving presence that is pure Heart Awareness. Engaging regularly with this stone, more perhaps than any other, brings about an ever-more-conscious relationship with the Soul of the World. As this occurs, one is inspired to love and care for the world and all beings in the world, for in doing so, one is caring for Sophia. As the relationship deepens one can be initiated into an alchemical co-creative union with Her for the transmutation of self and world into the Cosmos of Love.

Rosophia harmonizes with all stones. The most important combination is with White Azeztulite, through which the Light of Heaven meets the Earth's Love in one's own heart, fulfilling the Divine plan.

ROYAL SAHARA JASPER

KEY WORDS Vitality, fertility, will,
courage, creativity, prophetic vision
CHAKRAS All **ELEMENT** Earth
PHYSICAL Supports digestive system,
liver, spleen; increases energy level **EMOTIONAL** Lends courage to express one's
truth and to act from love **SPIRITUAL** Stimulates visions of the future; aids
self- discipline, persistence

ROYAL SAHARA JASPER is a microcrystalline variety of Quartz, a silicon
dioxide with a hardness of 6.5 to 7. It occurs in rounded nodules with vivid
patterns of tan, black and brown. It was found in North Africa.

Royal Sahara Jasper is stabilizing to the chakras, tending to bring the
whole system into balance. It stimulates the first three chakras, enhancing
one's vitality, creative fertility and will. It resonates with the heart, engendering gentle, loving energy there. At the throat, it activates one's capacity to
courageously speak (or write) the truth of one's heart. These stones also vibrate
strongly at the third eye. In meditation, Royal Sahara Jasper can bring perceptions of spiritual shifts and changes coming in the future. This is a stone of
the "New Jerusalem"—the Earth in its soon-to-be transformed state, with the
spiritual and material worlds in full conjunction. Meditation with this stone
can facilitate visions in which one can glimpse what is to come as we approach
that great conjunction. At the crown chakra, Royal Sahara Jasper can help to
awaken one's inner link to the Divine, opening one to receive the awareness of
"I Am That I Am." In self-development, these stones encourage persistence
and self discipline.

Royal Sahara Jasper works harmoniously with Moldavite, Guardianite,
Master Shamanite, Prophecy Stone, Rosophia, Astaraline, Mystic Merlinite,
Shantilite, Agnitite and all of the Azeztulites.

RUBY

KEY WORDS Life force, courage, passion, strength, enthusiasm, adventurousness, protectiveness **CHAKRAS** Root (1st) **ELEMENT** Earth **PHYSICAL** Increases the *chi* in the body, stimulates health in all organs and systems **EMOTIONAL** Inspires self-confidence, zest for life, trust and willingness **SPIRITUAL** Instills spiritual courage and altruism, brings forth heroism

Ruby is a red variety of corundum, an aluminum oxide with a hexagonal crystal system and a hardness of 9. Rubies have been mined in Sri Lanka, Burma, Thailand, India, Brazil and the USA.

Rubies emanate the pure Red Ray with an unsurpassed vibrancy. They are powerful tools for stimulating the root chakra and bringing in additional life force. Ruby energizes and activates one's physical, mental and emotional bodies. Rubies enhance passion and fortitude, allowing for the wholehearted pursuit of one's aspirations. They eliminate feelings of hopelessness or defeat, and they open the wellspring of optimism and determination needed to accomplish difficult goals. They impart a feeling of power, improving self-confidence and adventurousness. Rubies vibrate with an enthusiasm for life, instilling an openhearted willingness to make whatever leaps of faith are required. It is a magnet for novelty and adventure. Its vibrations attract opportunities for unexpected shifts of scenery and/or situation. Ruby is a stone of courage. It assuages doubt and assists one in dealing with anxiety. Ruby inspires the protective aspects of one's character. It encourages one to stand up for those who are threatened. Ruby helps you be the kind of person you would look up to.

Ruby harmonizes with Blue Sapphire, Proustite, Cuprite, Zincite Rose Quartz and Morganite.

RUBY FUCHSITE

KEY WORDS Strong emotional body, valuing of oneself, increased life force **CHAKRAS** Base (1st), Heart (4th) **ELEMENT** Water **PHYSICAL** Infuses body with *prana;* supports bowels, heart, cells, organs **EMOTIONAL** Encourages self-esteem, aids healing of relationship issues **SPIRITUAL** Inspires one to heal oneself, instills awareness of the deep Self

RUBY FUCHSITE is a natural composite of red Ruby and green Fuschite, which is a chrome mica. It is found in South India.

The energies of Ruby Fuchsite combine the courage, strength and passion for which Ruby is known with the calming, nourishing, heart-based currents of Fuchsite. Ruby Fuchsite is both empowering and strengthening to the emotional body. It fosters a strong sense of overall health and well-being in regard to both the emotional and physical self. It can be an aid to overcoming illnesses related to dysfunctional emotional patterns. It encourages one to face the future with an attitude of trust and confidence. Ruby Fuchsite stimulates the root and heart chakras, bringing an infusion of life force into the body. It energetically clears the bowels and stimulates proper regulation of the elimination process. It dispels sluggish energies from the heart, encouraging the body to clear arterial blockages. It brings additional *prana* into the bloodstream, providing vibrational support for the cells, organs and systems. Ruby Fuchsite works to clear the emotional body of psychic debris left over from past relationships. It encourages one to value oneself and to hold high standards in choosing emotional partners. It reminds one of the presence of the Self deep within, and of the Self's eternal love, which can never be lost.

Ruby Fuchsite harmonizes with Rosophia, Crimson Cuprite, Anandalite, Guardianite, Dioptase, Zincite and Astaraline.

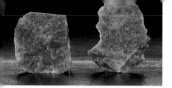

RUBY KYANITE

KEY WORDS Life Force, courage, passion, intuition, psychic ability, inspiration, visionary awareness **CHAKRAS** All, especially Root (1st), and Third Eye (6th) **ELEMENTS** Earth, Storm **PHYSICAL** Supports the brain and nervous system, as well as the sexual organs, bowels and intestines **EMOTIONAL** Quickens the formation of intimate relationships and enhances mutual attraction **SPIRITUAL** Stimulates intuitive awareness and inner visions; enhances courage, passion and commitment to spiritual development

RUBY KYANITE is a combination of red Ruby and blue Kyanite, found in South India. Ruby is a red corundum with a hardness of 9. Kyanite is an aluminum silicate with a hardness varying from 4.5 to 7.

Ruby Kyanite can increase one's Life Force, courage, passion and strength. It stimulates intuition, psychic abilities, the awareness of the wisdom of dreams, and one's ability to navigate in the spiritual realms. It facilitates expanded awareness and spiritual sensitivity, while enhancing courage, strength and sense of adventure. It stimulates the root chakra and the third eye, enhancing visionary awareness as well as physical vitality and Life Force. Ruby Kyanite helps one integrate high spiritual energies into the physical body, and to "walk the talk" of one's spiritual life in the everyday world.

Ruby Kyanite increases one's passion while helping maintain an enhanced sensitivity. It is an ideal stone for lovers, or to give to someone to whom one is attracted. In everyday life, it can increase vitality, allowing one to work long hours without exhaustion. It stimulates inspiration and insight, revealing new visions of one's purpose and potential. In self-healing, Ruby Kyanite supports the brain, spinal cord, sexual organs, bowels and intestines.

Ruby Kyanite harmonizes with Blue Sapphire, Cuprite, Zincite, Rose Quartz, Morganite, Moldavite, Phenacite, Ruby Fuchsite and Azeztulite.

RUTILATED QUARTZ

KEY WORDS Programmable for attunement, amplification, acceleration, expanding awareness, quickening and grounding manifestation **CHAKRAS** All **ELEMENT** Storm **PHYSICAL** Supports a speedy healing process, aids hair growth and quality **EMOTIONAL** Intensifies feelings, quickens emotional catharsis, breeds optimism **SPIRITUAL** Aids telepathy and intuition, amplifies one's power of manifestation

R UTILATED QUARTZ is a silicon dioxide mineral with a hexagonal crystal system and a hardness of 7, with inclusions of Rutile, a titanium oxide mineral. Most Rutilated Quartz comes from Brazil or Madagascar.

Rutilated Quartz simply sizzles with energy—it feels almost electrified. It is very programmable, and can be used to magnify the energy of practically any intention or affirmation. When doing this, one is advised to also visualize the energy of the programmed intent to be whizzing along the Rutile threads like electric energy singing through the wires of a circuit. Then visualize the crystal, with one's point of awareness still inside, broadcasting the programmed energy into the Universe as an antenna broadcasts radio waves.

Rutilated Quartz helps one instantly know if a person or situation carries good or bad "vibes." It amplifies intentions and emotions. It quickens the processes of manifestation, intuition, emotional catharsis, psychic opening, consciousness expansion and interdimensional travel.

Rutilated Quartz harmonizes with all types of Quartz. It can amplify the energies of the Synergy Twelve—Moldavite, Phenacite, Tanzanite, Danburite, Azeztulite, Herderite, Brookite, Satyaloka Quartz, Petalite, Natrolite, Scolecite and Tibetan Tektite. It also harmonizes with interdimensional stones such as Merkabite Calcite and Elestial Calcite.

RUTILE

KEY WORDS Attunement, amplification, acceleration, expanding awareness, quickening manifestation **CHAKRAS** All **ELEMENT** Storm **PHYSICAL** Aids digestive system, helps overcome addictions **EMOTIONAL** Inspires active, enthusiastic engagement with life; dispels passivity **SPIRITUAL** Enhances meditative journeying, dream recall, link with higher realms

RUTILE is a titanium oxide crystal with a tetragonal crystal system and a hardness of 6 to 6.5. The color is golden yellow, reddish brown, red or black. Most Rutile crystals are found in Brazil and Madagascar.

Rutile crystals are like radio antennas tuned to the frequency of Divine intention. They assist one in seeing the cosmic flow, thus allowing one to enhance synchronicities and experiences of grace. Rutile helps one raise one's antennae of psychic sensitivity. Rutile intensifies one's capacity to sense good or bad "vibes." Just as it is an antenna, Rutile is also an amplifier. It can magnify and accelerate the effects of one's intention and is an aid to manifestation. Rutile can amplify the energy of consciousness, opening access to the higher worlds. Similarly, Rutile is an accelerator, quickening the activities of manifestation, intuition, emotional catharsis, psychic opening, consciousness expansion, interdimensional travel, learning and the creative process. It assists one in making leaps of insight and enhances one's ability to synthesize information. It can help writers and artists find new inspiration. In business, it can accelerate the accumulation of wealth and the implementation of new ideas.

Rutile harmonizes with high-vibration stones like the Synergy Twelve. With interdimensional stones such as Phenacite, Merkabite Calcite, Danburite, Elestial Calcite, Herderite and Brookite, Rutile can work to bring about an instant linkage to the higher realms.

SAPPHIRE, BLUE

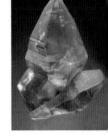

KEY WORDS Awareness, discipline **CHAKRAS** Third Eye (6th),
Throat (5th) **ELEMENT** Wind, Earth **PHYSICAL** Aids
healing of headaches, vertigo, earaches, vision problems
EMOTIONAL Encourages inner strength and confidence
SPIRITUAL Enhances psychic abilities, mental clarity and insight

BLUE SAPPHIRE is a variety of corundum, an aluminum
oxide with a hexagonal crystal system and a hardness of 9. It is found in
Thailand, Madagascar, India and the USA.

Blue Sapphire is a stone of mental and psychic activation, an enhancer
of insight, ESP and mental agility. It is believed to help one see below surface
appearances to the underlying truth and to speak clearly with the voice of
inner wisdom. Astrologically, Blue Sapphire is associated with the planet Saturn, the archetype of order, structure, limitation and discipline. It is an ideal
ally for organizing one's ideas and perceptions and bringing them into form.
The strong Blue Ray of these Sapphires is ideal for facilitating the integrated
awakening and utilization of the throat and third eye chakras. With these two
chakras working in unison, one has the capacity of inner vision, the focus to
use this inner vision like a laser beam and the lucidity to communicate one's
vision to others. Blue Sapphire can stimulate psychic abilities and activate
one's higher intelligence. It opens the channels for communication of one's
highest wisdom and allows one to act as a conduit for information from the
higher planes.

Blue Sapphire can be combined with Lapis Lazuli, Azurite, Lazulite,
Iolite and Blue Scapolite for increased enhancement of psychic abilities and
mental acuity. With Rose Quartz and other heart stones, it brings loyalty and
fidelity into love relationships.

SAPPHIRE, YELLOW

KEY WORDS Abundance, strength of will
CHAKRAS Solar Plexus (3rd) **ELEMENT** Fire
PHYSICAL Aids the body's vitality and digestion, supports
the spleen **EMOTIONAL** Allows one to playfully enjoy
one's work and creative activity **SPIRITUAL** Strong ally
for manifestation of wealth and one's highest visions

YELLOW SAPPHIRE is a variety of corundum, an aluminum oxide with a hexagonal crystal system and a hardness of 9. It is found primarily in Sri Lanka and India.

Yellow Sapphire has long been known as a stone of prosperity. In India, merchants wear fine Yellow Sapphire gems to enhance their success. In the West, metaphysical practitioners use Yellow Sapphire to assist in bringing not only financial abundance, but also in manifesting one's visions. Yellow Sapphires provide the ideal vibration of the third chakra, seat of the will. With them, one can focus one's intention for the achievement of almost any aim. The power of one's unbending intent is not fully recognized by most people, often because their wills are unfocused and little manifests through them. Many people have weak third chakras. Part of this comes from not being taught how and why to focus intention. With the help of Yellow Sapphire, those who clearly sustain their visions long enough will discover that their own thoughts can indeed come into being. This sustaining of one's vision is sometimes called faith, but one might as readily describe it as will, the awakened third chakra.

Yellow Sapphire harmonizes with Ruby, Herkimer "Diamond" and all other Sapphires. It works synergistically with Libyan Gold Tektite, Moldavite and Tibetan Tektite. It has a strong affinity for the visionary stone Phenacite, which works with Yellow Sapphire for manifestation.

SAPPHIRE, PADPARADSCHA

KEY WORDS Creativity, sexuality and zest for life, loving creation **CHAKRAS** Sexual/Creative (2nd), Heart (4th) **ELEMENT** Fire **PHYSICAL** Enhances sexual energies, supports reproductive health **EMOTIONAL** Encourages playfulness, sociability, zest for life and love **SPIRITUAL** Inspires creative expression, brings liveliness into spiritual life

PADPARADSCHA SAPPHIRE is a variety of corundum, an aluminum oxide with a hexagonal crystal system and a hardness of 9. It was originally found in Sri Lanka. The name means "lotus flower" in Sinhalese.

Padparadscha Sapphires blaze with the fire of life force and creative energies. They are highly activating and purifying to the second chakra, seat of one's sexual energies as well as the fountain of creativity in all areas of life. Padparadscha Sapphire can help one feel at home in the physical world, encouraging one to revel and delight in the exquisite sensory experiences of life. It can aid one in finding greater zest and enthusiasm in one's sex life, as well as opening the floodgates of one's creative nature. Padparadscha Sapphire is a solar stone, bringing warmth and physical comfort. It is also related to Mars, the planet of action, and its energy can enhance one's ability to move forward with projects or stand firm against opposition. It can assist those with weak constitutions in developing more vitality, and it can help one overcome distraction, confusion and flightiness. It is fitting that the name Padparadscha derives from words meaning "lotus blossom," for this gem can help one to discover "the jewel in the lotus" when used in meditation.

Padparadscha Sapphire harmonizes with Zincite, Carnelian, Orange Calcite, Satyaloka Rose Azeztulite, Himalaya Red-Gold Azeztulite, Russian Red Quartz, Rosophia and Proustite.

SAPPHIRE, PINK

KEY WORDS Love, forgiveness
CHAKRAS Heart (4th) **ELEMENT** Water,
Fire **PHYSICAL** Supports heart and
bloodstream, vibrationally helps balance
blood sugar and glucose metabolism **EMOTIONAL** Encourages gentleness and
compassion in relationships **SPIRITUAL** Provides courage to love without fear
and to act with generosity

Pink SAPPHIRE is a variety of corundum, an aluminum oxide with a hexagonal crystal system and a hardness of 9. It is found in Sri Lanka, Thailand, Burma and India.

Pink Sapphire might also be rightly called "pale Ruby," and energetically it appears as a softer, lighter version of Ruby's passionate emotional intensity. Pink Sapphire stimulates the gentle emotions of love, forgiveness, acceptance and release. It holds the power of vulnerability. It encourages one to be yielding and pliable. The strength it engenders is the strength of resilience. It is an ideal stone of emotional and psychic protection for situations in which one does not have the authority to direct events, but from which one cannot simply depart. Pink Sapphire allows one to weather the storms of life without damage. It also assists in healing the wounds of past emotional traumas, and it facilitates compassion for others, even those who have wronged us. Pink Sapphire evokes the energy of the heart and conjoins it with the power of the disciplined mind. It is excellent for bringing heart and mind into balance. Pink Sapphire teaches the lessons of appreciation and gratitude, reminding us that love is its own reward and that the longing of our hearts for the Divine is identical to the longing which the Divine feels for us.

Pink Sapphires works well with Rose Quartz, Rosophia, Morganite, Kunzite, Rhodocrosite, Pink Azeztulite and Rhodonite.

SAPPHIRE, WHITE

KEY WORDS Awareness, clarity, discernment
CHAKRAS Third Eye (6th), Crown (7th)
ELEMENT Wind **PHYSICAL** Stimulates pineal
and pituitary glands, energetically aids brain
function **EMOTIONAL** Aids in overcoming fear of fulfilling one's spiritual purpose **SPIRITUAL** Supports mental and spiritual clarity, link with the Higher Self

WHITE SAPPHIRE is a variety of corundum, an aluminum oxide with a hexagonal crystal system and a hardness of 9. It is found in Sri Lanka, Thailand, Burma, India and other localities.

White Sapphire is a colorless Sapphire easily mistaken for Diamond. Its energies are pure and refreshing, assisting one in clearing one's thoughts and coming to new tasks with a clean slate. Its balanced energies can enhance one's objectivity, facilitating successful discrimination between alternative paths. White Sapphire opens the powers of the mind and strengthens the conduit of communication with Spirit. It is a stone which helps one combine spiritual insight with earthly tasks or dilemmas, helping one to bring a higher perspective to bear when faced with difficult decisions. It stimulates the third eye and crown chakras and activates the lesser energy meridians in the brain, helping one to tune in to spirit guides, angels and even humans who have "crossed over." It assists one in developing the qualities of fairness, discernment and objectivity, and in maintaining a spiritual perspective in all situations.

White Sapphire combines synergistically with Phenacite for deepening one's insights and enhancing the clarity of inner visions. Petalite, Danburite, Satyaloka Azeztulite and White Azeztulite help White Sapphire in opening the doors of the angelic realm. Moldavite and White Sapphire combine to bring clarity to the experience of transformation.

SATYA MANI QUARTZ

KEY WORDS Spiritual truth and enlightenment
CHAKRAS Third Eye (6th), Crown (7th)
ELEMENT Wind **PHYSICAL** Stimulates the
neural links between heart and brain **EMOTIONAL** Promotes nonjudgment,
kindness, compassion and love **SPIRITUAL** Inspires commitment to truth,
triggers experiences of *satori*

S ATYA MANI QUARTZ is a silicon dioxide mineral with a hexagonal crystal
system and a hardness of 7. It is found in southern India. *Satya Mani* is a
Sanskrit phrase meaning "Truth Stone" or "Gem of Truth."

Satya Mani Quartz is, as its name implies, a stone of spiritual truth
and initiation. It attunes one to hear the inner call of one's path of destiny.
It brings the joy that comes from recognizing that the appearances of the
solid-seeming material world are simply the manifestations of deeper, living
currents from the spiritual realms. Satya Mani Quartz can help one awaken
to the truth of one's existence as soul and spirit, and the deeper truth of the
interrelatedness of all beings. Satya Mani Quartz is a stone of enlightenment,
bringing the light of Truth into one's mind by virtue of its connection to the
heart. It inspires the expression of truth and the commitment to kindness,
clear awareness, nonjudgment and compassion. The currents of Satya Mani
Quartz intensify the circuit of consciousness between the heart and the high
brain, leading to a single unified awareness.

Satya Mani Quartz also works harmoniously with Phenacite, Natrolite,
Danburite, Brookite, Herderite, Tibetan Tektite, Azeztulite, Petalite, Scolecite
and other high-vibration stones. It has a special affinity for Moldavite and
enhances that stone's powers of spiritual transformation. It intensifies the
potential benefits of all other silica-based minerals, especially those in the
Quartz family.

SCAPOLITE

KEY WORDS Insight, persistence, self-discipline, willpower, self-transformation, liberation
CHAKRAS All **ELEMENT** Storm
PHYSICAL Helps bring the Divine blueprint of health into integration with the body **EMOTIONAL** Encourages pride in accomplishment, inspires dedication to one's highest aspirations **SPIRITUAL** Supports the achievement of one's destiny and freedom

SCAPOLITE is a sodium, calcium, silicon, aluminum, oxygen, chlorine, carbon and sulfur mineral with a tetragonal crystal system and a hardness of 5 to 6. Scapolite crystals are found on every continent.

Scapolite helps one set one's mind on a goal and persist until the goal is attained. It is wonderful for developing the self-discipline and willpower to attain inner freedom. Its planetary influence is Saturn, the planet of structure and discipline, and this stone can help one create the forms and structures that allow us to fulfill our dreams. Scapolite's key phrase is "strength of purpose." It is thus a stone of destiny, of *dharma*. It helps one to hear the voice of the Higher Self and carry out the blueprint of one's evolutionary plan for this life. It can also illuminate the memory of past lives in which patterns of self-sabotage may be rooted. It not only helps one to embrace new patterns—it also allows one to release old ones which no longer serve one's highest good.

Scapolite is also a stone of insight. It is a stone of deep delving, and it assists one in going down into the psyche to discover what is holding one back and what must be overcome to break through to freedom.

Scapolite works well with Moldavite and any kind of Sapphire. With Blue Sapphire it aids self-discipline; with Yellow Sapphire it assists with prosperity; with Padparadsha Sapphire it stimulates creativity.

SCOLECITE

KEY WORDS Inner peace, relaxation, tranquillity, interdimensional travel, awakening the heart
CHAKRAS Third Eye (6th), Crown (7th)
ELEMENT Wind **PHYSICAL** Spiritually supports stable brain function and serotonin levels
EMOTIONAL Aids emotional stability, brings feelings of tranquility and serenity
SPIRITUAL Facilitates interdimensional and time travel, link to higher realms

SCOLECITE is a zeolite mineral with a monoclinic crystal system and a hardness of 5 to 5.5. It can be colorless, white or yellowish. It has been found in Teigarhorn, Iceland, and Poona, India.

The phrase that best summarizes the energy of Scolecite is "inner peace." These stones emanate a deep peace that resonates through one's entire auric field. For those who wish to enhance meditation, sleep more restfully or dream more sweetly, Scolecite is highly recommended.

The uplifting, relaxed state brought about by Scolecite is ideal for healing sessions, meditations, lucid dreaming or restful sleep. It offers protection from the intrusion of negative astral energies, as it lifts one to the higher vibrational planes. Scolecite is a very interdimensional stone. Contact with intelligences from far-flung inner and outer domains is possible when Scolecite is used for journeying. It also assists time travel, allowing one to access knowledge from ancient and even "future" civilizations.

Emotionally, Scolecite enhances heart energies, encouraging the spontaneous expression of love. It is a good stone to be exchanged between lovers, helping to establish a constant invisible connection between hearts.

Scolecite harmonizes with Phenacite, Herderite, all Azeztulites, Danburite and Apophyllite. Its best ally is Natrolite, which is nearly identical to Scolecite in its molecular structure.

SEDONALITE

KEY WORDS Balance, inner harmony, psychic
sensitivity, inspiration, optimism, awakening
CHAKRAS All **ELEMENT** Storm **PHYSICAL**
Supports brain and nervous system **EMOTIONAL**
Inspires optimism, enthusiasm, willingness to transform **SPIRITUAL** Enhances
psychic ability, past-life recall, visionary experience, interdimensional communication

SEDONALITE is a red sandstone concretion found in the red-rock mountains
and desert surrounding Sedona, Arizona, a location famous for its powerful energy vortexes. The stone sometimes occurs in natural spheres from one-
half to two inches in diameter, and it is also found in amorphous chunks.

Sedonalite can both charge and harmonize the meridian system, and
it can bring one's astral and subtle bodies into resonant alignment with the
physical. The stones are both grounding and stimulating, engendering a
heightened sense of sensitivity and alertness. They can be used to activate
any of the chakras as well as the meridians.

Sedonalite heightens one's psychic capacities, enhancing any natural
sensitivities and adding dimensions. It can clear away mental fog, fatigue
and dullness, and jumpstart one's enthusiasm. It carries a highly optimistic
energy, inspiring one to get going on manifesting one's dreams.

Sedonalite is intimately linked with the environment of Sedona, Arizona,
and all the phenomena that occur there. It can trigger spontaneous spiritual
experiences including past-life recall, visions of spirit beings and extraterrestrials, and the awakening of one's ability to channel. It offers a quick acceleration of one's spiritual growth, and can facilitate extraordinary visions.

Sedonalites work synergistically with Moldavite, Azeztulite, Amazez, and
all the stones of Vibrational Ascension.

SELENITE

KEY WORDS Spiritual activation, communion with the Higher Self, spirit guides and angels   **CHAKRAS** Third Eye (6th), Crown (7th), Etheric (8th–14th)   **ELEMENT** Wind   **PHYSICAL** Clears energy blockages, induces inner alignment, facilitates healing   **EMOTIONAL** Inspires one to release insecurity and reach for one's desires   **SPIRITUAL** Facilitates auric cleansing, upper chakra activation, spiritual attunement

SELENITE is a hydrous calcium sulfate mineral with a monoclinic crystal system and a hardness of 2. It is a form of gypsum, called Selenite if it is clear and well formed. The best clear Selenites come from Mexico.

Selenite quickly opens and activates the third eye and crown chakras, and the Soul Star chakra above the head. Its intensity is greater than almost any other stone for the upper chakras. A Selenite wand pointed at the third eye sends energy that can feel like a gust of wind going through the forehead and out the top of the head. Selenite is fast and effective at cleansing the auric field, and it can clear congested energies or negativity from one's physical and etheric body. Selenite can lift one's awareness to higher planes, making it possible to consciously meet one's spirit guides and guardian angels. It facilitates the experience of receiving inner guidance. Placing a Selenite wand upon one's back, along the spine, one can achieve an energetic alignment of the vertebrae and the chakras as well. Selenite is also an excellent stone for building energy grids. A group of six or more wands arranged around one's body puts one into a mini energy vortex!

Selenite amplifies and harmonizes with most other stones. It has a special affinity for the Synergy Twelve—Moldavite, Phenacite, Tanzanite, Danburite, White Azeztulite, Brookite, Herderite, Scolecite, Natrolite, Petalite, Tibetan Tektite and Satyaloka Azeztulite.

SERAPHINITE

KEY WORDS Self-healing, regeneration, wholeness, angelic connection   **CHAKRAS** All   **ELEMENT** Earth
PHYSICAL Supports cellular health, can be used in spiritual healing to reduce the activity of cancer cells
EMOTIONAL Aids release of toxic emotions, encourages a joyful attitude   **SPIRITUAL** Assists communication with angels, devas, Nature spirits

S ERAPHINITE is a variety of Clinochlore, a hydrous magnesium iron aluminum silicate with a monoclinic crystal system and a hardness of about 4. It is found only in the Lake Baikal region of Siberia.

Seraphinite is among the most powerful stones for bringing all the elements of the nonphysical bodies into alignment along the "I am" column of the spinal cord. It is both centering and energizing, and its beautiful green shades show how well it is suited to the heart chakra. It can move blocked energies in the meridians and can be combined with acupuncture for this purpose. Seraphinite imbues the auric field with the vibrations of wholeness and well-being. Seraphinite is very evolved and will bring one along rapidly in one's own evolution.

It is no mistake that Seraphinite's name derives from the Seraphim. These stones resonate strongly with all levels of the angelic domain, even the highest. Those who wish to meet the angels in meditation or dreaming can use this stone to facilitate the necessary attunements.

Seraphinite's energies are feminine in tone, and they can help one experience a greater awareness of the Divine Feminine.

Seraphinite harmonizes with Moldavite, Phenacite, Rosophia, Scolecite, Petalite, Tanzanite, Danburite, Azeztulite, Herkimer "Diamonds," Tibetan Tektite and Charoite. Azeztulite and Rosophia assist in making the connection with the Divine Feminine.

SERIPHOS GREEN QUARTZ

KEY WORDS Awareness of the Earth as Paradise, joyful acceptance of physical life, healing **CHAKRAS** Heart (4th) **ELEMENT** Earth **PHYSICAL** Supports enjoyment and love of the body, dispels negative attachments, aids in rejuvenation **EMOTIONAL** Inspires a joyful embrace of life and the Earth **SPIRITUAL** Transmits the regenerative, ecstatic energies of Nature

S ERIPHOS GREEN QUARTZ is a deep green, leaf-shaped Quartz crystal, a silicon dioxide mineral with a hexagonal crystal system and a hardness of 7. It is found only on the tiny Greek island of Seriphos.

Seriphos Green Quartz crystals emanate a most heavenly energy, and one can imagine the flower beds of the higher realms budding with just such as these. But the paradise of the Seriphos Green Quartz is right here on Earth! Holding, wearing or laying-on these stones brings one into the awareness of Earth as Paradise. They emanate a sweet, strong vibration that evokes the state of wholesome enjoyment of physical life and facilitates the attainment of vibrant good health. Seriphos Green Quartz helps the user or wearer be grounded in the best possible way—through love for the material world and one's place within it. It reminds us that we too are blooms brought forth from the womb of the fertile Earth, and our experience of life can be exquisite when we bring our attention to its beauty and pleasure. These stones are helpful to those who feel uncomfortable in their bodies or are distressed at the hardships of life on Earth, helping them to recognize the Earth as Home.

Seriphos Green Quartz harmonizes with Green Apophyllite, Rosophia, Amethyst, Turquoise and Moldavite. Combining it with Phenacite or Azeztulite brings awareness of the higher dimensional aspect of oneself into alignment with one's earthly life.

SERPENTINE

KEY WORDS Awakening of higher brain
functions, connection with Nature,
kundalini awakening **CHAKRAS** All
ELEMENT Earth **PHYSICAL** Aids in
rewiring neural pathways so higher brain areas predominate and guide behavior
EMOTIONAL Helps one release fear of change and embrace transformation
SPIRITUAL Assists in awakening kundalini energies for personal evolution

SERPENTINE is a magnesium silicate mineral with a monoclinic, orthorhombic or hexagonal crystal system and a hardness ranging from 2 to 5.5.
Major deposits are in England, South Africa, Brazil and the USA.

Serpentine is one of the best stones for rousing the kundalini energies—
the "serpent power" said to reside at the base of the spine. Serpentine is also
a good stone to place on the meridian points for clearing blocked energies
and allowing the healthy, natural flow to be reestablished. It is powerful for
working energetically to bring the old reptilian part of the brain into the
service of the higher brain. In many people, due to psychic wounds from one's
family and culture, the reverse is the case. Carrying, wearing or meditating
with Serpentine can help establish the order intended by Nature, bringing
peace and joy to the individual and reverberating into the outer world.

Serpentine harmonizes with Seraphinite for the rewiring of unhealthy
brain patterns. Herderite, Phenacite, Natrolite, Scolecite and Azeztulite can
all help this process by stimulating the higher brain areas. Anandalite and
Tibetan Tektite reinforce Serpentine's energies in the kundalini awakening
process. Other stones that harmonize with Serpentine are Amethyst, Moonstone, Libyan Gold Tektite, Golden Labradorite, Zincite, Tiger Eye, Emerald,
Green Jade, Purple Jade and Strombolite.

SHAMAN STONE

KEY WORDS Shamanic journeying, soul retrieval, polarity balancing, psychic protection, intuition   **CHAKRAS** All   **ELEMENT** Earth   **PHYSICAL** Supports the thyroid and adrenals, can be programmed to assist any organ or system   **EMOTIONAL** Helps one overcome fear of death through discovery of the spiritual worlds   **SPIRITUAL** Powerfully aids inner journeys, provides protection and discernment

SHAMAN STONES are sandstone concretions found on the north rim of the Grand Canyon in southern Utah. They are naturally spherical, and they range from a half inch to over two inches in diameter.

Shaman Stones are excellent tools and talismans for those engaged in shamanic journeying, rebirthing, holotropic breathwork or other intense forms of transformational inner work. These stones help guide one to the experiences which will be most beneficial to healing the soul and advancing one on the path of spiritual growth. Shaman Stones offer psychic protection to inner journeyers. They provide an energetic shield that keeps negative entities from attaching themselves. They also increase one's intuitive perception, making it easier for one to perceive the approach of all types of beings, both positive and negative. This can help those unfamiliar with shamanic work to perceive and connect with one's power animal and other helpers and guides. Shaman Stones also help balance the polarities of one's vibrational field, as well as harmonizing the energies of the meridian system. They aid the alignment of all the chakras as well as their proper attunement to the etheric and astral bodies.

Shaman Stones work well with Prophecy Stone, Alexandrite, Oregon Opal, Scolecite, Apophyllite, Phenacite and all Azeztulites.

SHANTILITE

KEY WORDS The "peace that passes understanding," inner silence, harmony   **CHAKRAS** All
ELEMENT Wind, Fire   **PHYSICAL** Supports recuperation from injury and illness, dispels stress
EMOTIONAL Quiets worry and anxiety, leads one into profound peace
SPIRITUAL Aids meditation and prayer through quieting the mind

SHANTILITE is the name of a gray Agate from Madagascar. It is a silicon dioxide with a hexagonal crystal system and a hardness of 7. The name comes from the Sanskrit "shanti," meaning Divine peace.

Shantilite's currents enter the body like a "whoosh" or wave of energy rushing through. With that wave comes an immediate flow of peace throughout the body, instilling a state of profound relaxation. Shantilite is an excellent stone for meditation. It can bring one into a state of deep inner silence, aiding one in feeling attuned with the living Silence of the spiritual realms. It stills the inner dialog, because its peace is so attractive to the psyche that the "thought train" tends to dissipate. Shantilite can help one clear the repeating loops of worry and anxiety. Its deep, slow, loving resonance works to dissolve the vicious circle of tension and worry. As a stone of deep peace, Shantilite can be of benefit to those working spiritually to alleviate all sorts of stress-related pathologies. Because it is strong enough to be felt throughout the etheric body, it is ideal for those recuperating from any illness or injury. Shantilite can be an aid to prayer, as it quiets the mental side and draws one's attention to the sacred. It helps one find communion with the angelic realm, and it aids in the Ascension process by bringing one's vibrational field into a state of quiet receptivity and harmony.

Shantilite works well with all of the Azeztulites, as well as Anandalite, Guardianite, Rosophia, Scolecite, Danburite and Petalite.

SHATTUCKITE

KEY WORDS Intuition, communication, channeling, mediumship, work with oracles   **CHAKRAS** Heart (4th), Throat (5th), Third Eye (6th)   **ELEMENT** Water, Wind   **PHYSICAL** Supports proper balance of the visceral organs and their fluids   **EMOTIONAL** Aids one in embracing truth and releasing fears, especially fears of the spirit realms   **SPIRITUAL** Aids attunement to inner guidance and spirit communication

SHATTUCKITE is a copper silicate hydroxide mineral with an orthorhombic crystal system and a hardness of 3.5. It is found in copper mines in Argentina, Congo, Namibia, South Africa and the USA.

Shattuckite assists in understanding and communicating information from Spirit. It can open one's psychic channel, enabling one to "hear" messages from inner guides and teachers as well as the spirits of the deceased. If one wishes to work as a medium, Shattuckite is an ideal ally. It vibrates to the tone of truth, so it can also aid in making sure one's interpretations of messages from the "other side" are accurate. Shattuckite stimulates the throat chakra, enhancing one's skills in communication. Shattuckite's highest use is in the communication of wisdom and information from the higher realms. It facilitates the practice of automatic writing as well as vocal channeling. It helps one find the right words to express the communications from spirit guides and teachers. It facilitates one's sense of synesthesia and can stimulate mental and intuitive abilities. This makes it most helpful for those studying intuitive disciplines such as astrology, tarot, runes, palmistry, the *I Ching* and other oracular guides.

Shattuckite works well with Turquoise, Chrysocolla, Larimar and Ajoite for throat chakra activation. For stimulating the third eye, Phenacite, Natrolite, Lazulite and Merkabite Calcite are ideal stone allies.

SHIVA LINGAM

KEY WORDS Kundalini activation, vitality and *prana*, spiritual transformation and rebirth, enlightenment, oneness with the All **CHAKRAS** All **ELEMENT** Earth, Wind, Water, Fire, Storm **PHYSICAL** Stimulates all one's energy systems, treats impotence and infertility **EMOTIONAL** Helps one to merge ecstatically with the Divine **SPIRITUAL** Can awaken Kundalini energies and bring about *samadhi*

SHIVA LINGAMS are egg-shaped stones of crypto-crystalline Quartz (with impurities), a silicon dioxide mineral with a hardness of 7. Shiva Lingams originate at the Narmada River in western India.

Shiva Lingams are named after the Hindu god Shiva, and they resonate deeply with the energies of the Earth, yet they also carry strong energies of Water, Wind and even Fire. In fact, the fire energy of these stones is so strong that they are capable of activating kundalini energies and charging the entire chakra system. For those who feel they need a boost of vitality and *prana* energies, meditating or sleeping with a Shiva Lingam is highly recommended.

Esoteric legends suggest that there is a field of invisible knowledge in which the stored psychic energy of human ritual and belief may reside. When one makes a connection to some portion of this field, one can tap into the energy of all the past consciousness that has contributed to it. Thus, when one works with a sacred object like the Shiva Lingam, one can receive the benefit of the efforts of all those who have used such stones in spiritual pursuits throughout history. This is especially true because these stones are composed primarily of microscopic Quartz. Through crystal resonance, any Shiva Lingam can connect to all others throughout the world, in all places and times. Through this power, Shiva Lingams can be emblems of inner transformation.

SHUNGITE

KEY WORDS Cleansing and purification, infusion of spiritual Light, activation of the Light Body, adherence to truth **CHAKRAS** All **ELEMENTS** Fire, Wind, Storm **PHYSICAL** Purifies the body, preparing it to be transformed by an infusion of spiritual Light **EMOTIONAL** Rids one of negative emotional patterns, can generate emotional rebirth **SPIRITUAL** Prepares one for Light Body activation, cleansing, balancing and aligning all the particles of the body

SHUNGITE is a combination of amorphous graphite, crystalline silicate and other minerals, and is found near Shunga, Russia. Its hardness is 3.5.

Shungite clears the energies of the entire body and opens one to receive spiritual Light. Shungite operates vibrationally on the molecular level, freeing the atoms of one's body from their bondage to negative patterns and energies. Shungite can clear the body of dysfunctional patterns manifesting as disease, emotional difficulties or various types of negativity. Shungite aids ungrounded people to better connect with the Earth. It provides an aura of psychic protection, primarily because of the energetic alignment it facilitates.

Shungite is a stone of truth; under its influence, one cannot act or speak falsely without becoming very uncomfortable. This is because Shungite dispels negativity and brings in so much spiritual Light that one immediately feels the unpleasant sensation of disharmony if a negative or false thought or statement is introduced. The clearing influence of Shungite tends to dispel one's self-harming or self-defeating habitual patterns. On an emotional level, it is excellent for letting go of deep-seated feelings of fear, guilt or shame.

Shungite resonates profoundly with Healerite, Lithium Light, crystallized Lepidolite and all forms of Azeztulite including Azozeo super-activated stones. All of these add beneficial currents to Shungite's infusion of spiritual Light.

SIBERIAN BLUE QUARTZ

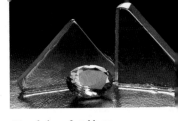

KEY WORDS Psychic awakening, mediumship, mental clarity and insight, feeling at home on the Earth **CHAKRAS** Third Eye (6th), Throat (5th) **ELEMENT** Wind, Water **PHYSICAL** Supports brain function and healing, aids with memory issues **EMOTIONAL** Helps "Star Children" and sensitives feel comfortable on Earth **SPIRITUAL** Opens latent capacities for receiving information from Spirit

SIBERIAN BLUE QUARTZ is the name given to a cobalt blue lab-grown Quartz created in Russia. It is a silicon dioxide material with a hexagonal crystal system and a hardness of 7.

Siberian Blue Quartz carries a great deal of energy. There is no other gemstone that so strikingly exhibits the Blue Ray as does Siberian Blue Quartz. It activates both the throat chakra and the third eye in a blended harmony that both awakens the insights of the higher mind and facilitates the eloquent communication of its knowledge. The Wind element energy of this stone evokes psychic awakening, and it can be of assistance to those who wish to develop the powers of clairvoyance, clairaudience, clairsentience, prophecy, psychokinesis, mediumship and interdimensional communication. The stones provide a balancing and calming influence. Siberian Blue Quartz connects one to the Water element and to the domains of emotion and Spirit. It can be a healing stone for those who feel misunderstood or ill-at-ease on the Earth plane, or for anyone who feels alienated from others. These stones illuminate the common humanity we share on the emotional and spiritual planes, and they help us remember and communicate that truth.

Siberian Blue Quartz harmonizes with Danburite, Amethyst, Moldavite, Oregon Opal, Blue Aragonite, Shattuckite and Phenacite. Its psychic activations are further enhanced by Iolite and Owyhee Blue Opal.

SILLIMANITE

KEY WORDS Unification and harmonization of the chakras, focus and self-discipline, self-mastery and magic, bringing order from chaos **CHAKRAS** All **ELEMENT** Earth **PHYSICAL** Supports bodily order and harmony, can be used to combat illnesses in which part of the body attacks itself **EMOTIONAL** Stimulates optimism and happiness through bringing coherence to one's thoughts, energies and actions **SPIRITUAL** Helps to unify one's energies and actions, aids in creating order, and feeds one's enthusiasm for life

SILLIMANITE is an aluminum-silicate mineral with a hardness of 6.5 to 7.5. It was named after the American geologist Benjamin Silliman

Sillimanite stimulates and unifies the chakras, making them flow more strongly. Placing a Sillimanite on a weakened area can strengthen it by uniting it with the other chakras and meridians. Sillimanite draws one into an inner unity from which the expression of self-discipline is natural and even pleasurable. It helps us keep our intentions and actions in alignment. It is a stone of self-mastery and therefore of magic, aiding one with manifestation.

Sillimanite encourages the emergence of order from chaos, and helps one achieve mental and emotional clarity. It encourages a calm and positive attitude. It can stimulate the release of endorphins, and is in that sense a feel-good stone. It encourages optimism and enthusiasm to flourish. Its energy supports and unifies all of one's organs and systems. Its healing energies can help in situations in which part of the body has departed from its unity with the whole, as with cancer and autoimmune illnesses.

Sillimanite works well with Kyanite, Andalusite and Anandalite. It allies with Sapphire for inner strength and Ruby for enhancing courage. It synergizes with Anandalite, and with all of the Azeztulites, for Light Body activation.

SMITHSONITE

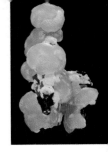

KEY WORDS Soothing the emotions, release of stress, deepening of love and compassion, relaxing into deeper perception **CHAKRAS** All **ELEMENT** Water **PHYSICAL** Aids in weight reduction, increases vitality, supports endocrine system and reproductive organs **EMOTIONAL** Helps eliminate fear, anxiety and tension; encourages trust and relaxation **SPIRITUAL** Opens psychic channels, instills awareness of cosmic Oneness

SMITHSONITE is a zinc carbonate mineral with a rhombohedral or hexagonal crystal system and a hardness of 5. Its color can be blue, pink, purple, green, yellow, white, gray or brown. Deposits of Smithsonite have been found in Greece, Mexico, Africa, Spain and the USA.

Smithsonite is one of the premier stones for soothing the emotional body and relieving stress. It cools anger and resentment, allowing one to reestablish the awareness of Oneness. It unwinds tension and dispels anxiety. It emanates an oceanic feeling of calm and clarity, encouraging one to view difficult situations with fresh, compassionate eyes. It allows one to see Light even in dark times of depression. Carrying or wearing Smithsonite is like having a caring friend by one's side.

Smithsonite assists one in entering the state of meditation by calming and relaxing the mind. It facilitates friendship and good feeling in relationships. It promotes relaxation during healing and body layouts. Smithsonite is a stone for stimulating psychic capacities, such as remote viewing, psychometry and telepathic communication. Smithsonite helps one connect with one's spirit guides for information and healing.

For relaxation and relief of stress, Smithsonite harmonizes with Lepidolite, Aquamarine, Kunzite, Chrysoprase and Rosophia. Iolite and Phenacite support its enhancement of psychic abilities.

SMOKY QUARTZ

KEY WORDS Grounding, transmutation of negative energies, practicality, organization, manifestation of one's dreams and inspirations **CHAKRAS** Root (1st) **ELEMENT** Earth **PHYSICAL** Offers spiritual protection from radiation, supports healing from sunburn, dispels the physical effects of negative energies **EMOTIONAL** Helps spiritual people feel positively engaged with physical life **SPIRITUAL** Protective and grounding, manifests the spiritual in the physical

Quartz is a silicon dioxide mineral with a hexagonal crystal system and a hardness of 7. It can vary in color from very pale tan to deep chocolate brown. Smoky Quartz is found in many countries.

Smoky Quartz is one of the premier grounding stones. It can help even the spaciest individuals get their "land legs" so they can fully function as physical beings. It also aids the grounding of spiritual information. Smoky Quartz enhances practicality and organization. It can help one avoid extravagance, except when it comes to purchasing Smoky Quartz! It offers protection from negative energies in one's environment. It can absorb and transmute almost unlimited amounts of negativity.

Smoky Quartz has a way of drawing the ethereal into manifestation. When one is wearing or carrying a Smoky Quartz, one is actually more likely to see such phenomena as ghosts, UFOs, fairies and spirit guides. Rather than raising one's vibration, it draws the entities or phenomena into one's auric field and down to one's level of perception. For similar reasons, Smoky Quartz is useful for helping one bring one's most potent dreams and inspired ideas into physical reality.

Smoky Quartz works in harmony with grounding stones such as Master Shamanite, Black Tourmaline, Jet and Obsidian. With Moldavite it draws the energy of transformation into the physical realm.

SODALITE

KEY WORDS Access to subconscious and intuitive abilities, enhanced insight and mental performance, deepened intuition   **CHAKRAS** Third Eye (6th)
ELEMENT Wind   **PHYSICAL** Supports maintenance of healthy blood pressure and hydration   **EMOTIONAL** Aids one's insight, allowing understanding of emotional issues   **SPIRITUAL** Conjoins mental acuity and psychic ability for wider awareness

SODALITE is a chloric sodium aluminum silicate with an isometric crystal system and a hardness of 5.5 to 6. The name refers to its sodium content. The largest Sodalite deposit is in Bahia, Brazil.

Sodalite is a stone of insight, helping one penetrate paradox and contradiction in order to form a new synthesis of thought. It enhances the mental powers of analysis, intuition, observation and creativity and is stimulating to one's latent genius. It facilitates self-discipline, efficiency, organization and structure in research and other mental pursuits. Sodalite provides insight into the self and a dispassionate assessment of one's motivations, strengths, weaknesses, desires, gifts and patterns of personal destiny. It can reinforce one's "witness" consciousness, and it brings a kind of stubborn courage into oneself, helping one stay on the Path during hard times. It stimulates psychic vision and multi-leveled understanding, sparking the "aha!" moments wherein one sees the pattern that connects the inner and outer worlds. Sodalite can aid astrologers, numerologists, tarot readers and all those who translate the archetypal patterns revealed in oracles.

For insight and mental ability, Sodalite harmonizes with Iolite, Lapis Lazuli, Siberian Blue Quartz, Blue Sapphire and Lazulite. Moldavite stimulates all of these. Phenacite, Natrolite, Herderite Scolecite and Danburite expand Sodalite's openings into higher dimensions.

SPHALERITE

KEY WORDS Physical strength, vitality, grounding, balance, discrimination **CHAKRAS** Root (1st), Sexual/Creative (2nd), Solar Plexus (3rd) **ELEMENT** Earth, Fire **PHYSICAL** Supports immune system, increases stamina and energy level **EMOTIONAL** Helps one discern the truth and overcome emotional bias **SPIRITUAL** Enhances life force, sexuality, creativity, manifestation and will

SPHALERITE is a zinc sulfide mineral with a tetrahedral and dodecahedral crystal system and a hardness of 3.5 to 4. Its color ranges widely, including red, black, brown, yellow, green, gray, white and clear. Gem-quality Sphalerite is found in Spain and Mexico.

Sphalerite energizes the first chakra, increasing one's life force, courage, strength and vitality. It stimulates the second chakra, enhancing sexual energy, creative inspiration and zest for life. It strengthens the third chakra, for greater success in manifestation, clearer thinking and more willpower. It helps one draw energy and vitality up from the Earth and release excessive energy down into the Earth. It can be useful in bringing energetic balance and grounding. Sphalerite is also a stone of discrimination. Meditating with Sphalerite, one can easily distinguish between guidance and fantasy, between true spiritual insights and wishful thinking. Using it in body layouts, one can more easily detect whether problems are physical or energy-based. In counseling, it sharpens one's perceptions so that one's "truth detector" is working at its best. It can aid those who consult oracles in making correct interpretations.

Sphalerite works well with Zincite, Black Tourmaline, Smoky Quartz and Blue Sapphire. Libyan Gold Tektite and Heliodor enhance Sphalerite's capacity to strengthen willpower and manifestation. Carnelian focuses Sphalerite's energies on improving the sexual and creative aspects of one's being.

SPHENE

KEY WORDS Mental clarity and quickness, accelerated learning, intuition, focused will **CHAKRAS** Third Eye (6th), Solar Plexus (3rd) **ELEMENT** Storm, Wind **PHYSICAL** Supports the bones, hearing and vision; stimulates the brain **EMOTIONAL** Instills enjoyment of mental activity, pride in accomplishment **SPIRITUAL** Enhances willpower and manifestation, attunes to Christ consciousness

SPHENE is a calcium titanium silicate mineral with a monoclinic crystal system and a hardness of 5 to 5.5. Its color is yellow or yellow-green. It has been found in Russia, Europe, Madagascar and the USA.

Sphene works to clear the mind and stimulate thinking. It is excellent for clearing mental cobwebs. It assists memory and helps one make connections between new material and one's base of knowledge. It can assist in learning a new language or a completely new discipline. It strengthens one's intuitive abilities and is useful in learning esoteric disciplines such as astrology, numerology or kabbalah.

Sphene also empowers the will. As a brilliant stone of the pure Golden Ray, it can activate the solar plexus chakra, increasing one's capacity to manifest one's projects, dreams and desires. It inspires practical solutions to problems. On a deeper level, the Golden Ray of Sphene resonates with Christ consciousness. It can help one link to the higher realms to absorb wisdom. It can aid in making intuitive leaps to decipher the meanings of esoteric texts. It also aids one in moving readily in the conscious state among the inner realms.

Sphene harmonizes with Lapis Lazuli, Iolite, Lazulite, Heliodor, Golden Labradorite, Sunstone and Citrine. Imperial Topaz, Satyaloka Yellow Azeztulite and Himalayan Gold Azeztulite can enhance one's focus on the Golden Ray and the mystical connection to Christ consciousness.

SPINEL

KEY WORDS Revitalization, inspiration, new hope, victory, re-energizing all levels of the self **CHAKRAS** Crown (7th), Solar Plexus (3rd) **ELEMENT** Storm
PHYSICAL Supports convalescence; overcoming fatigue, trauma, illness **EMOTIONAL** Encourages optimism and hopes, dispels negative thoughts **SPIRITUAL** Loosens past limitations, inspires self-transformation

SPINEL is a magnesium aluminum oxide mineral with a cubic crystal system and a hardness of 7.5 to 8. Its colors are red, blue, green, clear, black and brown. It is found in Madagascar, India and Sri Lanka.

Spinel is a stone of revitalization. It can stimulate any of the chakras, as well as the meridian system, bringing fresh energy where it is most needed. It is excellent for reducing fatigue, replenishing depleted energies and recovering from illness or trauma. In regard to emotions, Spinel is a stone of new hope. It can relieve the burden of negative thoughts and remind one that life is a gift. Mentally, Spinel can be a catalyst for inspiration and new ways of thinking. It assists one in generating and articulating new ideas. Spinel can even facilitate the process of building a new self-image. It loosens the grip of entrenched, limiting ideas about one's attractiveness, talents and capacities for new growth, allowing one to free the mind and transform into one's highest self. Spinel is a stone of victory. It inspires one to accept life's challenges and to do what is necessary to achieve them. It can increase one's endurance and persistence beyond what one had believed was possible. It aids in focusing oneself on the desired goal and continuing until it is won.

Spinel harmonizes with Rhodizite, Nuummite and Crimson Cuprite. Natrolite and all the Azeztulites take Spinel's energies to higher spiritual levels. Rosophia helps it with emotional replenishment.

SPIRALITE GEMSHELLS

KEY WORDS Preservation of life, longevity, access to information on higher levels, telepathic link with cetaceans and other sea creatures, DNA evolution **CHAKRAS** Third Eye (6th), Crown (7th) **ELEMENTS** Water, Earth **PHYSICAL** Supports bodily stamina, recovery from illness, longevity and the evolution of DNA **EMOTIONAL** Evokes the feeling of kinship with all living things and with crystalline life as well **SPIRITUAL** Brings the spiraling energies of universal vitality into one's consciousness, energy systems and cells

SPIRALITE GEMSHELLS are unique agatized spiral seashell fossils from India. The colors range widely through white, tan, brown and gray shades. Many specimens have hollow areas in which druzy crystals have formed.

Spiralite Gemshells bridge the boundary between the animal and mineral worlds, making it much easier for one to access crystal energies. These stone shells carry the memory of life in Earth's ancient times, and can be refreshing to the etheric body, offering healing benefits to one's whole being. They carry the energies of the Great Spiral, one of the fundamental forms of existence. They bring one's consciousness into a powerful focus, increasing access to spiritual information from higher levels. They are excellent stones for channelers, healers and intuitives—from medical seers to prophetic visionaries. These stones aid one in accessing the Akashic Records, recalling past lives, and communicating with spiritual beings. They are powerful aids to telepathic communication with beings of the sea such as whales, dolphins and even fish! Spiralite Gemshells support the preservation of life. They are powerful stones of longevity, and can "teach" the spiritual aspect of one's DNA to evolve itself while retaining its essential stability.

Spiralite Gemshells resonate with the Azeztulite, Deva Quartz, Phenacites, Anandalite, Nirvana Quartz, Mystic Merlinite and Auralite-23.

SPIRIT QUARTZ

KEY WORDS Merging with the Higher Self, purification, protection, spiritual evolution, freedom from fear
CHAKRAS Crown (7th), Solar Plexus (3rd)
ELEMENT Storm **PHYSICAL** Shields etheric body, keeps negative energy from causing disease
EMOTIONAL Cleanses the emotional body, instills inner peace **SPIRITUAL** Links one with the Higher Self, strengthens one's will forces

SPIRIT QUARTZ is a silicon dioxide mineral with a hexagonal crystal system and a hardness of 7. Its form is candle-shaped, covered with small Amethyst or Citrine points. It is found only in South Africa.

Spirit Quartz is a stone for bringing Spirit into play with all aspects of one's inner and outer life. It aligns the everyday "local self" with the Higher Self, and assists the Higher Self in manifesting through one's human form. Amethyst-colored Spirit Quartz links one's conscious mind to the Higher Self, allowing one to comprehend and express the knowledge one receives. The Citrine variety works through the third chakra, causing one to act directly from the will of the Higher Self. In meditation, Spirit Quartz can bring peace of mind and freedom from fear. The Amethyst form can dispel negative attachments and entities, repair "holes" in the etheric body, balance the astral body and bring the chakras and meridians up to their optimal level of functioning. It stimulates the crown chakra, so one can receive spiritual information and communication from guides. The Citrine form clears and stimulates the third chakra. It frees the will from the inhibitions of one's upbringing so one can focus on attaining one's chosen goals and those of the Higher Self.

Spirit Quartz works harmoniously with all members of the Quartz and Beryl families. Moldavite has the capacity to speed up the effects of Spirit Quartz. Guardianite helps it purify negative energies.

STAUROLITE

KEY WORDS Grounding and physical well-being, linking with the near realms of fairies, devas, animal and plant consciousness
CHAKRAS Root (1st), Heart (4th), Third Eye (6th), Crown (7th)   **ELEMENT** Earth   **PHYSICAL** Helps one stop self-destructive habits, aids cleansing practices   **EMOTIONAL** Opens one to the beauty and love of the soul of Nature   **SPIRITUAL** Enhances astral travel, animal communication, lucid dreaming

STAUROLITE is a complex mineral containing iron, magnesium, zinc, aluminum and silicon. Its hardness is 7 to 7.5, and its crystal system is monoclinic. The twinned crystals have been given the nickname "fairy crosses." It is found in the USA, Brazil, Russia and Switzerland.

Staurolite vibrates to the frequencies of the other dimensions closest to our own. It can act as a key to the astral plane, the devic realm, and the domain of the fairies, and it can be used to communicate with plant and animal spirits. Keeping the vibration of Staurolite in one's energy field helps to open one's eyes to invisible worlds that exist in symbiosis with the physical Earth. As a crystal which often manifests as a symbol of the four directions, Staurolite also contains the invisible link to the "fifth direction," which is the vertical inner direction by which one experiences and navigates the other worlds. Sleeping with a Staurolite crystal in the pillowcase can initiate astral travel or lucid dreaming. Meditators can use Staurolite to make fine vibrational discriminations among various inner doorways. Staurolite can also aid in giving up self-destructive habits and going through cleansing regimens.

Staurolite's power is increased by Ruby. Green Kyanite and Green Apophyllite assist one in attuning to the fairy and devic realms. Blue Kyanite increases its enhancement of the psychic senses.

STIBNITE

KEY WORDS Attunement with new frequencies, transformation, new perspectives, prosperity, enhancement of personal power **CHAKRAS** All **ELEMENT** Earth **PHYSICAL** Supports healing of infections, parasitic invasions, skin eruptions **EMOTIONAL** Helps overcome feelings of powerlessness and fear **SPIRITUAL** Aids in manifestation of wealth, facilitates self-transformation

STIBNITE is a lead sulfide mineral with an orthorhombic crystal system and a hardness of 2. The color is metallic gray and tarnishes to black. It is found in Romania, Japan and the Hunan Province in China.

Stibnite is a stone carrying the power of the underworld. It is associated with Pluto—both the planet and the god—and it emanates Pluto's energy of transformation, death and rebirth, new perspectives, great wealth and power. However, a highly focused intention is necessary when working with Stibnite. If one manages only a wandering attention, one may experience unexpected, undesired results. But for those who know what they truly want, Stibnite can help manifest it in abundance.

Stibnite can assist one in making profound changes in the self. If one dreams of a completely different career, spiritual life, self-image or outer personality, Stibnite can magnetize the experiences, people and synchronicities to make it so. In regard to acquiring wealth, Stibnite can be effective in attracting new opportunities through which this can happen.

Stibnite's power must be appropriately guided. Sodalite can enhance intuitive knowing, offering good hunches about potential choices. Sphalerite activates one's inner "truth detector," helping one discern when an offer is indeed too good to be true. Visionary stones like Phenacite, Azeztulite and Herderite can help one choose worthy goals. Cuprite, Heliodor and Zincite will enhance Stibnite's energy and power.

STICHTITE

KEY WORDS Kundalini activation, love
and forgiveness, compassion, spiritual
protection, emotional and physical resilience
CHAKRAS Heart (4th), Crown (7th), Root (1st)   **ELEMENT** Wind
PHYSICAL Supports neurological health, regeneration of neural pathways
EMOTIONAL Inspires love and compassion, helps overcome timidity
SPIRITUAL Encourages spiritual service, appreciation of the joy of life

STICHTITE is a hydrated magnesium chromium carbonate mineral with a trigonal crystal and a hardness of 1.5 to 2. Stichtite's color is a pinkish purple. It is found on the island of Tasmania, Australia.

Stichtite blends the vibrations of love, forgiveness and spiritual illumination, linking the heart and crown chakras. Stichtite emanates energies of protection from negativity, putting the wearer inside an "egg of Light" which shields the emotional body. It is a stone of forgiveness, and it can soften hardened attitudes, allowing one to release unreasonable stubbornness and see things from another's point of view. It encourages the spontaneous display of affection, dispelling shyness or hesitation. It helps clear one's karma and instills commitment to a life of spiritual service. It stimulates kundalini, the energy of enlightenment and evolution. Stichtite is a stone of emotional and physical resilience, allowing one to recover quickly from illness, trauma, disappointment, anger or depression. It rekindles the joy of life for its own sake. It helps one remember to see with the eyes of a child, joyful and free from expectation. Stichtite supports the regeneration of neural pathways, aiding recovery from spinal injury, dementia, Parkinson's and Alzheimer's.

Stichtite harmonizes with Moldavite, Amethyst, Sugilite, Serpentine, Scolecite, Gem Silica, Phenacite, Seraphinite and Morganite. Tibetan Tektite intensifies its kundalini energies.

STILBITE

KEY WORDS Clear thinking, expansion of self-sense, inner peace, enhancing one's dreams
CHAKRAS Heart (4th), Third Eye (6th), Crown (7th)
ELEMENT Wind   **PHYSICAL** Supports brain function, balances brain's electrical activity
EMOTIONAL Calming and expansive, opens one to experiences of bliss
SPIRITUAL Gently increases awareness, enhances dream life, awakens joy

S TILBITE is a zeolite mineral, a sodium calcium hydrous aluminum silicate with a monoclinic crystal system and a hardness of 3.5 to 4. The color is white, pinkish, gray, yellowish, reddish, orange or brown. It is also found in Poona, India; in Iceland; the Faeroe Islands and Scotland.

Stilbite crystals emanate a quiet and unceasing joy, and they are clearly stones of the love vibration. They are both opening and healing to the heart chakra, and they help one maintain openness and emotional vulnerability even in the most difficult situations. When used in meditation, Stilbite can bring about an expansion of the sense of self, starting in the heart center and increasing until one has grown past the confines of the body, becoming a sphere of awareness, connected to the body by a cord of Light. At night, Stilbite can help one drift into sleep. In meditation, Stilbite brings an inner peace that frees the Self. With issues of loss or grief, it can be a balm to the emotions. Keeping a Stilbite in the pillowcase or on the bedside table, one can experience an increase in the vividness and profundity of one's dreams.

When Stilbite and Apophyllite are together, the interdimensional access provided by the Apophyllite is gentler and more comfortable. Stilbite also harmonizes with Scolecite, Natrolite, Apophyllite, Heulandite, Morganite, Satyaloka Quartz, Celestite, the Azeztulite group and other stones of the heart and the higher spiritual dimensions.

STONEHENGE BLUESTONE

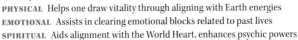

KEY WORDS Attunement to ancient knowledge, geomancy, shamanism **CHAKRAS** Base (1st), Third Eye (6th), Crown (7th) **ELEMENT** Earth
PHYSICAL Helps one draw vitality through aligning with Earth energies
EMOTIONAL Assists in clearing emotional blocks related to past lives
SPIRITUAL Aids alignment with the World Heart, enhances psychic powers

STONEHENGE BLUESTONE is a mixture of spotted dolerite, blue dolerite, rhyolite and volcanic ash, which is of high silica content. Its color is bluish gray with white spots. It is found in the Preseli Mountains of Wales.

Stonehenge Bluestone hearkens back to the prehistoric mysticism of the days of Britain's mysteries. When one meditates with this stone, there is a sensation of seeing far through distance and time. These stones are useful in attuning to the ancient Akashic records, facilitating intuitive viewing of the knowledge and histories of past civilizations.

They reveal a history of their use going back before Stonehenge, perhaps to the times of Atlantis. Stonehenge Bluestones resonate very readily with the "dragon currents," or ley lines in the Earth. They can be helpful in locating the best spots for constructing buildings, digging wells, erecting temples and outdoor altars or simply meditating. They facilitate shape-shifting and shamanic journeying. They can aid in dousing and scrying, as well as with attuning to past lives. They are one of the most powerful stones for all sorts of geomancy. Stonehenge Bluestone can be utilized for drawing energies from the Earth's meridian system, of which Stonehenge itself is a part. A piece of Stonehenge Bluestone can act as a vibrational talisman, allowing one to feel the "heartbeat of the world" and to move into harmony with that World Heart.

Stonehenge Bluestone resonates powerfully with Moldavite, Nuummite, Cryolite, Tugtupite and all of the Azeztulites.

STRONTIANITE

KEY WORDS Strength and confidence, enthusiasm for life, increased vitality and sexuality, decisiveness and self-control **CHAKRAS** Solar Plexus (3rd), Third Eye (6th), Sexual/Creative (2nd) **ELEMENT** Storm
PHYSICAL Supports muscle strength and coordination, healing of muscle diseases
EMOTIONAL Instills confidence, fairness, self-esteem; enhances sensuality
SPIRITUAL Inspires commitment to life, dispels hesitancy and fear

STRONTIANITE is a strontium carbonate mineral with an orthorhombic crystal system and a hardness of 3.5. Its colors include white, yellowish, brownish and colorless. It is found in Scotland and Germany.

Strontianite is a stone of strength and confidence. It clears and opens the third chakra, allowing for the full expression of one's personal power. It channels spiritual energy into the body, giving one increased vitality and endurance. It recharges the auric field. It inspires certainty in one's choices and commitment in one's activities. It encourages thrift and helps one organize and budget one's time, money and energy. Strontianite initiates a positive attitude, eliminating doubt and hesitation. It helps one overcome fears by facing and accepting facts. It enhances the senses, dissolving feelings of numbness and isolation. It increases one's receptivity to pleasure, quiets one's inner judge and increases self-esteem. It enhances one's receptivity to and enjoyment of others. It opens one's eyes to our common humanity and encourages friendship. Strontianite promotes healthy sexuality. It encourages the appreciation one's partner and the enjoyment of romance. Strontianite is a stone of self-control, influencing one to listen carefully before making decisions.

Strontianite harmonizes with Celestite, which softens its willfulness. It works well with all Calcites and with Spanish Aragonite. Libyan Gold Tektite increases its capacity to energize the third chakra.

SUGILITE

KEY WORDS Dreams, spiritual protection and purification, becoming a "beacon of Light"   **CHAKRAS** Third Eye (6th), Crown (7th), Etheric (8th–14th)   **ELEMENT** Wind
PHYSICAL Provides a purifying, protective influence; supports healing from cancer   **EMOTIONAL** Instills a positive, hopeful attitude; clears emotional body   **SPIRITUAL** Dissolves negativity, helps one receive and spread Divine Light

SUGILITE is a rare potassium sodium lithium iron manganese aluminum silicate mineral with a hexagonal crystal system and a hardness of 6 to 6.5. Its color ranges from pale lilac to deep purple. Almost all Sugilite on the market comes from manganese mines in South Africa.

Sugilite offers a multitude of beneficial properties—protection from negative influences, enhancement of one's ability to ground spiritual energies, the awakening of the crown chakra, the emanation of the pure Violet Ray of purification and a strong influence for healing. Carrying or wearing a piece of Sugilite sets up a "shield of Light" around the wearer. It is the most powerful stone for calling in the Violet Flame of purification, which can burn away "gray spots" in the auric field, removing negative attachments and karmic influences. It initiates an energetic cleansing process, eliminating toxic influences from one's inner and outer environment. Sugilite works to stimulate and open the crown chakra for grounding spiritual Light on Earth, making one a "beacon of Light." It can enhance the depth and meaning of dreams.

Sugilite works exceptionally well with the transformational energies of Moldavite. Phenacite, Natrolite, Herderite, Brookite and Scolecite all assist in intensifying the visionary component of Sugilite's energies. All the Azeztulites greatly enhance Sugilite's crown chakra opening and one's channeling and grounding of the Divine Light.

SUNSET GOLD SELENITE

KEY WORDS Creating through the will, integration of the brain hemispheres, unification of brain/mind and heart/wisdom **CHAKRAS** Solar Plexus (3rd), Heart (4th), Third Eye (6th), Crown (7th) **ELEMENT** Fire, Wind **PHYSICAL** Supports systems of digestion and elimination, vision and hearing **EMOTIONAL** Aids in recovery from addictions and wounds to one's personal power **SPIRITUAL** Initiates one's potential for cocreating, stimulates inner vision

SUNSET GOLD SELENITE is a hydrous calcium sulfate mineral with a hardness of 2. It is named because of its golden color and radiance. These crystals were discovered in Texas in 2007.

Sunset Gold Selenite quickly opens and activates the third eye and solar plexus chakras. When it is held to the third eye, its currents move up also to the crown, stimulating its opening. Sunset Gold Selenite aids in developing the creating activity of the will. It stimulates one's vision and one's will to create. This creating activity is first and foremost an activity of trust. Through trusting the unknown while holding the essence of our heartfelt intention, we engage in cocreation with the World Soul. Sunset Gold Selenite can aid in self-healing in these areas: digestive difficulties, bowel sluggishness, impaired vision and hearing, muscle weakness and addictive behaviors. Addictions and other sorts of bad habits are, from a certain perspective, diseases of the will. The enhancement of will forces offered by Sunset Gold Selenite can help one break through all sorts of old stuck patterns.

Sunset Gold Selenite resonates with Agni Gold Danburite, Golden Labradorite, Phenacite, Herderite, Himalaya Gold Azeztulite, Satyaloka Yellow Azeztulite and other high-vibration stones. Its power is magnified when it is combined with Guardianite or Master Shamanite.

SUNSTONE

KEY WORDS Leadership, benevolence, strength, abundance of blessings, enlightened male energy **CHAKRAS** Sexual/Creative (2nd), Solar Plexus (3rd) **ELEMENT** Fire
PHYSICAL Warms the body; increases metabolism, digestion and vitality; supports endocrine and reproductive systems
EMOTIONAL Encourages a positive, benevolent attitude; overcomes self-doubt
SPIRITUAL Inspires responsibility, conviction, benevolence; aids prosperity

SUNSTONE is an oligioclase feldspar with a triclinic crystal system and a hardness of 6 to 6.5. Its color is orange to red-brown, mixed with white. It comes from India, Canada, Norway, Russia and the USA.

Sunstone is a stone of personal power, freedom and expanded consciousness. It reflects the qualities of Solar Light—openness, benevolence, warmth, strength, mental clarity and capacity to bestow blessings. Sunstone can kindle the fire of leadership within those who wear or carry it. It helps leaders find the inner conviction and self-discipline to move forward. It melts away the sense of unworthiness that can keep one from fully being who one is. Sunstone engenders a sense of abundance in regard to all one's needs and desires, and it can assist one in manifesting prosperity, acquiring knowledge and attaining wisdom. It can bring the heart's wisdom into alignment with the mind's inspirations. Meditating with Sunstone on the third eye will help one to see one's highest path of action in any situation. Sunstone energizes the second and third chakras, stimulating leadership and will, creativity and sexuality. It can bring exuberance and innovation into one's romantic and/or artistic expressions.

Sunstone's *yang* balances Moonstone's *yin*, making a beautiful harmony. It also harmonizes with Labradorite, Moldavite, Amber, Selenite, Golden Labradorite, Prasiolite, Jet, Danburite, Larimar and Quartz.

TANGERINE QUARTZ

KEY WORDS Creativity, sexuality, passion, curiosity, inspiration, playfulness, innocence **CHAKRAS** Sexual/Creative (2nd) **ELEMENT** Fire **PHYSICAL** Supports healthy function of sexual organs and adrenals **EMOTIONAL** Encourages a playful, adventurous enthusiasm; dispels fear **SPIRITUAL** Inspires originality, courage; brings a great infusion of creativity

TANGERINE QUARTZ is a silicon dioxide mineral with a hexagonal crystal system and a hardness of 7. It has an orangy coloration caused by inclusions or coatings of iron. It is found in Brazil and Madagascar.

Tangerine Quartz activates the second chakra, stimulating one's creativity and sexual energies, blending them to enhance spiritual growth. The currents of these stones can trigger great bursts of creative power. Meditation with Tangerine Quartz can facilitate an upwelling of new ideas and inspirations from deep within the self, and these crystals can help one find the zest and energy to implement them. Tangerine Quartz can be used for activation of sexual desire as well, especially if the stone is placed at or near the second chakra. Partners can meditate or sleep within a grid of these crystals for enhancement of mutual creativity and inspirations to pursue together. Such a grid may increase the level of eroticism in the relationship. If one prefers to focus on only one of these activations, one can program the crystals to enhance only the desired energies. One can use Tangerine Quartz to enhance a creative endeavor by meditating with the stone and asking for assistance.

The currents of Tangerine Quartz are amplified by Orange Calcite, Zincite, Carnelian and Padparadsha Sapphire. Cuprite brings in additional life force, and Golden Labradorite empowers the will. Phenacite, Azeztulite and Herderite can be added to increase spiritual creativity.

TANZANITE

KEY WORDS Linkage of the mind and heart, enhanced spiritual perception, compassionate self-expression, adherence to truth **CHAKRAS** Heart (4th), Throat (5th), Third Eye (6th), Crown (7th), Soul Star (8th) **ELEMENT** Wind **PHYSICAL** Supports thyroid and adrenals, enhances neural links between brain and heart **EMOTIONAL** Encourages compassion, calms the mind, inspires joy **SPIRITUAL** Aids in knowing and expressing the wisdom of the heart

T ANZANITE is a calcium aluminum silicate with an orthorhombic crystal system and a hardness of 6.5 to 7. The color is mostly blue or blue-violet, though some crystals are yellow. It comes from Tanzania, Africa.

Tanzanite integrates the energies of the mind and heart. It opens a cascade of thoughts and insights, but it keeps one calmly anchored in the heart's wisdom. The integration of mind and heart offered by Tanzanite takes place through the linkage and attunement of the heart and third eye chakras. Bringing the heart into communion with the mind is essential to achieving wholeness. Tanzanite helps by making the heart's promptings more noticeable to the mind and connecting a circuit between the heart and third eye. One feels this circuit as a fluttering vibration of joy and pleasure. Another effect of Tanzanite's linking the mind and heart occurs at the throat chakra. Tanzanite's energy makes it easier to speak the heart's truth with eloquence, and makes it difficult to conceal or deny what one knows in one's heart.

Tanzanite is one of the Synergy Twelve stones, along with Moldavite, Phenacite, Danburite, Azeztulite, Herderite, Tibetan Tektite, Petalite, Brookite, Natrolite and Scolecite. It harmonizes with Larimar, Charoite, Ruby-Zoisite and most Quartz. It has a powerful affinity for Satyaloka Rose and Satyaloka Yellow Azeztulite, which link mind and heart.

TEKTITE (COMMON)

KEY WORDS Connection with ETs, telepathic communication, raising one's vibrational level
CHAKRAS All **ELEMENT** Storm
PHYSICAL Supports the body in integrating high-frequency energies **EMOTIONAL** Helps Starborns overcome homesickness and loneliness **SPIRITUAL** Increases psychic sensitivity, enhances telepathic link to ETs

Tektites are glassy objects associated with meteoric impacts. Their hardness is from 5.5 to 6.5, and their crystal system is amorphous. The name comes from the Greek word *tektos,* meaning "molten." The common Tektites discussed here are from Indochina and China.

Tektites carry extraterrestrial streams of communication and information. They vibrate with high-frequency pulsations which can put one in touch with ETs. A being known as Ashtar, who has been named as a benevolent ET guardian, is believed to use Tektites to facilitate telepathic communication with humans. For those interested in this, it is recommended that one sleep or meditate with a Tektite taped to the third eye or placed near the head. Experiencing this connection can feel like a homecoming to Starborns and others who feel kinship to extraterrestrial beings. Tektites can heighten psychic sensitivity, clairaudient experiences, frequency of synchronicities and "seeing through the veil" of the physical world. Tektite's increase of one's inner Light may attract people seeking friendship, counsel and kindness. Such experiences may account for Tektite's fame as a stone of good luck.

Tektites harmonize and magnify one another. The common Tektites are intensified by Moldavite, Libyan Gold Tektite and Tibetan Tektite. Lapis Lazuli, Jasper, Chalcedony, Opal, Petrified Wood and nearly all forms of Quartz crystals combine harmoniously with Tektite.

THULITE

KEY WORDS Joy, pleasure, affection, healing of negative patterns, generosity, kindness, centering in the heart, linkage of heart and mind **CHAKRAS** Heart (4th), Sexual/Creative (2nd), Solar Plexus (3rd), Throat (5th) **ELEMENT** Water, Wind **PHYSICAL** Supports and integrates the heart and digestive systems **EMOTIONAL** Dispels judgment of self and others, inspires kindness **SPIRITUAL** Enhances empathy, encourages one's full commitment to love

THULITE is a calcium aluminum silicate with an orthorhombic crystal system and a hardness of 6.5 to 7. The color is pink to reddish pink. It is found in Thule, Norway, as well as Australia and South Africa.

Thulite stimulates the second, third, fourth and fifth chakras, seats of sexuality and creativity, will and action, love relationship, and communication. Thulite encourages happiness, contentment, enthusiasm, affection, pleasure and joy. It assists in seeing the fundamental goodness of the world and oneself. It initiates rapport between people. It is excellent for making new friends or initiating a romantic relationship. It encourages empathy, diffuses tensions and facilitates finding common ground. Thulite is ideal for children, helping them feel safe, happy and at home in the world. For people of all ages, it encourages self-love. It supports healthy habits and assists in breaking self-destructive patterns. This can be true for addictions such as smoking, and for emotional imbalances such as shame and self-judgment. Thulite aids one in speaking sincerely and acting generously. It allows one to break through unhealthy emotional walls. It teaches one to love first and ask questions later.

Thulite harmonizes with all heart-chakra stones, especially Rose Quartz, Rosophia, Morganite and Dioptase. Moldavite can accelerate all of Thulite's effects. Iolite magnifies Thulite's enhancement of insight.

TIBETAN BLACK QUARTZ

KEY WORDS Spiritual protection and purification, enhancement of meditation, balancing chakras and meridians, clearing and energizing the aura
CHAKRAS All **ELEMENT** Storm
PHYSICAL Balances and energizes the Liquid Crystal Body Matrix
EMOTIONAL Clears negative energy patterns, initiates emotional balance
SPIRITUAL Offers spiritual cleansing, protection; enhances meditation

T IBETAN BLACK QUARTZ is a silicon dioxide with a hexagonal crystal system and a hardness of 7. The crystals are usually double-terminated and contain black inclusions. They are found in Tibet and Nepal.

Tibetan Black Quartz crystals are powerful stones of spiritual protection. Their currents create a "bubble of Light" around the body, allowing only positive vibrations to penetrate the auric field. Sleeping with Tibetan Black Quartz protects one from lower astral energies and disturbing dreams. It can energetically purify and cleanse one's living space. In meditation, Tibetan Black Quartz emanates a silent "om," and it can awaken the third eye. In addition, Tibetan Black Quartz crystals can activate and balance the chakras and meridian system, clearing energy blockages. One can use these stones to make crystal grids around one's bed or meditation space, creating a mini-vortex of good vibrations. Also, placing them at the outside corners of one's home, as well as at each door or window, can enhance the subtle energies of the entire environment. Rituals done with Tibetan Black Quartz will be amplified in power and pure in their positive effects.

Tibetan Black Quartz harmonizes with Moldavite, Lemurian Seed Crystals, Lithium Quartz and Faden Quartz. Combining these stones with any or all of the Azeztulites will bring in angelic energies, and using them with Phenacite can enhance visionary experiences.

TIBETAN TEKTITE

KEY WORDS Opening the chakra column, attunement to the Supramental Force, accelerated evolution, Light Body awakening **CHAKRAS** All **ELEMENT** Storm **PHYSICAL** Aids with spinal alignment, brings Light into the cells **EMOTIONAL** Inspires the joy and wonder of spiritual awakening **SPIRITUAL** Gently awakens kundalini, allows "downloads" of spiritual Light

TIBETAN TEKTITES are glassy objects with an amorphous crystal system and a hardness of 5.5 to 6.5. They are found in Tibet and southern China. Tibetan Tektites are believed to have formed in meteoric impacts. More than two thousand years ago, the Chinese writer Liu Sun gave Tektites the name *Lei-gong-mo*, meaning "Inkstone of the Thundergod." Australian Aborigines refer to them as *Maban*, which means "magic," and they believe that finding a Tektite brings good luck. In India the stones have been known as *Saimantaki-mani*, the "sacred gem of Krishna."

Tibetan Tektites are among the most powerful stones for opening the chakra channel along the spine. To do this, one can have a partner rotate one Tibetan Tektite clockwise above one's head while bringing a second stone slowly up along the spine. The results are very powerful and felt by almost everyone. This is the ideal beginning to a session in which one will work with other stones, as it opens the energy field. In opening the crown chakra and the column, Tibetan Tektites facilitate the descent of the Supramental Force, the Divine energy of evolution. As this energy penetrates deeply with repeated use of Tibetan Tektite, it can lead to the kindling of the Body of Light.

Tibetan Tektites harmonize with Light Body stones such as Phenacite, Herderite, Spanish Aragonite and all forms of Azeztulite. Astaraline and Guardianite protect the developing Light Body.

TIGER EYE

KEY WORDS Balance between extremes, discernment, vitality, strength, practicality, fairness **CHAKRAS** Solar Plexus (3rd), Sexual/Creative (2nd), Root (1st) **ELEMENT** Fire and Earth **PHYSICAL** Supports hormonal balance, enhances general vitality **EMOTIONAL** Facilitates finding emotional harmony with others **SPIRITUAL** Instills spiritual balance, stamina, creativity and clarity

TIGER EYE is a silicon dioxide mineral with a hexagonal crystal system and a hardness of 7. It has shimmering bands of yellow-brown to golden color. It is found in South Africa, India, Australia and the USA.

Tiger Eye is a solar stone of vitality, practicality and physical action. It stimulates the root chakra and solar plexus, assisting one in taking effective actions and remaining grounded, calm and centered. Tiger Eye is a stone of mental clarity. It activates and whets the intellect, sharpening the sword of logic. It also opens the mind to embracing paradox. Tiger Eye energizes the body to accomplish the imperatives of the will. It can lend one the strength to overcome fatigue or discouragement. It activates and aligns the lower chakras so one's actions draw upon the full spectrum of primal strength, creativity and enlightened intention. As a stone of balance, Tiger Eye allows one to find the harmonious center between all types of polarities. It helps one see both sides in disagreements. Those going through difficult negotiations are encouraged to bring along a Tiger Eye. One's own ability and willingness to find common ground with the other will often inspire a similar response.

Tiger Eye harmonizes with all the crystalline members of the Quartz family, as well as Malachite, Charoite, Seraphinite and most types of Jasper. Moldavite adds positive transformational energy that helps one move through "stuck" places, assisted by Tiger Eye's vitality and strength.

TIGER IRON

KEY WORDS Strength, stamina, focused will, physical energy and strength, self-healing, grounding
CHAKRAS Root (1st), Sexual/Creative (2nd), Solar Plexus (3rd) **ELEMENT** Fire and Earth
PHYSICAL Benefits physical vitality; supports kidneys, lungs, intestines and pancreas **EMOTIONAL** Increases self-confidence, helps overcome self-sabotage
SPIRITUAL Enhances personal power, focus, mental clarity, groundedness

TIGER IRON is a banded stone containing layers of Tiger Eye, Jasper and Hematite. Tiger Iron derives its name from the presence of Tiger Eye and iron-rich Hematite. It is found in Australia.

Tiger Iron is a stone of strength, stamina and courage. It combines three powerful stones, amplifying and blending their effects. Tiger Eye enhances vitality, practicality and physical action. Red Jasper increases vitality and endurance. Hematite is highly effective for grounding. These three minerals together make the most energetically dynamic of all the grounding stones. Tiger Iron is very useful for self-healing, especially from chronic illnesses. It can help one become physically stronger. It reinforces the patterns of health, personal power, focused will, mental clarity and groundedness. Tiger Iron encourages creative expression, especially in areas of performance such as music and acting. It helps those who are energetically or psychically sensitive to remain comfortably in the body. It can instill vibrational harmony in the kidneys, lungs, intestines and pancreas. It aids in strengthening the blood and muscle tone. It assists one in maintaining the willpower for giving up bad habits and sticking to diet and exercise programs.

Tiger Iron works synergistically with Heliodor, Red Garnet, Golden Labradorite, Cerussite, Sphalerite, Quartz and Jasper. It resonates with Spider Jasper for enhancement of agility, endurance and strength.

TITANIUM QUARTZ

KEY WORDS Increased life force and vitality, activation of the Rainbow Body of Light, humor and relaxation, enjoyment of life **CHAKRAS** All **ELEMENT** Fire and Storm **PHYSICAL** Supports endocrine system, energizes a sluggish immune system **EMOTIONAL** Enhances confidence, increases amusement and enjoyment of life **SPIRITUAL** Energizes all of the chakras, helps awaken the Rainbow Body of Light

Titanium quartz is the name given to a Quartz that has been placed in a chamber in which vaporized titanium and other metals are introduced and bonded with the Quartz. The result is Quartz displaying vivid multi-colored reflections and unusual energies.

Titanium Quartz projects strength, mental acuity and physical power. The currents of Titanium Quartz can make one more focused, more confident, more aware of one's environment, more amused by life in general and more ready to cope with whatever needs one's attention. One is able to take on greater responsibilities without feeling them to be a burden. One may also notice an activation of one's mental abilities, especially the analytical, rational side, as well as an enhancement of one's sense of fun. One can receive a great deal of vitality from this material. Those who already have a good supply of the energies provided by Titanium Quartz may enjoy it for the increase in zest and enjoyment of life they feel with it. Titanium Quartz can stimulate humor and relaxation, helping one take life more lightly. These are stones of Hermes, the god of quick intelligence and wit, and they can sharpen both in those who use it.

Titanium Quartz harmonizes with Moldavite, Cacoxenite, Lapis Lazuli, Blue Sapphire, Iolite and Lazulite. Strombolite augments its focus on one's appreciation and expression of humor.

TOPAZ, WHITE

KEY WORDS Spirituality, psychic gifts, mental clarity
CHAKRAS Crown (7th), Etheric (8th – 14th)   **ELEMENT** Fire
PHYSICAL Supports manifestation of one's vision of one's
health or illness   **EMOTIONAL** Helps one learn faith more
easily, teaches gratitude   **SPIRITUAL** Aids in envisioning and
realizing one's highest spiritual path

WHITE TOPAZ is an aluminum silicate fluoride hydroxide crystal with an orthorhombic crystal system and a hardness of 8. It frequently forms prismatic crystals, often eight-sided with striations along the length. It is found in Brazil, Sri Lanka, Russia, Burma, Australia, Japan, Madagascar, Mexico, Africa and the USA.

White Topaz works to help one in the process of clarifying one's intention, aligning it with Divine Will and manifesting it in the physical world. It is neutral in its magnification of whatever energy is focused through it. Therefore, it is important to hold positive intentions. Manifestation works largely through focus. Where we put our attention determines what we receive. In our world, vibrations move more slowly than on the higher planes, so there is usually a period of time between one's vision and its fulfillment. Often, people do not hold a clear focus long enough to manifest anything except their fears and worries. Faith is simply holding one's focus while remaining in a state of expectation and gratitude. As we learn this process and trust it more and more, things fall together, our synchronicities increase and we learn that we can be conscious cocreators with the Divine. The magic of White Topaz is that it can be used to speed up the vibrational energy of one's intention, shortening the time period between initial focus and fulfillment of one's vision.

White Topaz amplifies all other stones. Third chakra stones like Libyan Gold Tektite and Golden Labradorite aid with manifestation.

TOPAZ, GOLDEN

KEY WORDS Manifestation of personal intention, will and desires
CHAKRAS Solar Plexus (3rd) , Heart (4th)   **ELEMENT** Fire
PHYSICAL Supports the small intestines, kidneys, bladder and
colon   **EMOTIONAL** Helps align one's desires with Divine Will
for true emotional satisfaction   **SPIRITUAL** Opens the door to
Christ consciousness and Heart Ascension

GOLDEN TOPAZ is an aluminum silicate fluoride hydroxide crystal with an orthorhombic crystal system and a hardness of 8. It frequently forms prismatic crystals, often eight-sided with striations along the length. The gemstone's name is the Sanskrit word *tapaz*, which means "fire." It is found in Brazil, Sri Lanka, Russia, Pakistan and the USA.

Golden Topaz is a stone of great value for the enhancement of one's creativity, personal will and ability to manifest one's desires. It differs from White Topaz in that its energies move more slowly and are more grounded. It is an excellent stone for creating abundance within the context of what is appropriate for one's highest path. It helps one guide one's desires into alignment with Divine Will and bring a joyful acceptance and understanding of the operation of Divine Will in one's life. Golden Topaz is a carrier of the Gold/Pink ray of Christ consciousness, and it can be used to aid one in connecting with that frequency in meditation. It can help one open the heart in combination with the will, uniting the third and fourth chakras. This unity was a key aspect of Christ's mission, and when these centers function as one, the way is cleared for the Ascension of the Heart, in which the Will, Heart and Mind are in accord, initiating a state of permanent enlightenment.

Golden Topaz harmonizes with Citrine and Golden Labradorite. For Christ consciousness, it combines most powerfully with Golden Azeztulite, Himalaya Gold Azeztulite and Satyaloka Yellow Azeztulite.

TOPAZ, BLUE

KEY WORDS Enhancement of mind and communication
CHAKRAS Throat (5th), Third Eye (6th) **ELEMENT** Fire
PHYSICAL Supports healing of sore throat, speech impediments,
hyperactive thyroid **EMOTIONAL** Aids clear communication of
one's deepest feelings **SPIRITUAL** Enhances meditation, psychic
abilities, communication of deep insights

BLUE TOPAZ is an aluminum silicate fluoride hydroxide crystal with an
orthorhombic crystal system and a hardness of 8. It frequently forms prismatic crystals, often eight-sided with striations along the length. It is found in
Brazil, Sri Lanka, Russia, Madagascar, Africa and the USA. Sometimes crystals
are treated with radiation to deepen the color.

Blue Topaz can clearly provide an enhancement of one's mental processing and verbal skills, as well as improving one's attention span and ability to
concentrate on mental tasks. It can help one conceive and achieve perfection
in various projects and aspirations, as well as assisting one in making clear
discriminations about what one does and doesn't want in one's life. It can
clear and activate the throat chakra, enhancing one's ability to articulate one's
ideas and insights. Blue Topaz is a natural magnifier of psychic abilities, and
it can aid those who wish to attune to inner guidance, as well as those who
hope to serve others through doing readings or spiritual healing work. In fact,
these stones should be used in gemstone healing layouts because they are
resonant with the perfected pattern of the human body and energy system.
Though it is difficult to find naturally occurring Blue Topaz stones, their energies make them desirable to anyone who is able to do so. For spiritual work
and healing, it is much better to use natural rather than irradiated crystals.

Blue Topaz harmonizes with Aquamarine, Owyhee Blue Opal, Moldavite,
Danburite, Lapis Lazuli, Sodalite and Satya Mani Quartz.

TOURMALINE, BLACK

KEY WORDS Purification, protection   **CHAKRAS** Base (1st)
ELEMENT Earth   **PHYSICAL** Supports purification of the
body, eliminating toxic substances   **EMOTIONAL** Helps
dispel, worry, judgment, fear, anger, shame and other toxic
emotions   **SPIRITUAL** Aids with grounding and cleansing
of the energy field

Black Tourmaline is a complex aluminum borosilicate with a hexagonal crystal system and a hardness of 7 to 7.5. Its color is opaque black. It is found in Brazil, China, Pakistan, Africa and the USA.

Black Tourmaline crystals offer psychic protection for anyone who must work or live in challenging places or circumstances. It can keep one's auric field clear of imbalance even in the presence of destructive energies. Black Tourmaline crystals act like etheric vacuum cleaners, clearing oneself and one's surroundings of negativity and disharmony. Another application for Black Tourmalines is etheric purification. Carrying one of these stones in the pocket, holding one in meditation or sleeping with one in the pillowcase will provide a refreshing dose of cleansing for the auric field and the etheric body. This clearing can even echo down into the physical form. Black Tourmalines are also recommended for ridding oneself of negative thoughts, anxieties, anger, self-judgment and ideas of unworthiness. A small number of Black Tourmalines are double-terminated. These are the ideal specimens for body layouts because the linear flow of energies is enhanced equally in both directions along the crystalline form. Healing practitioners who utilize crystals are especially advised to use these with their clients.

Black Tourmaline's protective energies are enhanced by combining it with Jet, Obsidian, Black Andradite Garnet, Smoky Quartz, Sugilite, Charoite and Amethyst. Its grounding can be increased by Hematite.

TOURMALINE, PINK

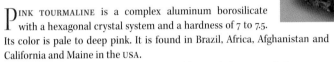

KEY WORDS Love, emotional healing **CHAKRAS** Heart (4th)
ELEMENT Water **PHYSICAL** Supports the heart, lungs and
parasympathetic nervous system **EMOTIONAL** Helps repair holes
in the auric field from emotional wounds **SPIRITUAL** Encourages
one to become a living beacon of love energies

PINK TOURMALINE is a complex aluminum borosilicate
with a hexagonal crystal system and a hardness of 7 to 7.5.
Its color is pale to deep pink. It is found in Brazil, Africa, Afghanistan and
California and Maine in the USA.

Pink Tourmaline is the quintessential heart-chakra stone. It is a representative of the feminine, or *yin* energies. It is unsurpassed for healing old emotional wounds, particularly those of childhood. It emanates a soft, soothing energy that engenders feelings of comfort, safety and nurturance. In meditation, one should hold or place a Pink Tourmaline upon the heart chakra, visualizing a pink light radiating from the stone and encompassing one in a pink cloud or bubble. This will infuse the entire emotional body with love and can restore a sense of wholeness.

Pink Tourmaline can be used to repair "holes" in the auric field created by negative attachments or past abuse. It can assist one in releasing stress, worries, depression and anxiety. It can help the emotionally numb recover their passion and zest for life. It strengthens the link between the heart and crown chakras. It can help the timid find the courage to love, and it can increase gentleness. Wearing Pink Tourmaline turns one into a beacon of its loving and healing energies, influencing others toward greater kindness and tolerance.

Pink Tourmaline works with Rose Quartz, Morganite, Kunzite, Thulite, Rosophia, Rhodochrosite, Malachite, Dioptase Pink Calcite and Satyaloka Rose Azeztulite for healing the heart and restoring love.

TOURMALINE, RUBELLITE
(Red Tourmaline)

KEY WORDS Alignment of the individual and Universal heart, healing the heart and emotions, rekindling one's passion for life **CHAKRAS** Heart (4th), Root (1st) **ELEMENT** Water, Earth **PHYSICAL** Spiritually supports heart health and recovery from heart attack **EMOTIONAL** Rekindles emotional sensitivity, passion and enjoyment of life **SPIRITUAL** Helps one attune to Cosmic Love through the Universal heart

Rubellite (aka Red Tourmaline) is a beryllium aluminum silicate with a hexagonal crystal system and a hardness of 7 to 8. Its color is deep pink to red. It is found in Brazil, Africa and the USA.

Rubellite strengthens one's heart and links it to the heart of the Earth. It can open one to the love that permeates the Universe. It is recommended to those with heart ailments because it carries and emanates the perfected vibrational pattern of the heart. Because it can link the individual heart to the Universal heart, it helps one tap into that energy for healing. Rubellite benefits the emotional heart as well. It facilitates healing emotional wounds and helps one overcome numbness and rediscover one's zest for living. Rubellite makes an excellent gift for one's romantic partner because of its capacity to fan the flames of passion. Rubellite stimulates the root chakra as well as the heart. It brings an increased flow of *prana*. Like Ruby, it stimulates courage and inspires one to protect what one loves. It enhances one's capacity to make and fulfill commitments if they are inspired by love.

Rubellite harmonizes with all other Tourmalines, as well as Rose Quartz, Morganite, Kunzite, Rosophia, Pink Azeztulite, Satyaloka Rose Azeztulite, Rhodonite, Rhodocrosite, Gaia Stone, Danburite, Petalite and Satyaloka Rose Azeztulite and White Azeztulite.

TOURMALINE, GREEN

KEY WORDS Healing, strength, vitality, wholeness
CHAKRAS Heart (4th) **ELEMENT** Water **PHYSICAL** Supports
healthy heart function, emanates *prana* for all living things
EMOTIONAL Aids in achieving inner peace through centering in
the heart **SPIRITUAL** Encourages one to embrace the spirituality
of physical life

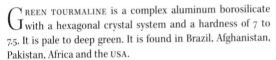

GREEN TOURMALINE is a complex aluminum borosilicate
with a hexagonal crystal system and a hardness of 7 to
7.5. It is pale to deep green. It is found in Brazil, Afghanistan,
Pakistan, Africa and the USA.

Green Tourmaline is one of the premier stones for self-healing. It centers
the energies at the heart chakra, and it is more connected to the denser vibrations of physical life than is its heart-oriented cousin, Pink Tourmaline. The
physical heart in humans is a powerful generator of bioelectricity, creating
a measurable energy field that extends twelve to fifteen feet around the body.
Green Tourmaline emanates a subtle-energy field that can harmonize with
that of the heart, engendering wholeness, dynamic balance and stability.
Because the heart is the center of one's being, bringing harmony to that
chakra creates a flow of wholesome energy to all parts of the self. Green Tourmaline is beneficial to all living things. It can be used to enhance gardens and
house plants and to connect with the spirits of plants and animals. It can be
used in meditation to commune with Nature spirits. Green Tourmaline can
enhance vitality and stamina, and it can evoke courage and strength. It helps
spiritual people embrace and enjoy life in the physical world.

Green Tourmaline's energies are enhanced by Aventurine, Emerald, Hiddenite, Peridot, Tsavorite Garnet and Uvarovite Garnet. Tiger Iron helps it
restore health and vitality and will link the heart with the lower chakras.

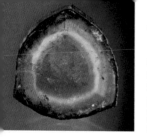

TOURMALINE, WATERMELON

KEY WORDS Calm, joy   **CHAKRAS** Heart (4th)
ELEMENT Water   **PHYSICAL** Supports the physical
heart, eases stress, stimulates release of endorphins
EMOTIONAL Fills the emotional body with a radiance of
joy, calms worry and fear   **SPIRITUAL** Stimulates the
awakening of the true Self in the "higher heart"

WATERMELON TOURMALINE is a beryllium aluminum silicate with a hexagonal crystal system and a hardness of 7 to 8. Its crystals have pink centers and green edges. It is found in Brazil, Africa and the USA.

Watermelon Tourmaline is particularly well suited to working simultaneously with the physical, emotional and spiritual components of the heart. It can awaken the "higher heart," the energy center just above the heart chakra, also known as the "seat of the soul." Watermelon Tourmaline teaches one the meaning of joy—that unbounded happiness which is not caused by any external circumstance but is instead the natural condition of being. This is also the source of Watermelon Tourmaline's capacity for healing. When one is attuned to the natural frequency of joy, there is a resulting harmonization of all aspects of oneself, from the auric field to the physical body. Life may continue to bring its moments of sorrow, but even they can be experienced with joy. The perception of beauty almost universally experienced by those who see or touch a fine Watermelon Tourmaline is in part a connection with one's own higher heart and the frequency of joy.

Watermelon Tourmaline works harmoniously with Thulite, Oregon Opal, Andean Pink Opal and Pink Calcite. Satyaloka Rose Azeztulite and Rosophia contribute greatly to the activation of the higher heart. Ruby can bring an intensity of passion to Watermelon Tourmaline's joy.

TOURMALINE, BLUE (Indicolite)

KEY WORDS Higher awareness, communication, healing **CHAKRAS** Throat (5th), Third Eye (6th) **ELEMENT** Water, Wind **PHYSICAL** Supports attunement to healing spirits, helps with headaches **EMOTIONAL** Aids clear expression of deep feelings, emotional cleansing **SPIRITUAL** Facilitates spirit communication, opens the mind to higher awareness

BLUE TOURMALINE is a complex aluminum borosilicate with a hexagonal crystal system and a hardness of 7 to 7.5. Its color is deep blue. It is found in Brazil, Africa, Pakistan, Afghanistan and the USA.

Blue Tourmaline, or Indicolite, helps one develop the psychic gifts—clairvoyance, clairaudience, clairsentience, prophecy and spirit communication. It is particularly useful for those who wish to become channels and mediums because it enhances one's ability to see and hear through the veil that separates us from the deceased and our spirit guides. Placing a Blue Tourmaline upon the sixth chakra enables one to open the third eye and "tunnel through" to the other world. Blue Tourmaline energizes the throat chakra, helping one translate psychic impressions into verbal communication. In everyday communication, Blue Tourmaline aids one in gracefully expressing deep feelings and insights. Blue Tourmaline also aids in attuning to and channeling the healing energies offered from higher dimensions. It facilitates contact with benevolent spiritual beings and the reception of their blessings. Meditation with Blue Tourmaline can open the doors to the highest spiritual realms, offering experiences of ecstatic rapture. If one has difficulty returning to the grounded state, Black Tourmaline is recommended.

Blue Tourmaline's energies are beneficially augmented by combining it with Blue or Indigo Kyanite, Lapis Lazuli, Blue Chalcedony, Lazulite, Aqua Aura Quartz, Siberian Blue Quartz and/or Sodalite.

TOURMALINE, GOLDEN

KEY WORDS Will, confidence, inner strength   **CHAKRAS** Solar Plexus (3rd)   **ELEMENT** Water   **PHYSICAL** Supports healing of digestive problems, ulcers, nausea, bowel problems   **EMOTIONAL** Encourages recognition of one's personal power, dispels fear   **SPIRITUAL** Inspires benevolent use of power, helps create prosperity

GOLDEN TOURMALINE is a complex aluminum borosilicate with a hexagonal crystal system and a hardness of 7 to 7.5. Its color is a rich yellow. It is found in Brazil and Africa.

Golden Tourmaline is a powerful aid for those who wish to repair damage to the third chakra. It can help one reduce and eventually eliminate feelings of visceral fear aroused by confrontations with others. It assists in "holding one's own" in all situations, helping timid individuals find the courage to face previously threatening experiences. In past-life therapy, it helps one relive and release traumas that have turned into repeating negative patterns. If worn or carried, it creates a "wheel of fire" at the solar plexus that acts as a shield from the "power trips" of others and enhances one's ability to focus and achieve one's aims.

Golden Tourmaline promotes clear thinking, goal setting, confidence, creative problem solving, perseverance, self-worth and a positive attitude. Because it helps bring one into a feeling of one's own worthiness and strength, it also supports tolerance, benevolence and the empowerment of others. From this place of confidence and benevolence, it is possible to easily create abundance and prosperity.

Golden Tourmaline's third chakra energies are increased by combining it with Golden Azeztulite, Satyaloka Yellow Azeztulite, Heliodor, Golden Labradorite and/or Libyan Gold Tektite. It can be used with Yellow Sapphire and Phenacite for the manifestation of prosperity.

TOURMALINE, DRAVITE
(Brown Tourmaline)

KEY WORDS Self-acceptance, self-healing, bringing the
Shadow self to consciousness, self-love **CHAKRAS** Root (1st),
Heart (4th) **ELEMENT** Earth, Storm **PHYSICAL** Aids in
over-coming addiction and self-judgment, supports the body's purification systems,
helps overcome digestive disorders **EMOTIONAL** Encourages self-acceptance and
self-love **SPIRITUAL** Powerful ally for healing and integrating one's dark side

D RAVITE (Brown Tourmaline) is a complex aluminum borosilicate with
a hexagonal crystal system and a hardness of 7 to 7.5. Its color is dark
brown. It is found in Brazil, Pakistan, India and Afghanistan.

Dravite is the ideal gemstone ally to initiate and accompany one on the
essential journey of understanding and integrating one's Shadow. In meditation, it can aid one in bringing Shadow material into conscious awareness
without rejecting or judging what one finds. Dravite is highly grounding and
will counter attempts to "ascend" before one is ready. It is nourishing to the
life-force energies, lending stamina to those doing deep inner work. It inspires
courage and persistence, and it even helps one see the humor in some of life's
darkest situations. Dravite is also an aid to those who feel numb—those who
have difficulty moving into grief or other heartfelt emotions. Its vibrations
can aid in removing energetic armoring around the heart. Dravite, like the
repairman who unclogs the sewer, is unappreciated until one realizes one
truly needs help. Then it is seen as the great blessing it truly is.

Dravite works well with Black Tourmaline, Jet, Black Obsidian, Aegirine
and Smoky Quartz, all of which provide grounding and psychic protection.
Mystic Merlinite is another ally for bringing the Shadow out of exile. Moldavite can help speed the process of inner transformation which Dravite
initiates and supports.

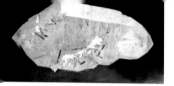

TOURMALINED QUARTZ

KEY WORDS Purification, recovery from negative influences **CHAKRAS** All **ELEMENT** Storm **PHYSICAL** Purifies one's environment, cleanses the body of negative energies **EMOTIONAL** Helps one overcome self-destructive emotional patterns **SPIRITUAL** Creates a protective, purifying field around one's aura and body

TOURMALINED QUARTZ is Clear Quartz with thin crystals of Black Tourmaline running through it. It is found primarily in Brazil, and the Quartz component can range from completely cloudy to water clear.

For anyone who has ever wished for a psychic vacuum cleaner to return one's energy field to the pristine, unpolluted state, Tourmalined Quartz is an ideal ally. Clear Quartz, with its easy programmability, can be a wonderful and versatile tool. However, Clear Quartz can sometimes pick up and amplify disharmonious energy. But in this material, the Black Tourmaline exerts a cleansing and grounding influence that keeps the Quartz clear of negativity. The Quartz in turn amplifies Black Tourmaline's purifying energies, making Tourmalined Quartz one of the most powerful tools for dispelling negative energies, repairing the auric field, restoring balance to the chakras and promoting general well-being. Tourmalined Quartz facilitates clear thinking. It is beneficial to people who need help staying on the spiritual path, especially those who have indulged in negative behaviors, such as crime or drug abuse. Wearing or carrying Tourmalined Quartz creates a "bubble of Light" around the body, screening out destructive energies. It is ideal for psychic protection because it keeps negative forces at bay while enhancing awareness.

Tourmalined Quartz's protective and purifying qualities are amplified by Moldavite, Master Shamanite, Guardianite, Aegirine, Nuummite, Charoite, Sugilite, Black Obsidian and Jet.

TREMOLITE

KEY WORDS Access to higher knowledge, calm and clarity, higher-mind activation, mystic rapture **CHAKRAS** Crown (7th), Soul Star (8th), Etheric (9th–14th) **ELEMENT** Wind **PHYSICAL** Increases *prana*, helps one diagnose ailments intuitively **EMOTIONAL** Helps release stress and anxiety, encourages calm and clarity **SPIRITUAL** Facilitates access to morphogenic fields of the Divine Mind

Tremolite is a calcium magnesium iron silicate with a monoclinic crystal system and a hardness of 5 to 6. Its color is white, gray, pink, green or brown. The best pieces are found in Pakistan and Afghanistan.

Tremolite can be used to activate the pineal gland and link it with the surrounding neural circuitry, leading to the opening of the third eye and crown chakras and conscious access to morphic fields of knowledge. When this occurs, one has only to wonder about something, and the answer appears in the mind. This is the consciousness of the "kingdom of heaven," the state in which one merely needs to "ask and it shall be given." Tremolite facilitates a sense of calm and clarity. It allows one to release stress and anxiety and to face even difficult times with equanimity. It can help one to alleviate depression and worry. Tremolite affects the unused neural circuitry of the neocortex. Holding this stone to the third eye, it can activate dormant mind centers meant for the next phase of human evolution. When this shift is made, many of the seemingly complicated problems of life dissolve because they simply do not exist at this higher level. It is like waking up from a dream.

Tremolite harmonizes with Phenacite, Brookite, Danburite, Petalite, Herderite and Beryllonite. Its stimulation of spiritual awakening is powerfully augmented by all of the Azeztulites. Rosophia aids in keeping one's expanded consciousness attuned to the heart.

337

TUGTUPITE

KEY WORDS Intense and passionate love, deep heart activation, mystic rapture, grief, emotional transformation
CHAKRAS Heart (4th), Throat (5th), Third Eye (6th), Crown (7th) **ELEMENT** Storm **PHYSICAL** Strengthens the nervous system, auric field and heart
EMOTIONAL Awakens the inner fire of love, ecstatic activation of the emotional body **SPIRITUAL** Opens one to Cosmic Love and passionate love of the Earth

TUGTUPITE is a sodium aluminum beryllium silicate with a tetragonal crystal system and a hardness of 4. It was discovered in Tugtup Agtakorfia, Greenland, in 1962.

Tugtupite is a stone of the deepest energies of the heart. Its vibrations can reawaken lost passion and forgotten love. It can also put one in touch with suppressed grief and sorrow, allowing the cleansing expression and release of these emotions. Tugtupite, for better or worse, releases the pure emotion of love in all its uncontrollable intensity. Those who wear or carry it may experience many things, but numbness is not likely to be one of them. Tugtupite simply opens the heart, all the way. The full activation of the heart chakra, for some people, is expressed in a rapturous experience of Nature and an upwelling of love for the Earth. In others, it may manifest as an ineffable joy with no object at all. As Tugtupite opens the floodgates of the heart, the upper chakras receive the rising tide of energy and are opened and energized. This can lead to the harmonious and integrated functioning of the heart, third eye, throat and crown chakras, in which all are enlivened.

Tugtupite harmonizes with Rose Quartz, Kunzite, Morganite, Emerald, Dioptase and Rosophia. Moldavite helps turn passion into transformation. Satyaloka Rose Azeztulite lifts the vibration from human to cosmic love.

TURQUOISE

KEY WORDS Wholeness, communication and spiritual
expansion **CHAKRAS** Throat (5th) **ELEMENT** Storm
PHYSICAL Increases life force in the body, supports
blood oxygenation **EMOTIONAL** Encourages self-
forgiveness and the release of useless regrets
SPIRITUAL Inspires one to act out of truth, compassion and forgiveness

Turquoise is a copper aluminum phosphate mineral with a triclinic crystal structure and a hardness of 5 to 6. Its striking blue color is caused by copper. The name means "Turkish stone."

Turquoise is a stone of wholeness and truth, and it aids in the communication and manifestation of those qualities. It stimulates and harmonizes the throat chakra, making it easier for one to articulate one's deepest wisdom. Because it is a stone of wholeness, Turquoise is also beneficial to overall well-being. It is balancing and induces a sense of serenity and peace. Holding or wearing Turquoise can help one restore depleted vitality and lift sagging spirits. This stone has the capacity to heal the emotional body, relieve stress and bring the focal point of awareness to its proper center in the heart. Turquoise teaches the wisdom of compassion and forgiveness. Through its heightening of emotional intelligence, Turquoise demonstrates that when one releases one's insistence on "justice" and views others through the lens of compassion and forgiveness, one immediately receives those gifts through one's own heart.

Turquoise works harmoniously with Gem Silica, Shattuckite, Chrysocolla, Ajoite, Malachite, Azurite and most other copper-based minerals. It is also on friendly terms with all types of Calcite, Smithsonite and Hemimorphite. Larimar and Rosophia work well with Turquoise in soothing and healing the emotional body.

ULEXITE

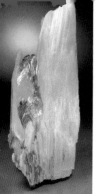

KEY WORDS Intuition, inner vision, telepathy, clairvoyance, imagination, creativity, mental agility   **CHAKRAS** Third Eye (6th)   **ELEMENT** Wind   **PHYSICAL** Supports the eyes and vision, helps overcome eye fatigue   **EMOTIONAL** Inspires feelings of exhilaration about one's visions and insights   **SPIRITUAL** Lifts the veil from one's inner eye for multiple psychic and spiritual experiences

ULEXITE is a sodium calcium borate mineral with a triclinic crystal structure and a hardness of 2.5. Much of it is found in the desert of the American Southwest.

Ulexite enhances clairvoyance. It is a stone of "far seeing." This can manifest as viewing events of the probable future, present happenings in distant places or past episodes that affect current issues. It acts upon the third eye to open interdimensional gates, so one may see and interact with beings from the higher planes. It also can be programmed to allow one to connect with extraterrestrials, guides and other entities.

Ulexite activates latent intuitive abilities. It sensitizes the self to be able to "read" the energies and intentions of others. Ulexite is a stimulant to both imagination and creativity. As it activates the third eye, numerous meaningful images and visions will appear. Telepathy is one of the inner potentials that can be awakened through meditating or sleeping with Ulexite. It is also a boon to other intuitive powers. It can quicken mental processes, allowing one to see the answers to complex problems instantly. It can enhance memory and give one a clearer grasp of concepts.

Ulexite works synergistically with Selenite, Celestite, Angelite and Mystic Merlinite for linking with higher dimensions. Moldavite and Satyaloka Azeztulite add power to its awakening of intuitive capacities.

VANADINITE

KEY WORDS Accomplishment of work, stamina, grounding, creativity, discipline, link to Earth energies   **CHAKRAS** Root (1st), Sexual/Creative (2nd), Solar Plexus (3rd), Third Eye (6th)   **ELEMENT** Fire   **PHYSICAL** Provides spiritual protection from radiation, stimulates proper hormone production   **EMOTIONAL** Encourages the adventurous spirit, playfulness, *joie de vivre*   **SPIRITUAL** Increases determination, discipline; expands intuitive awareness

V ANADINITE is a mineral combining lead, vanadium, oxygen and chlorine. Its hardness is 3, and its crystal system is hexagonal. Vanadinite is found in Morocco, as well as New Mexico and Arizona in the USA.

When one has a load of work to do, and there is no way to put it aside, one is advised to acquire some Vanadinite. This stone activates the lower three chakras, giving one the added endurance, persistence, power and will needed to see big projects through to completion. It stimulates the mind centers and links them with the lower chakras, enhancing clear thought, organization, determination and vitality. For those whose work entails intuitive readings, channeling or mediumship, Vanadinite can provide stamina and grounding. The same is true for healers. Vanadinite helps one stay linked with the body and the Earth without diminishing one's link to higher vibrational realms. Vanadinite provides a direct link to the Earth energies, and it can increase one's sensitivity to elemental forces. Vanadinite stimulates creative and sexual energies. It can help one find needed inspiration and the arousal to action. It helps one connect with the animal self and relish the experience of physical life.

Vanadinite harmonizes with Zincite, Cerussite, Carnelian and Orange Calcite, Golden Labradorite, Iolite, Tiger Iron and Lapis Lazuli.

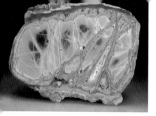

VARISCITE

KEY WORDS Inner peace, love and compassion, alignment of the physical and Light bodies, simplicity, clarity, emotional healing **CHAKRAS** Heart (4th) **ELEMENT** Water **PHYSICAL** Encourages positive brain states; enhances learning, cognition, reasoning and logic **EMOTIONAL** Opens the heart and kindles long-lasting emotional well-being **SPIRITUAL** Inspires one to release negative patterns into the Light, instills inner harmony

Variscite is a hydrous aluminum phosphate mineral with an orthorhombic crystal system and a hardness of 4 to 5. Variscite is found in Utah and Nevada in the USA, as well as Queensland, Australia.

Variscite is immediately soothing, bringing peace to the heart and tranquillity to the mind. It is an excellent stone for relieving stress. It aligns the Light Body and opens the channels to release all internal disharmonies into the Light. Variscite is cleansing to the auric field and the physical body. Its vibration is harmonious with the human energy field, and it closely matches the pattern of the Earth's energy field, so it can provide a resonant link between the human being and the Earth. Variscite brings about a strong activation and stabilization of the heart chakra. This generates positive emotional states and helps one establish them as one's normal way of being. Instead of seeing joy as a peak experience, it can become a way of life. In emotional healing, Variscite lends courage to the heart, so one can face the past without fear. It helps one to appreciate simplicity and let go of unnecessary complications. It allows one to discharge unhealthy emotional obsessions and self-destructive habits. It encourages one to take the steps to change unhealthy patterns.

Variscite works harmoniously with Tsavorite, Uvarovite Moldavite, Chrysoprase, Danburite, Rose Quartz, Rosophia and Pink Calcite.

VESUVIANITE

KEY WORDS Uniting the heart and the will, enthusiasm for life, release of negative attachments, the courage to change **CHAKRAS** All **ELEMENT** Earth **PHYSICAL** Supports muscle strength, especially in the legs and feet **EMOTIONAL** Encourages one to take joy in following one's true calling **SPIRITUAL** Helps one recognize, follow and persist in the heart's desires

VESUVIANITE, also known as Idocrase, is a calcium aluminum magnesium silicate mineral with a tetragonal crystal system and a hardness of 6 to 7. It has been found in Canada and in the USA.

Vesuvianite is a highly energetic stone, capable of affecting any of the chakras, though the predisposition of a certain specimen will vary according to color. Yellow-green Vesuvianites can help stimulate and integrate the solar-plexus and heart chakras, making it easier for individuals to align personal will with the promptings of the heart. This Vesuvianite is also useful for the manifestation of the heart's desires here on earth. It is supportive of one's taking one's true path or calling in life. If one feels unsure of one's heart's desire, the pink-purple variety of Vesuvianite may make one more aware. Vesuvianite is useful for combatting negative thoughts and bringing enthusiasm back into one's life. It helps one achieve the insights that inspire one to move forward in one's spiritual development. Vesuvianite helps those going through transformational work such as psychotherapy, breath work and past-life regression. Its ability to bring hidden material to consciousness and its enhancement of courage make it a most useful ally.

Vesuvianite harmonizes with Moldavite, Libyan Gold Tektite, Golden Labradorite, Heliodor, Emerald, Morganite, Dioptase, Tsavorite, Nuummite, Labradorite, Jet, Azeztulite, Kunzite and Tugtupite.

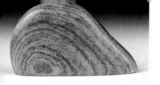

VITALITE

KEY WORDS Life Force, replenishment, joy, well-being, love, courage, emotional cleansing, generosity, creativity, spiritual awakening **CHAKRAS** Heart (4th), Third Eye (6th), Crown (7th) **ELEMENTS** Water, Earth **PHYSICAL** Supports heart, lungs, circulatory system, liver and digestive system; increases Life Force on all levels **EMOTIONAL** Aids in releasing negative emotions; helps cultivate joy **SPIRITUAL** Uplifts one into joy and remembrance of one's Divine Nature

VITALITE is comprised of quartz, muscovite, piemontite. It was discovered in New Zealand. It has layers of pink-red that appear as swirling patterns in a background of sparkling white. Its hardness is about 6.

Vitalite replenishes one's Life Force through the infusion of *prana*. When one holds this stone to the heart, it is easy to feel its flow of refreshing, revitalizing currents. Vitalite stimulates one's overall sense of well-being, helping to alleviate stress, anxiety, irritability and depression. As one feels one's body and energy field becoming enlivened, one's mood lightens and one is ready to face the world again. It stimulates courage and love, and can kindle the spiritual experience known as the Ascension of the Heart. In spiritual self-healing, Vitalite supports the heart, circulatory system, lungs, liver and digestive system. The chi in this stone is so strong that it affects the entire body on the cellular level, encouraging a healthy flow of Life Force in every cell, organ and system. Emotionally, Vitalite is a cleansing influence, and a stone of generosity. It stimulates imagination and will to help one receive inspiration and carry one's visions into manifestation. It is a stone of spiritual awakening, reminding us that we are as divine as the Universe itself.

Vitalite harmonizes with Vortexite, Kaurilite, Lilac Lepidolite, Piemontite, Crimson Cuprite, Petalite, Lithium Light, Aragonite, Rosophia, Azumar, Healerite, Revelation Stone, Empowerite and all Azeztulites.

VIVIANITE

KEY WORDS Compassion, love, inner peace, gentleness, refreshment, inspiration, mystic awakening   **CHAKRAS** Heart (4th)
ELEMENT Earth, Water   **PHYSICAL** Promotes cellular regeneration and the healing of wounds   **EMOTIONAL** Dispels negativity, opens one to the heart's ocean of love   **SPIRITUAL** Encourages one to live from the heart, enlightened compassion

VIVIANITE is a hydrous iron phosphate mineral with a monoclinic crystal system and a hardness of 1.5 to 2. The stones can be colorless, blue-green or deep blue. Fine Vivianite occurs in Bolivian tin mines.

Vivianite helps one to dive deeply into the pool of the heart. It assists one in achieving inner silence during meditation and helps one to hear the wordless voice of the heart's urgings. Vivianite allows one to enter a state of enlightened compassion. It helps to remove negativity from one's thoughts and clear one's auric field. It works below one's level of awareness to dispel self-inflicted wounds and low self-esteem. It supports feelings of altruism and kindness, and it inspires generosity. Vivianite can re-inspire those in the helping professions who suffer from exhaustion and burnout. Caregivers can receive a refreshing boost from simply sitting and holding one of these stones. Through its kindling of the heart, Vivianite can remind one of the love that dwells behind all things. It offers the heart a thread leading to its own essence. If one goes all the way, one discovers an ocean of love.

Vivianite's energy blends well with Morganite, Rose Quartz, Rhodochrosite, Moldavite, Emerald, Kunzite and Pink Calcite. Natrolite, Scolecite, Herderite and Phenacite bring the mind into resonance with the enlightened heart energy of Vivianite. Tugtupite brings passion and intensity to Vivianite's heart opening.

VORTEXITE

KEY WORDS Dynamic equilibrium, balance, refreshment, empowerment, strengthening inner energy vortices, links to Earth energies **CHAKRAS** All, especially Heart (4th) and Third Eye (6th) **ELEMENTS** Earth, Water, Fire **PHYSICAL** Supports nervous system, DNA, cellular self-repair **EMOTIONAL** Supports flow of feeling, relieves stress **SPIRITUAL** Aids attunement to Earth, Galactic and Universal energy vortices; can trigger the Ascension of the Heart

Vortexite is a combination of spherulitic rhyolite and deep-red quartz discovered in New Zealand by Peter Marden. It is volcanic in origin, produced millions of years ago from eruptions on New Zealand's North Island.

Vortexite's strong, comforting vibrations bring all of one's chakras and bodily energies into alignment. This stone is linked to the Life Force of the Earth, and brings a fresh charge of that energy into one's body, mind and spirit. Holding, carrying or wearing Vortexite helps charge, balance and attune us to our highest potential, allowing us to function as joyful and powerful spiritual human beings. Also, if one makes a journey to an energy vortex site, taking Vortexite along is sure to intensify the experience, while helping one remain balanced and grounded. Vortexite is ideal for constructing energy tools and meditation grids. Their charging and balancing effect extends to other stones as well as one's environment. In spiritual self-healing, Vortexite supports DNA self-repair and the strengthening of cell membranes. Its currents stimulate the nervous system and encourage neuronal health and regeneration. It acts as a tonic to the emotional body and aids in recovery from stress.

Vortexite works in synergy with Vitalite, Red Fire Azeztulite, Pakulite, Prophecy Stone, Sedonalite, Z Stone, Revelation Stone, Phenacite, Danburite, Vivianite and all of the Azeztulites.

WHITE PHANTOM QUARTZ

KEY WORDS Access to Akashic records, morphogenic fields and past-life memories, connection with spirit guides, energy cleansing
CHAKRAS Third eye (6th), Crown (7th) **ELEMENT** Storm
PHYSICAL Aids in healing issues that appear as "echoes" of past-life traumas **EMOTIONAL** Encourages one to free oneself from bonds to past-life patterns **SPIRITUAL** Open the spiritual archives of past knowledge and past lives

WHITE PHANTOM QUARTZ is a silicon dioxide mineral with a hexagonal crystal system and a hardness of 7. White Phantoms exhibits within the crystal body a white outline of a smaller crystal. The best White Phantom crystals are found in Brazil and in Arkansas, USA.

White Phantom Quartz crystals are ideal for moving into the archives of the past. Through meditative attunement, one can work with these stones to tap into the Akashic records with great specificity. White Phantoms can make it easier for inward journeyers to specify the goal of their search and to be sure of arriving there. Such goals can include—but are not limited to—retrieving information from forgotten past civilizations such as Atlantis and Lemuria. White Phantom Quartz assists one in attuning the mind for receiving information from the morphogenic fields of knowledge containing all histories. The field of one's own past includes the memories, wisdom and knowledge of one's previous incarnations. These, too, can be accessed with the help of White Phantom Quartz. This stone is also good for cleansing one's auric field and environment of negative energies. It can initiate contact with spirit guides and inner teachers. It helps one regain energies lost in past traumatic experiences, allowing one to relive and release the distress.

White Phantom Quartz works well with Amethyst, Rose Quartz, Owyhee Blue Opal, Alexandrite and Lemurian Seed Crystals.

WILLEMITE

KEY WORDS Interdimensional travel, adventures in the astral body, connection with higher astral beings **CHAKRAS** Third Eye (6th) **ELEMENT** Earth, Fire **PHYSICAL** Provides energetic protection from radiation and cellular mutation, enhances sexual function **EMOTIONAL** Encourages optimism and eagerness to improve one's life **SPIRITUAL** Stimulates consciousness for travels beyond the body

Willemite is a zinc silicate mineral with a hexagonal crystal system and a hardness of 5.5. Willemite is a rare mineral and occurs in combination with Franklinite and Zincite from New Jersey, USA.

Willemite is a stone of spiritual initiation. It opens the doors of many of the nearer higher realms, allowing one to begin learning how to move in consciousness beyond the Earth plane. It provides a dimensional doorway to the higher astral realm, where benevolent spirits concerned with the Earth reside. These beings will offer enthusiastic greetings to all humans who arrive in their world, because it is a big step for a human being to move consciously beyond the body, and these beings are caretakers of humanity who are encouraging our evolution. Willemite activates the third eye chakra and stimulates inner visions, as well as interdimensional travel. It assists astral travel by stabilizing both one's focused awareness and its manifestation as an astral body. The two go together—the more coherent the consciousness, the more stable the form. As one learns to move and function in the higher realms, one is limited in how "high" one can go mainly by one's success in maintaining a strong, awake sense of self.

Willemite from New Jersey occurs naturally in combination with Zincite, Franklinite and White Calcite. This natural combination of stones is ideal for those wishing to begin exploring the inner worlds.

WULFENITE

KEY WORDS Creativity, manifestation, determination, sexuality, alchemy, Earth connection   **CHAKRAS** Sexual/Creative (2nd), Solar Plexus (3rd)   **ELEMENT** Fire
PHYSICAL Stimulates metabolism, enhances sexual function and enjoyment   **EMOTIONAL** Inspires one to create, and to love the Earth and life's adventures
SPIRITUAL Aids self-transformation, artistic creativity, personal power

WULFENITE is a lead molybdenum oxide mineral with a tetragonal crystal system and a hardness of 2.5 to 3. The color is usually orange or yellow. Deposits exist in Morocco and in Arizona, USA.

Wulfenite is highly attuned to the Earth. In working with this stone, one can easily come into resonance with the planet's core vibration, or energetic heartbeat. Those who receive the full gift from Wulfenite will almost certainly be changed by the experience, and many will become activists on behalf of the living Earth. Wulfenite can aid in the alchemy of personal development—the transmutation of the "leaden" self into spiritual "gold." It can also assist in artistic creation. It stimulates both inspiration and persistence, assisting one in carrying projects through to completion. Wulfenite is a stone of originality, bringing new ideas and visions for painting, music, poetry and other art forms. Since it also activates one's sexual energies, Wulfenite's penchant for originality can lead to new adventures in love as well as art. Wulfenite stimulates the third chakra, activating one's personal power and will. It strengthens one's capacity for knowing what one wants and acting to make it happen. It helps rid one of hesitancy and fear.

Wulfenite harmonizes best with Zincite, Padparadsha Sapphire, Libyan Gold Tektite, Cerussite, Vanadinite and Yellow Sapphire.

ZINCITE

KEY WORDS Life force, creativity, sexuality, personal power, manifestation **CHAKRAS** Root (1st), Sexual/Creative (2nd), Solar Plexus (3rd) **ELEMENT** Fire **PHYSICAL** Stimulates the sexual organs and endocrine system, enhances sexual desire and performance **EMOTIONAL** Instills awareness of one's power, ignites one's enthusiasm and sense of fun **SPIRITUAL** Inspires courage, passion, creativity, willpower, enjoyment

ZINCITE is a zinc oxide crystal with a hexagonal crystal system and a hardness of 4. The color is red to orange-yellow. Natural Zincite from New Jersey, USA, occurs with Calcite, Willemite and Franklinite. Some Zincite crystals were accidentally formed in smelters in Poland.

Zincite is an ideal stone for those who need the fire of the lower-chakra energies in order to bring their aspirations into reality. Zincite strongly stimulates the first, second and third chakras and moves those energies upward to link them with the upper chakras. Zincite increases life force, courage, passion, creativity, will and personal power. It is one of the really strong stones that even people who are not usually sensitive to crystal energies can feel. Its stimulation of the base chakra brings one's consciousness firmly into the body, while providing an abundance of new energy for physical accomplishments. Its energy operates on the second chakra in a way that kindles the fires of both creativity and sexuality. Zincite charges the third chakra, increasing one's reservoir of determination, perseverance, focus of intention and capacity for manifestation. The increase in emotional, mental and spiritual energies that results from Zincite's activation of the chakras and meridians can be put to use in ways that truly revitalize one's life.

Zincite harmonizes with Carnelian, Heliodor, Golden Labradorite, Libyan Gold Tektite, Moldavite and Himalaya Red Azeztulite.

ZIRCON

KEY WORDS Stimulation of all the chakras, increased life force, grounding ideals in the physical world
CHAKRAS All **ELEMENT** Storm **PHYSICAL** Helps clear the body of common toxins and stress, supports adrenals **EMOTIONAL** Helps one overcome disillusionment and to work for one's ideals **SPIRITUAL** Aids transmutation of spiritual energies into physical reality

Z IRCON is a zirconium silicate mineral with a tetragonal crystal system and a hardness of 6.5 to 7.5. Its color is brownish red to brownish yellow. Large crystals have been found in Madagascar and Canada.

Zircon is a stone of high intensity and precise focus. It can be used to stimulate sluggish energies in any of the chakras or meridians. One of its special capacities is for transmuting spiritual energies into the physical plane. It also helps those who tend to be ungrounded to "get real" in taking care of the necessities of earthly life. Zircon is excellent for those who do not wish to give up their ideals but who need to focus on how to take those ideals out of the head and bring them into form in the world. Zircon lends energy and strength of purpose to those who might otherwise be overwhelmed by the conflict between their desire to change the world and the fear that their dreams are impossible.

In energy work, raw Zircon crystals can be used to activate any of the linkage points between the physical and etheric bodies, and they assist one in bringing the physical and spiritual self into union. Zircon can work as a talisman of spiritual protection. Its vibration acts as a "shield of Light" around the wearer, keeping intrusive or dangerous energies away.

Zircon harmonizes with Prophecy Stone for spiritual energies in the body. With Moldavite, the positive transformation is accelerated. With Phenacite, Zircon's intense energies initiate visionary experience.

351

ZOISITE (with Ruby)

KEY WORDS Increase in inner and outer development, awakening of the true self, joyful engagement with life, healing, increase in life force **CHAKRAS** Root (1st), Heart (4th), Third Eye (6th) **ELEMENT** Storm **PHYSICAL** Infuses the body with *chi*, supports optimal health and vitality **EMOTIONAL** Aids in overcoming negative states, promotes zest for life **SPIRITUAL** Facilitates the powerful, dramatic opening of the heart

ZOISITE is a calcium aluminum silicate mineral with an orthorhombic crystal system and a hardness of 6.5 to 7. Colors of Zoisite are varied, but this variety from India is green and is mixed with Ruby.

Zoisite with Ruby is one of those truly fortunate natural mineral combinations. Green Zoisite emanates an energy of growth and fertility, and it strengthens the neural and energetic connections between the brain and the heart. Ruby is a stone of life force, courage and passion. It stimulates the root chakra, providing an infusion of vitality which can make one feel rejuvenated and enthusiastic for life. When Ruby and Zoisite are combined, the root, heart and third eye chakras are strongly stimulated and harmonized. Zoisite with Ruby energizes the body and creates a sense of well-being. It facilitates the dramatic opening of the heart chakra. It supports one's optimal state of health and aids in the vibrational treatment of depression, chronic fatigue syndrome, fainting spells, sluggish thyroid and exhaustion of the adrenals. It can assist one in becoming aware of suppressed grief and releasing it. Zoisite with Ruby increases the potency of one's energy field, strengthening the etheric body and cleansing the astral body of negative attachments.

Zoisite with Ruby harmonizes with Tanzanite, Apophyllite, Tugtupite, Satyaloka Rose Azeztulite and all forms of Sapphire.

Z STONE

KEY WORDS Interdimensional travel, magic, sacred geometry, Merkaba vehicle **CHAKRAS** Third Eye (6th), Crown (7th) **ELEMENT** Storm **PHYSICAL** Stimulates the brain and nervous system **EMOTIONAL** Inspires interest in other dimensions **SPIRITUAL** Opens awareness of astral realm, enables travel as a point-of-consciousness, engenders spiritual visions

Z STONES are pseudomorph concretions found in the Sahara Desert. Their color is blackish-brown, and they display a wide variety of strange forms. Some specimens contain embedded fossils.

For those who wish to travel interdimensionally and explore the subtle realms of consciousness, Z Stones could provide an interesting ticket. They powerfully stimulate the third eye and crown chakras, widening one's awareness and allowing one to see and explore the nearer realms that are normally overlooked in our everyday state. The astral realm can be readily accessed with Z Stones. Another more rarified realm—that of the "living geometries"—can be reached by using Z Stones along with meditative focus on the Merkaba or other forms of sacred geometry. If one works to visualize the Merkaba vehicle while holding a Z Stone at the third eye, one may experience a much quicker and more vivid transition to the "traveling" state—moving as a point of consciousness, anywhere in the universe, almost instantaneously.

Z Stones can be helpful for those wishing to work with elemental currents, helping influence the manifestation of energy. They can be excellent tools for working magically, especially in the area of sympathetic magic.

Z Stones harmonize with Danburite, Anandalite, Rosophia, Black Tourmaline, Black Andradite Garnet, Guardian Stone and Merlinite. High-vibration stones such as Azeztulite channel Z Stones' influence to altruistic purposes.

APPENDIX I

HOW TO MEDITATE WITH A STONE: CIRCULATION THROUGH THE HEART

This is the meditative practice I use with all of the stones I write about. It is the one with which I begin all new relationships with a stone or group of stones. I like it because it is simple, direct, and heart-centered. Many other processes can be tried afterwards, with a huge array of results. For me, though, it all begins with this:

1. Sit in a quiet room in a comfortable chair. Hold the stone in your hand. Look it over carefully. Feel the texture, sniff it, notice its color and form. Focus all of your usual senses on the stone.

2. Hold the stone in front of your face and blow your breath across it. While doing so, imagine your breath to be an offering of yourself into relationship with the stone being. Next, inhale, drawing your breath across the stone and into your lungs. Imagine that you are taking in the stone's offer of relationship to you.

3. Now hold the stone over your heart. Continue the inner gesture of self-offering with the exhale, and an invitation or opening to the stone with each inhale. Feel the stone currents entering your chest and your heart as you inhale. Allow your energies to go out to the stone (and through the stone to the Soul Being of the stone) as you exhale.

4. Continue the inhale and exhale gestures as you breathe. Keep your awareness centered in your heart. Notice what occurs, and whether there is a building-up of the intensity of the currents between the stone and your heart. Notice where the currents of the stone go in your body.

5. Keep the exchange flowing as you breathe. Notice any shifts in your consciousness. Invite the stone to tell or show you its nature and purpose. Be aware of any inner pictures, sounds, words, ideas, smells, or tastes. Even things like song lyrics can be messages.

6. Stay with your heart as you keep on with the breathing, offering, and receiving, allowing the free exchange of energies between you and the stone. Ask questions if you wish, by "thinking" them in your heart. Pay attention to the next words you hear, or to the images you are given.

7. Continue as long as you wish, or until the experience feels complete. Some of these meditations can be profoundly rewarding. Stones such as Rosophia and Morganite can bring one into an almost unbearable sweetness. Others can be nurturing (Astaraline), expansive (Herderite), transformative (Moldavite), awakening (Azeztulite), or any of a wide array of inner states.

8. When the meditation is complete, hold the stone in front of you again, offering thanks with your outbreath flowing across the stone, taking in the inbreath with a sense of being receptive to whatever the stone may wish to offer you.

I hope that some readers who try this meditation will write and let me know what you experience, and how you feel about it. Write me at **heavenandearth@earthlink.net.**

APPENDIX II

AZOZEO SUPER-ACTIVATED AZEZTULITES:
THE BEGINNING OF A NEW CRYSTAL ERA

Readers of this book will notice mention of some stones having undergone the "Azozeo *(ʼah-zah-ZAY-oh)* super-activation process," or their compatibility with other stones that have undergone it. Below is the story of Azozeo, and how it entered my world and that of others who work with stone energies.

In August of 2012, I received a vision. I was at my home in Vermont, where I have a labyrinth made out of Azeztulites and some Rosophia stones. As I sat looking at the labyrinth, I thought back upon the history of Azeztulite. It seemed miraculous to me, the way the appearance of these stones had been preannounced by angelic beings called the Azez. They had told Naisha, my coauthor of *The Book of Stones* (but at that time, someone I knew only as a friend) about the imminent arrival of Azeztulite, and they told her this was the name we must give the stones when they appeared.

Since then, for over twenty years, our company, Heaven and Earth, has been disseminating and discovering more types of Azeztulite—all in accordance with the plans and directions we received from the Azez so many years ago. More recently, we learned that the Azez intend for all the quartz on Earth to ultimately receive the vibration of the Nameless Light of the Great Central Sun—making all of the quartz into Azeztulite. My sense is that the fulfillment of that prophetic vision will coincide with the global awakening of the Earth as a Planet of Light, and with the mass enlightenment of humanity.

There had been many synchronistic affirmations along the way. One of the most startling and exciting for me was the discovery, back when I was doing research for my book *Stones of the New Consciousness*, of the ancient *Book of Ieou*. This was one of the apocryphal Gnostic Gospels, and was purported to have been a guide to the Ascension process, dictated by Jesus to the disciples after his own Ascension. At one point in the narrative, there is this description of one of the Ascension stages:

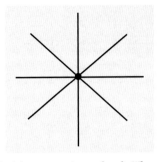

When you reach the fourth aeon, Samaelo and Chochochoucha (a pair of obstructing archons) will come before you. Seal yourself with this seal. This is its name: Azozeo. Say it once only. Hold this cipher—4555—in your hands. When you have finished sealing yourself with this seal and said its name once only, say these defenses also: "Withdraw yourselves, Samaelo and Chochochoucha, you archons of the fourth aeon, because I call upon Zozeza, Chozozazza, Zazezo." When you have finished saying these defenses, the archons of the fourth aeon will withdraw to the left. But you [will] proceed upward.

I was (and am still) struck by the above passage from this ancient book. Here was an actual 2,000-year-old manual for Ascension, describing the stages and beings involved. And, more to the point, the word used to invoke protection, and the names of the protective beings, all contain similarities to the word Azez—root of the name Azeztulite. And of course we were told at the beginning of our Azeztulite adventure that the name Azez means "the Nameless Light of the Great Central Sun," which is closely akin to the goal of the Ascension process in the *Book of Ieou*.

In that book, the disciples were being directed in how to ascend to the realms of Light (i.e., the Central Sun). And I feel sure that the names given in the book for the protective beings aiding humankind in this ascent—*Zozeza,*

Chozozazza, Zazezo—are referring to the same protective beings who have activated and guided the emergence of Azeztulite. They all sound similar to "Azez," their collective name. Further, they are engaged now in the Ascension of all humanity, and the Earth. It provokes awe in me to realize that when I hold an Azeztulite in my hands, I am, in a sense, touching those beings, and the Divine currents from the Great Central Sun. I am amazed to realize that these Beings of Light have been aiding the spiritual evolution of humanity and our world for at least 2,000 years, and that we can connect with them and our own great destiny through Azeztulite.

Let us return now to August of 2012. As I was sitting on my porch contemplating all this, I wondered whether there might be something more to be done. As powerful as Azeztulite is, I felt there might be another level, another octave of energy that could be accessed by those ready for it. I could imagine all the quartz on Earth vibrating as Azeztulite, but what about Azeztulite itself? Was it fully awakened, or could there be more?

I still recall vividly the moment when the vision came to me. It was powerful ... and simple. As I gazed at the Azeztulite labyrinth, I suddenly saw, with my inner eyes, a pyramid over the center of it, glowing with supernal Light. And in that moment, I knew what to do—I would construct a pyramid chamber in the labyrinth's center, placing Azeztulite stones inside it. The combined energy fields of the pyramid and the Azeztulite labyrinth might stimulate the stones inside to a higher level of activation.

But there was more to do. I felt a compelling inner urge, as if I were being told, to place two very large Phenacites in the energy field to be created. (I collect large Phenacites, and have two very large ones—a two-pound African Phenacite and an eighteen-pound single-terminated Brazilian Phenacite crystal, which I believe is the world's largest.) The two-pounder was to go at the apex of the pyramid, and the eighteen-pounder was to be placed in the center at the pyramid's base. The two would form a Circuit of Light, and the Azeztulite stones to be activated would be placed on a table between them.

It was clear that the two very large Phenacites were crucial to the process, and I suddenly understood why I had felt it so important to get the eighteen-pound Phenacite the previous February. (This crystal is the prize of my collection—a very tangible Stone Being with a joyful and luminous presence—and now I was beginning to learn about its purpose!) Phenacite has a close relationship with Azeztulite, and was actually initially used by the Azez, according to Naisha's original channelings, to vibrationally activate the first Azeztulites.

Two years prior, when building the Azeztulite labyrinth, I had felt a powerful inner intensity around doing it. Now that intensity seized me once again. I erected a copper pyramid (its pipes filled with Azeztulite and Rosophia stones) in the center of the labyrinth, and then placed the Phenacites as I had been directed. I brought a glass table into the center, where the Azeztulites to be activated were to be placed. Then there was one last touch—my inner guidance said I needed to use the ancient word of invocation of the Azez—"Azozeo."

Following my inner voice, I printed out the words and attached them on all four sides of the table, for the four directions. Then I walked the labyrinth in ritual consciousness, carrying the Azeztulite stones to be treated, holding them to my heart, and focusing on the intention that they be activated to their highest potential for the good of all. At the center, after placing the stones on the table, I uttered words of invocation and said "Azozeo" to each of the four directions, and silently to the fifth direction. The ritual was complete. Now was the time of waiting.

After exiting the labyrinth I went into the house and sat gazing back at the labyrinth, wondering if all this guidance had been as real as it seemed. In my thirty years of working with crystals and minerals, I had only attuned myself to whatever vibrations were already being emanated by the stones. I had never tried to do anything to increase their energies or power. I had never really imagined that anything like that was possible.

I wondered how long to leave the stones on the table in the labyrinth-pyramid. An inner voice said, "For one cycle of night and day." So, twenty-four hours later, I walked the labyrinth again to retrieve the Azeztulites.

When I brought the Azozeo-treated stones into the house, I sat down with one to check out whether anything had happened. Immediately, I caught my breath. Yes! There was a difference—a big difference! The already-powerful Azeztulites had more than doubled in their intensity, and the frequency of their pulsations was much faster! In seconds, the currents I felt in my hands moved to the third eye, the crown chakra, and then all through my body, and finally to my feet, where a strong charge seemed to go through me and into the Earth.

The longer I held the stone, the stronger the currents in my body became. I experienced a vision of entering a spiral of Light and traveling to the Great Central Sun. I felt spiraling currents of Celestial Fire spinning down into my body from above, entering the crown and spreading out into a web that infused every cell with Divine Light. I suddenly understood that this is what Light Body activation feels like. A wave of elation spread through me, and with that wave came the recognition that the whole tale of the Azez and the enlightenment of the world contained new chapters, which were being written in that very moment and which will continue to unfold in the months and years to come.

I felt a bit stunned by what was happening. It seemed to me that I had made a great discovery, and received a great gift. For the first time, I understood that it is possible to work with stones in a cocreative way that affects them energetically and helps the Stone Beings to fulfill their spiritual purpose. The power of it shocked and humbled me. I realized on a deeper level that the work with stones is beneficial to us, but not just for us—it is also for the beings in the world of Spirit, and for the Earth, for the fulfillment of our collective destiny with them.

I wondered what to do next, and I decided to see if someone else could feel the amazing difference in these Azeztulites. I brought one to my wife, Kathy, and she said, "Yes, definitely!" The next person to experience the Azozeo Azeztulite was our friend Leo McFee, a crystal teacher and maker of gemstone essences. He was affected just as powerfully as I had been, and we talked feverishly about our excitement at this new development, and about plans for bringing these super-activated stones out and spreading them through our network.

I began bringing home more pieces to treat in the Azozeo/pyramid/labyrinth/Phenacite field. At first, I had brought in only the original White Azeztulite, but now I began to try other varieties. I learned that all types of Azeztulite, as well as a few other kinds of crystals, could be enhanced through the Azozeo treatment. It is a painstaking process, because only a small quantity of stones can be activated at one time, but we have worked hard to charge a wide variety of Azeztulites and other receptive crystals in as many forms and shapes as possible.

I want to offer next some of the information I have received in inner visions regarding the properties of Azozeo Azeztulites:

Azozeo super-activated Azeztulites work as powerful conduits to bring through a flood of Celestial Fire—the Nameless Light of the Great Central

Sun—which has now begun to bathe the Earth. Although this Divine energy pours down upon us at all times (since it is the spiritual energy that animates and sustains the Universe), we are at the dawn of a new Golden Age in which a great surge of Celestial Fire is making its influx. Like an incoming tide, this energy is destined to uplift all of humanity and the Earth to a new level of being.

As we stand here at the beginning of this new era, the Azozeo Azeztulites function as grounding wires through which the initial surges of Divine currents can pass. In order for this process to fulfill itself, human participation is necessary. We are urged to work with these stones and allow ourselves to be Pillars of Light, acting to conduct the Celestial Fire into the world through our own being. We can do this through meditation with these stones, through utilizing them in energy grids and healing layouts, through wearing them, or through planting them ritually in the Earth.

In regarding to this ritual "planting" of Azozeo Azeztulites, I want to mention that when I presented some of the Azozeo stones to my friend Robert Sardello, who wrote the introductions to both of my books, his immediate intuition was that the Azozeo Azeztulites are "going to be the means by which all of the quartz in the Earth becomes Azeztulite." His sense was that the higher level of activation present in these stones was what was necessary to create the "contagious currents" whereby unawakened quartz stones would begin to attune to the currents of Azeztulite. That insight resonated with me as well, and I have committed myself to planting these stones in strategic places around the world. Already we have recruited helpers to do this with us.

Many additional qualities of Azozeo Azeztulites have presented themselves to my intuitive vision. I see these stones as bringing in not only subtle energies but also subtle matter from the spiritual realms. When one spends time attuning to Azozeo Azeztulite, the currents one feels entering the body are not mere ephemeral energy—they are streams of subtle matter that bond to the gross matter in every cell and molecule of the body in a way that spiritualizes and aligns them, teaching them to open themselves to the Light. This can rapidly increase the development of the mind of the body. This is an intelligence that resides in the entire Liquid Crystal Body Matrix, and is an aspect of enlightenment.

We have three intelligences within us—mental intelligence based in the brain, soul intelligence based in the heart, and universal intelligence based throughout all the cells of the body. The mental intelligence is what we are taught to believe is all we have. During the spiritually dark times of recorded history it predominated, and we lost touch with our wholeness.

The soul intelligence of the heart was never totally lost, and it has been in the process of reawakening in some people during the past few decades. The heart is the seat of our divine imagination, the center from which we can know truth and act with generosity and certainty.

While it is true that crystals (and especially Azeztulites) have the capacity to enhance our mental and heart/soul intelligence, their greatest boon is to the universal intelligence of the body. When this is fully activated, as the Celestial Fire or Nameless Light fully engulfs our world, we will begin to know things with our bodies without needing to learn them. What we now call inspiration and intuition will become pure vision, and we will see and know whatever we wish to understand simply by attending to it and feeling the knowledge in our cells. This capacity will be brought about by the influx of subtle matter bonding to the gross matter of the body, transforming every cell into an antenna for receiving pure knowledge.

Azozeo Azeztulite facilitates many enhancements of mind, heart, and body. It increases psychic vision, heals and seals the etheric body, brings a great infusion of Life Force into the cells, opens the gateways to angelic communication, stimulates inspiration, facilitates interdimensional travel, opens the doors for recollection of past lives and resolution of karma, dispels dysfunctional habits and patterns in the emotional body, organs, and bodily systems, frees the heart from suppression by the mental, and displays Divine Light to the inner eye. It increases the amount of chi circulating through the meridians, and enhances the power of the will to manifest one's spiritual goals. If two people hold hands with an Azozeo stone in their mutual grasp, they can experience an empathy so deep that it is nearly telepathy. These stones portend great hope for humanity and the world.

Here are two quotes about the Azozeo Azeztulites:

"I got the (Azozeo Azeztulite) you sent. Thank you. And yes, definitely very different, very powerful. In contemplation—all intense, intense white light, radiating from a center outward. Then the image changes, and there begins to be series of light forms structured like various kinds of quartz forms—single, double-terminated, clustered—but as light, not as in image representation. These are accompanied with the feeling that this Azeztulite is the "holder and transformer" of all quartz into Azez-to-Light." —Robert Sardello

"I sat in meditation today with the Azozeo pumping waves up my arms to my skull—that stuff is powerful!" —Birch Gerke

OTHER AZOZEO STONES

As we worked to activate some of each kind of the Azeztulites in the Azozeo energy field, we wondered if it might be possible for any other stones to take on the Azozeo energies if we placed them in the same field. We found that indeed there were several crystals that were also super-activated by exposure to the field. They include Auralite-23, Nirvana Quartz, and Lemurian Light Crystals. All of them jumped to a much faster rhythm of pulsation and a higher intensity of overall energy when they were left for twenty-four hours in the Azozeo/pyramid/labyrinth/Phenacite field. We continue to experiment to find other crystals and stones that can be enhanced through the Azozeo process.

Readers interested in following the progress of this work are encouraged to check in periodically at the Heaven and Earth website: **www.heavenandearthjewelry.com**. Those who are working with Azozeo stones are encouraged to share their experiences and insights by sending emails to **heavenandearth@earthlink.net**.

STONE PROPERTY REFERENCE INDEX

This index is divided into two sections—physical correspondences and emotional/spiritual correspondences. Those interested in working with stones to facilitate physical, emotional or spiritual self-healing are encouraged to use their intuition and discrimination in such explorations. Working with stones for any sort of self-healing is experimental and speculative, and the authors of this book do not intend to suggest that such practices will lead to any specific results. Both author and publishers recommend that readers do not use stones in place of traditional medical or psychological care.

PHYSICAL CORRESPONDENCES

acid Shattuckite; Tourmaline, Golden

acne, *see* skin problems

activation stone Moldavite

acupuncture Magnetite

ADD/ADHD Amblygonite; Cerussite; Lepidolite; Petalite; Stilbite

addiction Agate, Dendritic; Astrophyllite; Galena; Ruby; Dravite; Zircon

adrenal glands Adamite; Amazonite; Azeztulite, Honey and Cream; Cacoxenite; Chrysocolla; Ocean Jasper; Tangerine Quartz; Tanzanite; Topaz, Golden; Zircon; Zoisite

aging Calcite, Blue; Jasper, Mook; Staurolite; Vanadinite

agoraphobia Cerussite

alcohol use Dolomite; Jasper; Unakite; Nebula Stone

allergy Aquamarine

ALS Eudialyte; Natrolite

Alzheimer's disease Diaspore; Eudialyte; Natrolite; Stichtite

anemia Ajoite; Bloodstone; Magnetite; Meteorite, Pallasite; Peridot; Tiger Iron

angina, *see* heart issues

anxiety Cerussite; Gaia Stone; Lemurian Aquatine Calcite; Lithium Quartz; Molybdenite Quartz; Petalite; Rhodochrosite; Shantilite; Vitalite

appetite Celestite; Dolomite; Gaspeite

arterial blockage Calcite, Green

arthritis Angelite; Jade, Blue; Lilac Lepidolite; Malachite

asthma Diopside; Gem Silica; Jade, Blue; Opal, Common (Blue); Tremolite

assimilation Healer's Gold; Pyromorphite; Rutile; Scapolite, Yellow

athletic performance Jade, Red; Sphalerite

attraction between mates Agate, Fire; Tugtupite

auric field Amazez Azeztulite; Celestite; Tugtupite

auto-immune disorders Aventurine, Red; Azeztulite, Black; Azeztulite, Pink Fire; Rainbow Hematite; Sillimanite

back pain Agate; Dendritic

bed-wetting Celestite; Golden Labradorite; Opal, Precious, Oregon

bile Shattuckite

birth Calcite, Red

bladder Azeztulite, Himalaya Red-Gold; Pakulite

blockage Epidote; Fulgurite

blood Ajoite; Apache Tears; Azeztulite, Himalaya Red; Azeztulite, Red Fire; Kaurilite; New Zealand Carnelian (Azozeo Super-Activated); Novaculite

blood cell production Aventurine, Red; Meteorite, Nickel-Iron; Tiger Iron

blood formation Staurolite

blood oxygenation Azeztulite, Red Fire; Healer's Gold; see also oxygenation

blood pressure Petalite; Sodalite; Stichtite

blood purification Cinnabar; Dravite; Meteorite, Pallasite; Piemontite

blood strengthener Fulgurite; Goethite; Hematite; Lepidocrocite; Petrified Wood; Seraphinite; Tiger's Eye

blood, diseases of Bloodstone; Meteorite, Chondrite

blood-sugar level Calcite, Honey

"blue babies" Aventurine, Blue

boils Cinnabar; Marcasite; Stibnite

bonding between mother and infant Calcite, Pink Transparent

bone density, see Osteoporosis

bone issues Aragonite Star Clusters; Azeztulite, Himalaya Red; Elestial Quartz; Fluorite; Kyanite; Opal, Common (Brown or Black); Seriphos Green Quartz; Sphene

bone loss and degeneration, see Osteoporosis

bone growth Jasper, Picture

bone marrow Azeztulite, Himalaya Red; Bixbite; Bloodstone; Goethite; Hematite; Magnetite; Petrified Wood

bone regeneration Jasper, Picture

bones, broken Celestial Quartz; Faden Quartz; Kyanite; Obsidian, Rainbow; Quartz (Clear)

bowels Bumblebee "Jasper"; Cuprite; Healer's Gold; Ruby Kyanite; Spinel, Black; see also intestinal disorder

brain Alexandrite; Azeztulite, Red Fire; Azurite; Cinnazez (Cinnabar Azeztulite); Diaspore; Ruby Kyanite; Sedonalite; Tibetan Black Quartz; Z Stone

brain balance and imbalance Amethyst; Goshenite; Herderite; Kyanite, Indigo;

Muscovite; Phenacite

brain chemistry Barite; Fluorite; Scapolite; White-Gray

brain damage Natrolite; Phenacite; Purpurite

brain disease Barite; Diaspore; Kyanite; Obsidian, Peacock; Variscite

brain, evolution Benitoite; Heulandite, White

brain function Amethyst; Astrophyllite; Cryolite; Euclase; Herderite; Phenacite; Pietersite; Purpurite

brain hemispheres Calcite, Merkabite; Darwinite

bronchial conditions Gem Silica; Jade, Blue; Tremolite, Blue; Tremolite

bruising Obsidian, Rainbow

burns Agate, Ellensburg Blue

caffeine stress and withdrawal Rhodochrosite; Rutile; Zircon; see also addiction

calcification of joints Angelite; see also skeletal system

cancer Bixbite; Clinochlore; Elestial Quartz; Epidote; Galena; Jasper, Unakite; Obsidian, Snowflake; Prophecy Stone; Pyromorphite; Seraphinite; Sillimanite; Tourmaline, Green

capillaries, blood flow Fulgurite

cardiovascular system
see heart

cataracts Calcite, Blue

cell function Tourmaline, Green

cell growth Garnet; Grossular; Prasiolite; Tourmaline, Green; Willemite

cellular purification Auralite-23; Piemontite; Violet Flame Opal

cell regeneration Amazonite; Aragonite, Spanish; Azeztulite, Pink Fire; Azeztulite, White; Azumar; Seraphinite; Serpentine; Vivianite

cell repair Aventurine, Green; Vortexite

cellular respiration Seraphinite

chemotherapy Galena; Prophecy Stone; *see also* cancer

chi Clinochlore; Rhodonite

chronic fatigue syndrome Adamite; Zoisite

chronic physical problems Auralite-23; Coromandel Stonewood

circulation Agate, Moss; Calcite, Pink Opaque; Cuprite; Green Taralite; Ruby, Star

circulatory system Aventurine, Green; Clinochlore; Golden Healer Quartz; Greenstone (Pounamu); Halite,

Magnetite; Meteorite, Chondrite; Piemontite; Prehnite; Vitalite

cleansing Herkimer Quartz "Diamond"

cleansing regimens Staurolite

colon function Azeztulite, Himalaya Red; Malachite

concentration issues Stibnite

connective tissue Azeztulite, Himalaya Red; Benitoite

cough Opal, Common (Blue)

Crohn's disease Dravite

cysts Dream Quartz; Opal, Common (White); Opal, Precious (Black); Seriphos Green Quartz

Cystitis Chrysanthemum Stone; Epidote; Metals: Copper; Nebula Stone

death Zoisite

death experience, conscious Fulgurite

degenerative diseases Apophyllite, Green; Chrysoprase

dementia Siberian Blue Quartz; Stichtite

detoxification Agnitite; Apatite, Green; Astrophyllite; Calcite, Red; Carnelian; Dolomite; Galena; Golden Labradorite; Hematite; Jade, Green; Jasper, Rainforest; Malachite; Molybdenite Quartz; Obsidian, Mahogany; Rhodonite; Spinel, Black; Zircon

diabetes Gaspeite; Sapphire, Pink

digestive issues Agate, Fire; Agate, Moss; Amber; Ametrine; Apatite, Golden; Azeztulite, Sanda Rosa; Bustamite; Cacoxenite; Calcite, Orange; Celestite; Citrine; Eisen Quartz; Empowerite; Golden Labradorite; Heliodor; Libyan Gold Tektite; Lithium Light; New Zealand Carnelian (Azozeo Super-Activated); Obsidian, Gold Sheen; Opal, Common (Brown or Black); Prasiolite; Pyromorphite; Royal Sahara Jasper; Rutile; Sapphire, Yellow; Scapolite, Yellow; Scapolite, Pink; Shaman Stone; Spinel, Black; Stichtite; Sunset Gold Selenite; Sunstone; Tourmaline, Golden; Vitalite

dizziness, *see* vertigo

DNA Coromandel Stonewood; Kyanite, Orange; Petrified Wood; Spiralite Gemshells; Vortexite

drug use Dolomite; *see also* addiction

eating disorders Prasiolite; Stichtite

eczema, *see* skin problems

electromagnetic field Infinite; Metals: Titanium; Rainbow Hematite; Smoky Quartz

elf fields Vanadinite

elimination of waste Black Merlinite; Healer's Gold;

Onyx; Opal, Common
(Brown or Black); Scapolite,
Yellow; Spinel; Sunset Gold
Selenite

emphysema Calcite, Blue;
Diopside; Tremolite;

endocrine system Ametrine;
Apatite, Golden;
Bloodstone; Brazilianite;
Bustamite; Calcite, Orange;
Calcite, Red; Cavansite;
Citrine; Crocoite; Garnet,
Spessartine; Iolite-Sunstone;
Lepidocrocite; Ocean Jasper;
Opal, Precious (Fire); Pyrite;
Rutile; Sunstone; Tiger's Eye;
Titanium Quartz; Zincite

energy Cuprite; Diamond;
Infinite; Iolite-Sunstone;
Serpentine; Smithsonite;
Tektite; Metals: Gold

energy blockage Calcite,
Clear; Elestial Angel Calcite;
Glendonite; Tibetan Tektite

energy replenishment
Chrysoberyl; Heliodor;
Vitalite

exercise Marcasite; Sphalerite

extremities, blood flow
Fulgurite

eye problems Apatite, Blue;
Celestite; Gaia Stone; Her-
kimer Quartz "Diamond";
Hollandite Quartz; Iolite;
Onyx; Rhodizite; Sapphire,
Blue; Scapolite, Blue; Ulexite

fainting Zoisite

fascia Magnesite

fatigue, chronic Opal,
Precious (Fire)

feet Vesuvianite;
see also skeletal system

fertility Agate, Fire; Chrysan-
themum Stone; Cinnabar;
Crocoite; Cuprite; Garnet,
Spessartine; Lepidocrocite;
Ruby; Willemite; Zincite

fetal growth Jasper, Red

fever Agate, Ellensburg Blue;
Larimar

fibroid masses Chrysanthemum Stone; Magnesite;
Opal, Common

fingernails, see nails

food assimilation,
see digestion

food issues Rutile; Stichtite;
see also eating disorders

gallbladder Aegirine; Apatite,
Golden; Chrysoberyl; Golden
Labradorite; Petrified Wood;
Pyromorphite; Rhodonite;
Scapolite, Yellow

gardening Apophyllite, Green;
Seriphos Green Quartz

gastric disorders Cacoxenite;
Gaia Stone; Heliodor; Libyan
Gold Tektite; Malachite;
Obsidian, Gold Sheen;
Spinel, Green/Blue

genetic disorders Phenacite

gland function Amber;
Calcite, Honey; Ocean
Jasper; Prehnite; Rhodonite;
Tangerine Quartz

glucose metabolism Sapphire,
Pink; see also blood sugar

gout Amazonite

hair Amazonite; Apache Tears;
Opal, Precious (White);
Rutilated Quartz; Topaz,
White

hair growth, see hair

hair loss, see hair

headache Apatite, Blue;
Calcite, Blue; Cavansite;
Elestial Angel Calcite; Fairy
Wand Quartz; Gaia Stone;
Glendonite; Goshenite;
Herderite; Lazulite;
Merlinite; Muscovite;
Onyx; Rhodizite; Sapphire,
Blue; Stibnite; Stichtite;
Tourmaline, Blue

headaches, hormone-related
Hemimorphite; Herderite

healing Amulet Stone;
Apatite, Green; Amazez
Azeztulite; Aventurine,
Green; Azeztulite, Red
Fire; Diopside; Green
Taralite; Herkimer Quartz
"Diamond"; Sugilite

health, general Agate,
Moss; Axinite; Beryllonite;
Crocoite; Jade, Red; Rainbow
Garnet

hearing Sphene;
Sunset Gold Selenite

heart, physical Amegreen;
Apatite, Green; Aventurine,
Green; Azeztulite, Red Fire;
Black Phantom Quartz;
Calcite, Pink Transparent;
Chrysoberyl; Emerald; Gaia
Stone; Garnet, Uvarovite;
Hiddenite; Jasper, Unakite;
Lepidocrocite; Merlinite;

Morganite; Obsidian, Rainbow; Piemontite; Prasiolite; Rainbow Garnet; Seraphinite; Tourmaline, Green; Tourmaline, Watermelon; Tugtupite

heartbeat Meteorite, Pallasite; Opal, Common (Pink); Rose Quartz; Tourmaline, Pink

heart, diseases Apatite, Green; Calcite, Pink Opaque; Chrysoberyl; Diopside; Dioptase; Jade, Green; Lilac Lepidolite; Meteorite, Pallasite; Peridot; Rose Quartz; Tourmaline, Pink; Rubellite

heart surgery Apatite, Green

heart, scar tissue Seriphos Green Quartz

heart weakness Heulandite, Green; Rose Quartz

heartburn Amblygonite; *see also stomach*

heavy metal elimination Dolomite; Halite, Blue; Halite, Pink; Tourmaline, Black

hemoglobin Azeztulite, Himalaya Red; Hematite, Specular; Malachite; Metals: Copper; see also blood

herpes Aquamarine; Cinnabar; Stibnite

HIV Cinnabar

hives, *see skin problems*

hormonal balance and imbalance Ajoite; Aventurine, Blue;

Bloodstone; Brazilianite; Calcite, Orange; Calcite, Red; Cuprite; Metals: Silver; Opal, Precious (Fire); Quartz; Sunstone; Tiger Eye; Vanadinite

hormonal shift Hemimorphite; Lepidocrocite; Moonstone

hot temper Agate, Ellensburg Blue

hydration Sodalite

hyperactivity Aventurine, Blue; Cerussite; Lepidolite; Scapolite, Yellow; Tourmaline, Pink; Tourmaline, Watermelon

hyperglycemia Sapphire, Pink

hypoglycemia Sapphire, Pink

immune system Apache tears; Aventurine, Red; Azeztulite, Himalaya Red; Calcite, Honey; Cinnabar; Crocoite; Eisen Quartz; Garnet, Black Andradite; Healerite; Kaurilite; Shadow; Metals: Silver; Titanium New Zealand Carnelian (Azozeo Super-Activated); Quartz; Vivianite

impotence Jasper, Red; Obsidian, Gold Sheen; Pakulite; Pyrite; Shiva Lingam

indigestion, *see gastric disorders*

infant and children, development Aventurine, Green

infections Amber; Celestite;

Cinnabar; Covellite; Galena; Jade, Black; Larimar; Marcasite; Meteorite, Pallasite; Opal, Precious (Owyhee Blue); Pyrite; Stibnite

infection, fungal Marcasite; Pyrite

infections, yeast Covellite

infertility, male and female Bixbite; Healer's Gold; Metals: Copper; Pyrite; Shiva Lingam; Tangerine Quartz; see also reproductive issues

inflammation Chalcedony, Blue; Jade, Blue; Larimar; Lilac Lepidolite; Malachite; Opal, Common (Blue); Opal, Precious (Owyhee Blue)

influenza Larimar

inhalant addiction Peridot

injury Jasper, Unakite

inner ear imbalance Sapphire, Blue

insomnia Glendonite; Goshenite; Jasper, Mook; Lepidolite; Sugilite

insulin levels, *see* diabetes

intestinal disorder Tiger Iron; *see also bowels*

irritable bowel syndrome Amblygonite; Dravite; Libyan Gold Tektite; Tourmaline, Golden

jet lag Azeztulite, Red Fire; New Zealand Carnelian, Vortexite

joints Angel Wing Blue Anhydrite; Lilac Lepidolite;

Mystic Merlinite;
see also skeletal system

karmic roots of disease
Lapis Lazuli; Novaculite

kidney infection Opal, Oregon

kidneys Azeztulite,
Himalaya Red-Gold;
Brazilianite; Bumblebee
"Jasper"; Celestite;
Chrysoberyl; Golden
Labradorite; Jet; Marcasite;
Obsidian, Mahogany; Opal,
Precious, Oregon; Pakulite;
Rhodonite; Scapolite,
Yellow; Tiger Iron;
Topaz, Golden

laryngitis Agate; Aquamarine;
Chrysocolla; Gem Silica;
see also throat

legs Onyx; Vesuvianite;
see also skeletal system

lesions Cinnabar

leukemia Bixbite

lethargy New Zealand
Carnelian, Crimson Cuprite

liver Aegirine; Aventurine,
Red; Bixbite; Bloodstone;
Bumblebee "Jasper"; Chryso-
beryl; Jasper, Rainforest;
Jet; Magnetite; Marcasite;
Obsidian, Mahogany;
Pakulite; Petrified Wood;
Pyromorphite; Rhodonite;
Royal Sahara Jasper; Vitalite

love-based physiology
Rose Quartz

lungs Aragonite, Blue; Azeztulite, Red Fire; Black Phantom
Quartz; Calcite, Blue;

Cuprite; Crimson Cuprite;
Diopside; Gaia Stone; Jasper,
Unakite; Lepidocrocite;
Opal; Common (Pink);
Opal, Common (Blue);
Seraphinite; Tiger Iron

lymphatic system Calcite,
Red; Halite, Blue; Kaurilite;
Novaculite; Prehnite; Dravite

memory Barite; Iolite;
Siberian Blue Quartz

menopause, female
Bloodstone; Cuprite;
Diopside; Vanadinite

menopause, male Vanadinite

menstrual irregularities
Covellite; Cuprite;
Moonstone; Papagoite

mental focus Aventurine,
Blue; Sillimanite;
Tourmaline, Pink

meridian system Calcite,
Orange; Obsidian, Black;
Rhodonite; Sedonalite

metabolism Apatite, Green;
Calcite, Orange; Celestite;
Citrine; Dolomite; Gaspeite;
Golden Labradorite; Halite,
Pink; Rhodonite; Rutile;
Sunstone; Wulfenite

microbial infections,
see infections

migraines Azurite; Cavansite;
Gaia Stone; Herderite;
Lazulite; Muscovite;
Papagoite; Rhodizite; Topaz,
Blue; Tourmaline, Blue

MS Eudialyte; Natrolite

multiple sclerosis, *see* MS

muscle issues Opal, Common
(Brown or Black); Sunset
Gold Selenite; Tiger Iron

muscle injuries Faden Quartz;
Jasper, Red

muscle spasm and twitches
Aventurine, Blue; Magnesite

muscular system Black
Phantom Quartz;
Empowerite; Staurolite

muscular tension Glendonite;
Magnesite; Stichtite

myelin sheath Black Phantom
Quartz; Rhodochrosite;
Tibetan Black Quartz

nail growth Apache Tears;
Opal, Precious (White);
Topaz, White

narcolepsy
Chalcedony, Purple

nausea Libyan Gold Tektite;
Tourmaline, Golden

neck Topaz, Blue

nerve disorders Amethyst;
Kyanite, Blue; Natrolite;
Phenacite

nerve ganglia
Tibetan Black Quartz

nerve strengthening Pietersite

nerves, severed Faden Quartz;
Kyanite, Blue

nervous breakdown Lilac
Lepidolite; Lithium Quartz

nervous exhaustion
Lithium Light, Healerite

nervous system Angel Aura
Quartz; Astrophyllite;
Azeztulite, Golden Crystals;

Benitoite; Black Phantom Quartz; Calcite, Merkabite; Cinnazez (Cinnabar Azeztulite); Dolomite; Elestial Angel Calcite; Eudialyte; Faden Quartz; Jade, Green; Jade, Purple; Lemurian Light Crystal; Lithium Light; Merlinite; New Zealand Carnelian (Azozeo Super-Activated); Novaculite; Rhodochrosite; Ruby Kyanite; Sedonalite; Tibetan Black Quartz; Tugtupite; Variscite; Vortexite; Z Stone

neural pathway regeneration Stichtite; Vortexite

neuronal activity Agate, Moss

nutrient assimilation Brookite; Cacoxenite; Calcite, Pink Opaque; Dravite; Prasiolite

nightmares Lepidolite; Lilac Lepidolite; Muscovite; Sugilite

nutrient absorption Libyan Gold Tektite

optic nerve Onyx; Rhodizite; Scapolite, Blue

osteoporosis Angelite; Black Phantom Quartz; Calcite, Red; Cryolite; Dolomite; Meteorite, Chondrite; Sphene

ovaries Carnelian; Garnet, Almandine; Pakulite; see also reproductive system

overeating, see weight issues

oxygenation Amethyst; Goethite; Healer's Gold; Lepidocrocite; Magnetite; Malachite; Papagoite; Sphalerite; Tremolite; Turquoise

pain relief Aragonite Star Clusters

palpitations Rose Quartz; Stibnite; see also heart

pancreas Calcite, Honey; Pyromorphite; Tiger Iron

parasites Jade, Black

parasympathetic nervous system Azeztulite, Honey and Cream; Kunzite

Parkinson's disease Diaspore; Eudialyte; Natrolite; Stichtite

pelvis New Zealand Carnelian

phantom pain Rutilated Quartz

physical energy Agate, Fire

physical evolution Kyanite, Orange; Pyromorphite

physical fitness Adamite

physical strength Hollandite Quartz; Jasper, Red; Ruby Kyanite

pineal gland Adamite; Alexandrite; Cavansite; Hemimorphite; Sapphire, White; Sphene; Magnesite

pituitary gland Adamite; Alexandrite; Cavansite; Hemimorphite; Sapphire, White; Sphene; Magnesite

PMS Adamite; Ajoite; Hemimorphite

poison Spinel

polyps Chlorite Phantom Crystals

pollution, environmental Tourmaline, Black

prana Cuprite

prefrontal lobes Azeztulite, Golden Crystals; Cryolite; Diamond; Siberian Blue Quartz; see also brain

pregnancy Calcite, Red; Jasper, Red; Jasper, Mook; Larimar

premier healing stone Seraphinite

prosperity Amber; Apatite, Golden; Aventurine, Green

prostate gland Crimson Cuprite; Healer's Gold

psoriasis, see skin problems

psychic surgery Amazez Azeztulite; Chlorite Phantom Crystals; Novaculite; Seriphos Green Quartz

purification Black Merlinite; Herkimer Quartz "Diamond"; Jet; Rhodonite; Tourmaline, Black

radiation Chlorite Phantom Crystals; Chrysoberyl; Galena; Herkimer Quartz "Diamond"; Hollandite Quartz; Prophecy Stone; Purpurite; Pyromorphite; Smoky Quartz; Vanadinite; Willemite

radiation poisoning,
  see radiation

rash, *see* skin problems

recovery from illness Amulet Stone; Azeztulite; Honey and Cream; Chrysoberyl; Empowerite; Rainbow Hematite; Shantilite; Spiralite Gemshells

red blood cells Magnetite; Malachite; Metals: Copper; Tiger Iron; see also blood

reflux Obsidian, Gold Sheen; Tourmaline, Golden; see also acid, digestive issues

regeneration Chrysoprase; Diopside; Jasper, Mook; Vortexite

removal of entities Shaman Stone

reproductive issues Calcite, Red; Covellite; Cuprite; Dioptase; Garnet, Spessartine; Lepidocrocite; Obsidian, Black; Shiva Lingam; Smithsonite; Sunstone; Vanadinite; Zincite

reproductive system, female Crocoite; Jasper, Mook; Metals: Copper; Smithsonite

respiratory illness Aragonite, Blue; Opal, Blue; Aragonite, Blue

respiratory system Calcite, Blue; Clinochlore; Gem Silica

rosacea, *see* skin problems

SAD Adamite; Amber

seasonal affective disorder, *see* SAD

seizure Kyanite

self-abuse Dravite

self-destructive habits Astaraline; Shungite; Staurolite

self-discovery Astrophyllite

serotonin levels Scolecite

sexual abuse, *see* sexual issues

sexual energy Agate, Fire; Sapphire, Padparadsha

sexual intimacy Azeztulite, Himalaya Red-Gold; Calcite, Red; Pakulite; Ruby Kyanite

sexual issues Cinnabar; Dioptase; Fulgurite; Jasper, Red; Quartz; Ruby; Sapphire; Quartz; Padparadsha (Orange Sapphire); Tangerine Quartz; Willemite; Wulfenite; Zincite

sexual organs Bixbite; Brazilianite; Bustamite; Calcite, Orange; Cuprite; Eisen Quartz; Kyanite, Orange; New Zealand Carnelian (Azozeo Super-Activated); Pakulite; Ruby Kyanite; Strontianite

sexual repulsion Eisen Quartz

sinusitis Goshenite

skeletal system Angel Wing Blue Anhydrite; Angelite; Black Phantom Quartz; Empowerite; Petrified Wood; Tiger Iron

skin problems Aquamarine; Jade, Purple; Marcasite; Opal, Common (Blue);

Opal, Precious (White); Pyrite

sleep disorders Amulet Stone; Iolite; Lepidolite; Muscovite

social issues Cerussite

sore throat Agate; Chalcedony, Blue; Chrysocolla; Gem Silica; Larimar; Topaz, Blue

speech disorders Euclase; Topaz, Blue

spine Mystic Merlinite; Petrified Wood; Stichtite; Tibetan Tektite

spleen Aegirine; Apatite, Golden; Azeztulite, Himalaya Red; Brazilianite; Eisen Quartz; Golden Labradorite; Pyromorphite; Royal Sahara Jasper; Sapphire, Yellow; Shattuckite

spontaneous natural purging Staurolite

sports injury Hematite

stagnation Magnesite

stamina Aegirine; Agate, Fire; Citrine; Hollandite Quartz; Meteorite, Nickel-Iron; Rutile; Spiralite Gemshells

stomach issues, *see* gastric disorder

"stone of youth" Chrysoprase

strength Hollandite Quartz; Jasper, Red; Malachite; Meteorite, Nickel-Iron; Onyx

stress Agate, Dendritic; Amazonite; Amblygonite; Angel Aura Quartz; Aqua Aura Quartz; Calcite, Pink

Transparent; Cavansite; Chrysoberyl; Chryso-colla; Dolomite; Gaia Stone; Glendonite; Jade, Purple; Kunzite; Lemurian Aquatine Calcite; Lemurian Golden Opal; Lilac Lepidolite; Lithium Quartz; Petalite; Rhodochrosite; Shantilite; Vortexite

stroke Herderite; Kyanite

stuttering Euclase

substance abuse Tourmalined Quartz; *see also* alcohol, drugs, tobacco

sunburn Chrysoberyl; Purpurite

surgery, recovery Calcite, Pink Opaque; Faden Quartz; Quartz (Clear)

swelling Jade, Blue

systemic illness Seraphinite

teeth Fluorite

tension Magnesite

terminal prognosis Cassiterite

testes Carnelian; Garnet, Almandine; Healer's Gold

throat problems Aquamarine; Chalcedony, Blue; Opal, Precious (Owyhee Blue); Topaz, Blue

thymus gland Agate

thyroid gland Adamite; Agate; Amazonite; Cacoxenite; Chrysocolla; Ocean Jasper; Shaman Stone; Tanzanite; Topaz, Blue; Zoisite

tinnitus Amethyst; Azurite

tissue regeneration and repair Calcite, Pink Opaque; Jade, Green; Jasper, Unakite; Malachite; Metals: Copper; Ocean Jasper; Seriphos Green Quartz

tobacco use Dolomite; Jasper, Rainforest; Peridot; Rutile; Zircon

tonic stone Jade, Red

toxic emotion Agate, Dendritic

toxic energy and pollution from electrical systems Jasper, Unakite; Pyromorphite

toxin elimination Aegirine; Halite, Blue; Halite, Pink; Piemontite; Prehnite; Prophecy Stone; Pyromorphite; Tourmaline, Black; Spinel

trauma (physical) Amazonite; Amegreen; Dioptase; Goethite; Kunzite; Kyanite; Quartz (Clear); Vivianite

tumors Dream Quartz; Epidote; Opal, Precious (Black); Seriphos Green Quartz

ulcers Amblygonite; Libyan Gold Tektite; Scapolite, Pink; Tourmaline, Golden

urinary issues Celestite; Opal, Precious (Oregon); Prehnite; Topaz, Golden

vein issues Vesuvianite

venous and arterial walls Aventurine, Blue; *see also* circulatory system

vertigo (dizziness) Apatite, Blue; Azurite; Fairy Wand Quartz; Fluorite; Muscovite; Sapphire, Blue; Stibnite

vibrational healing Shaman Stone

virus, *see* infection

vision issues Fairy Wand Quartz; Lazulite; Scapolite, Blue; Sphene; Ulexite; Sunset Gold Selenite

vitality Adamite; Agate, Fire; Axinite; Azeztulite; Himalaya Red-Gold; Azeztulite, Honey and Cream; Clinochlore; Crocoite; Cuprite; Healer's Gold; Jasper, Red; Kaurilite; Kyanite, Green; Malachite; Ruby; Sapphire, Yellow; Spiralite Gemshells; Stonehenge Bluestone; Sunstone

vitamin assimilation Brookite; Magnifier Quartz

vocal cords Gem Silica; Chalcedony, Blue

warts Cinnabar

water retention Hanksite; Moonstone; Sodalite

weakness Jasper, Red

weight lifting and body building Jasper, Red; Metals: Copper; Onyx

weight loss, *see* weight management

weight management
Adamite; Angelite; Apatite,
Golden; Astrophyllite;
Calcite, Clear; Calcite,
Red; Celestite; Cerussite;
Citrine; Dolomite; Dream
Quartz; Garnet, Spessartine;
Gaspeite; Hollandite Quartz;
Iolite-Sunstone; Jasper,
Red; Jasper, Rainforest;
Jasper, Unakite; Magnetite;
Marcasite; Onyx; Rhodonite;
Ruby, Star; Smithsonite

wounds, *see* trauma

SPIRITUAL/EMOTIONAL CORRESPONDENCES

absent healing
Calcite, Pink Opaque

abundance Agate, Moss;
Apatite, Green; Azeztulite,
Himalaya Red-Gold;
Cassiterite; Chrysoberyl;
Clinochlore; Emerald; Uvaro-
vite Garnet; Jade, Green; Jet;
Obsidian, Mahogany; Yellow
Sapphire; Topaz, Golden;
Tourmaline, Golden

abuse of power
Obsidian, Gold Sheen

acceleration Rutilated Quartz;
Rutile; Tibetan Tektite

acceptance
Calcite, Pink Transparent;
Seriphos Green Quartz

action, graceful
Rutilated Quartz

action, productive
Iolite-Sunstone; Jade, Red;
Pyrite; Quartz (Clear)

activation stone Moldavite

adaptability Diaspore

**addiction, behavior and
recovery** Aegirine; Agate,
Moss; Amethyst; Black
Andradite Garnet; Jade, Red;
Lepidocrocite; Ocean Jasper;
Sunset Gold Selenite

adventure Bumblebee
"Jasper"; Pakulite; Ruby;
Sunstone

aging, slowing Jasper, Mook

agni mani (fire pearl)
Moldavite; Tektite

agoraphobia
Pallasite Meteorite

"aha" experience
Calcite, Blue; Sodalite

Akashic records Alexandrite;
Angelite; Apatite, Blue;
Calcite, Stellar Beam;
Cavansite; Celestial Quartz;
Chalcedony, Purple; Cin-
nazez (Cinnabar Azeztulite);
Covellite; Creedite; Datolite;
Elestial Quartz; Euclase;
Goethite; Heulandite;
Kaurilite; Labradorite; Lapis
Lazuli; Libyan Gold Tektite;
Magnesite; Chondrite
Meteorite; Papagoite;
Petrified Wood; Spiralite
Gemshells; Stonehenge
Bluestone; White Phantom
Quartz

alchemy Azeztulite, Black;
Cinnabar; Cinnazez
(Cinnabar Azeztulite);
Cuprite; Wulfenite

alchemical transformation
Azeztulite, Red Fire;
Cerussite

alignment with Divine plan
Cacoxenite

alignment, Will with Heart
Chrysoberyl

alignment, physical and light
Variscite

alignment, energies
Magnetite

alternate lives Nuummite

alternate realm
Azeztulite, Satyaloka Clear

altruism Calcite, Green;
Chrysoprase; Kunzite;
Rhodonite; Vivianite

ambition Pyrite

amplification
Magnifier Quartz; Quartz
(Clear); Rutilated Quartz;
Rutile

ananda Azeztulite, Satyaloka
Clear; Celestite

ancient civilizations
Chalcedony, Purple;
Almandine Garnet;
Greenstone; Heulandite;
Jasper, Picture; Petrified
Wood; Quartz, Clear

ancient knowledge
Coromandel Stonewood;
Cuprite; Papagoite; Spiralite
Gemshells

angelic communication
Ajoite; Angel Wing Blue
Anhydrite; Angelite;
Celestine; Cinnazez
(Cinnabar Azeztulite);
Clinochlore; Danburite; Elestial Angel Calcite; Elestial
Quartz; Lemurian Aquatine
Calcite; Opal, Owyhee Blue;
Prehnite; Shantilite; Violet
Flame Opal

angelic connections
Seraphinite

angelic domain Celestite;
Creedite; Elestial Quartz;
Fairy Wand Quartz; Opal,
Common; Seriphos Green
Quartz

angelic entities
Hemimorphite; Lemurian
Seed Crystals; Morganite;
Smithsonite

angelic guides Benitoite;
Celestite; Metals: Platinum;
Purpurite

angels Agate, Ellensburg Blue;
Amethyst: Chrysoberyl;
Covellite; Gem Silica;
Herkimer Quartz
"Diamond"; Metals:
Platinum; Phenacite;
Selenite; Seraphinite

angels in human form
Angel Wing Blue Anhydrite

anger Angel Wing Blue
Anhydrite; Aquamarine;
Danburite; Jade, Black;
Larimar

animal communication
Jasper, Mook; Spiralite
Gemshells

anxiety Andalusite; Amulet
Stone; Chalcedony, Blue;
Cuprite; Crimson Cuprite;
Danburite; Sauralite
Azeztulite Smithsonite;
Tourmaline, Pink; Tremolite

anxiety, financial
Grossular, Garnet

aphrodisiac
Calcite, Orange; Rubellite

appreciation Sapphire, Pink

**archetypal masculine and
feminine** White Azezulite
and Rosophia (together)

Arthurian legends Iolite

Arthurian times Merlinite

artistic expressions
Agate, Fire; Iolite

artists, *see* creative people

Ascended Masters Prehnite

ascension Azeztulite,
Pink; Azeztulite, White;
Azeztulite, Satyaloka Rose;
Azeztulite, Satyaloka
Yellow; Barite; Brookite;
Calcite, Stellar Beam;
Calcite, Merkabite;
Heliodor; Herkimer Quartz
"Diamond"; Rainbow
Hematite; Shantilite;
Vortexite

Ascension stone
Natrolite; Ashtar; Tektite

assertiveness Heliodor; Jade,
Red; Vesuvianite

astral energies Opal, Owyhee
Blue; Tibetan Black Quartz;
astral entities Pyromorphite;
Willemite

astral parasites Angel Aura
Quartz; Apache Tears

astral planes Scapolite;
Sphene; Staurolite; Stilbite;
Z Stone

astral projection Jet

astral travel Benitoite;
Calcite, Blue; Covellite;
Dream Quartz; Herkimer
Quartz "Diamond"; Kyanite,
Green; Labradorite; Lazulite;
Natrolite; Obsidian,
Peacock; Opal, Common;
Quartz (Clear); Rhodizite;
Blue Sapphire; Sphene

astrology Herderite; Iolite

Atlantean connection
Brazilianite

Atlantis Calcite, Stellar Beam;
Cathedral Quartz; White
Phantom Quartz

attachment, releasing negative
Azeztulite, Black; Barite;
Lepidocrocite; Master
Shamanite; Quartz (Clear);
Vitalite

attention, focus Onyx

attraction
Epidote; Spessartine

attunement Azumar; Green
Taralite; Jade, Purple;
Jade, Lavender; Obsidian,
Snowflake; Rutile; Tibetan

Tektite; Vortexite

aura balancing Hemimorphite

aura cleansing Chalcedony,
Purple; Smoky Quartz;

aura, healing Lithium Quartz

aura, holes Chalcedony, Blue;
Tourmaline, Pink

aura, purification Marcasite

auras, seeing Calcite, Clear

auras, strengthening
Green Heulandite

auric field Aragonite Star
Clusters; Faden Quartz;
Infinite; Phenacite

auric field cleansing Selenite

auric field stabilization
Guardianite, Auralite-23

auric leaks
Seriphos Green Quartz

automatic writing Shattuckite

awakening Agnitite;
Azeztulite, Black;
Azeztulite, White; Fulgurite;
Glendonite; Kyanite, Indigo;
Moldau Quartz; Moldavite;
Muscovite; Satyaloka
Quartz; Sauralite Azeztulite;
Scolecite; Sedonalite;
Tibetan Tektite; Vitalite;
Vivianite; Zoisite

awareness, expansion
Adamite; Angel Aura
Quartz; Angelite; Agnitite;
Azeztulite, Sanda Rosa;
Creedite; Darwinite;
Moldavite; Petalite; Ruby
Kyanite; Rutilated Quartz;
Rutile; Blue Sapphire;
Sapphire, White

**awareness of
earth-as-paradise**
Seriphos Green Quartz

bad dreams Amulet Stone

bad habits Jasper, Unakite

balance Amethyst;
Chalcedony, Blue; Diopside;
Dolomite; Healer's Gold;
Jasper, Unakite; Lepidolite;
Molybdenite Quartz;
Sedonalite; Shungite;
Sphalerite; Tiger Eye;
Tourmaline, Pink; Vortexite

balancing polarities
Magnetite; Marcasite

beacon of light Sugilite

benevolence Elestial Quartz;
Heliodor; Sunstone

birth and death Cassiterite

blessings Azeztulite, Honey
and Cream; Sunstone

blockage Anandalite;
Calcite, Stellar Beam;
Hanksite; Hollandite
Quartz; Moldavite; Quartz
(Clear), Double-terminated;
Stonehenge Bluestone;
Zincite

boundaries Amazonite

brain evolution
Herderite; Natrolite

brain function Amethyst;
Lazulite; Lemurian Light
Crystal; Tugtupite

breaththrough Cavansite;
Obsidian, Peacock

breath work Aragonite, Blue;
Shaman Stone

**bridging higher and lower
worlds** Covellite

bubble of light Amethyst;
Tourmalined Quartz

business skills
Apatite, Golden

calm Agate, Blue Lace; Agate,
Ellensburg Blue; Ajoite;
Amblygonite; Aqua Aura
Quartz; Chalcedony, Blue;
Dolomite; Gel Lithium
Silica; Guardianite; Larimar;
Lemurian Golden Opal;
Opal, Common, Blue; Opal,
Owyhee Blue; Smithsonite;
Watermelon Tourmaline;
Tremolite

career changes
Cerussite, Cathars Iolite

causal dimensions
Obsidian, Peacock

cellular encoding
Elestial Quartz

cellular memory Almandine;
Coromandel Stonewood
Garnet; Ocean Jasper;
Quartz (Clear)

centeredness Agate, Blue
Lace; Chalcedony, Blue;
Dolomite; Molybdenite
Quartz

chakras, activation Amazez
Azeztulite; Moldavite;
New Zealand Carnelian
(Azozeo Super-Activated);
Sedonalite; Sillimanite;
Tibetan Tektite; Z Stone

chakras, clearing Angel Aura
Quartz; Healerite; Kyanite,
Orange; Quartz (Clear)

chakras, re-energizing
Hematite

channeling Angelite; Aqua Aura Quartz; Benitoite; Chalcedony, Blue; Creedite; Danburite; Dream Quartz; Gem Silica; Hemimorphite; Iolite; Iolite-Sunstone; Lazulite; Metals: Copper, Niobium; Shattuckite; Zircon

charisma Spessartine

chi Cinnabar; Greenstone (Pounamu); Jade, Green; Jade, Red; Jasper, Red; Manifest Light Crystals; Opal, Fire; Prehnite; Ruby; Spessartine; Zircon

children Lithium Quartz

Christ Rose Quartz

Christ consciousness
Golden Healer Quartz; Heliodor; Sphene; Tiger Eye; Topaz, Golden

clairaudience Cavansite; Celestite; Chalcedony, Purple; Dumortierite; Lazulite; Siberian Blue Quartz; Tourmaline, Blue

clairsentience Celestite; Chalcedony, Purple; Circle Stone; Dumortierite; Lazulite; Siberian Blue Quartz; Topaz, White; Tourmaline, Blue

clairvoyance and mediumship Adamite; Agate, Holly Blue; Angelite; Beryllonite; Calcite, Blue; Cavansite; Celestite;

Chalcedony, Purple; Circle Stone; Covellite; Diamond; Dumortierite; Gem Silica; Gray Moonstone; Halite; Heliodor; Hemimorphite; Herderite; Iolite; Jade, Blue; Jet; Labradorite; Lazulite; Lemurian Golden Opal; Merlinite; Metals: Niobium; Moonstone; Muscovite; Natrolite; Nuummite; Petalite; Shattuckite; Siberian Blue Quartz; Topaz, White; Tourmaline, Blue; Tourmaline, Blue; Ulexite

clarity Agate, Blue Lace; Amber; Amblygonite; Ametrine; Apatite, Golden; Calcite, Clear; Calcite, Red; Euclase; Fluorite; Golden Labradorite; Jade, Blue; Kyanite, Indigo; Lemurian Jade; Moonstone; Lemurian Jade, Shadow; Sapphire, White; Sillimanite; Smithsonite; Stilbite; Tremolite; Variscite

cleansing Andalusite; Azeztulite, Black; Brazilianite; Bumblebee "Jasper"; Halite; Moldavite; Quartz (Clear); Shungite; Sugilite; Vitalite; White Phantom Quartz

clear thinking Tanzan Aura Quartz; Tourmalined Quartz

clearing
Aegirine; Quartz (Clear)

clearing spaces
Calcite, Stellar Beam

"cloak of invisibility"
Malachite

cocoon of Light
Astaraline; Celestite

coincidence control
Labradorite

comfort, emotional
Andalusite; Astaraline; Azeztulite, Honey and Cream; Lithium Light; Vortexite

commitment Empowerite; Piemontite; Pyrite

communication Agate, Blue Lace; Agate, Ellensburg Blue; Amazonite; Angelite; Aqua Aura Quartz; Aquamarine; Aquamarine, Blue; Cavansite; Chalcedony, Blue; Chrysocolla; Gem Silica; Hemimorphite; Lapis Lazuli; Lepidocrocite; Quartz (Clear); Shattuckite; Smithsonite; Topaz, Blue; Tourmaline, Blue; Turquoise

communication with animals or plants Azumar; Diopside; Peridot; Serpentine; Spiralite Gemshells

communication with higher beings Amazez Azeztulite; Azumar; Elestial Angel Calcite; Kyanite; Obsidian, Black; Prehnite

communication with Spirit
Sapphire, White

communion with Creation
Brookite

compassion Ajoite;

Amazonite; Amegreen; Azeztulite, Golden Crystals; Azumar; Calcite, Green; Calcite, Pink Transparent; Celestite; Chrysoprase; Dioptase; Emerald; Gaia Stone; Green Taralite; Jade, Lavender; Morganite; Prasiolite; Quartz (Clear); Rhodochrosite; Rhodonite; Rose Quartz; Sapphire, Yellow; Smithsonite; Stichtite; Tangerine Quartz; Variscite; Vivianite

concentration
Agate, Moss; Amblygonite

confidence Aegirine; Agate, Blue Lace; Ajoite; Apatite, Golden; Aragonite Star Clusters; Aventurine, Green; Azeztulite, Red Fire; Calcite, Orange; Calcite, Honey; Carnelian; Empowerite; Golden Labradorite; Healer's Gold; Libyan Gold Tektite; Malachite; Metals: Gold; Morganite; Opal, Owyhee Blue; Pyrite; Rhodizite; Strontianite; Tourmaline, Golden

confusion, emotional
Kyanite, Indigo; Malachite

consciousness, expanding
Agate, Holly Blue; Amegreen; Astrophyllite; Azeztulite, Satyaloka Clear; Benitoite; Beryllonite; Calcite, Merkabite; Cavansite; Cinnazez (Cinnabar Azeztulite); Darwinite; Green Taralite; Lemurian

Light Crystal; Magnesite; Obsidian, Peacock; Quartz (Clear); Rainbow Hematite; Rutilated Quartz; Staurolite; Sunstone; Tibetan Black Quartz; Tugtupite

consciousness, multidimensional Papagoite; Z Stone

consciousness, pure
Azeztulite, Satyaloka Clear

consciousness, shadow self
Dravite

consciousness, visionary
Auralite-23; Diamond; Hypersthene; Ruby Kyanite

consciousness, wordless
Calcite, Red

contact with guides
Dream Quartz

contentment Andalusite; Coromandel Stonewood

cooling Aquamarine; Larimar

cords Novaculite; Quartz (Clear)

core beliefs Amazonite

cosmic attunement Angel Aura Quartz; Moldavite

cosmic connection
Metals: Platinum

cosmic energy Azeztulite, Satyaloka Clear

cosmic Overmind
Pallasite Meteorite

counseling Chalcedony, Blue

courage Apatite, Golden; Apophyllite, Clear; Bixbite; Black Phantom Quartz; Bloodstone; Bumblebee

"Jasper"; Carnelian; Cuprite; Emerald; Empowerite; Greenstone (Pounamu); Hematite; Heulandite; Iolite- Sunstone; Jade, Red; Lemurian Jade, Shadow; Marcasite; Master Shamanite; Molybdenite Quartz; New Zealand Carnelian (Azozeo Super-Activated); Obsidian, Snowflake; Peridot; Royal Sahara Jasper; Ruby; Sphalerite; Sugilite; Tiger Iron; Rubellite; Ruby Kyanite; Tourmaline, Golden; Dravite; Vesuvianite; Vitalite

creation Apatite, Golden

creative people
Agate, Ellensburg Blue; Iolite-Sunstone; Larimar

creativity Adamite; Agate, Fire; Amblygonite; Amegreen; Ametrine; Anandalite; Azeztulite, Himalaya Gold; Azeztulite, Himalaya Red-Gold; Black Andradite Garnet; Brazilianite; Bustamite; Calcite, Orange; Citrine; Crocoite; Eisen Quartz; Fairy Wand Quartz; Spessartine; Goethite; Golden Labradorite; Herderite; Jade, Red; Kyanite, Orange; Lepidocrocite; Malachite; Metals: Gold; New Zealand Carnelian (Azozeo Super-Activated); Pakulite; Pyrite; Quartz (Clear); Scepter Quartz; Rutile;

Sapphire, Yellow; Sapphire, Padparadsha; Rathbunite; Sodalite; Tangerine Quartz; Tiger Iron; Topaz, Golden; Ulexite; Vanadinite; Vitalite; Willemite; Zincite

crop circles Amber

curiosity Tangerine Quartz

Dark Goddess
Azeztulite, Black; Goethite

dark night of the soul
Apophyllite, Clear; Diamond

death ceremonies Cassiterite

decisiveness
Ametrine; Fluorite

deep journey Nuummite; Obsidian, Rainbow

demonic influences
Pyromorphite

density
Epidote; Quartz (Clear)

depression Amulet Stone; Andalusite; Elestial Quartz; Eudialyte; Gel Lithium Silica; Lepidocrocite; Metals: Gold; Molybdenite Quartz; Obsidian, Mahogany; Ocean Jasper; Opal, Common; Rosophia; Tourmaline, Pink; Rubellite; Tremolite; Vitalite

desire Topaz, Golden

desperation Chalcedony, Blue

destiny path Bumblebee "Jasper"; Green Taralite; Hollandite Quartz; New Zealand Carnelian (Azozeo Super-Activated); Nirvana Quartz; Rhodonite; Scapolite

determination Agate, Moss; Ruby; Wulfenite; Zincite

devas, devic beings
Agate, Moss; Amber; Chlorite Phantom Crystals; Chrysoprase; Hemimorphite; Infinite; Jade, Purple; Jasper, Rainforest; Merlinite; Peridot; Prehnite; Staurolite

development, inner and outer
Zoisite

Devic energies Apache Tears; Aventurine, Green

Devic realm Diopside; Fairy Wand Quartz; Pallasite Meteorite; Seriphos Green Quartz; Staurolite; Tourmaline, Green; Tourmaline, Watermelon

dharma (path of highest destiny) Petalite; Scapolite

diagnostic tools
Aragonite Star Clusters

dimensional doorways
Apophyllite, Green; Calcite, Stellar Beam; Herkimer Quartz "Diamond"; Quartz (Clear); Stilbite

direction Quartz (Clear)

discernment Jade, Purple; Novaculite; Sapphire, White; Tiger Eye

discipline Jasper, Fancy; Lazulite; Onyx; Blue Sapphire; Vanadinite

discrimination Heliodor; Jade, Blue; Sphalerite

disorientation Jasper, Picture; Magnetite

distress, emotional
Rose Quartz

divination Black Merlinite

Divine benevolence
Green Taralite

Divine bliss, *see* ananda

Divine blueprint
Agate, Dendritic; Agate, Fire; Agate, Moss; Azeztulite; Astaraline; Clinochlore; Flint; Healerite; Tibetan Tektite

Divine cocreation
New Zealand Carnelian (Azozeo Super-Activated)

Divine communication
Ajoite; Chalcedony, Blue; Covellite; Crocoite

Divine connection
Alexandrite; Amethyst; Azeztulite, Black; Lilac Lepidolite; Vitalite

Divine creation Wulfenite

Divine Father Metals: Gold

Divine Feminine Aquamarine; Cuprite; Larimar; Lemurian Jade; Lemurian Seed Crystals; Pakulite; Seraphinite

Divine guidance
Ajoite; Ametrine

Divine intention Rutile

Divine inspiration
Dumortierite; Lapis Lazuli

Divine knowledge Quartz (Clear); Sapphire, Star

Divine Love Alexandrite; Azeztulite, Pink Fire;

Calcite, Green; Clinochlore; Elestial Quartz; Kunzite; Lepidocrocite; Morganite; Smithsonite; Tugtupite

Divine mind Alexandrite; Dumortierite

Divine purpose Beryllonite; Cryolite; Heliodor

Divine source Danburite

Divine, union with Mani Stone; Rose Quartz

Divine Will Ametrine; Apatite, Golden; Calcite, Stellar Beam; Heliodor; Libyan Gold Tektite; Obsidian, Gold Sheen; Opal, Common; Prasiolite; Spirit Quartz; Topaz, White; Topaz, Golden; Tourmaline, Golden

divorce Dioptase

DNA Quartz (Clear)

doubt Jade, Black; Yellow Sapphire

downloading of spiritual information Celestine; Tibetan Tektite

dowsing Diopside; Infinite; Vanadinite

dream enhancement Azeztulite, Sanda Rosa; Dream Quartz

dream state Hemimorphite; Moldavite

dream stone Apatite, Blue

dream time Sphene

dreamwork Herkimer Quartz "Diamond"; Jade, Green; Jasper, Picture; Lazulite;

Rhodonite

dreams Azeztulite, Sanda Rosa; Bustamite; Goshenite; Herkimer Quartz "Diamond"; Heulandite; Jade, Purple; Moonstone; Quartz (Clear); Smoky Quartz; Stilbite; Sugilite

dysfunctional relationships Hemimorphite

earth changes Faden Quartz

earth consciousness Jasper

earth connection Diopside; Pakulite; Wulfenite

earth energies Jasper, Mook; Jet; Vanadinite; Vortexite

earth evolution Apophyllite

Earth Goddess Cuprite

earth healing Apophyllite, Green; Jasper, Rainforest; Obsidian, Gold Sheen

Earth Mother Ajoite; Chrysoprase; Moonstone; see also feminine, Goddess, High Priestess

Earth's love Jasper, Rainforest

ecstasy Azeztulite, Honey and Cream; Sauralite Azeztulite; Azumar; Coromandel Stonewood; Lithium Light; Opal, Fire

efficiency Sodalite

electromagnetic energy Astrophyllite; Hematite

elemental beings Apache Tears

elemental forces Merlinite; Nuummite

eloquence Gem Silica

emotional abuse Azeztulite, Himalaya Red-Gold; Calcite, Honey; Dioptase

emotional amplifier Magnifier Quartz; Opal, White Precious

emotional attachments, release Agate, Holly Blue; Novaculite

emotional baggage, release of Aquamarine

emotional balance Calcite, Green; Jasper, Red; Malachite; Rainbow Moonstone; Thulite

emotional body Ajoite; Andalusite; Apache Tears; Aqua Aura Quartz; Azeztulite, White; Manifest Light Crystals; Smithsonite; Tibetan Tektite; Topaz, Blue; Vortexite

emotional exhaustion Seriphos Green Quartz

emotional healing Amegreen; Amulet Stone; Apache Tears; Aragonite Star Clusters; Aragonite, Blue; Aventurine, Green; Azeztulite, Honey and Cream; Azeztulite, Pink Fire; Calcite, Pink Transparent; Eudialyte; Gaia Stone; Rhodolite Garnet; Gaspeite; Hemimorphite; Heulandite; Hypersthene; Kunzite; Lepidocrocite; Lepidolite; Mani Stone; Ocean Jasper; Opal, Common, Pink; Piemontite; Rainbow

Garnet; Rathbunite;
Rhodochrosite; Rose Quartz;
Shungite; Tourmaline, Pink;
Rubellite; Dravite; Variscite

emotional paralysis
Eisen Quartz; Staurolite

emotional patterns, destructive
Epidote; Kyanite, Blue

emotional perception
Aragonite, Blue; Turquoise

emotional polarities Ajoite

emotional protection Opal,
Common, Black and Brown

emotional soothing Cavansite

emotional stability
Pallasite Meteorite

emotional trauma
Obsidian, Mahogany

emotional turmoil
Calcite, Pink Opaque

empathy Aragonite, Spanish;
Azeztulite, Pink; Azeztulite,
Golden Crystals; Calcite,
Pink Opaque; Coromandel
Stonewood; Hemimorphite;
Kyanite; Lemurian Golden
Opal; Lepidocrocite; Thulite

endurance Agate, Moss;
Azeztulite, Red Fire;
Molybdenite Quartz; Spinel;
Vanadinite

energetic alignment Barite

energetic patterns Infinite

energetic overload
Lithium Light, Guardianite

energy Aegirine; Ruby;
Tiger Iron

energy, male, archetypal
Metals: Gold

energy, command of Crocoite

energy, creative
Hypersthene; Jasper, Red

energy drain Andalusite

energy, elemental Merlinite

energy, feminine, archetypal
Metals: Silver

energy fields Amethyst;
Aragonite Star Clusters;
Faden Quartz; Fluorite;
Kaurilite

energy infusion Aragonite,
Spanish; Elestial Quartz;
Novaculite

energy, loving Rhodochrosite

energy, lunar Metals: Silver

energy, magnification
Rhodizite

energy, male Pyrite, Sunstone

energy, negative Apache Tears

energy overload Hematite

energy, regenerative Seriphos
Green Quartz; Spinel

energy transmission
Quartz (Clear)

enlightenment Amazez
Azeztulite; Angel Aura
Quartz; Crocoite; Herderite;
Nirvana Quartz; Metals:
Platinum; Novaculite;
Pietersite; Quartz (Clear)

enthusiasm Adamite; Ruby;
Azeztulite, Red Fire;
Piemontite; Sedonalite;
Sillimanite; Strontianite;

Titanium Quartz;
Vesuvianite; Wulfenite

entity attachment
Muscovite; Opal, Common

entity removal Astrophyllite;
Quartz (Clear)

envy Jade, Black

ESP Apophyllite, Clear;
Lazulite

etheric attachments
Angel Wing Blue Anhydrite

etheric bandage Faden Quartz

etheric blueprint Calcite,
Stellar Beam; Faden Quartz;
Rutilated Quartz

etheric body Agate, Moss;
Darwinite; Faden Quartz;
Infinite; Violet Flame Opal

etheric "bodyguard"
Jade, Black

etheric chakras Selenite

etheric entity
Metals: Niobium

etheric guide Brookite

ETs Astrophyllite; Brookite;
Chrysoberyl; Libyan Gold
Tektite; Metals: Niobium;
Chondrite Meteorite; Natro-
lite; Prehnite; Stibnite;
Tektite

euphoria Lithium Light;
Lithium Quartz

"Eureka!" moment
Azeztulite, Honey and
Cream; Azeztulite, Sauralite;
Brookite

evolution, personal
Cerussite; Fulgurite;

Moldavite; Nirvana Quartz

exorcism Astrophyllite

expansiveness Agate, Ellensburg Blue; Healerite

experimentation Sunstone

extrasensory perception Blue Sapphire

extraterrestrial communication Chondrite Meteorite; Elestial Angel Calcite

extraterrestrial entities Calcite, Stellar Beam; Covellite; Ulexite; Zircon

"facing the shadow self" Jade, Black

faery Apache Tears; Diopside; *see also* fairy

faith Beryllonite

fairy Chlorite Phantom Crystals; Faden Quartz; Infinite; Pallasite Meteorite; Peridot; Prasiolite; Prehnite; Smoky Quartz; Staurolite; Ulexite

fatigue Spinel

fear Agate; Agate, Blue Lace; Ajoite; Andalusite; Aragonite Barite; Crimson Cuprite; Danburite; Darwinite; Empowerite; Spinel; Gel Lithium Silica; Sauralite Azeztulite; Jade, Red; Larimar; Lemurian Aquatine Calcite; Lepidocrocite; Moldavite; Molybdenite Quartz; Opal, Common; Opal, Owyhee Blue; Yellow Sapphire; Scapolite; Serpentine; Spirit Quartz; Staurolite; Tourmaline, Golden

fear of confrontation Black Phantom Quartz

fear of death Master Shamanite; Shaman Stone; Tourmaline, Blue

fear of falling Apatite, Blue

fear of flying Pallasite Meteorite

fear of heights Apatite, Blue

fear of pain Shaman Stone

fear of the unknown Gaia Stone; Iolite

fear of using personal power Black Phantom Quartz

feeling at home on the Earth Siberian Blue Quartz

female energy Ajoite

feminine Moonstone, *see also* Goddess, Great Mother; High Priestess

feminine power Larimar; Moonstone

flight Angel Wing Blue Anhydrite

forgiveness Ajoite; Angel Wing Blue Anhydrite; Astrophyllite; Calcite, Clear; Chrysoprase; Dioptase; Mani Stone; Sapphire, Pink; Stichtite; Turquoise

freedom Eisen Quartz; Greenstone (Pounamu); Novaculite; Purpurite; Sunstone

frequencies, attunement Stibnite

friendliness Green Taralite

fulfillment Rhodonite

future, key to Quartz (Clear)

future lives Quartz (Clear)

future time stream Cryolite; Muscovite

gemstone healing layouts Topaz, Blue

generosity Healerite; Rainbow Garnet; Rhodonite; Thulite; Vitalite

gentleness Rose Quartz; Vivianite

geomancy Diopside; Infinite; Vanadinite

ghosts Smoky Quartz Goddess Aquamarine; Lemurian Seed Crystals; Moldavite; Moonstone; Quartz (Clear); *see also* feminine, High

Priestess, Great Mother Goddess energy Chrysocolla; Gaia Stone; Gem Silica; Jasper, Picture; Larimar

Goddess stone, *see* stone of the Goddess

Golden Void Herderite

good fortune Chrysanthemum Stone

good luck Aventurine, Green; Gaia Stone; Tektite

gratitude Apatite, Green; Hiddenite; Moldau Quartz

Great Central Sun Azeztulite, Himalaya Gold; Azeztulite, Honey and Cream; Cinnazez (Cinnabar Azeztulite);

Golden Healer Quartz; Golden Labradorite; Pallasite Meteorite; Obsidian, Gold Sheen; Azeztulite, Satyaloka Clear; Sunstone Great Mother Gem Silica; Jasper, Rainforest; Lemurian Seed Crystals; Moonstone; Prehnite; Rose Quartz; Gaia Stone

grief Alexandrite; Apache Tears; Aquamarine; Cavansite; Danburite; Datolite; Gel Lithium Silica; Sauralite Azeztulite; Lepidocrocite; Rainbow Moonstone; Morganite; Piemontite; Stilbite; Dravite; Tugtupite; Zoisite

grounding Agate, Moss; Andalusite; Apache Tears; Black Obsidian; Chrysanthemum Stone; Crocoite; Dolomite; Black Andradite Garnet; Healer's Gold; Hematite; Jet; Magnetite; Metals: Copper; Molybdenite Quartz; Pakulite; Ruby; Shungite; Smoky Quartz; Sphalerite; Staurolite; Tiger Iron; Tourmaline, Black; Vanadinite; Zircon

grounding the Light Prophecy Stone

grounding the spiritual in the physical Celestial Quartz; Flint

growth Agate, Dendritic; Aventurine, Green; Chrysoprase; Petrified Wood

guardian angels Angelite

guilt, overcoming Agate, Dendritic

hall of records Calcite, Merkabite; Celestial Quartz

happiness Azumar; Green Taralite; Guardianite; Papagoite; Rainbow Garnet; Sillimanite

harmful vibrations Astrophyllite

harmony Amazonite; Amulet Stone; Aragonite, Blue; Azeztulite, Sanda Rosa; Healer's Gold; Guardianite; Lemurian Jade, Shadow; Rainbow Moonstone; Sedonalite; Sillimanite; Spirit Quartz; Violet Flame Opal

hatred Black Jade

healing a damaged root chakra Aegirine, Guardianite

healing Amber; Charoite; Clinochlore; Crocoite; Cuprite; Diopside; Emerald; Healer's Gold; Healerite; Iolite; Jasper, Fancy; Jasper, Unakite; Lemurian Seed Crystals; Seriphos Green Quartz; Tourmaline, Green; Zoisite

healing and love, broadcast Quartz (Clear)

healing energy Nebula Stone

healing from grief Empowerite; Goethite

healing, genetic Jasper, Mook

healing herbs Seriphos Green Quartz

healing, physical Faden Quartz

healing words Aragonite, Blue

health Calcite, Pink Opaque; Chrysoprase; Clinochlore; Grossular; Jade, Green; Jade, Red; Jasper, Red; Molybdenite Quartz

healthy habits Staurolite; Thulite

heart alignment Green Heulandite

heart, awakening Prasiolite; Scolecite

heart chakra, expansion Datolite

heart connection Calcite, Green

heart, courageous Rhodochrosite; Stichtite

heart frequency Quartz (Clear)

heart healing Azeztulite, Pink; Hiddenite; Malachite; Rose Quartz; Rosophia; Rubellite; Tourmaline, Watermelon

heart, kindling Gaspeite; Vivianite

heart knowledge Apatite, Green; Cryolite; Healerite; Kunzite; Lepidocrocite; Moldavite; Muscovite

heart, loving Hiddenite

heart of the Earth Tourmaline, Rubellite

heart opening Diopside; Eudialyte;

Lemurian Seed Crystals; Tugtupite; Vortexite

heart, Universal Rubellite; Tugtupite

heart wisdom Crocoite; Cryolite; Kaurilite; Magnesite; Piemontite; Rathbunite

heartbeat of the Earth Chlorite Phantom Crystals; Coromandel Stonewood; Gaia Stone

hidden talent Rhodonite

high heart Azeztulite, Pink Fire; Datolite; Dioptase; Emerald High Priestess Cuprite; Metals: Silver; Moonstone

high will Datolite

higher brain Herderite; Natrolite

higher-chakra awakening Brookite

higher consciousness Lemurian Jade, Shadow; Natrolite; Tourmaline, Blue

higher dimensions Celestite; Papagoite

higher guidance Gem Silica; Jade, Lavender; Labradorite; Opal, Owyhee Blue

higher knowledge Calcite, Stellar Beam; Calcite, Merkabite; Magnesite; Blue Sapphire; Tremolite

higher mind Aragonite Star Clusters; Metals: Titanium; Rutile; Scolecite; Tremolite

higher purpose Fulgurite

higher realms Agate, Ellensburg Blue; Apophyllite; Cinnazez (Cinnabar Azeztulite); Datolite; Jasper, Unakite; New Zealand Carnelian (Azozeo Super-Activated); Petalite; Phenacite

Higher self Agate, Moss; Amegreen; Apophyllite, Clear; Auralite-23; Barite; Chalcedony, Purple; Clinochlore; Elestial Quartz; Hollandite Quartz; Lithium Quartz; Mani Stone; Natrolite; Prasiolite; Sapphire, White; Scapolite; Selenite; Spirit Quartz; Tanzan Aura Quartz

higher vibrations Magnifier Quartz; Metals: Copper; Rainbow Hematite

"holy fire" Opal, White Precious

Holy Grail Moldavite

honesty Flint

hope Alexandrite; Beryllonite; Spinel

hope, rebirth Mani Stone; Rose Quartz

hopelessness Datolite

humiliation Obsidian, Mahogany

humility Dolomite

humor Eisen Quartz; Jade, Purple; Kaurilite; Pakulite; Rainbow Garnet; Rathbunite; Titanium Quartz

hyperactivity Gel Lithium Silica

hypnosis Blue Sapphire

hysteria Aquamarine; Staurolite; Rubellite

"I am" Cavansite; Azeztulite, Satyaloka Clear

imagination Citrine; Opal, Oregon; Ulexite

implants Quartz (Clear)

increase Peridot; Indicolite; Tourmaline, Blue; Tourmaline, Pink

indecision Calcite, Orange; Datolite; Empowerite

infusion with Light Astrophyllite; Azeztulite, Black; Azeztulite, White; Golden Healer Quartz; Shungite

initiation Bustamite; Phenacite; Purpurite

inner bridge Kyanite

inner child Azeztulite, Pink; Bustamite; Gaspeite; Lepidocrocite; Rainbow Garnet

inner exploration Diaspore

inner guidance Cathedral Quartz; Dumortierite

inner journey Jasper, Picture

inner king Diamond; Lapis Lazuli; Libyan Gold Tektite

inner knowledge Azeztulite, Sauralite; Lemurian Light Crystals

inner knowledge Tanzan Aura Quartz

Inner Light Azeztulite, Honey and Cream; Lemurian Light Crystal; Manifest Light Crystals

inner peace Cavansite; Celestite; Coromandel Stonewood; Cryolite; Fairy Wand Quartz; Green Taralite; Lithium Quartz; Petrified Wood; Prehnite; Scolecite; Stilbite; Variscite; Vivianite

inner queen Diamond; Lapis Lazuli; Libyan Gold Tektite

"inner radar" Shaman Stone

inner release Obsidian Mahogany

inner sight Quartz (Clear)

inner silence Agate, Blue Lace; Agnate Gold Danburite; Nirvana Quartz; Vivianite

inner strength Aventurine, Blue; Nuummite; Onyx; Tourmaline, Golden; Vortexite

inner truth Ajoite; Gem Silica

inner vision Ajoite; Angel Wing Blue Anhydrite; Azeztulite, Himalaya Gold; Barite; Calcite, Blue; Covellite; Diamond; Goshenite; Iolite; Lapis Lazuli; Lithium Quartz; Magnesite; Cat's Eye Moonstone; Sunset Gold Selenite; Ulexite; Willemite

inner work Agate, Dendritic

innocence Tangerine Quartz

insight Aragonite; Blue; Auralite-23; Calcite, Clear; Calcite, Honey; Cinnabar; Eisen Quartz; Green Taralite; Lazulite; Moonstone; New Zealand Carnelian (Azozeo Super-Activated); Obsidian, Snowflake; Pietersite; Purpurite; Rutile; Blue Sapphire; Scapolite; Siberian Blue Quartz; Sodalite

inspiration Bumblebee "Jasper"; Iolite-Sunstone; Muscovite; Ruby Kyanite; Rutile; Spinel; Tangerine Quartz; Tanzan Aura Quartz; Vitalite; Vivianite

inspired writing Iolite-Sunstone

instinct Jasper, Mook

integrity Crocoite; Metals: Gold

intellectual power Azeztulite, Red Fire; Calcite, Honey; Cinnabar

integration Hematite

integrity Amazonite; Euclase

intensity Bumblebee "Jasper"; Diamond; Elestial Angel Calcite

intention Azeztulite, Himalaya Gold; Empowerite; Manifest Light Crystals; Sillimanite; Topaz, Golden

interdimensional awareness Apophyllite, Clear

interdimensional beings Brookite; Stibnite

interdimensional communication Aqua Aura Quartz; Astrophyllite; Brookite; Metals: Platinum; Chondrite Meteorite; Cinnazez (Cinnabar Azeztulite); Sedonalite; Siberian Blue Quartz

interdimensional gates Cassiterite; Phenacite

interdimensional travel Barite; Calcite, Stellar Beam; Calcite, Merkabite; Cavansite; Danburite; Dream Quartz; Fairy Wand Quartz; Heulandite; Kyanite, Green; Natrolite; Pallasite Meteorite; Phenacite; Pietersite; Quartz (Clear); Rhodizite; Rutilated Quartz; Scolecite; Sphene; Willemite; Z Stone

interdimensional world Apache Tears

introversion Metals: Gold

intuition Agate, Holly Blue; Alexandrite; Amazez Azeztulite; Amegreen; Aragonite, Blue; Benitoite; Coromandel Stonewood; Euclase; Hypersthene; Iolite-Sunstone; Jade, Lavender; Lemurian Aquatine Calcite; Merlinite; Moonstone; Muscovite; Nuummite; Papagoite; Phenacite; Pietersite; Prehnite; Pyromorphite; Ruby Kyanite; Shaman Stone; Shattuckite; Sodalite; Sphene; Tektite;

Ulexite; Zoisite

invincibility
Cinnabar; Metals: Titanium

inward journeys Metals: Silver

isolation Andalusite

joy Adamite; Alexandrite; Anandalite; Apatite, Green; Astaraline; Auralite-23; Azeztulite, Black; Azumar; Beryllonite; Bustamite; Calcite, Pink Transparent; Cryolite; Dioptase; Elestial Angel Calcite; Gem Silica; Golden Healer Quartz; Green Taralite; Healerite; Hemimorphite; Jasper, Rainforest; Kyanite, Green; Nirvana Quartz; Ocean Jasper; Opal, Oregon; Piemontite; Rainbow Garnet; Rathbunite; Rose Quartz; Sauralite Azeztulite; Smithsonite; Stilbite; Thulite; Tibetan Tektite; Tourmaline, Pink; Tourmaline, Watermelon; Tugtupite; Vitalite

karmic patterns
Azeztulite, Black; Dioptase

karmic understanding
Aegirine; Euclase

kindness Rainbow Garnet; Thulite; Tourmaline, Pink

kinesiology Infinite

Kingdom of Heaven
Quartz (Clear); Tremolite

Knights Templar Iolite

Knowledge, access
Apatite, Blue; Cavansite;

Black Andradite Garnet; Sunstone

knowledge fields
Pallasite Meteorite

knowledge, higher Azeztulite, Satyaloka Clear; Spiralite Gemshells

Kundalini Anandalite; Auralite-23; Brookite; Cinnabar; Crocoite; Cuprite; Fulgurite; Almandine Garnet; Black Andradite Garnet; Infinite; Jasper, Red; Manifest Light Crystals; Moldavite; Moonstone; Nickel- Iron Meteorite; Opal, Fire; Ruby; Seraphinite; Serpentine; Shiva Lingam; Stichtite; Strontianite; Tangerine Quartz; Tibetan Tektite; Kwan Yin Calcite, Pink Transparent; Jade, Lavender; Quartz (Clear); Smithsonite

language of Light
Chalcedony, Blue

latent capacities, activation Anandalite; Herderite

leadership Heliodor; Iolite-Sunstone; Malachite; Sunstone

learning Apatite, Golden; Diopside; Dumortierite; Fluorite; Herderite; Rutile; Sphene; Ulexite

legal situations Cathedral Quartz; Lemurian Seed Crystals; Quartz (Clear); Lemuria White Phantom Quartz

Lemuria Coromandel Stonewood; Kaurilite; Lemurian Light Crystal

letting go Sapphire, Pink

ley lines Diopside; Infinite; Jasper, Picture; Stonehenge Bluestone

liberation Cryolite; Scapolite

life, enjoyment Cinnazez (Cinnabar Azeztulite); Ocean Jasper; Seriphos Green Quartz; Zoisite

life force Amber; Andalusite; Aventurine, Green; Azeztulite, Red Fire; Cuprite; Crimson Cuprite; Eudialyte; Greenstone (Pounamu); Guardianite; Jasper, Mook; Kaurilite; Kyanite, Orange; Marcasite; Pakulite; Ruby; Ruby Kyanite; Sphalerite; Titanium Quartz; Vitalite; Zincite; Zircon; Zoisite; see also prana, chi

light Amber; Amethyst; Apophyllite, Clear; Hollandite Quartz; Satyaloka Quartz

light activation Hemimorphite

Light Body Aragonite, Spanish; Azeztulite, Himalaya Red; Herderite; Lithium Light; Manifest Light Crystals; Piemontite; Phenacite; Shungite; Tibetan Tektite

light frequencies Aegirine

light in darkness Beryllonite; Azeztulite, Black

lightheartedness Gem Silica; Rainbow Garnet; Rathbunite

liminal threshold Cassiterite

linking higher and lower self Prasiolite

linking mind and heart Darwinite; Piemontite; Tanzanite; Thulite

Liquid Crystal Body Matrix Healerite; Lemurian Light Crystal; Violet Flame Opal

loneliness Andalusite; Lemurian Golden Opal

longevity Amber; Azeztulite, Red Fire; Coromandel Stonewood; Greenstone (Pounamu); Healerite; Kaurilite; Manifest Light Crystals; Rose Quartz; Spiralite Gemshells

loss Cavansite

lost information, retrieval Datolite

lost objects Staurolite

love Adamite; Azeztulite, Honey and Cream; Azeztulite, Pink Fire; Azumar; Bixbite; Clinochlore; Crocoite; Darwinite; Emerald; Gaia Stone; Kaurilite; Lepidocrocite; Lilac Lepidolite; Rathbunite; Rhodonite; Rose Quartz; Rosophia; Sapphire, Pink; Smithsonite; Stilbite; Tourmaline, Pink; Tugtupite: Vitalite

love and will, blending Healerite; Pyromorphite

love attractor Chrysoprase; Ruby Kyanite

love for the Earth Tugtupite

love, interpersonal Hiddenite

love, physical Almandine Garnet

love relationship Bixbite; Almandine Garnet; Pakulite

love, unconditional Azeztulite, Pink Fire; Calcite, Pink Transparent; Charoite; Lemurian Jade, Shadow; Scapolite; Tiger Eye

Love, Universal Smithsonite

loving-kindness Jade, Green

lucid dreaming Agate, Holly Blue; Auralite-23; Black Merlinite; Covellite; Dream Quartz; Goshenite; Kyanite; Lazulite; Lemurian Aquatine Calcite; Lemurian Golden Opal; Obsidian, Peacock; Rhodizite; Blue Sapphire; Scolecite; Sodalite; Staurolite; Sugilite

loyalty Goshenite; Greenstone (Pounamu); Molybdenite Quartz

magic Cerussite; Cinnabar; Greenstone (Pounamu); Jet; Labradorite; Merlinite; Mystic Merlinite; Nuummite; Onyx; Opal, Black Precious; Opal, Owyhee Blue; Pietersite; Sillimanite; Z Stone

magic, benevolent Pyromorphite

Magic Presence Chalcedony, Purple; Stichtite

Magician Cuprite

Magician archetype Cinnabar

magnetic therapy Magnetite

magnifier of intentions Amazonite; Gray Moonstone

manifestation Apatite, Golden; Azeztulite, Himalaya Gold; Brazilianite; Bumblebee "Jasper"; Calcite, Clear; Cinnabar; Citrine; Gaspeite; Heliodor; Hematite; Spessartine; Uvarovite Garnet; Kyanite, Orange; Lemurian Jade; Libyan Gold Tektite; Manifest Light Crystals; Obsidian, Gold Sheen; Opal, Black Precious; Petalite; Pyrite; Pyromorphite; Rathbunite; Rutilated Quartz; Rutile; Yellow Sapphire; Smoky Quartz; Tiger Iron; Topaz, Golden; Vitalite; Wulfenite; Zincite

manifestation and destruction Carnelian

marriage Moldavite

martial arts Jade, Red

mathematics Benitoite; Datolite; Goshenite

meditation Amethyst; Apophyllite, Clear; Aragonite, Blue; Azeztulite, Sanda Rosa; Black Merlinite; Brookite; Calcite, Green; Danburite;

Diamond; Diaspore; Dioptase; Dream Quartz; Gel Lithium Silica; Gem Silica; Halite; Healer's Gold; Herderite; Lemurian Golden Opal; Lemurian Light Crystal; Lilac Lepidolite; Lithium Quartz; Merlinite; Moonstone; Natrolite; Obsidian, Peacock; Opal, Common; Opal, Black Precious; Petalite; Phenacite; Prophecy Stone; Quartz (Clear); Quartz (Clear), Rhodizite; Rutilated Quartz; Blue Sapphire; Scolecite; Shantilite; Sodalite; Sphene; Staurolite; Stibnite; Tibetan Black Quartz; Tiger Eye; Tourmaline, Blue; Tremolite; Vivianite; Z Stone

mediumship, *see* clairvoyance

memory Coromandel Stonewood; Dumortierite; Herderite; Jasper, Red; Lazulite; Quartz (Clear); Sphene

memory, genetic Goethite

memorization Datolite

memory recovery Rhodochrosite

mental ability Cinnabar; Datolite; Blue Sapphire; Titanium Quartz; Ulexite

mental clarity Adamite; Citrine; Siberian Blue Quartz; Sphene; Topaz, White

mental discipline Dumortierite

mental discomfort Papagoite

mental energy Jasper, Fancy

mental enhancement Diaspore; Fluorite; Sodalite

mental focus Ametrine; Bumblebee "Jasper"; Lazulite; Libyan Gold Tektite; Sillimanite

meridians Anandalite; Magnetite; Moldavite; Sillimanite

Merkabah Vehicle of Light Papagoite; Z Stone

metanoia, *see* Divine, union with

mind Calcite, Pink Opaque; Heliodor; Topaz, Blue

mind/heart integration Amegreen

moderation Dolomite

morphogenic fields Pallasite Meteorite

mood swings Agate, Moss; Lithium Light; Obsidian, Rainbow; Rathbunite

morphic fields of knowledge Hypersthene; Tremolite; White Phantom Quartz

multi-level awareness Agate, Holly Blue; Calcite, Clear; Cathedral Quartz

multidimensional self Astrophyllite

music of the spheres Danburite; Elestial Angel Calcite; Elestial Quartz; Fairy Wand Quartz; Golden Labradorite

musicians, *see* creative people

mystery Metals: Silver; Moonstone

namaste Prasiolite

Nameless Light Azeztulite; Satyaloka Clear

nature connection Jasper, Rainforest; Kaurilite; Kyanite; Prasiolite; Serpentine

nature, heart of Serpentine

Nature spirits Agate, Moss; Apache Tears; Apatite, Green; Apophyllite, Green; Brookite; Chlorite Phantom Crystals; Gaia Stone; Hemimorphite; Jasper, Rainforest; Tourmaline, Green; Tourmaline, Watermelon

negative attachments Amazez Azeztulite; Lithium Quartz; Novaculite; Vesuvianite

negative energies Agate, Holly Blue; Aqua Aura Quartz; Jet; Obsidian, Gold Sheen; Rainbow Garnet; Pyromorphite; Smoky Quartz

negative entities, protection against Aegirine; Quartz (Clear)

negative influences Tourmalined Quartz

negative psychic "implants" Obsidian, Mahogany

negative thought patterns Anandalite; Citrine; Jade, Purple; Pyromorphite; Thulite

negativity, internalized
Charoite

negativity, purging Charoite; Jade, Black; Kyanite, Orange; Obsidian, Black; Ocean Jasper; Piemontite; Shungite

negativity, transformation Euclase

new directions Calcite, Honey

new paradigm Rose Quartz

newborns Cassiterite

night terror Aegirine; Guardianite; Lilac Lepidolite

nightmares Angel Aura Quartz; Charoite; Dream Quartz; Gaia Stone; Tibetan Black Quartz

nobility Heliodor

objectivity Iolite; Lapis Lazuli

observation Sodalite

om Tibetan Black Quartz

oneness with the All Shiva Lingam

opening the heart Halite

opportunity Willemite

optimism Agate, Ellensburg Blue; Angel Aura Quartz; Aventurine, Green; Azeztulite, Red Fire; Citrine; Eisen Quartz; Natrolite; Moonstone, Rainbow; Obsidian Rainbow; Opal, Fire; Pakulite; Ruby; Sedonalite; Sillimanite; Sugilite

oracles Pietersite; Shattuckite; Sodalite

order Fluorite; Sillimanite

organization Smoky Quartz

orgone generator Rhodizite

originality Wulfenite

out-of-body experience Astrophyllite; Calcite, Stellar Beam; Green Taralite; Papagoite; Rhodizite; Scapolite; Sphene

pain, release Aragonite Star Clusters; Sauralite Azeztulite

panic Chalcedony, Blue; Larimar; paradox Muscovite

paranormal abilities Benitoite; Diamond

paranormal activity Agate, Holly Blue;

passion Agate, Fire; Agnitite; Azeztulite, Himalaya Red; Azeztulite, Red Fire; Bixbite; Bumblebee "Jasper"; Crimson Cuprite; Crocoite; Jade, Red; Metals: Gold; Greenstone (Pounamu); New Zealand Carnelian (Azozeo Super-Activated); Opal, Fire; Ruby; Ruby Kyanite; Sapphire, Pink; Tangerine Quartz; Tugtupite; Zincite

passive aggressive behavior Calcite, Pink Opaque

past civilizations Cathedral Quartz; Heulandite

past life Amber; Anandalite; Angelite; Apatite; Blue; Black Shadow Quartz; Covellite; Dream Quartz; Elestial

Quartz; Iolite; Jet; Lazulite; Nuummite; Obsidian, Snowflake; Opal, Common; Opal, Oregon; Papagoite; Quartz (Clear); Scapolite; Sphene; Stonehenge Bluestone

past-life learning Almandine Garnet; Healerite

past-life memories Dioptase; Goethite; Kyanite; Labradorite; Lemurian Aquatine Calcite; Merlinite; Petrified Wood; Quartz (Clear); Sedonalite; Spiralite Gemshells; White Phantom Quartz

patience Dolomite; Kaurilite; Petrified Wood

path of service Charoite

pattern recognition Sodalite

peace Agate, Moss; Angel Aura Quartz; Aqua Aura Quartz; Dioptase; Gem Silica; Lilac Lepidolite; Lithium Light; Opal, Common; Shantilite; Smithsonite; Spirit Quartz; Sugilite; Turquoise

peacemaker Amazonite

perception Opal, Owyhee Blue; Smithsonite

perseverance Adamite; Jasper, Fancy; Obsidian, Black; Obsidian, Snowflake; Onyx; Zincite

persistence Agate, Moss; Calcite, Honey; Dravite; Goshenite; Jasper, Unakite; Molybdenite Quartz;

Pakulite; Pyrite;
Royal Sahara Jasper;
Scapolite; Vanadinite

personal power Empowerite;
Greenstone (Pounamu);
Pakulite; Petalite; Onyx;
Zincite

personal will Citrine

perspective Stibnite

phobias Larimar

**physical disruption,
protection** Faden Quartz

physical life, spiritualization
Herkimer Quartz "Diamond"

planetary consciousness
Azeztulite, Satyaloka Clear;
Azumar; Healerite

planetary healing
Jasper, Rainforest

playfulness Calcite, Orange;
Eisen Quartz; Opal, Fire;
Pakulite; Rainbow Garnet;
Rathbunite; Sapphire,
Padparadsha; Tangerine
Quartz; Vanadinite

pleasure Azeztulite,
Honey and Cream; Azumar;
Lemurian Light Crystal;
Rathbunite; Thulite

poets, *see* creative people

polarities, balancing Agate,
Dendritic; Manifest Light
Crystals; Shaman Stone

poltergeists Pyromorphite

positive outlook Agate,
Dendritic; Apache Tears;
Calcite, Blue; Guardianite;
Healer's Gold; Strontianite

positive patterns Epidote

potential, personal
Libyan Gold Tektite

**poverty consciousness,
overcoming**
Uvarovite Garnet

power Amblygonite;
Azeztulite, Black;
Azeztulite, Red Fire; Golden
Labradorite; Heliodor;
Metals: Titanium; New
Zealand Carnelian (Azozeo
Super-Activated); Purpurite;
Rainbow Hematite;
Rhodizite; Stibnite

power of the underworld
Stibnite

practicality Empowerite;
Flint; Strontianite

prana Azeztulite, Himalaya
Red; Calcite, Red; Cuprite;
Flint; Healer's Gold; Jade,
Red; Kaurilite; Shiva Lingam;
Tiger Iron; Rubellite;
Tremolite; Vitalite

prana yama Aragonite, Blue

prayer Fulgurite; Gel
Lithium Silica; Gem Silica;
Goshenite; Shantilite

pre-birth state
Calcite, Stellar Beam

precognition Pietersite

prescience Chalcedony,
Purple; Circle Stone

prefrontal lobes
Lazulite; Phenacite

probable futures Elestial
Quartz; Prophecy Stone

problem solving Muscovite

procrastination Amblygonite;
Ametrine; Calcite, Honey;
Spirit Quartz

programmability
Quartz (Clear)

prophecy Celestite; Chal-
cedony, Purple; Lemurian
Golden Opal; Siberian Blue
Quartz; Tourmaline, Blue

prophetic vision Apophyllite,
Clear; Black Merlinite;
Chrysoberyl; Dumortierite;
Phenacite; Prophecy Stone;
Royal Sahara Jasper

prosperity Cassiterite;
Chrysanthemum Stone;
Chrysoprase; Dioptase;
Emerald; Grossular;
Uvarovite Garnet; Jade,
Green; Jade, Red; Pallasite
Meteorite; Peridot; Quartz
(Clear); Ruby; Yellow
Sapphire; Stibnite; Sunstone;
Tourmaline, Golden;
Variscite

protection Aegirine; Amber;
Amethyst; Andalusite;
Apache Tears; Azeztulite,
Black; Charoite; Black
Andradite Garnet; Jade,
Black; Jet; Labradorite;
Malachite; Moldavite; Ruby;
Smoky Quartz; Spirit Quartz;
Stichtite; Tourmaline, Black

psychic abilities Agate,
Ellensburg Blue; Agate,
Holly Blue; Amazez
Azeztulite; Amegreen;
Amethyst; Anandalite;

Aragonite, Blue; Auralite-23; Benitoite; Calcite, Blue; Chalcedony, Purple; Chrysoberyl; Cinnabar; Covellite; Crocoite; Dream Quartz; Dumortierite; Flint; Fluorite; Halite; Herderite; Jade, Purple; Jade, Blue; Kunzite; Kyanite; Lazulite; Metals: Silver; Natrolite; Nuummite; Papagoite; Phenacite; Rainbow Hematite; Rathbunite; Rhodizite; Ruby Kyanite; Rutilated Quartz; Rutile; Blue Sapphire; Scapolite; Sedonalite; Siberian Blue Quartz; Tanzan Aura Quartz; Tektite; Topaz, Blue; Tugtupite; Zircon

psychic activation Apatite

psychic attack Andalusite; Aqua Aura Quartz; Dream Quartz; Muscovite; Obsidian, Mahogany; Opal, Common; Opal, Owyhee Blue; Scapolite

psychic attunement Angelite; Apache Tears; Aventurine, Blue; Iolite; Jade, Lavender; Merlinite

psychic awakening Benitoite; Rhodizite; Siberian Blue Quartz

psychic centers of the brain Agate, Holly Blue

psychic clearing Halite

psychic communication Brookite

psychic entities Marcasite

psychic gifts Iolite; Sapphire, White; Topaz, White; Tourmaline, Blue

psychic healers Adamite

psychic perception Agate, Ellensburg Blue; Angel Wing Blue Anhydrite; Eudialyte; Magnesite; Natrolite; Moonstone; Rainbow Moonstone

psychic powers Petalite; Rutile

psychic protection Andalusite; Apache Tears; Aqua Aura Quartz; Benitoite; Almandine Garnet; Labradorite; Lepidocrocite; Libyan Gold Tektite; Obsidian, Black; Obsidian, Peacock; Purpurite; Shaman Stone; Tourmaline, Black; Tourmalined Quartz

psychic reading Labradorite; Prehnite

psychic surgery Calcite, Stellar Beam

psychic vampirism Adamite; Infinite

psychic vision Calcite, Clear; Hypersthene; Pietersite; Quartz (Clear); Blue Sapphire; Sodalite

psychics Covellite; Metals: Niobium

psychokinesis Cavansite; Dumortierite; Lazulite; Phenacite; Siberian Blue Quartz

psychometry Cavansite; Chalcedony, Purple;

Dumortierite

purification Amethyst; Amazez Azeztulite; Auralite-23; Bloodstone; Cacoxenite; Chalcedony, Purple; Fulgurite; Hanksite; Herkimer Quartz "Diamond"; Jade, Black; Jet; Kaurilite; Lepidolite; Opal, Common, Pink; Opal, White Precious; Purpurite; Selenite; Spirit Quartz; Shungite; Sugilite; Tibetan Black Quartz; Tourmaline, Black; Tourmalined Quartz

purification, aura Jade, Purple

purification, energy field Agate, Dendritic; Violet Flame Opal

purifications, spiritual Agate, Ellensburg Blue; Violet Flame Opal

purpose Agate, Fire; Bumblebee "Jasper"; Golden Labradorite

qi gong Jade, Red

quickness Sphene

radiance Diamond; Greenstone (Pounamu)

Rainbow Body Metals: Niobium; Rainbow Hematite; Rainbow Moonstone; Titanium Quartz

rapport Thulite

rapture Clinochlore; Purpurite; Sapphire, Padparadsha;

Tourmaline, Blue; Tremolite; Tugtupite; Zoisite

reason Onyx

rebirth of hope, rebirthing Obsidian, Mahogany; Shaman Stone; Shiva Lingam

receptivity Cinnazez (Cinnabar Azeztulite); Kunzite

recovery of knowledge Benitoite

regeneration of the body Aragonite, Spanish; Cacoxenite; Chlorite Phantom Crystals; Hollandite Quartz; Seraphinite

reiki Danburite; Healer's Gold; Infinite

rejuvenation Azumar; Healerite; Mani Stone

relationships Clinochlore; Gaia Stone; Hiddenite; Lithium Quartz

relaxation Agate, Ellensburg Blue; Apatite, Green; Aqua Aura Quartz; Calcite, Green; Dream Quartz; Fairy Wand Quartz; Gil Lithium Silica; Healer's Gold; Lepidolite; Lithium Light; Ocean Jasper; Scolecite; Titanium Quartz; Tourmaline, Pink

release of anger Calcite, Pink Opaque

release of negativity Epidote

release of stress Dream Quartz; Lithium Light; Violet Flame Opal; Vitalite

relief Agate, Ellensburg Blue

remote viewing Apophyllite, Clear; Benitoite; Covellite; Diamond; Lazulite; Phenacite; Ulexite

resentment Angel Wing Blue Anhydrite; Danburite

resilience Sapphire, Pink; Stichtite

revitalization Apatite, Green; Spinel

retrieval of lost (ancient) information Andalusite

retrieval of lost soul parts Mystic Merlinite; Quartz (Clear)

"return to paradise" Lemurian Seed Crystals

revelation Cavansite

revitalization Rhodizite

risk-taking Agate, Fire; Eisen Quartz

romance Strontianite; Thulite

royal virtue Labradorite

sacred expression Chrysocolla

sacred geometry Z Stone

samadhi Angel Aura Quartz

scrying Merlinite; Obsidian, Black; Onyx; Stonehenge Bluestone

"seat of the soul" Tourmaline, Watermelon

security Almandine Garnet; Azeztulite, Honey and Cream

self-acceptance Angel Wing Blue Anhydrite;

Astrophyllite; Hypersthene; Nirvana Quartz; Dravite

self-confidence Azeztulite, Himalaya Red-Gold; Eisen Quartz; Heliodor; Pakulite; Ruby

self-discipline Aventurine, Blue; Flint; Iolite-Sunstone; Lazulite; Royal Sahara Jasper; Scapolite; Sillimanite; Sodalite

self-discovery Astrophyllite

self-doubt Empowerite; Eudialyte

self-esteem Azeztulite, Himalaya Red-Gold; Bixbite; Golden Labradorite; Opal, Oregon; Tanzanite

self-healing Sauralite Azeztulite; Azeztulite, Pink Fire; Azeztulite, Red Fire; Bumblebee "Jasper"; Chlorite Phantom Crystals; Dravite; Golden Healer Quartz; Hypersthene; Kaurilite; Lepidocrocite; Moldavite; Ruby Kyanite; Seraphinite; Tiger Iron

self-knowledge Amazonite; Astrophyllite; Empowerite; Hypersthene; Stilbite; Turquoise

self-judgment Black Phantom Quartz; Mani Stone

self-love Eudialyte; Greenstone (Pounamu); Pink Halite; Rhodochrosite; Thulite; Dravite

self-mastery Nuummite; Onyx; Sillimanite; Strontianite

self, positive Ocean Jasper

self-sabotage Apatite, Golden

self transformation Pietersite; Scapolite

self-worth Apatite, Golden; Rhodolite Garnet; Mahogany Obsidian; Spirit Quartz; Strontianite

sensory awareness Calcite, Red

sensual pleasure Ruby

seraphim Lemurian Seed Crystals; Seraphinite

serenity Angel aura Quartz; Azumar; Angelite; Celestite; Gel Lithium Silica; Jade, Lavender; Lepidolite; Lilac Lepidolite; Lithium Light; Scolecite; Seriphos Green Quartz; Variscite

"serpent power" Serpentine

service to the world Quartz (Clear)

sexual abuse Azeztulite, Himalaya Red-Gold; Calcite, Orange; Calcite, Honey; Kyanite, Orange

sexual energy Eisen Quartz; Jade, Red; Jasper, Red; Marcasite; Pakulite; Ruby; Sapphire, Padparadsha; Vanadinite; Willemite

sexuality Adamite; Agate, Fire; Azeztulite, Himalaya Red-Gold; Azeztulite, Red Fire; Bumblebee "Jasper"; Bustamite; Calcite, Orange; Carnelian; Kyanite, Orange; Spessartine; Marcasite;

Metals: Gold; Opal, Fire; Padparadsha Sapphire; Strontianite; Sunstone; Wulfenite

shadow Covellite; Hypersthene

shadow material Black Phantom Quartz

shadow, reclaiming Mystic Merlinite

shakti Jet

shamanic journey Amber; Black Merlinite; Iolite; Jade, Purple; Jade, Black; Obsidian, Peacock; Opal, Common; Opal, Owyhee Blue; Prophecy Stone; Shaman Stone; Sodalite; Sphene

shamanic practice Adamite; Jasper, Fancy; Opal, Black Precious; Prophecy Stone

shaman Moonstone; Quartz

shame Obsidian, Mahogany; Thulite

shape-shifting Cinnabar; Stonehenge Bluestone

shield of Light Sugilite

shyness Calcite, Orange Sirius Calcite, Stellar Beam

social phobias Calcite, Green

solar energy Amber; Heliodor

soothing Aquamarine; Gel Lithium Silica; Larimar

soothing the emotional body Azeztulite, Pink; Calcite, Blue; Darwinite; Lilac Lepidolite; Smithsonite;

Topaz, Blue

sorrow, release Alexandrite

sorrow, transmutation Papagoite

soul energy Crocoite

soul life Goethite

soul mate Chalcedony, Purple; Morganite

soul of the earth Gaia Stone

soul potential Cathedral Quartz; Tibetan Tektite; Vortexite

soul purpose Chrysanthemum Stone

soul retrieval Azeztulite, Honey and Cream; Azeztulite, Pink; Iolite; Jade, Black; Lepidocrocite; Mani Stone; Nuummite; Shaman Stone

sound healers Aragonite, Blue

sovereignty Diamond; Purpurite

speaking in tongues Chalcedony, Blue; Hematite; Spessartine, Garnet

spirit communication Black Merlinite; Master Shamanite; Merlinite; Obsidian, Snowflake; Obsidian, Peacock; Rainbow Hematite; Shattuckite

spirit guides Dream Quartz; Hemimorphite; Lemurian Aquatine Calcite; Master Shamanite; Metals: Platinum; Opal, Owyhee Blue; Selenite;

Smoky Quartz; White Phantom Quartz

spiritual activation Selenite

spiritual assistance Goshenite; Greenstone (Pounamu)

spiritual awareness Quartz (Clear); Rainbow Hematite; Strontianite; Tanzanite; Violet Flame Opal

spiritual commitment Euclase; Ruby Kyanite

spiritual connection Amegreen; Elestial Angel Calcite

spiritual courage Azeztulite, Himalaya Red; Phenacite

spiritual destiny Diamond

spiritual energy Quartz, (Clear)

spiritual enlightenment Apophyllite; Azeztulite, Satyaloka Clear; Azeztulite, Satyaloka Yellow; Cavansite; Datolite; Healerite; Moldavite; Nirvana Quartz; Novaculite; Rathbunite; Vivianite

spiritual evolution, rapid Azeztulite, Satyaloka Yellow; Bumblebee "Jasper"; Darwinite; Lithium Light; Magnifier Quartz; Moldavite; New Zealand Carnelian (Azozeo Super-Activated); Spirit Quartz; Tibetan Tektite

spiritual expression Gaspeite

spiritual growth Ametrine;

Sedonalite; Turquoise

spiritual guides Agate, Holly Blue; Angel Wing Blue Anhydrite; Apophyllite, Clear; Calcite, Stellar Beam; Covellite; Lepidocrocite

spiritual healing Angelite

spiritual history Serpentine

spiritual information Cathedral Quartz

spiritual initiation Willemite

spiritual insight Angelite; Apophyllite, Clear; Gaspeite; Herderite; Hollandite Quartz; Jade, Green; Jade, Blue; Jet; Quartz, (Clear); Sapphire, White

spiritual light Golden Healer Quartz; Green Taralite; Nebula Stone; Shungite

spiritual path Rainbow Garnet; Rhodolite Garnet

spiritual protection Green Taralite; Rainbow Hematite; Tibetan Black Quartz

spiritual strength Sapphire, White; Sugilite

spiritual transformation Fulgurite; Lithium Light; Shiva Lingam

spiritual truth Cryolite

spiritual twin Agate, Moss; Chalcedony, Purple

spiritual warrior Bloodstone

spirituality Green Taralite; Marcasite; Topaz, White

stability Agate, Moss; Aragonite, Blue; Gel Lithium

Silica; Molybdenite Quartz

stagnation, release Calcite, Clear

"stairway to heaven" Lemurian Seed Crystals

stamina Bixbite; Pyrite; Tiger Iron; Tourmaline, Green; Vanadinite

Star Seed Chondrite Meteorite; Quartz (Clear)

state of grace Papagoite; Stibnite

stimulant, mental Goshenite; Muscovite

stone energies Metals: Copper

stone of Avalon Black Merlinite; Mystic Merlinite

stone of eternal youth Agate, Fire

stone of miracles Benitoite

stone of Shambhala Moldavite; Tektite

stone of the Goddess Chrysocolla

stone of the Grail Moldavite

stone of the muses Ametrine; Iolite

stone of truth Hanksite

strength Aragonite Star Clusters; Bloodstone; Bumblebee "Jasper"; Almandine Garnet; Empowerite; Heliodor; Hematite; Jade, Red; Molybdenite Quartz; Petrified Wood; Ruby; Sphalerite; Strontianite; Sunstone; Tiger Eye; Tiger Iron

stress Amblygonite; Apatite, Green; Fairy Wand Quartz; Opal, Common; Tremolite

stress, release of Azeztulite, Pink; Calcite, Green; Danburite; Lepidolite; Lilac Lepidolite; Lithium Quartz; Ocean Jasper; Rose Quartz; Smithsonite; Staurolite; Tourmaline, Pink

structure, creating Flint; Sodalite

stubbornness Black Phantom Quartz

study Fluorite

subconscious Sodalite

subtle bodies Aegirine

subtle energies Infinite; Novaculite; Rainbow Hematite

subtle perception Diopside

subtle vision Datolite

supramental force Prophecy Stone; Tibetan Tektite

surrender Ajoite; Cryolite

synchronicity Benitoite; Charoite; Chrysanthemum Stone; Cinnazez (Cinnabar Azeztulite); Eudialyte; Malachite; Merlinite; Moldavite; Natrolite; Nuummite; Obsidian, Snowflake; Opal, Common; Quartz (Clear); Ruby; Willemite

Synergy Twelve stones Azeztulite, White; Brookite; Danburite; Herderite; Moldavite; Natrolite; Petalite; Phenacite;

Satyaloka Quartz; Scolecite; Tanzanite; Tibetan Tektite

synergy, heart-brain Darwinite; Nirvana Quartz

synesthesia Shattuckite

synthesis Dumortierite; Metals: Titanium; Sodalite

tai chi Jade, Red

tantric love-making Crocoite; New Zealand Carnelian (Azozeo Super-Activated)

tantric practice Calcite, Red

tarot Creedite; Dumortierite; Herderite; Iolite; Pietersite

teaching stone Chrysocolla

telekinesis Natrolite; Onyx

telepathy Apophyllite, Green; Auralite-23; Calcite, Blue; Chalcedony, Blue; Diamond; Gaia Stone; Hemimorphite; Kyanite; Labradorite; Lazulite; Lemurian Aquatine Calcite; Lemurian Golden Opal; Muscovite; Natrolite; Petalite; Phenacite; Pietersite; Quartz (Clear); Rhodizite; Rutilated Quartz; Scapolite; Spiralite Gemshells; Tektite; Ulexite

telomere protection Coromandel Stonewood

therapy Chalcedony, Blue

third eye chakra Phenacite

third eye stimulation Angel Wing Blue Anhydrite; Phenacite

"thousand-petaled lotus" Magnesite

thrift Strontianite

time stream of the future Nirvana Quartz

time travel Coromandel Stonewood

total union, *see* samadhi

toxins, clearing Hanksite

tranquility Angel Aura Quartz; Angelite; Petalite; Scolecite

trance states Sodalite

transformation Azeztulite, Black; Azeztulite, Golden Crystals; Azeztulite, Satyaloka Yellow; Cerussite; Covellite; Crimson Cuprite; Metals: Platinum; Moldavite; New Zealand Carnelian (Azozeo Super-Activated); Quartz (Clear); Sedonalite; Tugtupite

trauma, emotional Cuprite; Lepidolite

trickster Stibnite

trust Nirvana Quartz

truth Ajoite; Aquamarine; Azeztulite, Golden Crystals; Azeztulite, Satyaloka Clear; Azeztulite, Satyaloka Rose; Azumar; Jasper, Red; Purpurite; Tanzanite; Turquoise

truth of the heart Kyanite

UFOs Smoky Quartz

unconscious Black Merlinite; Metals: Silver

union of heart and will Prehnite; Vesuvianite

unworthiness Rhodolite
Garnet; Hiddenite

verbal communication
Shattuckite

vertical dimension
Agate, Holly Blue

vibrational level Elestial
Angel Calcite; Tektite

victory Spinel

viewing, distance Rhodizite
Violet Flame Sugilite

visionary ability
Dumortierite; Iolite;
Iolite-Sunstone; Jade,
Lavender; Rhodizite

visionary experience
Azeztulite, Red Fire;
Beryllonite; Danburite;
Dream Quartz; Elestial Angel
Calcite; Herkimer Quartz
"Diamond"; Heulandite;
Lemurian Light Crystal;
Natrolite; Sedonalite;
Violet Flame Opal

vitality Agate, Fire; Agnitite;
Amber; Aventurine, Green;
Azeztulite, Red Fire; Bixbite;
Bustamite; Calcite, Red;
Carnelian; Clinochlore;
Coromandel Stonewood;
Crimson Cuprite; Eisen
Quartz; Eudialyte; Golden
Labradorite; Greenstone
(Pounamu) Jade, Red; Manifest Light
Crystals; Marcasite;
Metals: Gold, Titanium;
Molybdenite Quartz;
Pyrite; Ruby; Sphalerite;
Strontianite; Tiger Eye;
Tiger Iron; Titanium
Quartz; Tourmaline, Green;
Turquoise

Void of Potential
Nirvana Quartz

vulnerability Sapphire, Pink;
Stilbite; Tourmaline, Pink

walk-ins Astrophyllite;
Goethite; Metals: Platinum;
Pallasite Meteorite

warmth Amber; Peridot

wealth Agate, Moss;
Alexandrite; Azeztulite,
Himalaya Red-Gold;
Cinnabar; Emerald; Rutile;
Yellow Sapphire

well-being Apatite, Green;
Calcite, Pink Opaque; Green
Taralite; Healer's Gold;
Kaurilite; Peridot; Staurolite
White Light Phenacite;
Satyaloka Quartz; Vitalite

white magic
Black Andradite Garnet

wholeness Azeztulite, Honey
and Cream; Calcite, Pink
Opaque; Mani Stone;
Seraphinite; Tanzanite;
Tourmaline, Green;
Turquoise

will Agate, Fire; Amblygonite;
Azeztulite, Himalaya
Gold; Empowerite; Golden
Labradorite; Heliodor;
Kyanite, Orange;
New Zealand Carnelian
(Azozeo Super-Activated);
Opal, Owyhee Blue; Pakulite;
Pietersite; Yellow

Robert Simmons has been a student and investigator of many spiritual paths since a spontaneous mystical experience during his first year at Yale changed the course of his life. In 1986, he married Kathy Helen Warner and together they established their company, Heaven and Earth, which began as a small crystal and jewelry shop. Now their mail order and web business reaches thousands of people worldwide. Together Robert and Kathy published their first stone book *Moldavite: Starborn Stone of Transformation* in 1988.

Robert sometimes travels to present workshops or intensives on stone energies, spiritual evolution and other topics he enjoys. To contact him regarding a workshop or to share your story of spiritual awakening, (with or without the aid of stones), send an email to **heavenandearth@earthlink.net**.

To read Robert's new articles about stones, or to see the many items offered by Heaven and Earth, visit **www.heavenandearthjewelry.com**. To contact us for a free color catalog, send an email to **heavenandearth@earthlink.net**.

Bestselling Books by Robert Simmons!

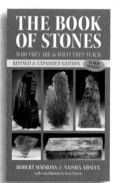